LANGUAGE AND LITERACY DEVELOPMENT IN BILINGUAL SETTINGS

CHALLENGES IN LANGUAGE AND LITERACY
Elaine R. Silliman and C. Addison Stone, *Series Editors*

LANGUAGE
and LITERACY
DEVELOPMENT
in BILINGUAL
SETTINGS

Edited by
Aydin Yücesan Durgunoğlu
Claude Goldenberg

Series Editors' Note by Elaine R. Silliman and C. Addison Stone

THE GUILFORD PRESS
New York   London

© 2011 The Guilford Press
A Division of Guilford Publications, Inc.
72 Spring Street, New York, NY 10012
www.guilford.com

Printed in the United States of America

This book is printed on acid-free paper.

Last digit is print number: 9 8 7 6 5 4 3 2 1

Library of Congress Cataloging-in-Publication Data
is available from the Publisher.

ISBN 978-1-60623-954-4

About the Editors

Aydin Yücesan Durgunoğlu, PhD, is Professor of Psychology at the University of Minnesota Duluth. She has worked as a high school teacher and as a college instructor of English as a foreign language. She also was a researcher at the Center for the Study of Reading at the University of Illinois at Urbana–Champaign. Since 1995, as a consultant for the Mother Child Education Foundation in Istanbul, Dr. Durgunoğlu has led the efforts to create the two levels of an innovative adult literacy program in Turkey. Since its development and implementation, this Functional Adult Literacy Program has been continuously evaluated and improved. It also has been modified to function as the resource for women's empowerment initiatives. The program has now reached about 100,000 individuals, mostly women, across the country and won a 2006 UNESCO King Sejong Literacy Prize. Dr. Durgunoğlu is coeditor (with Ludo Verhoeven) of *Literacy Development in a Multilingual Context: Cross-Cultural Perspectives* (1998). Her research on child literacy development in different languages as well as in bilingual contexts, adult literacy, and English literacy development of recent immigrants to the United States has been supported by the Spencer Foundation and the National Institutes of Health. She is currently serving as a member of a National Academy of Sciences Task Force on Adolescent and Adult Literacy.

Claude Goldenberg, PhD, is Professor of Education at Stanford University. He has taught junior high school in San Antonio, Texas, and first grade in a bilingual elementary school in Los Angeles. Prior to his Stanford appointment, he was at California State University, Long Beach, from 1994 to 2008. Dr. Goldenberg was a National Academy of Education Spencer Fellow and a corecipient (with Ronald Gallimore) of the Albert J. Harris Award from the International Reading Association. He was also on the Committee for the Prevention of Early Reading Difficulties in Young Children (National Research Council) and the National Literacy Panel, which synthesized research on literacy development among language-minority children and youth. Dr. Goldenberg is the author of *Successful School Change: Creating Settings to Improve Teaching and Learning* (2004) and coauthor (with Rhoda Coleman) of *Promoting Academic Achievement among English Learners: A Guide to the Research* (2010). His research on topics such as literacy development among English language learners, home–school connections with language-minority families, processes and dynamics of school change, and classroom literacy interventions for middle elementary and middle school students has been supported by the Spencer Foundation, the U.S. Department of Education, and the National Institutes of Health. Dr. Goldenberg is currently codirecting a project (with Edward Haertel, also of Stanford), funded by the Spencer and Grant Foundations, to develop a measure of classroom quality for English language learners.

Contributors

P. G. Aaron, College of Education, Indiana State University, Terre Haute, Indiana

Iuliana Baciu, Department of Psychology, Wilfrid Laurier University, Waterloo, Ontario, Canada

Laura Méndez Barletta, independent scholar/researcher, Palo Alto, California

Ellen Bialystok, Department of Psychology, York University, Toronto, Ontario, Canada

María R. Brea-Spahn, Speech and Theatre and Interdisciplinary Literacy Studies PhD Program, Middle Tennessee State University, Murfreesboro, Tennessee

Him Cheung, Department of Psychology, Chinese University of Hong Kong, Shatin, New Territories, Hong Kong

Alan B. Cobo-Lewis, Department of Psychology, University of Maine, Orono, Maine

Aydin Yücesan Durgunoğlu, Department of Psychology, University of Minnesota, Duluth, Duluth, Minnesota

Xiaojia Feng, Department of Applied Foreign Language Studies, Nanjing University, Nanjing, China

Esther Geva, Department of Human Development and Applied Psychology, University of Toronto/Ontario Institute for Studies in Education, Toronto, Ontario, Canada

Claude Goldenberg, School of Education, Stanford University, Stanford, California

Alexandra Gottardo, Department of Psychology, Wilfrid Laurier University, Waterloo, Ontario, Canada

Yan Gu, College of Business, University of Illinois at Urbana–Champaign, Champaign, Illinois

Kenji Hakuta, School of Education, Stanford University, Stanford, California

Linda Jarmulowicz, School of Audiology and Speech–Language Pathology, University of Memphis, Memphis, Tennessee

R. Malatesha Joshi, College of Education and Human Development, Texas A&M University, College Station, Texas

Janette K. Klingner, School of Education and Human Development, University of Colorado Denver, Littleton, Colorado

Adèle Lafrance, Psychology Department, Laurentian University, Sudbury, Ontario, Canada

Che Kan Leong, Department of Educational Psychology and Special Education, University of Saskatchewan, Saskatoon, Saskatchewan, Canada

Kim A. Lindsey, Driver Benefits, Torrance, California

Franklin R. Manis, Department of Psychology, University of Southern California, Los Angeles, California

Stefka H. Marinova-Todd, School of Audiology and Speech Sciences, University of British Columbia, Vancouver, British Columbia, Canada

Catherine McBride-Chang, Department of Psychology, Chinese University of Hong Kong, Shatin, New Territories, Hong Kong

Julie Mueller, Faculty of Education, Wilfrid Laurier University, Waterloo, Ontario, Canada

D. Kimbrough Oller, School of Audiology and Speech–Language Pathology, University of Memphis, Memphis, Tennessee

Michael J. Orosco, Graduate School of Education, University of California, Riverside, Riverside, California

Ana Laura Pauchulo, Sociology and Equity Studies, University of Toronto/Ontario Insitute for Studies in Education, Mississauga, Ontario, Canada

Barbara Z. Pearson, Department of Communication Disorders, University of Massachusetts Amherst, Amherst, Massachusetts

Leslie Reese, College of Education, California State University, Long Beach, Long Beach, California

Ali Rezaei, College of Education, California State University, Long Beach, Long Beach, California

Elaine R. Silliman, Communication Sciences and Disorders and Cognitive and Neural Sciences, University of South Florida, Tampa, Florida

Xiuli Tong, Department of Psychology, Dalhousie University, Halifax, Nova Scotia, Canada

Yuuko Uchikoshi, School of Education, University of California, Davis, Davis, California

Series Editors' Note

Since 2004, a total of nine volumes have been published as part of the Challenges in Language and Literacy series. The two purposes of these volumes have remained unchanged: (1) to unravel the complexity of oral–written language relationships by drawing on the collaborative contributions of multiple disciplines in order to promote effective outcomes for diverse students; and (2) to provide practitioners from a wide range of professional backgrounds, including speech–language pathology, literacy instruction, and special education, with informative and timely resources for meeting the individual educational needs of students who struggle with language and literacy learning.

In this tenth volume in the series, the coeditors, Aydin Yücesan Durgunoğlu and Claude Goldenberg, have admirably met the two aims of the series. They have brought together premier researchers in the bilingual arena from varied disciplines, including education, psychology, educational psychology, foreign language studies, communication disorders, and special education. Their orchestration of the chapters has resulted in an authoritative, but accessible, treatment of bilingual research that encompasses students whose first languages are Spanish or Chinese, as well as the family and community contexts that serve as the cultural "funds of knowledge" (Moll, Amanti, Neff, & González, 2005, p. 72) that students (and professionals) bring to the school milieu. At the same time, Durgunoğlu and Goldenberg place a strong emphasis on building sturdy bridges to professional practice and policy issues in the education of English language learners. The various contributions in the volume give prominence to assessment issues as well as the critical importance of attending to the national policy context regarding the evaluation of effective bilingual education programs.

Three important assets of this volume are its solid grounding in current theory and research, its accessibility to professionals from various disciplines, and its attention to second-language issues across a range of language families. The combination of these features assures that the recommendations for policy and practice contained in the volume rest on solid evidence, that they are sensitive to the changing demographics of our classrooms, and that they are forward-looking and sensitive to the emerging challenges facing educators. Given these assets, we are confident that this volume will make a valuable contribution to our collective work with English language learners.

ELAINE R. SILLIMAN
C. ADDISON STONE

REFERENCE

Moll, L., Amanti, C., Neff, D., & González, N. (2005). Funds of knowledge for teaching: Using a qualitative approach to connect homes and classrooms. In N. González, L. C. Moll, & C. Amanti (Eds.), *Funds of knowledge* (pp. 71–87). Mahwah, NJ: Erlbaum.

Preface

As summarized by Goldenberg, Reese, and Rezaei in Chapter 1, the linguistic landscape is changing rapidly in the United States. As a result, schools have many students who have different home languages and are developing proficiency in English. For both theoretical and practical reasons, it is essential to understand how these children progress in a second language (L2), and hence there is an ongoing discussion in many fields (education, communication disorders, psychology, social work, and linguistics, to name just a few) about dual-language learners (DLLs)[1]. In this book, our goal is to continue this discussion. There are several themes that run throughout the chapters:

- Learning an L2 is a complex process, very much affected by not only the learners' cognitive and linguistic processes, but also home, classroom, community, and societal contexts. This also implies that the very diverse backgrounds of DLLs pose a challenge for educators and other professionals working with them. DLLs can differ on dimensions such as the characteristics of their first language (L1), type of instruction in their L1 and L2, prestige of their L1 and L2, contexts of use for L1 and L2, and other factors.
- There are many parallels in L1 and L2 literacy development; hence, an L1 literacy foundation is quite useful. But there is also language-specific knowledge (e.g., L2 vocabulary) that needs to be learned. L1–L2 relationships are also complex, with instances of negative, positive, and no transfer from L1 to L2 language and literacy proficiencies.
- The L1–L2 parallels also imply that, because they overlap, L1 difficulties can be a window to diagnosing and remediating L2 difficulties.

- Having a lower vocabulary level compared to their L1-only peers does not put DLLs at risk for difficulties with cognitive processes such as recall, executive control of memory, decoding, or spelling, but does put them at risk for problems with reading comprehension and writing.
- Educational and cultural practices affect not only how L2 develops but also what happens to L1 as children increase L2 proficiencies.

The opening chapter by Goldenberg, Reese, and Rezaei, provides the big-picture context for dual-language development and emphasizes the complexity and interrelatedness of the relevant factors. The authors specifically highlight the role of family, school, and community contexts.

In the next section are chapters on the oral language development of young LLs. Marinova-Todd and Uchikoshi (Chapter 2) discuss the growth in English lexical and morphosyntactic knowledge of English language learners (ELLs) and how that is related to their L1s with different degrees of similarity to English. Using a finer-grained analysis, Brea-Spahn and Silliman (Chapter 3) analyze how vocabulary development is tied to the understanding of the distributional properties of the language, such as its common phonological and phonotactic patterns, and discuss nonword repetition as a possible diagnostic tool tapping into this understanding.

Oller, Jarmulowicz, Pearson, and Cobo-Lewis (Chapter 4) note that in early language learning there is a rapid shift to the L2 (English, in this case), and the children seem to understand but not produce their L1 (Spanish, in this case), as the data show a gap between receptive and productive proficiencies in L1. It is not entirely clear why such a rapid attrition in L1 occurs as children start school and become immersed in English, but this pattern has implications for language policies and practices.

Bialystok and Feng (Chapter 5) also focus on changes that occur as children become more proficient in L2, in terms of not only linguistic knowledge but also other cognitive processes. Bialystok and Feng first note that vocabulary levels in *either* language of bilingual children tend to be lower compared to their monolingual peers. However, they seem to develop basic decoding skills with relative ease. The lower vocabulary levels do not seem to affect the access and recall of lexical items or executive control of memory. In fact, these children show better executive control as indicated by fewer intrusion errors in a memory task.

In Part III, the focus is on the development of written language and its relationships with oral language. Since phonological awareness is one of the strongest predictors of literacy development in monolinguals, Gottardo, Gu, Mueller, and Pauchulo (Chapter 6) investigate the links among L1 and L2 phonological processing and L2 reading. They show that the following factors yield different patterns across studies: (1) language variables—phonological and orthographic characteristics of L1 and its distance to English; (2) child variables—child's nonverbal reasoning, context of language acquisition, and speech perception skills; (3) sociocultural contexts of language development—socioeconomic status and parental education; and (4) measurement and methodology issues—type of tasks, sample composition, and longitudinal or cross-sectional designs.

In the next two chapters, the context of language development is different. These two chapters are about ELLs in non-English-speaking countries (Korea and China). The sociocultural and educational contexts for L2 development are different from those discussed in the other chapters, so these two chapters provide an opportunity to observe universal versus context-specific aspects of English literacy development. Cheung, McBride-Chang, and Tong (Chapter 7) find that for Korean- and Chinese-speaking children, L1 syllable awareness is a strong predictor of their L1 reading, but L2 phoneme awareness is the predictor for English reading. In addition, depending on the language instruction, transfer across languages is possible only if comparable units are available across the L1 and L2 (e.g., phonemic-level awareness through alphabetic instruction in Chinese). Leong (Chapter 8) also illustrates how the holistic teaching and understanding of Chinese orthography influences English reading and spelling of Chinese-speaking children. English orthographic information plays a stronger role than English phonological information in English reading and spelling, indicating that L1 learning experiences affect L2 reading and spelling strategies.

Chapter 9, by Barletta, Klingner, and Orosco, moves beyond single words and reviews research on the writing acquisition of ELLs, including learner, home, and classroom variables. They examine the role of L1 writing proficiency and home and classroom contexts in facilitating L2 writing.

In Part IV, the authors review the basic cognitive processes of L2 development and the implications for assessment and diagnosis. Geva and Lafrance (Chapter 10), in a longitudinal study, summarize the significant role of phonological awareness and rapid naming (rather than vocabulary and nonverbal reasoning) in spelling for both L1 and L2 learners and relate these factors to the assessment, diagnosis, and instruction of ELLs.

Along the same theme, in another longitudinal study, Manis and Lindsey (Chapter 11) investigate the cognitive and oral language contributors of reading disabilities. They report that patterns are quite stable across the grades and the two languages. For children who have difficulties in both English and Spanish word recognition and passage comprehension, there is evidence of phonological processing difficulties in both languages, yielding a typical disability pattern in both languages. However, for children who have reading difficulties in one language only, the factor to consider is the limited oral competence, possibly due to lack of sufficient exposure and/or instruction in that particular language.

Joshi and Aaron (Chapter 12) also start from a theoretical model of reading development and recommend using measures derived from such a theoretical model to assess literacy skills of both monolingual English speakers and ELLs. They provide examples of specific assessments and also discuss possible weaknesses.

In the final section of the volume, we conclude with the chapter by Hakuta (Chapter 13), moving us back to the big picture by providing a personal (and personable!) account of the history of bilingualism research in North America. Hakuta highlights how—for better or for worse—political undercurrents and policy contexts are always a big part of the research endeavors, when, in fact, it should be that the research findings inform policy and political stances.

ACKNOWLEDGMENTS

Special thanks are due to series editors Addison Stone and especially Elaine Silliman, who tirelessly reviewed and helped improve the chapters. Their contributions were above and beyond what one would expect from series editors. We also owe a debt of gratitude to our editor at The Guilford Press, Rochelle Serwator, for her patience. Special thanks to Ali Durgunoğlu for providing serenity and support amid some frustrations.

NOTE

1. We use the terms *dual-language learners* (DLLs) and *language learners* (LLs) interchangeably in this volume.

Contents

PART III. LITERACY AND DUAL-LANGUAGE LEARNERS

PART IV. ASSESSMENT AND DIAGNOSIS

PART V. CONCLUSION

PART I

Introduction

CHAPTER 1

■　■　■

Contexts for Language and Literacy Development among Dual-Language Learners

CLAUDE GOLDENBERG
LESLIE REESE
ALI REZAEI

The steady growth in the language-minority population—children and adults from non-English-speaking homes—constitutes an ongoing population shift with wide repercussions throughout the United States. The impact on schools has been and will continue to be especially pronounced, but no sector remains untouched. Health care and other social services, the judiciary, electoral politics, entertainment and the arts, the workforce, marketing, demands for goods and services—virtually all facets of U.S. society are undergoing important changes as a result of the changing linguistic landscape. More than ever, language has been catapulted into our collective awareness, becoming an increasingly complex and volatile topic as linguistic diversity is becoming a fact of life for more and more Americans.

The chapters that follow provide illustrations of the some of the work currently under way designed to deepen and broaden our understanding of language and literacy development in bilingual contexts. We set the stage by first sketching a broad statistical portrait of the language-minority populations in the United States and then providing a conceptual model for thinking about contextual influences on language and literacy development.

Finally, we use the model to report some findings from a large study of Spanish-speaking children in Texas and California.

The authors of the chapters in this book report on studies with many different types of populations and look at many different linguistic, psycholinguistic, and cognitive factors that might influence the course of language and literacy development among dual-language learners. The chapters focus largely on cognitive and psycholinguistic dimensions of language and literacy development, with some attention to contextual factors. We suggest that it is probably useful to keep in mind the larger social contexts in which children develop as we consider the theoretical and practical implications of the research reported here. The conceptual model we use here provides one way of doing so.

LINGUISTIC DIVERSITY IN THE UNITED STATES

"Dual-language learners" are children and youth who learn a language other than English at home and learn English simultaneously or sometime thereafter. Despite common characteristics, dual-language learners are highly diverse in many ways. This diversity is probably relevant for understanding the diversity of findings reported in the following chapters.

The number of *dual-language learners* in the United States has increased dramatically over the past decades. The most current estimates suggest that nearly 11 million children and adolescents—more than 20% of the 5- to 17-year olds enrolled in PreK to 12th grade—speak a language other than English at home (National Center for Education Statistics, 2008). Some dual-language learners are bilingual children whose English language skills are comparable to those of their English-only peers. However, nearly half of dual-language learners—5.1 million—are classified as *English language learners* (National Clearinghouse for English Language Acquisition, 2008), or ELLs. ELLs were formerly known as limited English proficient, or LEP. These students are limited in their English skills and therefore cannot benefit adequately from mainstream classroom instruction. About 10% of students in U.S. schools are ELLs and require some sort of instructional modification to assure they have meaningful access to the school curriculum.[1]

There are no reliable projections for how much either number—dual-language learners or the subset of English language learners—will grow,[2] but grow they surely will as the number of immigrants and children of immigrants continues to increase. Consider that by 2050:

- Nearly 1 in 5 U.S. residents will be foreign-born (compared with 1 in 8 in 2005).
- An additional 114 million U.S. residents will be immigrants or the children of immigrants.

- More than 1 in 3 children will be an immigrant or the child of an immigrant (compared with fewer than 1 in 4 in 2005).
- The number of foreign-born children ages 17 and younger will nearly double to almost 6 million, from just over 3 million in 2005 (Passel & Cohn, 2008).

Other developed countries have experienced and will continue to face growth in their immigrant—and therefore dual-language—populations, although the U.S. will continue to be by far the largest receiver of international migration in the world (United Nations, 2007). Children in the United States come from more than 400 different language backgrounds (Kindler, 2002). A large majority are Spanish speakers, but more than a million students speak one (or more) of dozens of other languages. Table 1.1 lists the 15 most common languages spoken by students who speak a language other than English at home. Of particular concern are those dual-language learners who are limited in their English proficiency. For educators charged with providing these students a comprehensive and comprehensible education, it is especially critical to understand the dynamics of dual-language development and its implications for literacy learning and other aspects of academic achievement.

The language-minority population is also socioeconomically diverse. Table 1.2 shows the income and education characteristics of Latinos and Asians in the United States. Not all Latinos and Asians are language minority, that is, speak a language other than English at home. Nonetheless, Latinos and Asians together comprise about 90% of the language minorities in the United States, so their characteristics provide a sense of how varied these populations are. Overall, Asians have higher incomes and levels of formal schooling than Latinos, but there is great diversity among Asian subgroups as well. For example, only 40% of Hmong have high school degrees and nearly 40% live below the poverty level; in contrast, among Filipinos, nearly 90% are high school graduates and only 6% live below the poverty level. Latino-origin subgroups also vary: Salvadorans have a 36% high school completion rate and higher than 20% poverty rate, while 63% of Cubans have high school diplomas and fewer than 15% are below poverty. Family education and income levels have important implications for children's educational outcomes, so the socioeconomic indicators shown in Table 1.2 also indicate likely differences in achievement levels across the subgroups. Children from some of the subgroups are clearly more at risk for poor school outcomes than others.

AN "UNRESTRICTED FIELD
OF PROFFERED EXPLANATIONS"

While few dispute the centrality of language, numerous long-standing disputes over language acquisition, development, influences, and relationship

TABLE 1.1. 15 Most Common Languages Spoken by ELLs

Home language	Estimated % of ELLs who speak this language[a]	Approximate number of ELLs who speak this language[b]	% of population 5–17 years old who report speaking English with difficulty[c]
Spanish	79.05%	4,031,300	37.8%
Vietnamese	1.95%	99,600	45.7%
Hmong	1.55%	79,281	54.5%
Chinese, Cantonese	1.02%	52,055	35.2%[d]
Korean	0.97%	49,258	33.6%
Haitian Creole	0.93%	47,316	27.6%[e]
Arabic	0.91%	46,244	22.9%
Russian	0.82%	41,627	30.1%
Tagalog	0.75%	38,239	25.4%
Navajo	0.59%	30,280	33.5%
Khmer	0.59%	30,041	39.5%
Chinese, Mandarin	0.49%	25,065	35.2%[d]
Portuguese	0.46%	23,287	22.0%
Urdu	0.41%	20,892	23.1%
Serbo-Croatian	0.38%	19,227	31.6%

Note. Adapted from Goldenberg and Coleman (2010). Copyright 2010 by Sage Publications. Adapted by permission.

[a]Data from Kindler (2002).

[b]Based on estimated 5.1 million school-age ELLs.

[c]Data from Census 2000 PHC-T-37. Ability to Speak English by Language Spoken at Home: 2000 (Tables 1a and 1b). Percentages were obtained by subtracting values for population age 18 and over from values for population age 5 and over and coverting to percents. Percentages indicate percent of respondents, ages 5–17 years , who speak a language other than English at home and who reported (or whose parent/guardian reported) they speak English less than "very well."

[d]Kindler (2002) reports Cantonese and Mandarin separately, but no distinction is made between them in the Census data.

[e]Data are for French Creole, which includes Haitian Creole.

to other developmental processes (such as cognition) have occupied scholars for years, with no end in sight. Bialystok (2001) calls the study of language acquisition an "unrestricted field of proffered explanations" (p. 51). Her explanation is that we have no commonly accepted way of defining what we mean when we say someone speaks a language well (or not so well): "There is no consensus regarding a definitive set of criteria or definition for language proficiency" (p. 50). What does it mean to say a speaker's pronunciation is good, their vocabulary expansive, or their grammar correct? And what does each of these presumed thresholds actually mean?

Nevertheless, we all seem to believe we know what we mean when we

TABLE 1.2. Education and Income Characteristics of Select Hispanic and Asian Populations

	Total population	Percentage of high school graduates	Percentage with a BA or more	Per-capita income[a]	Percentage below poverty
White non-Hispanic	194,552,774	85.5%	27.0%	24,819	7.9%
Hispanic/Latino	35,305,818	52.4%	10.4%	12,111	22.1%
Mexican	20,640,711	45.8%	7.5%	10,918	23.3%
Puerto Rican	3,406,178	63.3%	12.5%	13,518	25.1%
Cuban	1,241,685	62.9%	21.2%	20,451	14.3%
Salvadoran	655,165	36.1%	5.5%	12,349	21.2%
Asian	10,242,998	80.4%	44.1%	21,823	12.3%
Chinese mainland	2,314,537	76.2%	47.1%	23,642	13.1%
Filipino	1,850,314	87.3%	43.8%	21,267	6.2%
Vietnamese	1,122,528	61.9%	19.4%	15,655	15.7%
Korean	1,076,872	86.3%	43.8%	18,805	14.4%
Cambodian	171,937	46.7%	9.2%	10,366	29.8%
Hmong	169,428	40.4%	7.5%	6,600	37.6%

Note. Data from Goldenberg and Coleman (2010) based on data from 2000 Census (*www.census.gov/population/www*).

[a]1999 dollars

say a person is a competent speaker of a language. We associate high levels of language use and proficiency with competence; low levels are considered problematic, even symptomatic of some underlying adverse condition. The growing linguistic diversity of the United States makes it increasingly important that we strengthen our understanding of language development, more specifically *dual-language development*, and the many factors that can influence it. If we believe, as Brea-Spahn and Silliman (Chapter 3, this volume) assert, that "all language learning outcomes ... are experience driven," then we must consider the contexts in which children acquire and develop their language proficiencies, however these are defined.

CONTEXTS FOR DUAL-LANGUAGE AND LITERACY DEVELOPMENT

Family and Community Contexts

Our conception of contexts of language development derives from a language socialization perspective (Zentella, 2005), which examines how children become competent speakers of one or more languages. This perspective considers factors such as activities in which children engage with more competent speakers of the language and shared beliefs and assumptions surrounding appropriate uses of language that shape interactions during these activities. Researchers have studied many aspects of children's social contexts and their influence on language and literacy development. As a result there is a large body of empirical work going back for years that has studied numerous populations and identified a wide range of home and family factors that influence the language and literacy development of both dual-language learners and monolingual speakers. These factors include talking with and to children, reading and other literacy events, storytelling, books and other learning materials in the home, going to the library, doing homework with children or following up on school lessons, and home–school communications (e.g., Booth & Dunn, 1996; Delgado-Gaitan, 1990; Goldenberg, 1987; Hart & Risley, 1995; Hess & Holloway, 1984; Hoff, 2003; Kainz & Vernon-Feagans, 2007; Mercado, 2005; Oller & Eilers, 2002; Reese, Goldenberg, Loucky, & Gallimore, 1995; Roca, 2005; Valdés, 1996; Vasquez, Pease-Alvarez, & Shannon, 1994; Zentella, 1997, 2005).

Families do not raise children in isolation, however, and the ways in which children experience language at home presumably varies, at least partly in response to opportunities for and restrictions on language use in the settings outside of the home in which children participate. There are clear differences in community sociodemographic characteristics and language and literacy resources, any of which might enable or constrain children's language and literacy experiences (e.g., Neuman & Celano, 2001; Reese & Goldenberg, 2006; Reese, Linan-Thompson, & Goldenberg, 2008; Smith, Constantino, & Krashen, 1997). The literature on community influences on child language and literacy development (in fact, on child outcomes in general) is not as extensive as that on family influences. The research that does exist suggests that neighborhoods and communities have less impact on child outcomes than do families (Ellen & Turner, 1997; Klebanov, Brooks-Gunn, McCarton, & McCormick, 1998; Sanbonmatsu, Kling, Duncan, & Brooks-Gunn, 2006; Shonkoff & Phillips, 2000). Nonetheless, neighborhood and community characteristics might influence the language and literacy opportunities children have, even though for young children in particular we would expect those influences to be largely mediated by families.

For bilingual children growing up in U.S. contexts, the dynamics of language use in the home and community are necessarily more complex than are those for monolingual speakers of English. For example, Vasquez et al. (1994) documented ways in which immigrant families responded to the challenges of living in an English-dominant community, working together to maximize comprehension of unfamiliar English texts. Immigrant children are often called upon to serve as translators for their families in a variety of domains including legal, financial, residential, and religious (Orellana, Dorner, & Pulido, 2003; Orellana, Reynolds, & Dorner, 2003).

Home Language Use

The issue of language use in the home—specifically, whether and to what degree English or a non-English language is used—is, of course, unique to families that speak a language other than English. Thus, in addition to the many contextual factors that influence children's language and literacy development, we must also consider the language in which those factors play themselves out. For example, if reading with children and speaking with children promote literacy and language development, are the effects different depending on what language is used?

Saunders and O'Brien (2006) reviewed several studies that examined the relationship between family characteristics and child language development among English language learners. The most straightforward, and perhaps unsurprising, finding of these studies was that more English used in the home and with peers led to greater English proficiency among children. Goldenberg, Rueda, and August (2006) came to similar conclusions in their review of studies that examined family context effects on English learners' literacy achievement: Generally—but not in all studies—more English in the home was associated with higher literacy achievement in English.

This literature has several limitations; perhaps the most important is that it is almost exclusively correlational. It is therefore impossible to determine whether more English in the home and among peers leads to greater language and literacy attainment in English, or as children (and families) acquire more facility in English they engage more with others in English, or if some combination of the two explains the correlation. Three experimental studies of early literacy development suggest a more complex relationship than might at first appear and, indeed, point to the possible benefits—*in terms of second language outcomes*—of parents using the home language in their literacy interactions with young children.

Hancock (2002) studied the effects of kindergarten children taking home books in either English or Spanish to read with their parents. Providing reading materials in Spanish led to more enhanced preliteracy skills (e.g., concepts of print) in English than did providing English reading materials for children to take home. Consistent with these findings, Koskinen et al. (2000) found that sending home and promoting the use of books and tapes in English had *no* effect on first-grade English learners' English literacy development. More recently, Roberts (2008) reported two experiments involving Spanish- and Hmong-speaking children. Roberts compared the effects of sending home storybooks in English or a child's home language on children's acquisition of storybook vocabulary in English. In the first study, children who received the home-language storybooks learned more storybook vocabulary, as measured in English; in the second study there were no differences.

We should bear in mind that these studies did not manipulate the language generally used by parents and children in the home, but rather the language used during fairly circumscribed reading events. Limited as these manipulations were, the findings do suggest that enhancing home literacy experiences for English learners in their first language can have positive effects on early literacy development *in English*. Although we have far too little research to reach firm conclusions about the relative effects of first- and second-language use in the home, this finding is consistent with the school-based literature on the positive effects of home-language instruction on reading achievement in English (Goldenberg, 2008).

There are several possible explanations for these findings. One is that language, literacy, and cognitive skills are learned most easily in one's first language, and then transfer to one's second language, making this a more efficient pathway for literacy learning. Another possibility is that language, literacy, and cognitive skills learned in one's primary language promote enhanced language, literacy, and cognition in general, creating a stronger foundation for subsequent and ongoing development. (See Part II of August & Shanahan, 2006, "Cross-Linguistic Relationships in Second-Language Learners.")

Regardless, these data both challenge and support the complex findings reported in the chapters that follow of positive, negative, and no transfer across languages. Stated differently, we find evidence for the facilitating, interfering, and nil effects of L1 on L2 language and literacy acquisition (e.g., Brea-Spahn & Silliman, Chapter 3; Gottardo, Gu, Mueller, Faroga, & Pauchulo, Chapter 6; Méndez Barletta, Klinger, & Orosco, Chapter 9; Bialystok & Feng, Chapter 5; Oller, Jarmulowicz, Pearson, & Cobo-Lewis, Chapter 4, this volume). These chapters also address two additional complicating factors. One is transfer across languages with alphabetic and nonalphabetic scripts (e.g., Cheung, McBride-Chang, & Tong, Chapter 7; Leong, Chapter 8; Marinova-Todd & Uchikoshi, Chapter 2, this volume), where phonological representations and other linguistic features will differ; the relative importance of orthographic, lexical, and phonological processes in reading might also differ. The other is diagnosis and intervention when learners experience difficulties of different sorts (e.g., Brea-Spahn & Silliman, Chapter 3; Geva & Lafrance, Chapter 10; Joshi & Aron, Chapter 12; Manis & Lindsey, Chapter 11, this volume). In all cases, however, as Cheung et al. and others argue, instruction is likely to play an important role in facilitating the development of L2 literacy skills, regardless of the languages used and the challenges learners face. Where we need continued effort, as exemplified by the work of many of these authors, is in understanding the nature of that instruction and how and whether effective instruction differs for different groups of learners learning in different languages.

WORKING MODEL OF COMMUNITY
AND FAMILY INFLUENCES

Drawing on the literature briefly reviewed above, we present a working model that attempts to bring together a large number of potential community and family influences on children's developing language skills in their first and second languages. This is a functionalist perspective; that is, it assumes "language emerges out of children's ordinary experiences to fulfill specific cognitive, social, and communicative functions" (Bialystok, 2001, p. 40). In contrast to formalist language theories, which presume (or propose) that language is the result of innate structures, themselves the result of human evolutionary adaptation, functionalist theories are based on the premise that the language children learn is largely the result of interactions with their environments. Formalist theories such as Chomsky's (1965) argue that all children will acquire language, given some (usually undefined) threshold of environmental stimulation. Functionalist theories, in contrast, presume more of a direct association between environmental input and/or demand on the one hand and children's acquisition of language on the other.

The model derives from considerable theoretical and empirical work centered in the child development literature (e.g., Bronfenbrenner, 1979; Shonkoff & Phillips, 2000) and research in literacy and language socialization (e.g., Delgado-Gaitan, 1990; Zentella, 1997, 2005), families as learning environments (e.g., Booth & Dunn, 1996; Hart & Risley, 1995; Hess & Holloway, 1984), and community and neighborhood influences on developmental outcomes (e.g., Lara-Cinisomo, Pebley, Vaiana, & Maggio, 2004; Sanbonmatsu et al., 2006). The constructs and variables depicted in the model were derived from a conceptual analysis of this literature.

In brief, the model maps out eight broad classes of variables; four at the community level—demographics, language, language of literacy, and literacy resources—and four analogous classes of variables at the family level—characteristics, language practices, language of literacy, and literacy practices. The model was developed to try to bring together a large number of community and family contextual factors into a single coherent framework. This framework can be used to guide data collection and analysis in order to determine the relative impact of factors at the community (boxes 1–4) and family (boxes 5–8) levels. Each box in Figure 1.1 contains examples from the class of variables within the box.

There are many possible paths of influence illustrated in the model—for example, community demographics can influence community language and literacy resources, which in turn can influence family language and literacy practices, which then affect child outcomes. Family characteristics might also influence language and literacy practices, which then influence child outcomes. Alternatively, children's proximal experiences with language and literacy might be independent of community demographics and family characteristics. The model only provides a framework to address the question of contextual influences on children's language and literacy development. We are far from a clear and comprehensive understanding of how the dimensions represented in Figure 1.1 actually function to influence dual-language learning outcomes.

FINDINGS FROM A STUDY
OF SPANISH-SPEAKING DUAL-LANGUAGE LEARNERS

We have used this model to analyze qualitative and quantitative data from a sample of approximately 1,400 Spanish-speaking children in 35 communities from the time they entered kindergarten until they finished second grade. The communities are located in urban and suburban settings in Southern California and urban, suburban, semirural and border Texas.

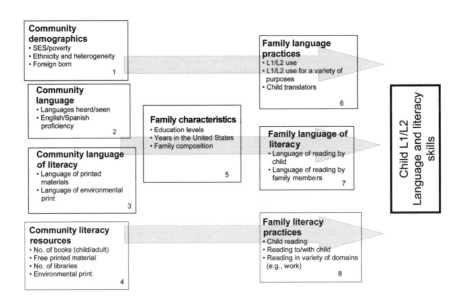

FIGURE 1.1. Community and family influences on language and literacy.

Children attended one of four types of instructional programs (for sampling frame, see Reese & Goldenberg, 2006, 2008; Reese, Goldenberg, & Saunders, 2006). Some of the children were in *all-English* instruction (sometimes called English immersion). Other children were in one of three bilingual programs, where they received instruction in Spanish for substantial portions of the school day. The three bilingual programs were *early transition* (children learn literacy and academic skills in the home language for the first few years of elementary school, then transition to English instruction); *maintenance (or developmental) bilingual* (students continue with Spanish instruction even after beginning to receive substantial amounts of instruction in English); and *dual-language (or two-way)* (Spanish-speaking children and English-speaking children receive instruction in both languages, the goal being bilingualism and biliteracy for both groups). Table 1.3 provides a breakdown of children by program and geographic region.

Data for this study came from different sources. We used "American Factfinder" on the U.S. Census website (*census.gov*) to gather data on community income and education, ethnic composition, and percent foreign-born. Data on language use and availability of literacy materials in the community were collected as part of day-long area surveys conducted by teams of two or three researchers. We noted and rated (e.g., 1–5 scale, with 1 = all Spanish and 5 = all English) the prevalence of English and Spanish use and the amount of written materials in either English or Spanish that was available in the community.

Family-level data were collected through parent questionnaires sent home by the children's teachers. Questionnaires asked about family demographics (e.g., occupation, income, family size, place of birth, and time in the United States) and language and literacy practices in the home (e.g., language spoken with the child by various interlocutors, reading frequency and language by child and others in the household, frequency of child's translating for family members). The return rate for the surveys was 76%.

Children's language and literacy achievement, in English and Spanish, was measured using the Woodcock Language Proficiency Battery—Revised

TABLE 1.3. Participating Children, by Program and Region

	All English	Early transition	Maintenance bilingual	Dual language
Border Texas	77	239	0	133
Urban Texas	82	363	0	60
Urban California	267	78	84	34
Total	426	680	84	227

(WLPB-R; Woodcock, 1991; Woodcock & Muñoz-Sandoval, 1995). The WLPB-R is perhaps the most widely used assessment of language and literacy achievement in the United States. It has parallel forms in English and Spanish, thereby permitting comparisons of achievement within and across languages.

Diversity across Communities

One theme that clearly emerges from our analyses is community diversity. The communities where the young dual-language learners in our sample resided and attended school are diverse in virtually every respect defined by our working model (Figure 1.1; boxes 1–4)—socioeconomic and ethnic characteristics, language use, availability of literacy materials in English and Spanish (Reese & Goldenberg, 2006; Reese et al., 2006, 2008). For example:

- Median family income (adjusted for cost of living, which itself varied considerably across the sample) in the communities ranged from $12,000 to nearly $80,000 (mean = $32,000).
- Percent high school completion among Latinos in the community ranged from 12.3% to 91.5% (mean = 39.4%).
- Percent of population that speaks only English in the community ranged from 3.0% to 91.4% (mean = 30.3%).
- Language heard when walking around the community ranged from only Spanish to only English, with most communities falling somewhere in between.
- Signs, newspapers, and free printed material in the communities ranged from being mostly in Spanish to only in English.
- Percent of reading material for sale in Spanish ranged from 0% to 100% (mean = 21.9%).
- Number of books and magazines estimated to be available in public places (libraries, bookstores, etc.) ranged from 0 in communities with no library, bookstore, or any local store with books and magazines for sale, to more than 1 million in communities with a library, bookstores, and grocery and drug stores with books and magazines for sale (mean = 51,000 books and magazines).

Diversity across Families

Families were sampled from a population that is predominantly Spanish speaking and low in socioeconomic status (see Table 1.2). Nonetheless, as would be expected, there was also some diversity among families along the dimensions identified in the model (boxes 5–8). For example:

- Reported annual family incomes ranged from below $10,000 (nearly one quarter of the sample) to more than $40,000 (nearly 11%), with some families reporting annual incomes above $60,000.
- Parents' level of schooling ranged from only having finished elementary school (approximately 35% of parents) to receiving post–high school vocational training or university education (approximately 15% of parents). Nearly 30% had at least a high school degree or its equivalent.
- Approximately 82% of parents were foreign-born, all but a handful in Mexico; in contrast, 84% of children were born in the United States.
- Parents reported that they or an older sibling read to children approximately two to three times per month in Spanish and an equal amount of time in English; the range for both was zero to daily.
- Parents' reading language tended to be mostly in Spanish, but the reported range was from only Spanish to only English.
- Books for children in the home ranged from 0 to 700, with a mean of 46; for adults the range was 0 to 900, with a mean of 40.

Associations with Student Outcomes

We are, of course, interested in seeing the degree to which the dimensions identified in our analytical model predicted student language and literacy achievement, as measured by the WLPB-R. Analyses are incomplete and still under way, but a number of patterns are emerging (Grunow, Goldenberg, Reese, & Bryk, 2008; Reese & Goldenberg, 2008; You, Reese, Rumberger, & Goldenberg, 2009). Results are complex and to some extent depend on the type of analysis. In addition, relationships between predictor variables and child outcomes varied depending on the language being measured.

Community-level variables were at best weakly associated with student outcomes. This is consistent with the literature on community influences on child outcomes (e.g., Ellen & Turner, 1997; Sanbonmatsu et al., 2006; Shonkoff & Phillips, 2000). However, *family-level variables* were associated with variations in student outcomes. Home language environments predicted children's oral language scores, and home literacy predicted reading scores. In Bronfenbrenner's (1979) terms, the "microsystem" comprising those factors closest to the child on a daily basis has the most effect on child outcomes.

Language-Specific Correlations

There were language-specific associations in both reading and oral language. That is, home language use and literacy activities in English tended to predict higher English language and literacy scores and lower Spanish scores among the children (at each grade level); conversely, home language and literacy in Spanish predicted higher Spanish and lower English scores. For example, greater prevalence of English in the home (e.g., oral language use, television viewing, reading language) was associated with higher English oral language and lower Spanish oral language scores when children began kindergarten. However, the effect of language use in the home was not uniform. There were also interlocutor effects that varied by language: Language spoken with adults predicted Spanish (but not English) scores; language spoken with children predicted English (but not Spanish) scores. This finding resonates with what Oller et al. (Chapter 4, this volume) report regarding the role of peers in language shift.

As we discussed previously, these are correlations, so we must be cautious about interpretations. It is very difficult to tease out cause and effect: More use of English might produce higher English—and lower Spanish—achievement, but it can also be the case that as children develop more facility in English they tend to use English more (particularly with friends) and Spanish less; and of course both can be true—language use and language facility might affect each other in reciprocal fashion. Some variables, however, suggest a particular direction of effects. For example, correlations between parents' reading language and children's reading and language scores were language specific, as described above. The direction of effects is more likely to be from parents' reading language (or whatever aspect of the home environment that variable indexes) to child language and literacy outcomes rather than the reverse. But even here we must be very cautious: Parents' reading language was correlated with other measures of home-language use, so it is impossible to know whether the correlations between parents' reading language and children's language scores indicate a possible cause–effect relationship or are spurious; that is, the result of causal relations between children's oral language and other variables, all of which are associated with parents' reading language.

Family SES and Student Outcomes

The relationship between family SES (income and parent occupation and education) and child outcomes depended on language and the type of analysis. In simple bivariate correlations, SES predicted higher scores in English oral language and reading but was only weakly and inconsistently associated with scores in Spanish. In contrast, an analysis using hierarchical linear modeling (HLM), which takes into account the "nested" structure of the data (i.e., children are not randomly distributed among communities), found that SES was significantly associated with oral language scores in both English and Spanish at the beginning of kindergarten (Grunow et al., 2008). But an analysis using structural equation modeling (SEM)—which can analyze Spanish and English outcomes simultaneously while also taking into account that children are nested within community—found (1) no SES effect on Spanish oral language in kindergarten, but (2) a significant effect on English oral language in kindergarten (You et al., 2009). Neither analysis found that SES contributed to language growth between kindergarten and second grade. Growth analyses on reading outcomes have not yet been conducted.

Translating by Children

Children are sometimes asked to translate for family members who are more limited in their English proficiency. Studies of adolescents have suggested that this language-intensive activity might have positive effects on children's language development (e.g., Orellana, Dorner, et al., 2003; Orellana, Reynolds, et al., 2003). In our study we found that children as young as kindergarten were called upon to translate for family members an average of approximately one to two times/month and that frequency of translating was associated with higher language scores. Associations were stronger and more consistent for Spanish than for English. That is, kindergarten children who translated more frequently for family members had significantly higher Spanish language scores than children who translated less frequently or not at all. English language scores were also higher for children who translated more frequently, but the effect was not as strong or consistent.

The magnitude of the associations depended on the analysis. In the HLM analysis, the association between translating and English oral language did not quite reach significance, whereas the association with Spanish oral language did. In the SEM analysis, translating effects on Spanish were significant at $p < .001$; they were significant, but weaker, for English. We are still not certain why the inconsistency. It might be because outcomes in both languages are analyzed simultaneously in SEM, thereby applying better statistical control and better isolating the relationship between translating and English oral language. In any case, it seems as if Spanish language proficiency, more so than English, is implicated in children's translation activities in the family. Again, we cannot separate correlation from causation: It might be that children with stronger language skills (particularly in Spanish) are asked to translate; it might also be that translating promotes stronger language skills; or both might be true.

Oral Language Growth from Kindergarten Entrance to End of Grade 2

In analyses of oral language growth in English and Spanish, we have found that several variables predicted growth, either positively or negatively:

whether children were born outside the United States, how prominent English was in the home, how much literacy was in the home, whether parents read or told stories in Spanish to children, and the number of people in the household. Neither SES nor translating was associated with language growth in either language. The relationships we found were complex and hard to encapsulate simply; they sometimes varied by time of the year (academic year vs. summer). For example:

• Children born outside the United States gained more in English than children born in the United States This accelerated gain was only observed during the summer, not during the academic year. The first part of this finding is explained by the fact that children born outside the United States began kindergarten with lower levels of English proficiency; they then tended to "catch up" relative to their U.S.-born peers. But it is unclear why this should happen only in the summer. In a related finding, children born in the United States and whose parents were also born in the United States showed greater growth in Spanish, reflecting the fact that they began with lower levels of Spanish oral language and between kindergarten and second grade tended to catch up with children born outside the United States or whose parents were born outside the United States. There were no differences in growth rates between the academic year and summer

• Children living in homes where there was greater prevalence of English showed slower oral language growth in Spanish. This finding is easily understood if we assume that more exposure to English means less exposure to Spanish, which then leads to decreased Spanish language growth. However, there were two findings that seemed somewhat contradictory—or at least create a more complex picture:

• First, there was no effect of *English prevalence* in the home on oral language *English growth*. A possible explanation is that although there was more English in the homes of some of the children, homes were still heavily Spanish dominant. There might not be sufficient English use, or quality of English use, to affect English oral language growth on the WLPB-R, which tends to gauge academic rather than what is sometimes called everyday or "conversational" language (Saunders & O'Brien, 2006).

• Second, greater frequency of telling or reading stories *in Spanish* to children led to greater oral language growth *in English* (but only during summers). This finding is consistent with experimental findings (and theory regarding L1 to L2 transfer) reported previously, indicating that home literacy events in the home language—in contrast to L2 home literacy events—produce stronger effects on English literacy outcomes. However, this finding is *not* consistent with the language-specific effects of home language and literacy use we reported previously. Associations between home language use and oral language development thus seem to be different depending on whether "language development" is gauged at one point in time (consistent language-specific correlations) or as growth trajectories over different times of the year (more complex picture).

• Children living in larger households gained less in Spanish than children living in smaller households, but only during the academic year. Again, we can explain part of this finding fairly easily: Parents mostly spoke Spanish to their children, and adult use of Spanish, and relative absence of English, was a significant predictor of child language scores in Spanish. Family size is known to correlate negatively with child language skills and other achievement outcomes, probably because more children in the family diminishes the amount of verbal interaction between parents and any one child (e.g., Blake, 1989; Qi, Kaiser, Milan, & Hancock, 2006). However, again, it is unclear why this effect was found during the academic year and not in the summer. It is also unclear why family size had an effect on Spanish language *growth* but not on language skills at kindergarten entry.

Taken together, this set of findings suggests that family factors associated with achievement and growth in one language typically do not play the same role for another language the child is learning. For example, children in families that use more English have higher English oral language scores but lower Spanish language scores at kindergarten entry; more English in the home is then associated with slower growth in Spanish oral language but is unrelated to language growth in English. Interlocutors also seem to matter differently for different languages. Moreover, some associations varied by time of the year: some family variables predict language growth during the academic year, others during the summer, and yet others show no difference across the year. These and other findings summarized here suggest that family context effects on dual-language learners matter, but they matter in complex and myriad ways, some of which we do not yet fully understand.

Relationship with School Program

In analyzing potential influences and correlates of student language and literacy development, we have also found that different school programs draw from different populations of families (Goldenberg, 2006; Reese et al., 2006). For example, two-way programs are in more affluent, English-speaking communities; transition programs are in poorer, more heavily Spanish-speaking communities. Moreover, compared to families in primary language programs, families in English immersion programs have higher incomes; parents have been in the United States longer and read more in English, and families use more English and less Spanish. Finally, compared to families in other types of programs, families in dual-language programs have higher incomes; parents have more formal education, higher occupation levels, and are more likely to be U.S.-born; and children are more likely to have attended preschool.

Readers should keep in mind that our sample of California and Texas students was heavily—75%—Mexican-origin; almost all the rest were either U.S.-born or born in Central America. It is possible that the relationships among background characteristics and language program could be different for different populations of Latino families. For example, whereas the Mexican-origin population tends to have income and education levels below national means, Cuban Americans in Miami are much closer to mainstream norms (Oller & Eilers, 2002; see also Table 1.2, above). These and other population differences, as well as differences in programs in states other than Texas and California, could limit the generalizability of our findings. Nonetheless, the more important point suggested from data regarding children's school program and family characteristics is that, without controlling for family background characteristics, comparisons among different language programs are likely to be misleading.

Particularly noteworthy in this regard is our finding that children who are in English-only programs begin kindergarten with higher English and lower Spanish oral language scores (Grunow et al., 2008; You et al., 2009). However, although children began school with greater proficiency in English, over the next 3 years, being in an English immersion program did not predict growth in English oral language. On the other hand, being in an English immersion program did predict declining Spanish oral language growth (You et al., 2009). Additional analyses have found that the growth patterns differ during the academic year and summers: During the academic year, being in an English immersion program predicted higher growth in English oral language than being in a Spanish language program. During the summer, however, children in English immersion programs essentially lost whatever gains were observed during the school year (Grunow et al., 2008). The net result was no difference in English growth as a result of being in an English immersion program, but a negative effect on Spanish oral language growth (You et al., 2009).

CONCLUSION: TOWARD A MORE ENLIGHTENED LANGUAGE POLICY

Dual-language learners in the United States represent a large and growing segment of our school-age population. They live and go to school under very different conditions and circumstances, some far more supportive of language and literacy growth in one or more languages than others. We need continued, comprehensive efforts to understand influences on and mechanisms of language and literacy development; to document ways in which two (or more) languages interact and influence the other—both positively and negatively; and to determine how home, school, and possibly community conditions can promote high levels of proficiency. We should strive for high levels of proficiency in two or more languages, given the potential social, economic, cultural, and intellectual advantages of bilingualism (Bialystok, 2001; Saiz & Zoido, 2005). Such a goal is not only appropriate for dual-language learners but also for the monolingual English population.

To accomplish this, we must be mindful of what Kenji Hakuta discusses in his provocative and insightful concluding chapter (see Chapter 13). That is, due to the volatile and contentious debates over language of instruction, language education policy seems to proceed largely oblivious to the findings of scientific research. English-only advocates, convinced that use of the home language in school necessarily means a degradation of English attainment, or perhaps worse, a dilution of Anglo-American culture, have spearheaded efforts at the national and state level to eliminate the use of languages other than English in school. This is indeed a shame, since it means that the linguistic resources of 11 million dual-language learner children in U.S. schools are not used to good effect. These resources can both help them acquire literacy in English *while* maintaining their home language, thereby becoming functioning bilingual, biliterate citizens and residents. Discounting these linguistic resources is a loss not only to them but also to the society as a whole. We can only hope that at the beginning of the second decade of the 21st century a more progressive view of language and language policies will be begin to emerge, guided by research such as that in the following chapters.

ACKNOWLEDGMENTS

This work was partly supported by Grant No. P01 HD39521, "Oracy/Literacy Development in Spanish-Speaking Children," from the National Institute of Child Health and Human Development and the Institute of Education Sciences. Our thanks to Elaine Silliman and Aydin Durgunoğlu for their helpful comments.

NOTES

1. In a landmark 1974 case, *Lau v. Nichols* (414 U.S. No. 72-6520, pp. 563–572), the Supreme Court ruled that schools are required to teach ELLs so that they have "a meaningful opportunity to participate in the public educational pro-

gram" (p. 563). The court did not specify what kind of pedagogy must be used, but "sink or swim" was deemed unconstitutional and a violation of students' civil rights.

2. In previous publications (e.g., Goldenberg, 2008), we have cited a figure of 1 in 4 as the projected ELL population by 2025, based on comments made several years ago by former U.S. Department of Education Secretary Margaret Spellings (retrieved February 14, 2006, from *www.ed.gov/news/speeches/2005/12/12012005.html*) and contained in a report by the U.S. Department of Education (2005). However, we have been unable to confirm this number with statisticians and analysts at the U.S. Census Bureau, National Center for Education Statistics, National Clearinghouse for English Language Acquisition, and Office of English Language Acquisition (U.S. Department of Education).

REFERENCES

August, D., & Shanahan, T. (Eds.). (2006). *Developing literacy in second-language learners: Report of the National Literacy Panel on language-minority children and youth.* Mahwah, NJ: Erlbaum.

Bialystok, E. (2001). *Bilingualism in development: Language, literacy, and cognition.* New York: Cambridge University Press.

Blake, J. (1989). *Family size and achievement.* Berkeley: University of California Press.

Booth, A., & Dunn, J. (1996). (Eds.). *Family and school links: How do they affect educational outcomes?* Mahwah, NJ: Erlbaum.

Bronfenbrenner, U. (1979). *The ecology of human development: Experiments by nature and design.* Cambridge, MA: Harvard University Press.

Chomsky, N. (1965). *Aspects of the theory of syntax.* Cambridge, MA: MIT Press.

Delgado-Gaitan, C. (1990). *Literacy for empowerment.* New York: Falmer.

Ellen, I., & Turner, M. (1997). Do neighborhoods matter? Assessing recent evidence. *Housing Policy Debate, 8,* 833–866.

Goldenberg, C. (1987). Low-income Hispanic parents' contributions to their first-grade children's word-recognition skills. *Anthropology and Education Quarterly, 18,* 149–179.

Goldenberg, C. (2006, April). *Family contexts and the language and literacy achievement of Spanish-speaking children.* Paper presented at the International Reading Association Annual Convention, Chicago, IL.

Goldenberg, C. (2008). Teaching English language learners: What the research does—and does not—say. *American Educator, 32*(2), 8–23, 42–44.

Goldenberg, C., & Coleman, R. (2010). *Promoting academic achievement among English learners: A guide to the research.* Thousand Oaks, CA: Corwin Press.

Goldenberg, C., Rueda, R., & August, D. (2006). Sociocultural influences on the literacy attainment of language-minority children and youth. In D. August & T. Shanahan (Eds.), *Developing literacy in second-language learners: Report of the National Literacy Panel on Language Minority Children and Youth* (pp. 269–347). Mahwah, NJ: Erlbaum.

Grunow, A., Goldenberg, C., Reese, L., & Bryk, A. (2008, April). *Home and com-*

munity resources for oral language development of Spanish-speaking students: A multilingual multi-level analysis. Paper presented at the Annual Meeting of the American Educational Research Association.

Hancock, D. R. (2002). The effects of native language books on the pre-literacy skill development of language minority kindergartners. *Journal of Research in Childhood Education, 17,* 62–68.

Hart, B., & Risley, T. R. (1995) *Meaningful differences in everyday experiences of young American children.* Baltimore: Brookes.

Hess, R. D., & Holloway, S. (1984). Family and school as educational institutions. In R. D. Parke (Ed.), *Review of child development research, 7: The family* (pp. 179–222). Chicago: University of Chicago Press.

Hoff, E. (2003). The specificity of environmental influence: Socioeconomic status affects early vocabulary development via maternal speech. *Child Development, 74,* 1368–1378.

Kainz, K., & Vernon-Feagans, L. (2007). The ecology of reading development for children in poverty. *Elementary School Journal, 107,* 407–427.

Kindler, A. (2002). *Survey of the states' limited English proficient students and available educational programs and services, 2000–2001 summary report.* Washington, DC: U.S. Department of Education. Accessed September 10, 2009, from *www.ncela.gwu.edu/files/rcd/BE021853/Survey_ofthe_States.pdf.*

Klebanov, P., Brooks-Gunn, J., McCarton, C., & McCormick, M. (1998). The contribution of neighborhood and family income to developmental test scores over the first three years of life. *Child Development, 69,* 1420–1436.

Koskinen, P. S., Blum, I. H., Bisson, S. A., Phillips, S. M., Creamer, T. S., & Baker, T. K. (2000). Book access, shared reading, and audio models: The effects of supporting the literacy learning of linguistically diverse students in school and at home. *Journal of Educational Psychology, 92,* 23–36.

Lara-Cinisomo, S., Pebley, A., Vaiana, M., & Maggio, E. (2004). *Are L. A.'s children ready for school?* Santa Monica, CA: RAND.

Mercado, C. (2005). Seeing what's there: Language and literacy funds of knowledge in New York Puerto Rican homes. In A. C. Zentella (Ed.), *Building on strength: Language and literacy in Latino families and communities* (pp. 134–147). New York: Teachers College Press.

National Center for Education Statistics. (2008). Table A-8-2. Number and percentage of children ages 5–17 who spoke a language other than English at home and who spoke English with difficulty, by selected characteristics: 2007. Retrieved August 17, 2009, from *nces.ed.gov.*

National Clearinghouse for English Language Acquisition. (2008). *How has the English Language Learner population changed in recent years?* Washington, DC: Author. Retrieved September 6, 2009, from *tinyurl.com/nyekev.*

Neuman, S., & Celano, D. (2001). Access to print in low-income and middle-income communities: An ecological study of four neighborhoods. *Reading Research Quarterly, 36,* 8–26.

Oller, D., & Eilers, R. (Eds.). (2002). *Language and literacy in bilingual children.* Clevedon, UK: Mulilingual Matters.

Orellana, M., Dorner, L., & Pulido, L. (2003). Accessing assets: Immigrant youth as family interpreters. *Social Problems, 50,* 505–524.

Orellana, M. F., Reynolds, J., & Dorner, L. (2003). In other words: Translating or "para-phrasing" as a family literacy practice in immigrant households. *Reading Research Quarterly, 38,* 12–34.

Passel, J., & Cohn, D. (2008). *U.S. population projections: 2005–2050.* Washington, DC: Pew Research Center. Retrieved September 8, 2009, from *pewhispanic.org.*

Qi, C. H., Kaiser, A. P., Milan, S., & Hancock, T. (2006). Language performance of low-income African American and European American preschool children on the PPVT-III. *Language, Speech, and Hearing Services in Schools, 37,* 5–16.

Reese, L., & Goldenberg, C. (2006). Community contexts for literacy development of Latina/o children: Contrasting case studies. *Anthropology and Education Quarterly, 37,* 42–61.

Reese, L., & Goldenberg, C. (2008). Community literacy resources and home literacy practices among immigrant Latino families. *Marriage and Family Review, 43,* 109–139.

Reese, L., Goldenberg, C., Loucky, J., & Gallimore, R. (1995). Ecocultural context, cultural activity and emergent literacy of Spanish-speaking children. In S. Rothstein (Ed.), *Class, culture and race in American schools: A handbook* (pp. 199–224). Westport, CT: Greenwood.

Reese, L., Goldenberg, C., & Saunders, W. (2006). Variations in reading achievement among Spanish-speaking children in different language programs: Explanations and confounds. *Elementary School Journal, 106,* 362–366.

Reese, L., Linan-Thompson, S., & Goldenberg, C. (2008). Variability in community characteristics and Spanish-speaking children's home language and literacy opportunities. *Journal of Multilingual and Multicultural Development, 29,* 271–290.

Roberts, T. (2008). Home storybook reading in primary or second language with preschool children: Evidence of equal effectiveness for second-language vocabulary acquisition. *Reading Research Quarterly, 43,* 103–130.

Roca, A. (2005). Raising a bilingual child in Miami: Reflections on language and culture. In A. C. Zentella (Ed.), *Building on strength: Language and literacy in Latino families and communities* (pp. 110–117). New York: Teachers College Press.

Saiz, A., & Zoido, E. (2005). Listening to what the world says: Bilingualism and earnings in the United States. *Review of Economics and Statistics, 87,* 523–538.

Sanbonmatsu, L., Kling, J., Duncan, G., & Brooks-Gunn, J. (2006). *Neighborhoods and academic achievement: Results from the Moving to Opportunity experiment* (Working Paper 11909). Cambridge, MA: National Bureau of Economic Research. Available at *www.nber.org/papers/w11909.*

Saunders, W., & O'Brien, G. (2006). Oral language. In F. Genesee, K. Lindholm-Leary, W. Saunders, & D. Christian (Eds.), *Educating English language learners* (pp. 14–63). New York: Cambridge University Press.

Shonkoff, J., & Phillips, D. (Eds.). (2000). *From neurons to neighborhoods: The science of early childhood development.* Washington, DC: National Academy Press.

Smith, C., Constantino, R., & Krashen, S. (1997). Differences in print environment for children in Beverly Hills, Compton, and Watts. *Emergency Librarian,* 24(4), 8–9.

United Nations. (2007). *World population prospects: The 2006 revision highlights.* Working Paper No. ESA/P/WP.202, Population Division of the Department of Economic and Social Affairs of the United Nations. Retrieved September 13, 2009, from *www.un.org/esa/population/publications/wpp2006/WPP2006_ Highlights_rev.pdf.*

U.S. Department of Education. (2005). *Education in the United States: A brief overview.* Washington, DC: Author. Retrieved September 5, 2009, from *www. ed.gov/international/edus.*

Woodcock, R. W. (1991). *Woodcock Language Proficiency Battery—Revised* (English form). Chicago: Riverside.

Woodcock, R., & Muñoz-Sandoval, A. F. (1995). *Woodcock Language Proficiency Battery—Revised* (Spanish form). Chicago: Riverside.

You, S., Reese, L., Rumberger, R., & Goldenberg, C. (2009, January). *Modeling oral language development in Spanish and English.* Paper presented at the University of California Linguistic Minority Research Institute Biliteracy Development Forum.

Valdés, G. (1996). *Con respeto.* New York: Teachers College Press.

Vasquez, O., Pease-Alvarez, L., & Shannon, S. (1994). *Pushing boundaries: Language and culture in a Mexicano community.* New York: Cambridge University Press.

Zentella, A. C. (1997). *Growing up bilingual: Puerto Rican children in New York.* New York: Blackwell.

Zentella, A. C. (2005). Premises, promises, and pitfalls of language socialization research in Latino families and communities. In A. C. Zentella (Ed.), *Building on strength: Language and literacy in Latino families and communities* (pp.13–30). New York: Teachers College Press.

PART II

∎ ∎ ∎

Oral Language and Dual-Language Learners

CHAPTER 2

■　■　■

The Role of First Language in Oral Language Development in English

The Case of Both Alphabetic and Nonalphabetic Languages

STEFKA H. MARINOVA-TODD
YUUKO UCHIKOSHI

Anyone who has ever studied a second language (L2) must have been puzzled by the apparent arbitrary nature of some aspects of the L2's grammar or lexicon. It appears as if throughout history speakers of different languages randomly have picked and chosen different categories from the vast number of possibilities. For example, why does the English language have at least nine basic verb tenses (or tense and aspect combinations), while there are arguably four in Russian, and none in Chinese? Even more puzzling is the case of grammatical gender, which is present in many languages (e.g., three genders in Bulgarian and German, two in French) and all but completely lost in English. Finally, the verbalizing of the sounds animals make is the most amusing example of nonequivalent lexical representation across languages. In particular, the rooster makes exactly the same sound across the globe, but this sound is represented quite differently across languages (e.g., *cocorico* in French, *koke-kokko* in Japanese, *kukareku* in Russian, *kuk-kurri-guuu* in Bulgarian and, most bewildering of all, *cock-a-doodle-doo* in English).

When a learner embarks upon the task of learning a new language, he or she not only needs to learn the new grammatical rules and vocabulary items, but also to let go of some of the restraints imposed by the first language (L1), because often there is no direct transfer of grammatical rules and lexical items from one language to the other. Therefore, once the first language has been fully acquired, the task of learning an L2 could be even more difficult, since the new language is constantly being compared and contrasted to the L1. On the other hand, advanced L1 knowledge may assist in understanding L2 constructs, especially when the two languages are similar (Snow, Burns, & Griffin, 1998).

In this chapter, we examine the transfer of two components of oral proficiency,[1] vocabulary and morphosyntax, in both the oral and print domains for alphabetic and nonalphabetic languages. These two components have been considered to be strong predictors of reading outcomes, reading being one of the main domains of academic performance in elementary schools. Effective reading comprehension requires substantial vocabulary and background knowledge to understand and make inferences about the text being read (Konold, Juel, McKinnon, & Deffes, 2003; Lesaux & Siegel, 2003; Snow et al., 1998). Vocabulary size has been identified as a good predictor of future reading achievement (Snow et al., 1998; Ordóñez, Carlo, Snow, & McLaughlin, 2002). Similarly, studies have considered the processing and production of morphosyntactic knowledge and have found both to be equally predictive of reading success, especially in the early grades (Snow et al., 1998).

We first present the few studies in applied linguistics examining the role of L1 on oral language development in the L2 and discuss the role of L2 oral proficiency on L2 literacy development. Wherever possible, we focus on research on preschool and early elementary school children. Findings are summarized based on what L1s have already been considered and how their degree of similarity to and difference from English affects children's development in English. We also present recent findings from our own research on the English performance as well as the L1 skills of kindergarten children whose L1 is Chinese and Spanish. We compare the children's proficiency in their two languages and discuss how the differences and similarities between Chinese and Spanish, on the one hand, and English, on the other, could explain some of the transfer effects we observed in the children's performance.

ENGLISH LANGUAGE LEARNERS
IN THE UNITED STATES AND CANADA

Both in the United States and Canada, children from homes where English is not the dominant language are faced with the task of learning English as a second language, usually sometime before entering school. Some of these children, however, are first exposed to English when they enter school. As a result, upon school entry, these children come with varying degrees of proficiency in English, but in most cases, they continue to acquire English as an L2; thus they are labeled English language learners (ELLs) in the United States and English as second language students (ESL students) in Canada. For the purpose of this chapter we use the American label to refer to these children.

Past research demonstrates that teachers inappropriately use oral language proficiency to gauge the child's overall academic performance (Limbos & Geva, 2001). Especially with ELLs, teachers, speech–language pathologists, and other educators often find it difficult to determine whether the observed language limitations fall within the normally expected range of variation for age and experience, or are evidence of a language or learning disorder. Data recently released by the National Center for Education Statistics (U.S. Department of Education, 2007) on the Early Childhood Longitudinal Study, Kindergarten Class of 1998–99 (ECLS-K) shows that Hispanic students are overrepresented in the learning disabilities category, but not in the language impairment category in proportion to their numbers in the U.S. school-age population. In other words, educational professionals are more likely to designate Hispanic ELLs as struggling with academic language in English, usually in the later grades, and are less likely to identify weaknesses in their oral proficiency early on. In Canada there is a similar trend for school personnel to misdiagnose and to misplace large numbers of different groups of ESL-learning students in special education classes (Cummins, 1984). Education experts in both countries have argued that this tendency was due to the inappropriate reliance on standardized tests designed and normed on monolingual English-speaking children (Cummins, 2000; Valdés & Figueroa, 1994). In order to accurately establish ELL children's levels of oral proficiency and academic performance, we need to understand the role of L2 oral proficiency on academic performance, as well as the effects of L1 oral proficiency on L2 oral proficiency.

VOCABULARY DEVELOPMENT IN ELL CHILDREN WITH PRIMARILY ALPHABETIC L1s

One of the most prominent measures of oral language proficiency/linguistic knowledge is vocabulary knowledge (Geva & Zadeh, 2006; Proctor, Carlo, August, & Snow, 2005). As the review of the literature focuses on Spanish–English bilinguals, this section mostly covers L1 Spanish and L2 English vocabulary knowledge of Spanish ELL children. Past research has shown that the size of a child's vocabulary is heavily dependent on the amount of input for monolinguals (Hart & Risley, 1995; Huttenlocher, Haight, Bryk, Seltzer, & Lyons 1991), and on input per language for bilinguals (De Houwer, 1995; Patterson, 2002; Pearson, Fernández, Lewedeg & Oller, 1997). Native English speakers from professional homes have around 1,100 English words in their lexicon by the time they turn 3 years old (Hart & Risley, 1995). With only half of the English input, it is difficult for bilinguals to achieve the same number of vocabulary words in the same amount of time. As such, studies have shown that, even when the socioeconomic status of ELL children was higher than that of the monolingual sample, the Spanish-speaking ELL children scored significantly lower than the mean of the monolingual sample in English (Umbel, Pearson, Fernandez, & Oller, 1992).

Although vocabulary knowledge is most often measured by number of words, there is a complexity in word knowledge (Nagy & Scott, 2000; Ordóñez et al., 2002). This complexity has several dimensions (Nagy & Scott, 2000; Ordóñez et al., 2002):

1. Word learning is incremental (Nagy & Scott, 2000). There is a continuum to knowing a word: from never seeing or hearing the word before, to being able to use the word in a sentence.

2. Word knowledge consists of multiple dimensions (Nagy & Scott, 2000). Sometimes children may know the definition of the word, but may be unable to use it in a sentence. The child must understand the syntactic structures in which the word can be used. The child must also be aware of the word's various morphological connotations. For example, the child may understand the word *inactive,* if he/she knows that it is related to the word *active.* The child must also realize the word's pragmatic uses, that is, knowing when to use the word. For example, some words may not be appropriate to use in certain situations; other words may be too formal to use in a casual context.

3. Words often have multiple meanings (Nagy & Scott, 2000). Often, the word has a main meaning, but depending on the context, that meaning may change.

4. Words are interrelated (Nagy & Scott, 2000). A child's knowledge of one word is not independent of that child's knowledge of other words. For example, if the child knows the word *up,* the child may have already acquired some of the components of the word *down,* even if he has never heard of that word before.

5. Word knowledge is heterogeneous (Nagy & Scott, 2000), in that what it means to know a word differs depending on the type of word. For example, knowing function words is different from knowing a noun or verb.

These five dimensions influence how much a child "knows" a word. For an ELL, this means that these five dimensions of complexity exist in both his L1 and L2 vocabulary. These five dimensions of complexity in English vocabulary play a critical role, especially for the ELL children ability to understand academic language and be successful in the upper grades. However, much of the work so far on ELLs' vocabulary development has focused on the size of vocabulary in L1 and L2, as can be seen in the following review. Only one study was found that showed ELL children to be disadvantaged in the complexity of vocabulary knowledge in both L1 and L2. For example, Verhallen and Schoonen (1993) reported that, when compared to 40 monolingual Dutch children, 40 bilingual Turkish children (ages 9 and 11) tended to have less extensive and less varied meanings for common, frequently occurring Dutch nouns. In a highly structured interview session, children were asked to express all the meaning aspects they could think of for each word. In a follow-up study, Verhallen and Schoonen (1998) examined these bilingual children's L1 Turkish vocabulary. Their results showed that the bilingual children were stronger in their L2 Dutch than L1 Turkish. That is, their L1 vocabulary, in both size and complexity, lagged behind their L2 vocabulary knowledge, in both size and complexity, which lagged behind the monolingual children's vocabulary knowledge.

The Role of L1 on L2 Oral Vocabulary Development

ELL children need to know the L2 vocabulary in order to understand L2 text. Whether vocabulary transfers from L1 to L2 appears to depend on the existence of cognate relationships between the two languages of the bilingual children. A summary of the research included in this section is provided in Table 2.1.

Cognates Assist in Transfer

Knowledge of cognate relationships that exist between Spanish and English has been found to assist in L2 English vocabulary development and L2 English reading comprehension in Spanish–English bilinguals (Hancin-Bhatt & Nagy, 1994; Nagy, Garcia, Durgunoğlu, & Hancin-Bhatt, 1993; Ordóñez et al., 2002). Research has found evidence of transfer effects at the lexical level for students in Grades 4, 5, and 6, when cognates exist in both languages. Ordóñez et al. (2002) found that Spanish superordinate performance was a significant predictor of English superordinate performance, as measured by providing definitions and descriptions of English and Spanish words. Children's depth of knowledge for high-frequency Spanish nouns was related to their depth of knowledge for similar English nouns. The authors suggested that there was a direct lexical effect, where students who knew the Spanish

TABLE 2.1. Role of L1 on L2 Oral Vocabulary Development

Authors	Purpose	Sample size and demographics	Outcome measures (partial listing)	Results
Hancin-Bhatt & Nagy (1994)	To evaluate Spanish ELL students abilities to translate cognates	196 Latino bilinguals in grades 4 ($n = 96$), 6 ($n = 41$), and 8 ($n = 59$)	Researcher-developed English–Spanish vocabulary task	• Abilities to translate cognates increased with age, controlling for any increases in vocabulary knowledge in Spanish and English.
Ordóñez, Carlo, Snow, & McLaughlin (2002)	To examine the ransfer of vocabulary skills among Spanish ELLs	38 fourth-grade and 50 fifth-grade Spanish–English bilinguals	• Peabody Picture Vocabulary Test • Researcher-developed word definition and description task	• Spanish superordinate performance was a significant predictor of English superordinate performance.
Uchikoshi (2006a)	To evaluate the best predictors of L2 English vocabulary	150 Spanish-speaking ELL kindergarteners	• Peabody Picture Vocabulary Test • Test de Vocabulario en Imágenes • Woodcock Language Proficiency Battery—Revised—picture vocabulary subtest	• Children who entered kindergarten with larger Spanish vocabulary also had larger English vocabulary at the beginning of kindergarten.
Verhoeven (1994)	To examine the transfer of various literacy skills	98 6-year-old Turkish children living in the Netherlands	• Researcher-developed receptive and productive vocabulary tasks	• No clear evidence of lexical transfer.

words, such as *animal* and *humano,* easily acquired and knew the equivalent English words, such as *animal* and *human.*

This ability to recognize cognates appears to increase with age. Hancin-Bhatt and Nagy (1994) showed that there was a developmental trend in bilingual children's ability to recognize cognates. Results showed that the students' abilities to translate cognates increased with age, controlling for any increases in vocabulary knowledge in Spanish and English. That is, there was a rapid increase between grades 4 and 8 in children's ability to translate cognates, even after controlling for English and Spanish vocabulary knowledge.

Spanish ELL Kindergarten Children

The above cognate studies on Spanish-speaking ELLs have been conducted on children in grades 4 through 8. Only one study was found that examined the influence of L1 Spanish vocabulary on the development of L2 English vocabulary understanding and production skills at an earlier age, in kindergarten (Uchikoshi, 2006a). In this study, Spanish vocabulary data were only collected at the beginning of the year in, October, while English vocabulary was followed longitudinally and collected at three time points during the academic year: October, February, and June.

Results on data analysis examining the growth of children's English vocabulary using initial Spanish vocabulary as a predictor indicated that children with higher initial Spanish vocabulary comprehension scores tended to start kindergarten with higher English vocabulary comprehension scores than those who had low initial Spanish vocabulary comprehension scores. This gap remained constant throughout their kindergarten year (Uchikoshi, 2006a). Thus there appeared to be an association between the children's L1 and L2 lexical comprehension knowledge even at school entry. Understanding more Spanish words led to understanding more English words. This may be due to the fact that there are many cognates in Spanish and English.

However, there was no relationship between L1 Spanish vocabulary comprehension scores and L2 English vocabulary production (Uchikoshi, 2006a). As described earlier in this chapter, there is a complexity in word knowledge (Nagy & Scott, 2000; Ordóñez et al., 2002). ELL children may have known some dimensions of English vocabulary that were tested; however, they may not have known them to a degree to be able to verbalize the word. A relationship may also not have been seen due to the words tested in the vocabulary production test. Many of the English words on the picture vocabulary subtest of the Woodcock Language Proficiency Battery—Revised did not share cognates with Spanish. Results may have been different had there been more cognates on the assessment.

No Transfer

Only one study was found that examined oral vocabulary transfer among bilinguals with languages other than Spanish and English (Verhoeven, 1994). In this study, there was no transfer between L1 vocabulary and L2 vocabulary (Verhoeven, 1994). Vocabulary size in L1 did not predict L2 lexical comprehension or production for Turkish–Dutch bilingual children, although transfer effects were seen between L1 and L2 at the pragmatic, phonological, and literacy levels.

In summary, the above studies suggest the importance of L1 oral vocabulary development for English L2 vocabulary development when cognate relationships exist between the two languages. Cognates appear to be a principal mechanism for L2 vocabulary, and ELLs can draw on L1 Spanish knowledge to develop L2 English vocabulary. This suggests that Spanish ELLs, especially those with a large L1 vocabulary, can benefit from direct instruction about cognate relationships between Spanish and English. Much more research is needed to explore these issues. Further research on the role of cognates, especially with different language pairs that have cognate relationships, is also needed.

The Role of L2 Vocabulary on L2 Literacy Development

Past research shows a relatively consistent positive correlation between language-specific L2 oral vocabulary and L2 reading comprehension (e.g. Carlisle, Beeman, Davis, & Spharim, 1999; Proctor et al., 2005). Although little has been examined on the relationship between language-specific L2 oral language and decoding at younger ages, the studies that do exist show a positive relationship between L2 English oral vocabulary and L2 English decoding skills (e.g. Geva & Zadeh, 2006; Uchikoshi, 2006b). In addition, research on ELLs' recognition and use of cognate relationships between L1 and L2 vocabulary has shown that ELLs can transfer the meaning of L1 vocabulary to determine the meaning of the L2 cognate vocabulary in L2 reading text (Nagy et al., 1993). This section discusses: (1) language-specific relationships between L2 oral vocabulary and L2 decoding; (2) language-specific relationships between L2 oral vocabulary and L2 reading; and (3) cognate–reading comprehension relationships. A summary of the research included in this section is provided in Table 2.2.

Language-Specific Relationships and L2 Decoding

Two recent studies have examined the relationship between L2 vocabulary and L2 decoding. Geva and Zadeh (2006) found the size of L2 oral vocabulary to be a significant predictor of L2 word and text reading among Canadian ELL children who were efficient readers. Children who had more oral English vocabulary were able to decode English text more easily than those who had less oral vocabulary.

In a second study, Uchikoshi (2006b) also found the size of L2 English vocabulary to have a significant effect on L2 decoding. Spanish ELL children who started kindergarten with larger L2 English vocabulary also started with better word decoding abilities, and their scores remained high

TABLE 2.2. The Role of L2 Vocabulary on L2 Literacy Development

Authors	Purpose	Sample size and demographics	Outcome measures (partial listing)	Results
Carlisle & Beeman (2000)	To examine the effects of teaching literacy skills to Hispanic ELL first-grade students in L1 Spanish or L2 English	36 Spanish–English first grade children; 17 receiving English instruction (EI), 19 receiving Spanish instruction (SI)	• Peabody Picture Vocabulary Test • Test de Vocabulario en Imágenes • Woodcock–Johnson Psycho-Educational Battery—Revised • Batería Woodcock Muñoz • Researcher-developed listening and reading comprehension measures	• L2 English reading comprehension at the end of first grade and beginning of second grade was affected by L2 English vocabulary size, but not additionally affected by language of instruction. • EI children had higher English oral language than SI children, but not on English decoding or reading comprehension.
Carlisle, Beeman, Davis, & Spharim (1999)	To investigate the developing metalinguistic capabilities (definition tasks) of Hispanic primary school children who are becoming bilingual but whose English reading achievement is below average	67 Spanish–English children in grades 1, 2, and 3 who were struggling readers	• Peabody Picture Vocabulary Test • Test de Vocabulario en Imágenes • Woodcock–Johnson Psycho-Educational Battery—Revised, listening comprehension and letter–word identification subtests • California Achievement Test, reading comprehension subtest • Definition Task (FDQ) • Test of Auditory Analysis Skill (TAAS)	• PPVT accounted for 13.5%, TVIP accounted for 15%, FDQ accounted for 5%, and TAAS accounted for 6% of the variance in CAT reading comprehension.

(continued)

TABLE 2.2. (continued)

Authors	Purpose	Sample size and demographics	Outcome measures (partial listing)	Results
Carlo et al. (2004)	To test the impact of an L2 English vocabulary enrichment intervention	142 bilingual Spanish ELL children from nine fifth-grade classrooms; 94 received academic vocabulary instruction intervention	• Peabody Picture Vocabulary Test • Researcher-developed polysemy production task • Researcher-developed reading comprehension, vocabulary, word association, and morphology tasks	• Systematic L2 English vocabulary instruction over a 2-year period during grades 4 and 5 for Spanish ELLs had positive effects on their English reading comprehension.
Geva & Zadeh (2006)	To examine the word- and text-reading efficiency skills of monolingual English speakers and ELL students, and examine whether individual differences can be understood in terms of similar underlying component processes	183 Canadian ELL children with a mean age of 7.25 years and first languages of Cantonese, Punjabi, Tamil, or Portuguese	• Expressive One-Word Picture Vocabulary Test—Revised (Gardner, 1990) • Biemiller Test of Reading Processes (Biemiller, 1981)—Word efficiency subtest and text reading subtest • Woodcock Reading Mastery Test—Revised—word attack subtest • Wide Range Achievement Test—Revised, word recognition subtest	• L2 oral vocabulary explained 7% of the variance in both L2 word efficiency and L2 text reading efficiency for skilled readers. • When the language used in the reading materials is below or perhaps just at the level of oral proficiency (Chall, 1996), L2 oral proficiency contributes only marginally to word- or text-reading efficiency
Manis, Lindsey, & Bailey (2004)	To explore the development of English and Spanish reading skills in Spanish ELL children in grades K–2	251 Spanish ELL children followed from kindergarten through grade 2	• Woodcock Language Proficiency Battery in Spanish and English • CTOPP in English and adapted in Spanish	• Expressive L2 English skills, including oral vocabulary, in grade 1 contributed significantly to L2 English text comprehension in grade 2.

Study	Purpose	Sample	Measures	Findings
Nagy, Garcia, Durgunoglu, & Hancin-Bhatt (1993)	To investigate how Spanish ELL students' knowledge of L1 Spanish vocabulary and ability to identify cognates relate to their L2 English reading comprehension	74 Spanish ELLs in grades 4, 5, and 6	• Researcher-developed English reading comprehension and vocabulary tests	• Transfer of L1 Spanish lexical knowledge to English, resulting in relationship between L1 vocabulary knowledge and L2 reading comprehension.
Proctor, Carlo, August, & Snow (2005)	To examine the predictors of L2 reading comprehension using a structural equation model	135 Spanish ELL fourth-grade children	• Computer-Based Academic Assessment System • Woodcock Language Proficiency Battery	• L2 vocabulary directly and indirectly (through L2 listening comprehension), along with L2 fluency, L2 listening comprehension, and L2 alphabetic knowledge predicted L2 reading comprehension.
Uchikoshi (2006b)	To examine the effect of *Between the Lions*, an educational television show, on Spanish ELL children's L2 phonological awareness and decoding skills	150 Spanish-speaking ELL kindergarteners	• Peabody Picture Vocabulary Test • Woodcock Language Proficiency Battery—Revised—letter-word identification subtest	• L2 English vocabulary had a significant effect on L2 English decoding.

through their kindergarten year. Strong correlations were found between L2 English vocabulary and L2 decoding variables throughout the kindergarten year.

Language-Specific Relationships and L2 Reading Comprehension

Other studies have shown the size of L2 English vocabulary to be important in L2 English reading comprehension. Carlisle et al. (1999) showed that the size of L2 vocabulary predicted L2 reading comprehension with Spanish–English children in grades 1, 2, and 3 who were struggling readers. Proctor et al. (2005) found the same results with grade 4 Spanish ELL children. Furthermore, Manis, Lindsey, and Bailey (2004) showed that expressive L2 English skills, including the size of oral vocabulary, in grade 1 contributed significantly to L2 English text comprehension in grade 2 for Spanish ELL children.

In addition, although L2 English reading comprehension was influenced by the size of L2 English vocabulary, it was not further affected by language of instruction (Carlisle & Beeman, 2000). When ELL children attending English instruction classrooms were compared to Spanish instruction classrooms, the former had more English oral vocabulary than the latter, but their English decoding and reading comprehension scores were not significantly different.

However, Carlo and colleagues (2004) found that systematic L2 English vocabulary instruction over a 2-year period during grades 4 and 5 for Spanish ELLs had positive effects on their English reading comprehension. This intervention combined direct English word instruction with instruction in English word-learning strategies. It also gave Spanish translation equivalents for English words and text. At the end of the 2-year period, the ELL children in the intervention group performed as well or even better than the English-only control group.

Cognate–Reading Comprehension Relationships

Nagy et al. (1993) found that the ability of upper elementary students to recognize cognates had an effect on the relationship between L1 vocabulary knowledge and L2 reading comprehension. When Spanish–English bilingual students knew the word in L1 Spanish and were able to identify the L2 English word as a cognate, students were able to understand the L2 vocabulary word in context. Specifically, when students knew the Spanish cognate, they identified 67% of the English words, whereas if they did not know the Spanish cognate, they correctly answered only 37% of the English words. Thus L1 vocabulary cognate knowledge transfers to L2 vocabulary knowledge, as discussed earlier, which in turn has a relationship with L2 reading comprehension.

In summary, review of the literature suggests that, for Spanish–English bilinguals, cognates are a principle mechanism for L2 vocabulary development, which further influences L2 reading comprehension. This ability to recognize and utilize cognates appears to develop with age and has major implications for practice. Cognate instruction may be a key factor to developing Spanish–English bilingual children's L2 vocabulary and reading skills, especially since ELL children's abilities to recognize cognate relationships increase substantially after grade 4. The literature also suggests that the size of L2 English oral vocabulary predicts L2 English decoding in children with various L1s, including those that do not have cognates with the L2 English, therefore more studies need to be conducted to find best practices to increase the size of L2 vocabulary. Unfortunately, very few studies have examined the complexity of word knowledge and the development of this complexity in ELL children.

THE DEVELOPMENT OF MORPHOSYNTAX IN ELL CHILDREN WITH PRIMARILY NONALPHABETIC L1s

Knowledge of grammar, or morphosyntax, refers, on one hand, to how morphemes (e.g., content words: *dog, jump,* and the affixes that change their meaning: *dog-s, jump-ed*) are used in a particular language; and, on the other hand, to the rules by which words are combined into sentences (e.g., in English the subject always precedes the main verb). Morphosyntax is another area of oral proficiency that has been established as a necessary skill for reading (Plaza & Cohen, 2003) especially in the early grades (Snow et al., 1998; Lipka, Siegel, & Vukovic, 2005). Morphosyntactic awareness has been defined as "the ability to reason consciously about the syntactic aspects of language, and to exercise intentional control over the application of grammatical rules" (Gombert, 1992, p. 39). Knowing the morphosyntactic rules of a language allows the reader to make predictions about the words that come next in a sentence, thus leading to more fluent and efficient reading of a text (Siegel, 1992). For example, children tend to use their L1 syntactic knowledge when trying to decipher unknown L2 vocabulary in L2 contexts (Nagy, McClure, & Mir, 1997). Nagy et al. (1997) showed that Spanish–English bilingual students in grades 7 and 8 used their Spanish grammatical knowledge to make guesses about the meanings of unfamiliar English words in context. Therefore, this strategy has proven to be particularly effective for reading comprehension in the L2. In the following sections studies that have examined possible transfer effects in the domain of morphosyntax are reviewed, in order to identify which grammatical structures, if any, are transferable between the two languages of a bilingual individual.

The Role of L1 on L2 Morphosyntactic Development

The Nature of Cross-Linguistic Transfer of Morphosyntactic Skills

In the case of ELLs, the effects of morphosyntax on reading are complicated by the presence of two languages—the language spoken in the home (L1) and the language of instruction at school (L2). By nature, ELLs are bilingual children; thus they are subjected to transfer effects or cross-linguistic influences (Hulk & Müller, 2000) from their L1 to the L2 and vice versa. It is common for bilingual children to produce mixed utterances that contain words or grammatical structures of one language in the other. These mixed utterances were initially considered as evidence that children do not always separate their languages in the early stages of bilingual language development (e.g., Volterra & Taeschner, 1978; Taeschner, 1983). More recently, research on bilingual language development, especially for balanced bilinguals—those who exhibit equivalent levels of proficiency both in their L1 and L2—has shown that, early in the acquisition process, children are able to differentiate between their two languages (De Houwer, 1990; Genesee, 1989; Meisel, 1989). Despite the fact that the two languages in a bilingual child may develop independently (Genesee, Nicoladis, & Paradis, 1995), they can also influence each other or be subjected to "cross-linguistic influence" (Hulk & Müller, 2000). Hulk and Müller (2000) conceive of cross-linguistic influence as a process of facilitation/acceleration and delay or transfer and not as mixing or fusion of the two languages.

Often ELLs are children of recent immigrant families; thus they tend to fall into the much more common category of unbalanced bilinguals; that is, one of their languages tends to be stronger than the other, due to varying degree of exposure to each language and the amount of L2 use. In such cases cross-linguistic transfer is likely to occur. The suggestion is that syntactic transfer from one language to the other depends on either the dominance of one language (Yip & Matthews, 2000, 2006), or the syntactic ambiguity of the language input (Hulk & Müller, 2000; Müller, 1998). Language dominance is present when one of the child's languages is more advanced or developing faster than the other and is considered to be an important factor in predicting the direction of language transfer (Yip & Matthews, 2006), whereby bilingual children bring elements from the dominant language into the less dominant language (Gawlitzek-Maiwald & Tracy, 1996).

Alternatively, if the child perceives that one language has two possible structural analyses, and the other language only reinforces one of them, then there is an input ambiguity and the child is likely to produce nontarget structures in the former language that are transferred from the latter language (Hulk & Müller, 2000; Müller, 1998). In other words, transfer may occur when "two different grammatical hypotheses are compatible with the same surface string" (Müller, 1998, p. 153). In this case, transfer is unidirectional and the target language is the one that presents the child with input ambiguity, regardless of dominance (Döpke, 1998; Müller, 1998)

Transfer of Morphosyntactic Skills from a Nonalphabetic L1 to an Alphabetic L2

The majority of older studies on transfer were conducted on bilingual children whose languages were similar and shared the same alphabet, such as English, Dutch, German, French, and Spanish (e.g., De Houwer, 1990; Döpke, 1998; Müller, 1998; Nagy et al., 1997; Paradis & Genesee, 1996). More recent studies have examined bilingual children whose languages are not based on the same alphabetic writing system, such as English and Chinese (Chan, 2004; Yip & Matthews, 2000), or English on one hand, and Japanese and Korean on the other (Whong-Barr & Schwartz, 2002). Moreover, both English and Chinese are not morphologically rich languages, in that they rely on a very minimal set of affixes to change the meaning of content words. Japanese and Korean, on the other hand, are morphologically rich languages, and thus are different from English. It is possible, then, that the degree of morphological richness between two languages could further affect the presence and direction of transfer of morphosyntactic skills. A summary of the studies that have examined the role of L1 on the L2 morphosyntax is provided in Table 2.3.

In a study that compared morphologically reduced languages, Yip and Matthews (2000) examined a case study of a bilingual child from Hong Kong, who was dominant in Cantonese. Language samples were collected from the child during the period when he was 1 year and 5 months and 3 years and 6 months old. Their findings revealed evidence of transfer from Cantonese to English in three syntactic areas: (1) *wh-* in-situ interrogatives (*e.g.*, *Wh-* questions in English involve a syntactic movement of the *wh-* word to the beginning of the sentence: *What did you eat?*, while in Cantonese there is no syntactic movement: *You eat what?*; (2) null objects (e.g., Cantonese allows for null objects: *I like (it)*, while English requires that subjects and objects be always realized); and (3) prenominal relatives (e.g., in Cantonese relative clauses precede the head noun: *I know those people leave all*, whereas in English they follow the head noun: *The people I know have all left*). The directionality of transfer appeared to be due to language dominance, based on a greater mean length of utterance (MLU) in Cantonese, as well as language preference for and richer input in Cantonese. A close match was observed between the MLU value and transfer of all three syntactic areas that were investigated, a finding that led the authors to conclude that dominance in Cantonese was the major factor determining the directionality of transfer, while input ambiguity played only a minor role (its effect was revealed only in one of the syntactic areas, namely the case of null objects).

TABLE 2.3. The Role of L1 on L2 Morphosyntactic Development

Authors	Purpose	Sample size and demographics	Outcome measures	Results
Chan (2004)	• To study the extent to which the English production of ESL Chinese speakers was influenced by their L1 • To examine the nature and process of syntactic transfer in the English output of students from different proficiency levels	710 Hong Kong ESL learners at different proficiency levels	• Self-reports on the language in which subjects think • One-on-one interviews • Translation task from Chinese to English • Grammaticality–judgment task in English	• The extent of syntactic transfer was the largest for complex target structures and among learners of lower proficiency levels. • High-proficiency learners also relied on syntactic transfer from L1 when encountering difficulty in L2 output.
Whong-Barr & Schwartz (2002)	• To compare the acquisition of a morphosyntactic structure in English by children with different L1s • To examine whether L2 children transfer properties of the L1 grammar	• 6 L1 English (age range 6 years, 11 months–10 years, 10 months), 5 L1 Japanese (age range 7 years, 3 months–8 years, 11 months), and 5 L1 Korean (age range 6 years, 6 months–ten years, 2 months) speakers • All children exposed to English between 1 year, 3 months and 3 years, 11 months	• Picture-description task in English • Oral grammaticality–judgment task in English	• Found evidence for morphosyntactic transfer. • Japanese L1 children experienced more interference from their L1 than Korean L1 children. • Group differences explained with degree of similarity between L1 and L2.
Yip & Matthews (2000)	• To examine the degree to which syntactic transfer in bilingual acquisition is dependent on the degree of language dominance	A single case study of a Cantonese–English bilingual child whose stronger language was Cantonese	• Recorded spontaneous speech data for the period when subject was 1 year, 5 months and 3 years, 6 months	• Syntactic transfer was heavily dependent on the degree of language dominance. • Structures were transferred from Cantonese (dominant language) to English (weaker language).

Providing further evidence in support of the language dominance effect on the transfer of morphosyntax, Chan (2004) examined the presence of syntactic transfer from Chinese to English in 710 Hong Kong Chinese learners of English as an L2. The participants were either university or high school students and were at different proficiency levels in English. Data were collected through self-reporting, individual interviews, translations, and a grammaticality judgment task. An error analysis of the participants' L2 revealed the presence of surface structures typical for their L1, which the author considered to be evidence for language transfer from Cantonese to English. Furthermore, it was found that the degree of syntactic transfer was particularly large for complex L2 structures among learners with lower proficiency levels in English, although Chan hypothesized that the high-proficiency learners may also have relied on transfer when encountering difficult syntactic structures in the L2, further supporting the more limited role of input ambiguity on the directionality of transfer.

Finally, a different study examined bilinguals whose L1 was morphologically rich (either Japanese or Korean) and whose L2 was morphologically reduced (English). Whong-Barr and Schwartz (2002) studied ELLs who were more dominant in either Japanese or Korean and a comparison group of English monolingual children. The children were between the ages of 6 years and 6 months and 10 years and 10 months and had been exposed to English between 1 year and 3 months and 3 years and 11 months. All subjects were given a grammaticality judgment task that consisted of sentences that contained the to- and for- dative alternation in English (e.g., "show the results to someone" vs. "show someone the results"). On this morphosyntactic feature English and Korean are more similar than English and Japanese. Whong-Barr and Schwartz's (2002) results provided evidence for transfer from the L1, where the Korean children performed more similarly to the English monolinguals, while the Japanese children experienced more interference from their L1. Therefore, this study provided new evidence that, in addition to language dominance, the transfer of morphosyntactic skills also depends on the degree of similarity between the L1 and L2, especially in cases where the degree of morphological richness between the two languages was quite different.

The review of the oral language research above provides evidence for the presence of morphosyntactic transfer from the L1 to the L2 both for languages that share the alphabetic writing system, as well as for languages that use different writing systems. In both cases, ELLs tended to transfer morphosyntactic structures from their dominant language (usually the L1) to their weaker language, and in some cases they also relied on transfer when they were faced with an ambiguous input in the target language. In most cases, transfer effects that are readily observable tend to be defined as negative transfer, a case in which structures from the source language are inappropriately used in the target language, thus leading to errors in the learner's output. However, the degree of structural similarity between the L1 and L2 led to a positive transfer, the result of which was an L2 performance closer to the target performance of native speakers of the L2.

The Role of Morphosyntactic Awareness on L2 Literacy Development

Morphosyntactic knowledge is one aspect of oral proficiency, which also includes knowledge of word meanings, morphosyntactic structures, and pragmatic skill. Research has shown that more explicit *linguistic knowledge* is a significant precursor to reading, which includes both fluency and comprehension (Konold et al., 2003; Miller et al., 2006) and is correlated with later success in reading (Snow et al., 1998; Durgunoğlu, Nagy, & Hancin-Bhatt, 1993; Noonan, Hildebrand, & Yackulic, 1997; Proctor, August, Carlo, & Snow, 2006; Proctor et al., 2005). In particular, syntactic awareness was found to significantly correlate with reading and spelling in English (Plaza & Cohen, 2003). Moreover, in the case of ELLs, it is commonly inferred that their limited oral proficiency in English (including syntactic skills) is the main cause for any difficulties they may have with reading or language processing skills in school (Limbos & Geva, 2001; Moll & Diaz, 1985). Because the presence of negative transfer within the domain of morphosyntax has been established in the literature, the question in the case of ELLs is: How does this transfer affect young children's ability to learn to read and write in the L2? A summary of the studies that have examined the role of L1 and L2 morphosyntax on reading outcomes is provided in Table 2.4.

Between- and Within-Language Transfer of Morphosyntax and Reading

Some of the studies cited above (Durgunoğlu et al., 1993; Noonan et al., 1997; Proctor et al., 2005, 2006) revealed that reading is affected most strongly by oral proficiency in the same language, which has been considered as evidence for minimal cross-language transfer (Miller et al., 2006). Miller et al. (2006) argued that studies revealing some degree of transfer of oral language skills from one language to the reading skills in another have utilized a small number of variables that may be language specific and were often taken from standardized tests. Instead, Miller at al. (2006) contended that "assessment tools that are both equivalent across language and evaluate more language features are likely to discover patters of cross-language transfer (or lack of transfer)" (p. 30). In order to examine their prediction, Miller and his collaborators embarked on a large-scale study of 1,531

TABLE 2.4. The Role of Morphosyntactic Awareness on L2 Literacy Development

Authors	Purpose	Sample size and demographics	Outcome measures (partial listing)	Results
Lesaux & Siegel (2003)	To examine patterns of reading development between K and grade 2 in native English-speaking children and ELLs	790 monolingual speakers and 188 ELLs of various L1 backgrounds	Oral proficiency measure: • Researcher-developed oral cloze test of syntactic awareness Reading measures: • Wide Range Achievement Test–3—reading subtest • Woodcock Reading Mastery Tests–Revised—word identification and word attack subtests • Stanford Diagnostic Reading Test—reading comprehension subtest	• By grade 2 ELLs performed equivalently to the monolinguals on reading measures in English. • Syntactic awareness explained a small percentage of the variance in reading skill.
Lipka et al. (2005)	To review published studies on the English literacy of ELLs in Canada in order to understand their reading development and characteristics or reading disabilities in this population	Studies usually examined children from diverse L1 backgrounds in early and middle elementary grades	• Syntactic awareness measure: researcher-developed oral cloze test • A variety of experimental and standardized measures of reading, spelling, phonological awareness, and working memory	• Early school-age ELLs demonstrated poor performance on syntactic awareness tests compared to English monolinguals. • Older ELLs did not consistently show poor performance on syntactic awareness skills compared to English monolinguals. • Results were explained with the presence of implicit language learning knowledge in ELLs, in general, or with positive transfer when the L1 has a more heavily inflected structure than English.

(continued)

47

TABLE 2.4. (*continued*)

Authors	Purpose	Sample size and demographics	Outcome measures (partial listing)	Results
Low & Siegel (2005)	To examine the relative role played by three cognitive processes: phonological processing, verbal working memory, and syntactic awareness on English reading comprehension	884 English L1 children and 284 ELLs of various L1 backgrounds who were in grade 6 (mean age 11.43 years)	Word reading measures: • Wide Range Achievement Test–3 reading subtest • Woodcock Reading Mastery Tests–Revised: Word identification Reading comprehension measures: • Stanford Diagnostic Reading Test–reading comprehension subtest Syntactic awareness measure: • Researcher-developed oral cloze test	• The performance of both groups were comparable on measures of reading fluency, phonological processing, and verbal working memory. • ELLs had significantly lower scores on the syntactic awareness measure. • All three cognitive processes played a significant role in the development of English reading comprehension.
Miller et al. (2006)	To examine whether various measures of oral language predict reading achievement, both within and across languages for bilingual children	1,531 Spanish-speaking ELLs in K through grade 3 whose dominant language was Spanish and were enrolled in transitional educational programs	Oral language measure: • Narrative language samples using a wordless picture book Reading comprehension measure: • Woodcock Language Proficiency Battery–Revised—English and Spanish—passage comprehension subtest Word reading efficiency measure: • Test of Word Reading Efficiency	• Measures of English oral proficiency predicted readings skills in English. • Measures of Spanish oral proficiency predicted readings skills in Spanish. • Spanish and English oral language skills contributed to reading within and across languages—evidence of cross-language transfer.

48

Spanish-speaking ELLs who were attending kindergarten through grade 3 in Texas public schools. All children were Spanish dominant and were enrolled in transitional bilingual programs.

As a method for assessing oral proficiency, the children were asked to retell a story from a wordless picture book *Frog, Where are You?* by Mercer Mayer (1969) in both their L1 (Spanish) and L2 (English). The oral narratives were then transcribed and four oral language measures were developed based on the narrative transcripts. These measures were: (1) syntactic skill (measured in mean length of utterance), (2) vocabulary diversity (measured with number of different words produced in the narratives), (3) general language proficiency (measured with language fluency expressed in the number of words per minute), and (4) narrative structure (assessed with a scheme that consists of seven different categories designed to function as an index of the children's ability to produce coherent narratives). In addition, measures of reading comprehension and word reading fluency were used to assess the children's reading ability in both languages.

The descriptive results from this study revealed that the children's reading ability was increasing from grade to grade in both languages. In addition, there was clear evidence that the children were successfully acquiring their L2 and were showing no signs of loss of proficiency in their L1. A series of regression analyses revealed that the strongest relationships between the oral language skills and reading were within individual languages. However, the oral language skills in one language accounted for some portion of the variance in reading in the other language, thus providing evidence for cross-language transfer. Moreover, the transfer effects between languages were not symmetrical; that is, the transfer from Spanish to English was stronger than from English to Spanish. Based on this evidence, Miller et al. (2006) concluded that their study affirmed and further revealed the complex relationship between oral proficiency and reading in bilingual children.

Evidence from Research on ELLs in Canada

In a review of studies done in Canada with ELLs, Lipka et al. (2005) have shown that, in the domain of syntactic awareness, early school-age ELLs (in kindergarten through grade 2) tend to do worse than monolinguals on an oral cloze test designed to tap into these children's morphosyntactic knowledge in English. On simple reading tasks in English (e.g., letter identification and word decoding), however, the ELLs did not exhibit similar difficulty and generally tended to perform at a level equivalent to the monolingual groups. Lipka et al. (2005) concluded that, in the early stages of learning to read, poor morphosyntactic skills in the L2 were not related with poor L2 reading skills.

After reviewing studies that have examined the morphosyntactic awareness of students from specific language backgrounds, Lipka et al. (2005) found that there was an effect of the L1 on the outcomes in L2. In particular, Portuguese-speaking kindergarten students had lower scores on syntactic awareness as measured by the oral cloze test in English, and were not different from native English-speaking children on word recognition and phonological awareness tasks. The performance of older Portuguese-speaking students in grades 4, 6, and 8 was similar. On the other hand, Arabic- and Italian-speaking students of the same age had less difficulty with the oral cloze task. It appears, therefore, that ELLs' syntactic awareness in English varies for speakers of different L1s who are in the middle school years. However, there was no difference between the ELLs of all L1 backgrounds and native English speakers on word-reading tasks in English. Based on these findings, Lipka at al. (2005) hypothesized that, either ELLs need more time to develop full proficiency in the L2 morphosyntax, or that "there is a positive transfer when the grammatical system of the first language has a more heavily inflected structure than English, such as Arabic or Italian" (p. 45).

In summary, the review of the literature revealed modest transfer effects of L1 syntactic skills to the L2 literacy skills in ELLs of various languages. In the domain of morphosyntax, L2 learners tend to transfer knowledge acquired in one language to the other, and often the direction of transfer tends to proceed from the stronger to the weaker language. In addition, morphosyntactic skills are part of the larger set of oral language skills, which have been confirmed as strong predictors of literacy achievement. Unfortunately, very few studies have examined the effects of morphosyntax on literacy development and often they have included it in a global measure of oral proficiency and have not examined its individual contribution to literacy outcomes. In the line of research conducted by Linda Siegel and her collaborators (Lesaux & Siegel, 2003; Lipka et al., 2005; Low & Siegel, 2005) and reviewed above, the syntactic awareness of ELLs was consistently examined. ELLs tended to score significantly lower on a measure of morphosyntactic skill, and their scores on syntactic awareness predicted between 1.5% and 3% of the variance in their literacy skills. When specific L1s were considered, the effects of morphosyntax on literacy measures varied, which was seen as a possible indication of transfer across languages. Finally, the transfer of morphosyntactic skills seems to play a smaller role in the earlier stages of reading development, namely decoding, and a more significant role in the more advanced stages of reading development, namely comprehension. In addition, studies have repeatedly utilized the same limited set of formal measures of morphosyntax, such as grammaticality–judgment tasks or cloze tests. In the next section the results from a study are presented, which utilized a more spontaneous measure of morphosyntax in addition to the more formal cloze test.

The Role of Chinese (L1) on English (L2) Morphosyntax in the Spontaneous Discourse of Kindergarten Children

As the literature review above indicates, there is a dearth of research on the transfer effects of morphosyntactic skills in ELLs, and researchers have consistently called for a more systematic examination of the ELLs' oral proficiency skills in both their home and school language. In particular, focusing on kindergarten students, who have limited or no literacy exposure, would allow researchers to examine the effect of pure oral language skills on their literacy development in English. Moreover, most of the research to date has been done on ELLs of structurally similar languages, such as Spanish or French and English, and more research is needed to address the needs of ELLs of L1s different from English, such as Chinese. Finally, researchers have called for utilizing tasks that reflect language used in natural settings when examining children's linguistic knowledge. In order to address these needs, our recent line of research has examined the morphosyntactic knowledge both in English and Chinese in a group of Chinese–English ELLs, and we compared their performance in English to a group of English monolingual children. Both groups of children were enrolled in kindergarten classes in public schools in Vancouver, Canada (Campbell & Marinova-Todd, 2006a, 2006b). The data were collected as part of a larger project examining the oral proficiency and literacy development of ELLs of different home languages.

The sample consisted of 59 children in total: 21 English monolingual speakers (mean age 5 years and 8 months) and 38 Chinese ELLs (mean age 5 years and 7 months). The children attended schools in culturally diverse neighborhoods where the average SES of the parents was relatively low. As is standard in schools within the Vancouver district, monolingual English-speaking children attended half-day kindergarten classes, while the ELLs attended full-day kindergarten classes. All the instruction was conducted in English, and the ELLs did not receive any additional English language instruction.

Most of the previous studies used formal tests to assess morphosyntactic knowledge in English, such as grammaticality judgment tests, oral cloze tests, and standardized tests. Miller et al. (2006), on the other hand, argued that these tests are not sensitive enough to reveal any possible transfer effects of oral proficiency; thus they promoted the use of tools that elicited more natural language that was similar to the language used on a day-to-day basis. In their study, Miller et al. (2006) employed oral narratives that were elicited through a wordless picture book. For reliability purposes, we decided to include the oral cloze test originally developed by Siegel and Ryan (1988), adapting it in Chinese. In the context of this test, children heard a sentence with a missing element (e.g., "Betty _____ a hole with her shovel"). After hearing the sentence twice, the children were asked to provide the missing element in the sentence (in the above case: "dug"). But we also included oral narratives elicited in English through the same picture book as in the Miller at al. (2006) study as a more sensitive measure that mirrors real-life discourse more closely. In order to compare the groups' performance in a valid way, the potential influence of variability in the story length was controlled for in the following manner. First, the number of clauses from each narrative was tallied. A clause was defined as a verb and its arguments (e.g., "the boy is looking at his frog"). Then all narrative measures of interest were divided by the total number of clauses, thus creating proportions that controlled for any differences in the length of narratives produced by the children.

Our results supported previous findings by Siegel and her collaborators (Lesaux & Siegel, 2003; Lipka et al., 2005; Low & Siegel, 2005) by showing that the monolingual children did significantly better than the ELLs on the oral cloze test. Moreover, our data confirmed that, in the area of morphosyntax, the ELLs' oral proficiency was not equivalent to their monolingual peers. In addition, the oral cloze test scores of the Chinese ELLs in English and in Chinese were also compared. There was no significant difference between the two languages, which indicated that the Chinese ELLs had equivalent knowledge of morphosyntax in their L1 and L2. Moreover, there was a moderately high correlation ($r = .60$, $p < .01$) between their English and Chinese scores on the test, thus revealing a potential for transfer effects between the two languages in this group of children.

Upon examination of the grammatical errors exhibited in their English oral narratives, the Chinese ELLs produced significantly more morphosyntactic errors per utterance than the monolingual children, a result that confirmed our findings from the oral cloze test. Our error analysis further revealed that, when children made many errors, they tended to be of the same type. For example, if a child had difficulty with plural markings, he or she would make multiple errors on plurals (e.g., "many *bee*", "two *frog*", etc.), or if pronoun reference was an issue, the child would continually use pronouns without clarifying whom they refer to (e.g., "The boy and the dog went outside. *He* looked in the hole"). This indicated that ELLs lacked knowledge only in some aspects of English grammar, rather than having a more global deficit across the whole domain of English morphosyntax. On the other hand, the fewer and more varied errors of the monolingual children may have been due in part to lapse in attention, forgetting in what tense they were telling the story, or inconsistently describing the different animal characters (e.g., an "elk" may sometimes be called "deer" or "moose" by the same child).

Upon closer examination of the specific types of errors the two groups of children made, an interesting pattern was revealed. Overall, the ELLs made more errors of every type examined, but they made significantly more inflectional morphological errors. Inflectional morphemes are affixes that do not change the part of speech or the meaning of the word to which they are attached. For example, the ELLs omitted the plural morpheme on nouns ("many bee") or the past tense morpheme on verbs ("the boy went outside and close the door"), switched tense throughout the narrative, and made pronoun errors, such as using "she" and "her" to refer to a boy ("and then the boy closed her eyes and shout"). All of the ELLs' typical errors could be explained by the fact that these inflectional aspects of English morphosyntax are minimal or nonexistent in Chinese; thus it was possible that the Chinese ELLs were experiencing negative transfer from the L1 to their L2. On the other hand, reference errors, which were represented by reference gaps in the necessary presentation of characters, times, or places (e.g., "The dog was looking at a hole in the ground. The boy climbed a tree. *He* looked *inside*," an example of reference gap for characters *he*, and places *inside*), were equivalent in number across the two groups, which may be an indication that reference errors could be related to general language development, not to the language status of the child.

Since we used a formal measure of morphosyntax, the oral cloze test, and a less formal measure, the oral narrative, it was possible to examine any associations between the two measures. Our results revealed that, in the English monolingual group, the number of errors per utterance was negatively and significantly correlated with their score on the oral cloze test. In other words an increase in the number of morphosyntactic errors in the narrative was associated with lower scores on the cloze test. Therefore, when the morphosyntactic proficiency in the sample is generally high, the two measures could be treated as equivalent when determining the level of morphosyntactic skill in young children. The association between the error rate in narratives and the scores on the oral cloze test was weaker and not significant in the ELL group, which could be explained by the fact that they generally did very poorly on the oral cloze task, and there was very little variation in their distribution. If we were to make conclusions solely on the oral cloze test, the ELLs would have appeared as uniformly weaker in the domain of morphosyntax. Therefore, we concur with Miller et al. (2006) that it is even more important to utilize a more detailed analyses of the ELLs' errors, such as the oral narratives, in order to establish the exact areas of strength and weakness in this group.

In the context of the larger study we also measured some aspects of the children's literacy skills in English. Similarly to the studies reviewed by Lipka et al. (2005) we found that, despite a significantly lower oral proficiency in English, the ELLs performed as well or even better on a standardized (Wide Range Achievement Test–3 [WRAT-3]; Wilkinson, 1995) measure of reading in English which consisted of letter identification and simple word reading. Moreover, in the ELL group a correlational analysis revealed a moderate and positive association between their cloze test scores and reading scores within language, but no associations across languages. A somewhat weak, but significant correlation ($r = -.37$, $p < .05$) between the number of errors per utterance and the scores on the WRAT-3 further confirmed the trend that could only be confirmed with regression analyses on a much larger sample size. In the meantime, it appears that our findings are in line with previous research (Lipka et al., 2005; Miller et al., 2006) showing a modest contribution of English morphosyntactic skills to reading skills in English for the Chinese ELLs.

In summary, findings were discussed from our current research that compared a group of English monolingual speakers with a group of Chinese ELLs on their morphosyntactic knowledge and literacy skills in English. In addition, the ELLs' morphosyntactic skills in both their L1 and L2 were compared. A potential for cross-language transfer of morphosyntactic knowledge between Chinese and English was found in this group of ELLs. However, the cross-language transfer effects between morphosyntax and reading are far less clear. Unlike previous research, we utilized both formal and informal measures of morphosyntax in the L2. This approach demonstrated that, by utilizing the informal but more detailed measure, the areas of particular strength and weakness for the ELL group were revealed. The types of morphosyntactic errors common to the ELLs were different than the types of errors for the monolingual group. This pattern presented the possibility of transfer effects from the L1 to the L2 (which would not have been revealed from the cloze test results alone). Finally, the possibility was put forward that the ELLs' morphosyntactic skill in English, and not Chinese, may be an important, albeit modest, predictor of their reading achievement in English. These findings are in line with previous research and further contribute to our understanding of the oral language and literacy development of ELL children in North America.

GENERAL CONCLUSION
AND IMPLICATIONS FOR PRACTICE

The constantly growing number of ELLs across schools in North America necessitates research that is focused on describing the oral language skills these children bring to school entry and how these skills contribute to their literacy development in the language of instruction. Therefore, it is important to establish the degree of English oral proficiency of ELLs. In addition, due to their bilingual/multilingual status, the role of their home language needs to be determined too, especially the ways in which it could help ELLs to acquire better skills in English and ultimately achieve higher success in school. It is also crucial that we recognize and develop not only the size but also the complexity of ELL children's vocabulary knowledge for their future academic success. More research is necessary to examine the best instructional practices to create elaborated semantic networks that will assist in ELL children's understanding and use of academic language in later schooling.

In this chapter, research was reviewed in two important but less extensively studied domains of oral proficiency, namely, the lexicon and morphosyntax. In both domains, ELLs' skills in English were significantly lower than the skills of monolingual English-speaking children of the same age, especially in the early grades. In other words, ELLs come to school with lower English proficiency, which often may not be apparent during an informal conversation. Teachers and parents often erroneously assume that once ELL children sound like native-speaking children, then they have achieved native-like proficiency in their L2 and thus no extra support is needed in school. However, research consistently shows that, upon closer scrutiny, the ELLs' oral skills in English are lower than the skills of their monolingual peers, and it takes time for the ELLs to catch up with their monolingual counterparts.

Despite lower proficiency in their L2, ELLs have a benefit in speaking more than one language. ELLs can rely on language skills developed in their L1 when functioning in their L2 (usually English), and the facilitating links between the two languages could be further emphasized with effective instructional practices. Therefore, more intervention studies are needed to assess the outcomes of instruction in the explicit teaching of transfer strategies. In both domains that were examined, research revealed transfer effects from the L1 to the L2. In the domain of vocabulary, by utilizing cognates recognition, for example, ELLs improved their vocabulary scores in English. In the domain of morphosyntax, it was shown that structures present in the L1 can facilitate morphosyntactic knowledge in the L2. Some skills may be less transferable, even for bilinguals with two alphabetic languages; yet this may be balanced with other linguistic knowledge that is transferable. For example, only a limited number of vocabulary and syntactic structures transfer from L1 to L2, but metalinguistic skills repeatedly have been shown to transfer.

For languages that are structurally very different from each other, simply being aware of the main areas of disparity could help educators focus their instruction in those areas in the L2, thus helping students develop skills in the exact areas of weakness. This instructional strategy requires that teachers be familiar with the native language of their students. Due to the multicultural nature of North American classrooms (sometimes there are speakers of more than 10 L1s in a classroom), it is not possible that a single teacher could be knowledgeable about all the L1s present in the class. However, in both Canada and the United States there are large clusters of more or less homogenous groups of immigrant children who come from homes that speak the same language, for example, Chinese in Western Canada and Spanish across the United States. If we could initially address the needs of these children, we would make huge progress toward improving the educational experience of a large percentage of ELLs.

In addition to cross-language transfer of linguistic knowledge, there is also evidence confirming the within-language transfer of vocabulary and morphosyntactic knowledge to reading. In other words, stronger vocabulary and morphosyntactic skills in English tend to be associated with stronger reading skills in English. Therefore, it is equally important for ELLs and monolingual English-speaking children to develop strong oral language proficiency skills in English.

In conclusion, it is essential to be reminded of the extremely difficult task that ELLs face when being schooled in an L2 in which they are not very proficient. Therefore, we need to always acknowledge their achievement, even when it appears to be modest or not up to standard, since the standard is usually set by the average performance of monolingual children. On a daily basis, ELLs in kindergarten struggle to learn a new writing system, as well as to figure out how to put their limited number of words into a sentence that is understood by their teacher. But in addition, they also spend effort on disentangling linguistic conundrums set by their knowledge of one language, which is constantly being re-analyzed through their exposure to another language. It was one of our kindergarten ELLs who asked us the question: "Why does the rooster say '*cock-a-doodle-doo*' in English, when the rooster doesn't sound like that? NEVER!"

NOTE

1. We use the term *oral language* to refer to the language skills that children develop in preschool, that is, before they are explicitly taught reading and writing. When discussing children who are in first grade and older, we use the term *linguistic literacy* instead. With this distinction we emphasize the development of academic language as a result of literacy instruction; thus, language skills that were previously oral are now tightly connected with literacy development. Otherwise, when the age of the children is unknown or when referring to language skills generally, we will use the term *oral proficiency*.

REFERENCES

Biemiller, A. J. (1981). *Biemiller Test of Reading Processes*. Toronto, ON: University of Toronto Press.

Campbell, K., & Marinova-Todd, S. H. (2006a, May). *L2 Oral proficiency of Chi-

nese–English bilingual children. Presentation at the *Language Acquisition and Bilingualism (LAB): Consequences for a Multilingual Society,* Toronto, ON.

Campbell, K., & Marinova-Todd, S. H. (2006b, August). *Grammatical errors in narratives of Chinese–English bilingual children.* Paper presented at the 2006 Third International Conference on Speech Writing and Context, Edmonton, AB.

Carlisle, J. F., & Beeman, M. (2000). The effects of language of instruction on the reading and writing achievement of first-grade Hispanic children. *Scientific Studies of Reading, 4*(4), 331–353.

Carlisle, J. F., Beeman, M., Davis, L. H., & Spharim, G. (1999). Relationships of metalinguistic capabilities and reading achievement for children who are becoming bilingual. *Applied Psycholinguistics, 20,* 459–478.

Carlo, M. S., August, D., McLaughlin, B., Snow, C. E., Dressler, C., Lippman, D. N., et al. (2004). Closing the gap: Addressing the vocabulary needs of English language learners in bilingual and mainstream classrooms. *Reading Research Quarterly, 39,* 188–206.

Chall, J. S. (1996). *Stages of reading development* (2nd ed.). Orlando, FL: Harcourt Brace.

Chan, A. (2004). Syntactic transfer: Evidence from the interlanguage of Hong Kong Chinese ESL learners. *Modern Language Journal, 88,* 56–74.

Cummins, J. (1984). *Bilingualism and special education: Issues in assessment and pedagogy.* San Diego: College-Hill Press.

Cummins, J. (2000). *Language, power and pedagogy: Bilingual children in the cross-fire.* Toronto, ON: Multilingual Matters.

De Houwer, A. (1990). *The acquisition of two languages from birth: A case study.* Cambridge, UK: Cambridge University Press.

De Houwer, A. (1995). Bilingual language acquisition. In P. Fletcher & B. MacWhinney (Eds.), *The handbook of child language* (pp. 219–250). Oxford, UK: Blackwell.

Döpke, S. (1998). Competing language structures: The acquisition of verb placement by bilingual German–English children. *Journal of Child Language, 25,* 555–584.

Durgunoğlu, A., Nagy, W., & Hancin-Bhatt, B. (1993). Cross-language transfer of phonological awareness. *Journal of Educational Psychology, 85,* 453–465.

Gardner, M. (1990). *Expressive One-Word Picture Vocabulary Test—Revised.* Novato, CA: Academic Therapy.

Gawlitzek-Maiwald, I., & Tracy, R. (1996). Bilingual bootstrapping. *Linguistics, 34,* 901–926.

Genesee, F. (1989). Early bilingual development: One language or two? *Journal of Child Language, 16,* 161–179.

Genesee, F., Nicoladis, E., & Paradis, J. (1995). Language differentiation in early bilingual development. *Journal of Child Language, 22,* 611–631.

Geva, E., & Zadeh, Z. Y. (2006). Reading efficiency in native English-speaking and English-as-a-second-language children: The role of oral proficiency and underlying cognitive-linguistic processes. *Scientific Studies of Reading, 10*(1), 31–57.

Gombert, J. E. (1992). *Metalinguistic development.* Chicago: University of Chicago Press.

Hancin-Bhatt, B., & Nagy, W. E. (1994). Lexical transfer and second language morphological development. *Applied Psycholinguistics, 15*(3), 289–310.

Hart, B., & Risley, T. (1995). *Meaningful differences in the everyday experience of young American children.* Baltimore: Brookes.

Hulk, A., & Müller, N. (2000). Bilingual first language acquisition at the interface between syntax and pragmatics. *Bilingualism: Language and Cognition, 3,* 227–244.

Huttenlocher, J., Haight, W., Bryk, A., Seltzer, M., & Lyons, T. (1991). Early vocabulary growth: Relation to language input and gender. *Developmental Psychology, 27,* 236–248.

Konold, T., Juel, C., McKinnon, M., & Deffes, R. (2003). A multivariate model of early reading acquisition. *Applied Psycholinguistics, 24,* 89–112.

Lesaux, N., & Siegel, L. (2003). The development of reading in children who speak English as a second language. *Developmental Psychology, 39,* 1005–1019.

Limbos, L. M., & Geva, E. (2001). Accuracy of teacher assessments of second-language students at risk for reading disability. *Journal of Learning Disabilities, 34,* 136–151.

Lipka, O., Siegel, L. S., & Vukovic, R. (2005). The literacy skills of English language learners in Canada. *Learning Disabilities Research and Practice, 20*(1), 39–49.

Low, P. B., & Siegel, L. S. (2005). A comparison of the cognitive processes underlying reading comprehension in native English and ESL speakers. *Written Language and Literacy, 8,* 207–231.

Manis, F. R., Lindsey, K. A., & Bailey, C. E. (2004). Development of reading in grades K–2 in Spanish-speaking English language learners. *Learning Disabilities, Research and Practice, 19*(4), 214–224.

Mayer, M. (1969). *Frog, where are you?* New York: Puffin Books.

Meisel, J. (1989). Early differentiation of languages in bilingual children. In K. Hyltenstam & L. Obler (Eds.), *Bilingualism across the lifespan: Aspects of acquisition, maturity and loss* (pp. 13–40). Cambridge, UK: Cambridge University Press.

Miller, J. F., Heilmann, J., Nockerts, A., Iglesias, A., Fabiano, L., & Francis, D. (2006). Oral language and reading in bilingual children. *Learning Disabilities Research and Practice, 21,* 30–43.

Moll, L. C., & Diaz, S. (1985). Ethnographic pedagogy: Promoting effective bilingual instruction. In E. E. Garcia & R. V. Padilla (Eds.), *Advances in bilingual education research* (pp. 127–149). Tucson: University of Arizona Press.

Müller, N. (1998). Transfer in bilingual first language acquisition. *Bilingualism: Language and Cognition, 1,* 151–171.

Nagy, W., Garcia, G. E., Durgunoğlu, A. Y., & Hancin-Bhatt, B. (1993). Spanish–English bilingual students' use of cognates in English reading. *Journal of Reading Behavior, 25,* 241–259.

Nagy, W. E., McClure, E. F., & Mir, M. (1997). Linguistic transfer and the use of context by Spanish–English bilinguals. *Applied Psycholinguistics, 18*(4), 431–452.

Nagy, W. E., & Scott, J. (2000). Vocabulary processes. In M. L. Kamil, P. B. Mosenbatch, P. D. Pearson, & R. Barr (Eds.), *Handbook of reading research: Vol. III* (pp. 269–284). Mahwah, NJ: Erlbaum.

Noonan, B., Hildebrand, D., & Yackulic, R. (1997). The effects of early oral language skills and other measures on subsequent school success: A longitudinal study. *Alberta Journal of Educational Research, 43*, 254–257.

Ordóñez, C., Carlo, M., Snow, C., & McLaughlin, B. (2002). Depth and breadth of vocabulary in two languages: Which vocabulary skills transfer. *Journal of Educational Psychology, 94*(4), 719–728.

Paradis, J., & Genesee, F. (1996). Syntactic acquisition in bilingual children: Autonomous or interdependent? *Studies in Second Language Acquisition, 18*, 1–25.

Patterson, J. (2002). Relationships of expressive vocabulary to frequency of reading and television experience among bilingual toddlers. *Applied Psycholinguistics, 23*, 493–508.

Pearson, B., Fernández, S., Lewedeg, V., & Oller, D. K. (1997). The relation of input factors to lexical learning by bilingual infants. *Applied Psycholinguistics, 23*, 493–508.

Plaza, M., & Cohen, H. (2003). The interaction between phonological processing, syntactic awareness, and naming speed in the reading and spelling performance of first-grade children. *Brain and Cognition, 53*, 287–292.

Proctor, C. P., August, D., Carlo, M., & Snow, C. (2006). The intriguing role of Spanish language vocabulary knowledge in predicting reading comprehension. *Journal of Educational Psychology, 98*(1), 159–169.

Proctor, C. P., Carlo, M. S., August, D., & Snow, C. E. (2005). Native Spanish-speaking children reading in English: Toward a model of comprehension. *Journal of Educational Psychology, 97*, 246–256.

Siegel, L. S. (1992). An evaluation of the discrepancy definition of dyslexia. *Journal of Learning Disabilities, 25*, 618–629.

Siegel, L. S., & Ryan, E. B. (1988). Development of grammatical sensitivity, phonological, and short-term memory skills in normally achieving and subtypes of learning disabled children. *Developmental Psychology, 24*, 28–37.

Snow, C., Burns, M., & Griffin, P. (Eds.). (1998). *Preventing reading difficulties in young children*. Washington, DC: National Academy Press.

Taeschner, T. (1983). *The sun is feminine: The study of language acquisition in bilingual children*. Berlin, Germany: Springer.

Uchikoshi, Y. (2006a). English vocabulary development in bilingual kindergartners: What are the best predictors? *Bilingualism: Language and Cognition, 9*(1), 33–49.

Uchikoshi, Y. (2006b). Early reading in bilingual kindergarteners: Can educational television help? *Scientific Studies of Reading, 10*(1), 89–120.

Umbel, V. M., Pearson, B. Z., Fernandez, M. C., & Oller, D. K. (1992). Measuring bilingual children's receptive vocabularies. *Child Development, 63*(4), 1012–1020.

U.S. Department of Education. (2007). *Demographics and school characteristics of students receiving special education in the elementary grades* (NCES 2007-005). Retrieved February 9, 2009, from *nces.ed.gov/pubsearch/pubsinfo. asp?pubid=2007005.*

Valdés, G., & Figueroa R. (1994). *Bilingualism and testing: A special case of bias*. Westport, CT: Ablex.

Verhallen, M., & Schoonen, R. (1993). Vocabulary knowledge of monolingual and bilingual children. *Applied Linguistics, 14*, 344–363.

Verhallen, M., & Schoonen, R. (1998). Lexical knowledge in L1 and L2 of third and fifth graders. *Applied Linguistics, 19*(4), 452–470.

Verhoeven. L. (1994). Transfer in bilingual development: The linguistic interdependence hypothesis revisited. *Language Learning, 44*, 381–415.

Volterra, V., & Taeschner, T. (1978). The acquisition and development of language by bilingual children. *Journal of Child Language, 5*, 311–326.

Wilkinson, G. S. (1995). *The Wide Range Achievement Test–3.* Wilmington, DE: Jastak Associates.

Whong-Barr, M., & Schwartz, B. (2002). Morphological and syntactic transfer in child L2 acquisition of the English dative alternation. *Studies in Second Language Acquisition, 24*, 579–616.

Yip, V., & Matthews, S. (2000). Syntactic transfer in a Cantonese–English bilingual child. *Bilingualism: Language and Cognition, 3*, 193–208.

Yip, V., & Matthews, S. (2006). Assessing language dominance in bilingual acquisition: A case for mean length of utterance differentials. *Language Assessment Quarterly, 3*, 97–116.

CHAPTER 3

■　■　■

Tuning In to
Language-Specific Patterns

Nonword Repetition and the Big Picture of Bilingual Vocabulary Learning

MARÍA R. BREA-SPAHN
ELAINE R. SILLIMAN

All language learning outcomes, including vocabulary learning, are experience driven. In developing possible word meaning, language learners extract information about language-specific phonological patterns through everyday social interactions that cultivate their attending to the distributional characteristics of the linguistic input (Ellis, 2002; Saffran & Thiessen, 2007). However, most of the research on language-specific pattern learning has been conducted with infants and young children from monolingual English-speaking homes. For instance, infants display sensitivity to English language word boundaries by 8 months (Saffran, 2001). As early as 9 months, infants can also distinguish between frequent and infrequent English phoneme sequences (Goldstein & Schwade, 2008; Jusczyk, Luce, & Charles-Luce, 1994). In addition, preschool children (ages 3 years to 6 years) were able to learn novel words that contained common English phoneme sequences more rapidly than novel words that contained rare phoneme sequences (Storkel, 2001). The influence of frequency on lexical acquisition continues as children's phonological representations become adult-like (Storkel & Rogers, 2000).

A second research strand on English vocabulary acquisition comes from the literature on language processing. Measures of language processing always include items that are either equally unfamiliar or equally familiar to all children. The principle guiding this approach is straightforward. The examination of how children manage specific types of linguistic input is a less culturally biased approach than is the use of assessment tools that are heavily experience based (Campbell, Dollaghan, Needleman, & Janosky, 1997), such as standardized vocabulary measures. Empirical support exists for a relationship between performance on language processing tasks, like nonword repetition (NWR) and word knowledge. In fact, more accurate repetition of nonwords has been found to correlate positively with vocabulary size in English-speaking children (Gathercole, 2007; Gathercole & Baddeley, 1989). Some NWR studies have been conducted with Spanish-speaking children who are English language learners (ELLs); however, these studies have two major limitations. One restriction is that NWR tasks tend to be administered in English only (e.g., Chiappe, Siegel, & Gottardo, 2002; Gottardo, 2002), while the second issue is that item construction of Spanish NWR tasks has not employed a systematic approach.

The aim of this chapter is to address the current state of knowledge on the relationship between Spanish-specific phonological knowledge of word forms and the developing bilingual lexicon. In the first section, we describe sociocultural factors affecting variations in bilingual vocabulary learning experiences. The next section provides a brief overview of working memory and NWR measures as potential indicators of the ease of new word learning. How NWR tasks have been applied to identifying oral language impairment in English-only and ELL children is examined in the third section. We then present an alternate framework in the fourth section. This framework is grounded in probabilistic learning that may guide research on relationships between language-specific lexical patterns and performance on language processing tasks, like NWR, in Spanish-speaking children. In the final segment, we offer some future directions for NWR research, as well as for clinical and educational practices, in the assessment of the bilingual lexicon.

FACTORS AFFECTING VOCABULARY DEVELOPMENT

How do working memory and NWR contribute to the vocabulary learning of bilinguals in both the oral and text domains? A starting point involves the oral vocabulary learning of bilingual children within the context of their language experience.

Role of Language Experience

The Language of Instruction

In comparison with English vocabulary learning, bilingual vocabulary learning is more complicated due to the multiple linguistic, sociocultural, and individual factors that influence bilingual lexical organization. Furthermore, identifying "the optimal conditions for L2 vocabulary acquisition" (Snow & Kim, 2007) is linked to the quality and nature of experiences with the language of instruction (English only, Spanish only, or bilingual). A number of individual studies of English reading performance, using a variety of research designs (August, Calderón, Carlo, & Eakin, 2006; August, Snow, et al., 2006; Calderón et al., 2005; Manis, Lindsey, & Bailey, 2004; Miller et al., 2006; Paez & Rinaldi, 2006; Proctor, Carlo, August, & Snow, 2005; Proctor, August, Carlo, & Snow, 2006; San Francisco, Carlo, August, & Snow, 2006), as well as a meta-analysis of 15 investigations that utilized experimental or quasi-experimental designs to study language of instruction (Francis, Lesaux, & August, 2006), have shown better outcomes for bilingual reading instruction in the early school years. In contrast to the large number of studies of reading instruction, a review of bilingual research by the National Literacy Panel (August & Shanahan, 2006) found only three studies on vocabulary instruction with Spanish-speaking children that met the empirical criteria for inclusion (Shanahan & Beck, 2006).

Home Experiences with Vocabulary Learning

Duursma et al. (2007), who employed a parent interview in a large-scale, cross-sectional study, identified three language-specific predictor variables for performance on English vocabulary measures at grade 5. One focus was low-income Hispanic families who enrolled their children in English as the language of initial instruction. These predictors were:

- Paternal preference for English use in the home.
- The extent to which parents assisted the child in English with homework or learning.
- Sibling interaction in English, which "had a much larger effect on English (vocabulary) proficiency than the language preferred by the parents" (Duursma et al., 2007, p. 185).

Maternal education level, as a stand-in for socioeconomic status, also appears to be another factor affecting vocabulary learning. In one of the few studies with Spanish-learning young children, all of whom had minimal exposure to English and were from low-income homes, children's oral vocabulary comprehension was positively correlated with mothers' level of education (Hurtado, Marchman, & Fernald, 2007). Those who were more lexically advanced had faster and more accurate responses to spoken Spanish object names (Hurtado et al., 2007). Moreover, toddlers with more robust vocabularies who had mothers with higher education levels were more accurate in their real-time language processing of object names. In contrast, toddlers with limited vocabularies who had mothers with lower educational levels were less proficient in their real-time spoken-language processing of object names. While no single factor can account for these vocabulary learning patterns (Pearson, 2007), one possibility is that the level of maternal education indirectly influences variation in the quantity and quality of the input that young children hear.

Acquisition of a Literate English Lexicon

Snow and Kim (2007) concede that there is still little persuasive evidence that vocabulary transfer from everyday conversational Spanish to everyday conversational English is a major mechanism for increasing the depth of the English lexical network (Bialystok, 2002; Carlo et al., 2004; Ordóñez, Carlo, Snow, & McLaughlin, 2002; Ouelette, 2006), much less a means for the transfer of strategies for the processing of more literate oral syntax (Clahsen & Felser, 2006). The literate lexicon required for processing and understanding written texts at a deep level likely originates from the frequency and quality of engagement in meaningful experiences across a range of literacy contexts (Fuste-Herrmann, Silliman, Bahr, Fasnacht, & Federico, 2006; Silliman, Wilkinson, & Brea-Spahn, 2004).

Language-specific experience is a powerful factor in developing a literate lexicon. A question concerns the pathway for the vocabulary–reading comprehension relationship. It is unclear whether linkages are unidirectional (one "causes" the other), bidirectional (each reciprocally influences the other), or result from the contributions of another factor, such as the expansiveness of metalinguistic awareness (Nagy, 2007; Wagner, Muse, & Tannenbaum, 2007).

ROLE OF WORKING MEMORY:
NWR AND WORD KNOWLEDGE

Consider the following set of instructions:

> I want you to listen to some made-up words.... After you hear each made-up word, I want you to say it exactly as you heard it and as clearly as you can. Even if it's hard to say, give it your best try. Listen carefully because I can't repeat the words. Okay? Let's try some: *ballop*. (from the Compre-

hensive Test of Phonological Processing [CTOPP]; Wagner, Torgesen, & Rashotte, 1999)

This example from a commonly used measure of phonological processing is a NWR task. These tasks[1] were originally devised to assess the efficiency of phonological memory, or the phonological loop, which serves a language processing function. As described by Baddeley and Hitch (1974), the phonological loop is a component of the working memory system where verbal information, including the decoding of print by beginning readers, is initially translated and held for temporary storage. According to Wagner et al. (2003), "efficient phonological memory helps the beginning reader by storing sounds they retrieve from permanent storage that are associated with letters and letter patterns in the to-be-decoded word" (p. 56).

Rationale for the Use of NWR Tasks

In assessing the integrity of phonological memory, NWR tasks are often selected for three reasons. First, performance on these tasks predicts word-level recognition ability and, second, in theory, NWR tasks are believed to minimize real word meaning (wordlikeness). Because meaning is unavailable, it follows that accurate word pronunciation depends primarily on phonological processing rather than lexical processing (Wagner et al., 2003). A final reason is a pragmatic, although challengeable, assumption. A NWR task "is very simple, which makes it easy to explain to individuals even without a thorough mastery of their native language" (Wagner, Francis, & Morris, 2005, p. 12).

In contrast to the primary phonological processing perspective on NWR tasks, Gathercole (1995) and colleagues (Gathercole, Service, Hitch, Adams, & Martin, 1999) suggest a broader view of NWR performance, which is that NWR ability is linked to vocabulary learning. Results from the multiple cross-sectional and longitudinal studies conducted by Gathercole and colleagues (summarized in Gathercole, 2006) have led to the premise that phonological memory mediates the scope (breadth) of children's vocabulary learning, at least before age 5. Moreover, because NWR performance is a product of phonological memory processes, the premise is that the accuracy of performance is less dependent on individual language experience (Gathercole, 2006), unlike vocabulary assessments, which represent language-specific knowledge. For example, for Spanish-speaking children acquiring English as a second language in school, variations in their language experience in both languages combined with their English proficiency may obscure the meaning of their performance on vocabulary measures (Kohnert, Windsor, & Yim, 2006).

NWR as a Dual Index of Verbal Working Memory and New Word Learning

The ability to repeat orally unfamiliar phonological forms, like *ballop* (Wagner et al., 1999) is simultaneously a measure of verbal working memory and, on another level, a proxy for the rate of new oral word learning in the first language (L1). Although word knowledge involves skills that extend well beyond naming, establishing associations between lexical and phonological representations of a word is an essential initial step in building a lexicon. In effect, "Every word we now know was once unfamiliar to us, and on many occasions will have started its journey into our mental lexicon via such a repetition attempt" (Gathercole, 2006, p. 513).

However, repetition by itself is not the source of the connection for novice language learners. It is believed that the linkage between the meaning and phonological (form) components of a spoken word, whether real or a nonword, are temporarily stored in the phonological component of working memory. Gathercole (2007) suggests that phonological storage, which accumulates phonologically represented information on a short-term basis, is one aspect of working memory that, in turn, is linked with the coordinating functions of a central executive component.

The distinction between real (familiar) words and nonwords is important since, in theory, nonwords do not activate lexical representations, while actual words must activate both lexical and phonological representations. From Gathercole's (2007) perspective, nonwords, not real words, provide a purer test of the quality of the phonological storage that "influences the ease of new word learning" (p. 522) and eventually influences the shift in lexical organization. This shift, from holistic to sublexical units such as syllables and phonemes, accommodates rapidly growing lexical representations. In this framework, the integrity of the phonological storage mechanism drives the developmental relationship between vocabulary knowledge and the repetition of both low- and high-familiarity NWRs of increasing syllable length. The same phonological storage mechanism is also responsible for the subsequent ability to engage in the segmental analysis critical for successfully breaking the alphabetic code.

NWR AND LANGUAGE IMPAIRMENT IN MONOLINGUAL ENGLISH-SPEAKING AND ELL CHILDREN

Monolingual English-Speaking Children with and without Language Impairment

Over the last 20 years, NWR tasks have become a popular research measure with monolingual English-speaking children who are typically developing and with children who exhibit atypical language development (Archibald & Gathercole, 2006; Campbell et al., 1997; Dollaghan, 1998; Dollaghan & Campbell, 1998; Edwards & Lahey, 1998; Munson, Kurtz, & Windsor, 2005; Snowling, 1981; Snowling, Goulandris, Bowlby, & Howell, 1986; Weismer et al., 2000). Measures are usually selected for two purposes (Beckman & Edwards, 2000; Bowey, 2001; Coady & Aslin, 2004; Edwards, Beckman, & Munson, 2004; Gathercole, 1995; Gathercole & Baddeley, 1990; Gathercole, Service et al., 1999; Gathercole, Willis, Emslie, & Baddeley, 1991a, 1991b; Michas & Henry, 1994; Wagner et al., 2005). These aims were to: (1) explore the functional integrity of the phonological loop and phonological working memory, and (2) investigate the perceptual, lexical, phonological, and articulatory elements involved in vocabulary learning.

Diagnostic Outcomes of NWR Performance

Despite variations across studies in NWR task construction and sample selection, the outcomes have been generally consistent: NWR seems to have diagnostic sensitivity in identifying children with language impairment (LI; Coady & Evans, 2008; Conti-Ramsden, 2003; Dollaghan & Campbell, 1998; Weismer et al., 2000) and/or a reading disability (Nation, Clarke, Marshall, & Durand, 2004; Snowling, 1981; Snowling et al., 1986). This result leads to the suggestion that NWR has potential as a tool for "leveling the (diagnostic) playing field" (Windsor & Kohnert, 2008). In effect, NWR tasks allow for a less biased exploration of children's accumulated phonological knowledge about words, regardless of their linguistic or cultural background. The findings across these studies converge on four major patterns:

- *Vocabulary links.* Performance on vocabulary and NWR measures is strongly correlated. Children with typical language development who obtain high scores on vocabulary measures tend to have better NWR performance in comparison to children with low vocabulary scores (Edwards et al., 2004; Gathercole & Adams, 1994; Gathercole & Baddeley, 1989, 1990; Gathercole, Willis, Emslie, & Baddeley, 1992). This relationship becomes stronger as children's vocabularies increase in breadth (size).

- *Wordlikeness.* Language-specific patterns influence NWR performance. The degree of linguistic similarity (or wordlikeness) between the nonwords and real words in a child's lexicon is a particularly salient pattern that may contribute to individual variation (Dollaghan, Biber, & Campbell, 1995; Edwards et al., 2004; Gathercole, 1995).

- *Language impairment.* Children with LI are typically less accurate on NWR tasks than are their age-matched and language ability-matched peers (Gray, 2006). Three hypotheses have been advanced to explain this divergence. One proposal is that children with LI will perform more poorly than age-matched controls, as they sacrifice working memory resources for linguistic processing; that is, because the input children with LI listen to in these tasks is unfamiliar and highly complex, they allocate more resources to comprehension processes. A consequence is that they fail to "rehearse" the NWR item sufficiently for active maintenance of the word's representations for retrieval purposes (Montgomery, 2002; Weismer, 1996). An alternate account suggests that perceptual, articulatory, and phonological encoding task demands are difficult for children with LI to coordinate simultaneously (Edwards & Lahey, 1998). A third perspective draws on the quality of phonological representations. Children with LI do not have sufficiently integrated phonological representations necessary for parsing the unfamiliar phonological patterns that support the repetition of nonwords (Munson, Edwards, & Beckman, 2005).

• *LI, NWR, and Fast Mapping.* The fourth trend offers a somewhat different perspective. In children with and without LI, NWR accuracy has been found to correlate positively with the fast mapping, or incidental learning, of lexical and semantic information about novel words (Alt & Plante, 2006). A speculation is that NWR performance may provide a snapshot of well-integrated phonological and lexical representations. These amalgamated representations then influence how effectively subsequent elaborated meanings are acquired. Elaborated meanings characterize a more literate lexicon.

A recent meta-analysis of NWR studies that included children with and without language impairment provides a significant caution (Graf Estes, Evans, & Else-Quest, 2007). Outcomes of the meta-analysis indicated a lack of homogeneity between varied versions of a NWR task. According to the authors, differing versions of NWR likely access dissimilar patterns of breakdown since the "characteristics of nonword repetition matter for the magnitude of the SLI [specific language impairment] deficit found" (Graf Estes et al., 2007, p. 192). As a result, the development of explanations for performance patterns in LI must be crafted with prudence. However, the task variation issue will be returned to in the discussion of NWR measures with ELL children.

ELL Children with and without LI

Seven studies to date have assessed working memory skill in Spanish-speaking children with typical and atypical language development. These studies (Calderón & Gutierrez-Clellen, 2003; Chiappe et al., 2002; Danahy,

Kalanek, Cordero, & Kohnert, 2008; Girbau & Schwartz, 2007, 2008; Gottardo, 2002; Gottardo, Collins, Baciu, & Gebotys, 2008) are examined below. As shown in Table 3.1, the seven studies are separated into three categories: (1) Assessment of NWR ability only in English to determine relationships between phonological working memory and English broad reading outcomes (n = 2); (2) assessment only in Spanish to establish whether a NWR measure might be diagnostic of phonological working memory problems in children with LI (n = 4); and (3) assessment only in Spanish to obtain preliminary performance data and develop a set of stimulus items that may be applied in clinical and research settings (n = 1).

Assessment in English Only

As displayed in Table 3.1, the Chiappe et al. (2002) study involved a large multilingual sample of kindergartners with a mean age of 5 years, 4 months. A variety of languages and proficiency levels was represented, from native-English-speaking children to emerging bilinguals who spoke two languages, including English in the home, to ELLs, who had a home language different from English. Children were assessed with measures targeting phonological awareness, syntactic awareness, print awareness, verbal short-term memory, and NWR assessed with the Sound Mimicry subtest of the Goldman, Fristoe, and Woodcock Sound–Symbol Test (Goldman, Fristoe, & Woodcock, 1974).

Significant differences in NWR ability were not found among the three major language groups; that is, the ELL group performed similarly to the bilingual and the native-English-speaking children in their reproduction of English nonwords. The participants in the three language groups showed growth in phonological processing, with the monolingual group outperforming the bilingual and ELL groups. Performance in the Sound Mimicry subtest predicted spelling ability, but not phonological awareness skills or other linguistic processing skills (e.g., syntactic processing). The absence of a relationship between phonological working memory and phonological awareness may contradict findings of previous studies, which have suggested that, to develop proficient decoding skills, an efficient and accurate set of phonological encodings is necessary (e.g., Snowling et al., 1986).

Unlike the multilingual sample of Chiappe (2002), Gottardo et al. (2002) included only Spanish-speaking children of Mexican origin, ages 5 to 8 years. Similar to Chiappe et al., NWR was assessed only in English. The rationale for the assessment of phonological memory in English only was its similarity to the process of English vocabulary acquisition that bilingual children faced daily. However, no significant correlations emerged between performance in the NWR task and raw scores on a standardized vocabulary test. Performance on the NWR task was related only to phonological aware-

TABLE 3.1. NWR Studies in ELLs Based on Language of Administration (English Only or Spanish Only)

Study	Language of administration	Participants/language	Nonword (language processing) measures
Chiappe, Siegel, & Gottardo (2002)	English only	N = 659 Subgroups: n = 540 English, n = 59 bilingual (English and another language as home languages), n = 60 second-language learners (home language other than English)	Phonological processing purpose: • Sound Mimicry subtest (Goldman et al., 1974)
Gottardo (2002)	English only	N = 92 Spanish Subgroups: n = 42 females n = 43 males	Phonological processing purpose: • N = 18 nonwords • Based on Dollaghan et al. (1995), Gathercole et al. (1991a), and Goldman et al. (1974) • Two to four syllables in length
Gottardo, Collins, Baciu, & Gebotys (2008)	English only	N = 72 Spanish–English bilingual grade 1 children (retested in grade 2) Subgroups: n = 42 females n = 37 males	Phonological processing purpose: • Same task as Gottardo (2002)
Calderón & Gutierrez-Clellen (2003)	Spanish only	N = 32 Spanish, low English proficiency, Mexican descent Subgroups: n = 16 typical language development n = 16 impaired language development	Diagnostic purpose: • N = 22 nonwords • Two to four syllables in length • Adapted Dollaghan and Campbell's (1998) scoring criteria
Girbau & Schwartz (2007)	Spanish only	N = 22 Spanish–Catalan bilinguals Subgroups: n = 11 typical language development n = 11 impaired language development	Diagnostic purpose: • N = 20 nonwords, one to five syllables in length • Medium-low frequency syllables • No diphthongs, but permissible Spanish clusters used

(continued)

TABLE 3.1. (continued)

Study	Language of administration	Participants/language	Nonword (language processing) measures
Girbau & Schwartz (2008)	Spanish only	N = 22 Spanish–English bilinguals Subgroups: n=11 typical language development n = 11 impaired language development	Diagnostic purpose: • Same task as Girbau and Schwartz (2007)
Danahy, Kalanek, Cordero, & Kohnert (2008)	Spanish only	N = 14 Spanish–English bilinguals Subgroups: n = 7 older n = 7 younger Older: 4;3–5;6 years Younger: 3;6–4;0	Obtaining normative data on performance: • N = 20 nonwords, one to five syllables in length • Adapted Dollaghan and Campbell's (1998) criteria Construction of syllables and assignment of primary stress followed typical patterns for Spanish • No later acquired consonants • No abutting consonants or consonant clusters

ness, a precursor to decoding abilities, measured by a phoneme deletion task in this case, and syntactic processing, as measured by a sentence completion measure. The latter outcome provided further support for suggesting a relationship between working memory skill and decoding, while at the same time contradicted the findings by Chiappe et al.

Nevertheless, Gottardo presented only correlative data between NWR performance and other measures of phonological awareness. No additional information detailing the quality of the participants' productions was provided. For example, error pattern analysis may be helpful in distinguishing typical mispronunciations that children may make from production errors induced by the level of phonological complexity characterizing the NWR items (Edwards et al., 2004). In the case of Spanish speakers who may be assessed with NWR in two languages, an error analysis may provide a point of comparison for the types of phonological patterns that are being learned in the first and second languages.

The disparity in results between these studies is a good illustration of how item characteristics influence task outcomes (Graf Estes et al., 2007). For example, a tentative explanation for the absence of a relationship between phonological working memory and phonological awareness is that the nonwords employed by Chiappe et al. (2002) contained linguistic components, such as syllables and phonemes, which were prearranged in a manner that violated English rules for phoneme placement within words. If so, this NWR test might involve more articulatory complexity. As a result, it might be tapping into skills other than working memory and language-specific exposure.

In another study, Gottardo et al. (2008) attempted to determine in a group of grade 1 Spanish–English bilinguals the language and literacy variables in Spanish (L1) that predicted consistency (either low or average) of their English (L2) word reading and vocabulary knowledge in grade 2. A sample of 115 children was assessed in grade 1; a year later, in grade 2, 79 participants from the original sample were reassessed. Sample attrition occurred, which the authors attributed to the migrant nature of this population; however, according to the authors "no significant differences on the grade 1 measures were found between the children who dropped out of the study and those who continued" (Gottardo et al., 2008, p. 14).

Measures of phonological awareness, rapid automatized naming, receptive vocabulary, and syntactic processing were administered in both languages. An English NWR measure was also used that was identical in description to the one administered in Gottardo's (2002) investigation. Gains in English vocabulary appeared to occur more consistently for children with "strong Spanish skills in the same area" (Gottardo et al., 2008, p. 20). However, in grade 1, the majority of children obtained vocabulary standard scores categorically identified as "low." In addition, little growth on these vocabulary breadth scores was found from grade 1 to grade 2. Finally, NWR accuracy predicted L2 vocabulary knowledge in grade 2. While the authors suggested that Spanish-speaking children who performed poorly on the English NWR were "good candidates for vocabulary-based interventions" (Gottardo et al., 2008, p. 22), they also cautioned that a NWR test that is valid, reliable, and diagnostically sensitive for use with Spanish-speaking ELLs had yet to be developed.

Assessment of NWR Ability in Spanish Only

To date, only a few studies have assessed NWR in languages other than English (e.g., Papagno & Vallar, 1995; Stokes, Wong, Fletcher, & Leonard, 2006; Thorn & Gathercole, 1999). Of the studies including Spanish-speaking children, only two (Calderon & Gutierrez-Clellen, 2003; Girbau & Schwartz, 2007) have used NWR as a diagnostic measure to identify children at risk for LI.

The Calderón and Gutierrez-Clellen (2003) measure, the Spanish Nonword Repetition Test (SNRT), was designed to differentiate 5-year-old Spanish-speaking children of Mexican descent with LI (n = 16) from Spanish-speaking children with typical language development (n = 16). Significant main effects were found for group and word length. The LI group performed significantly different from the typically developing language group. A length effect was also observed, with longer nonwords being produced less accurately than shorter nonwords. However, a group x length interaction was not significant, which contradicted previous results with English-speaking monolingual children. Calderón and Gutierrez-Clellen (2003) attributed this outcome to language-specific features of Spanish. The more frequent occurrence of multisyllabic words in Spanish may have resulted in children's being more attuned to repeating longer words, eradicating the potential difference between the groups in the repetition of the longer nonwords.

Although the SNRT appears to be sensitive to the identification of children with LI in a small sample, the power of the instrument is limited by at least two critical omissions in NWR construction: (1) prior ratings of wordlikeness for the nonwords were not obtained and (2) the effect of Spanish dialect patterns on NWR pronunciation was not considered. These variables singly or in combination could be the reason for the absence of a length interaction in this study.

The second study, Girbau and Schwartz (2007), assessed Spanish NWR in two groups of Spanish–Catalan bilingual children, ages 8 years, 3 months to 10 years, 11 months one group with a reported LI (n = 11) and another group consisting of age- and gender-matched controls (n = 11). The nonwords adhered to Spanish syllabification and stress patterns. Syllable frequency was manipulated in the construction of the items. Results replicated studies with English monolinguals: an effect of syllable length was significant. Regardless of language ability, children had more difficulty accurately repeating three-, four-, and five-syllable nonwords than repeating one- and two-syllable nonwords. Children with typical language development outperformed children with LI. Moreover, children with LI made more errors on vowels, consonants, and clusters via substitutions in comparison with the typically developing children, who did not produce any vowel errors. The relevance of this study is that a Spanish NWR measure containing nonwords consistent with Spanish phonotactics may be a potentially valuable screening assessment for LI. However, the influence of syllable frequency on these patterns of performance was not analyzed, and possible linguistic correlates for the error patterns remained unexplained. In addition, because the sample size was small, generalizability of results is limited.

In a subsequent study in which 22 bilingual Spanish–English children with and without LI participated, Girbau and Schwartz (2008) replicated the findings from their study in Spain. An effect of syllable length was observed again with accuracy of repetitions decreasing progressively from three-, to four-, and five-syllable nonwords. Children with LI exhibited significantly less accurate repetitions than did children with typical language development. The small number of nonword instances at each syllable length is one caveat that findings should be interpreted with care.

On a larger scale, the authors build the case that their NWR task appeared to identify language group membership accurately. Using the percentage of correct NWR at three-, four-, and five-syllable lengths, two accuracy metrics were calculated: positive and negative likelihood ratios, and test sensitivity and specificity. While both are measures of diagnostic (classification) accuracy related in part to the score cutoff between normal variation and impairment, they are independent of one another. Sensitivity concerns the proportion of a sample that is positive for the target impairment based on test performance, while specificity pertains to the proportion that is negative for the target impairment. Sensitivity and specificity are each determined separately. A significant problem with their application is that both are susceptible to disparities in the base rate of the target condition or the "percentage of people who have the disorder out of the entire sample of people who were assessed (i.e., the affected and unaffected people)" (Dollaghan, 2007, p. 92). For example, if the base rate is 50%, then prior to testing, the probability that any single person has the target condition is 50–50; but as sample size decreases, the probability increases that (1) fewer individuals will have the target impairment and (2) more persons will not be affected by it. While a base rate has been estimated for oral language impairment in English-only speaking children in the United States,[2] a comparable base rate value has yet to be ascertained for oral language impairment in bilingual children.

In contrast, likelihood ratios are less influenced by base rate variations because they are derived from the simultaneous consideration of sensitivity and specificity. They can be applied when the base rate is unusually low or exceptionally high (Dollaghan, 2007). Positive and negative likelihood ratios provide a degree of confidence that an individual's score is (Dollaghan, 2007) (1) most probably in the affected range, from a value of ≥ 10 (very positive) to a value of ≥ 3 (moderately positive but insufficient to diagnose the impairment) or (2) most probably in the unaffected range, from $\leq .10$ (extremely negative) to $\leq .30$ (moderately negative but insufficient to rule out the disorder).

Returning to the Girbau and Schwartz (2008) study, their use of likelihood ratios is problematic because a pretest base rate had not been determined; instead, Girbau and Schwartz relied on a preselected sample of bilingual children with and without LI, which most probably "inflated" (Girbau & Schwartz, 2008, p. 136) the likelihood ratios. The authors also reported a NWR test sensitivity of 0.82 and test specificity of 0.91. In the Plante and Vance (1994) rule of thumb, a measure intended for diagnostic purposes should demonstrate an overall accuracy of at least 90%, a standard that the Spanish NWR measure developed by Girbau and Schwartz (2007, 2008) did not meet.

More recently, Danahy and colleagues (2008) developed a set of one- to five-syllable Spanish nonwords. They administered their task to a small sample of typically developing Spanish-speaking preschoolers in an effort to obtain normative data on performance. Age and word-length effects were observed, although there were no significant differences in the repetition of one- to three-syllable nonwords. Rather, errors in repetition only occurred for the longer nonwords. Also, the authors emphasized that generalizations about age effects in their study were limited by the small number of participants in each sub-group. The nonwords that Danahy et al. (2008) developed followed the phonotactic and phonological patterns of Spanish. However, these items did not represent a range of wordlikeness. Because the authors used penultimate stress as the only prosodic pattern and embedded true monosyllabic words as constituent syllables in 12 of the nonwords, their stimuli are all likely to be relatively high in wordlikeness.

Summary: What We Know about NWR Performance

Three patterns of outcomes are discernable about NWR performance from the research to date. Of the three sets of results, the first two are yet to be replicated in studies involving Spanish language learners.

• *Repetition accuracy correlates with established word knowledge.* Monolingual English-speaking children with large vocabularies are more accurate in their repetitions of novel meaningless words than are children with smaller vocabularies. Multiple explanations, ranging from working memory capacity to children's ability to apply phonological patterns stored in their lexicons, have been proposed for this relationship between linguistic knowledge (or linguistic experience) and more accurate performance.

• *Precision in the repetition of nonwords depend heavily on the intrinsic characteristics of the NWR items comprising the task.* Items that contain phoneme sequences or phonetic transitions that are more frequent in a particular language are more accurately repeated. This outcome is not at all unexpected considering that, from a probabilistic perspective, infants first learn phonemes, phoneme sequences, and syllables that are more prevalent in and consistent with the patterns of their language (Pierrehumbert, 2003).

• *Language ability predicts NWR skill.* Children with LI, whether Spanish-speaking or English-only speakers, exhibit less accurate repetitions of novel meaningless words than do their chronological age- and language age-matched cohorts. Reduced accuracy has been attributed to limited working memory resources or even multitasking demands (Graf Estes et al., 2007). An example of multitasking in NWR tasks occurs for children with LI when they attempt to recruit underdeveloped phonological and lexical representations that, simultaneously, must be mapped into and programmed onto complex articulation patterns.

Last, if the intent is for NWR measures to be utilized for diagnostic aims with either monolingual English-speaking children or ELLs, then it is essential for studies to report likelihood ratios. In the case of ELLs, obtaining base rate values for oral LI appears to be a priority for reducing misclassifications of ELL children as LI.

AN ALTERNATIVE FRAMEWORK: INTEGRATING WORKING MEMORY AND NWR

In this section, we offer a different perspective on NWR, what it may be assessing, and why item construction is critical for deriving valid interpretations about the performance of ELL children.

Phonotactic Likelihood, Phonotactic Regularity, and the Wordlikeness Issue

Since great numbers of nonwords can be developed from a pool of available phonological units—from phonemes, allophones, subsyllabic components (e.g., onsets and rimes), to syllables—researchers can manipulate their inclusion or exclusion to control item complexity in a NWR task (Coady & Aslin, 2004; Dollaghan et al., 1995). The selection and combination of units is important considering that abundant evidence exists about the influence of language-specific patterns on individual performance during language processing tasks (Brea-Spahn & Frisch, 2006; Dollaghan et al., 1995; Edwards et al., 2004; Frisch, Large, & Pisoni, 2000; Storkel & Morrisette, 2002; Vitevitch & Luce, 1998). Some of these language-specific patterns include (1) *phonotactic likelihood*, the probability of occurrence of phonemes, onsets and rimes, and syllables within the words of a language; (2) *phonotactic regularity*, the patterns regulating the ordering of these elements within words.

Phonotactic likelihood and regularity affect the degree to which a nonword resembles the phonological composition of real words in children's lexicons. Consequently, both affect the accuracy with which nonwords are imitated in a repetition task. For example, a nonword with constituent phoneme sequences that are highly likely and frequent in English (such as /en/ as in *pain, main, rain, detain*) are considered more *wordlike* and thus more likely to be accurately repeated than a nonword composed of phonetic sequences or prosodic patterns that do not appear in the language (e.g., /kva/; Dollaghan et al., 1995; Gathercole, 1995). When nonwords are highly wordlike, adults and children may draw on their lexical repertoire and phonological representation of similar real words to support the accurate reproduction of the novel, meaningless item (Gathercole, 2006). Experience with the phonotactic properties of a language may scaffold the representation of unfamiliar phoneme sequences (Gathercole, Frankish, Pickering, & Peaker, 1999).

Frequency and Regularity Count in Building Language-Specific Experience: An Alternate View

Children learn about phonotactic patterns, including existing, possible, and impossible-to-produce phonological sequences, as they learn the words in which these patterns are embedded. Mastered articulatory routines scaffold the production of new words that have similar phonological constituents. Thus one account of word learning is that vocabulary grows while individuals accrue words that are phonologically similar to those already established (Storkel, 2001). This account of rapid acquisition would suggest that children become knowledgeable about the distributional regularities of the linguistic input and that this knowledge, in turn, has consequences for word learning (Hollich, Hirsh-Pasek, & Golinkoff, 2000).

The within-word phonological patterns that influence vocabulary learning vary in their frequency of occurrence in a specific language. There are two ways for counting frequency of occurrence in language: token frequency and type frequency. The frequency of occurrence of a word (i.e., how often it is used) is token frequency. On the other hand, the incidence of occurrence of a particular pattern (e.g., a syllable onset, a consonant cluster, or a stress pattern) is type frequency. Thus type frequency is "based on the number of items matching a particular pattern" (Bybee, 2001, p. 13).

Why Frequency Counts for Lexical–Phonological Learning

The frequency of specific phonotactic patterns affects children's learning of new words. For example in Storkel (2001), a group of 34 typically developing preschool children more accurately identified the referents for novel nouns with common sound sequences than novel nouns with rare sound sequences. The common sound sequence advantage in referent identification was larger for children with greater recognition vocabulary breadth, suggesting that the children were drawing on phonological regularities in their lexicons. Parallel findings were documented in a second study of verb learning in English (Storkel, 2003).

The Case for the Active Participation of the Lexicon in NWR Language Processing Tasks

Children, including ELLs, will perform differently on language processing tasks when they are presented with items that contain phonemic, subsyllabic, or syllabic arrangements that are frequently represented in their native language lexicons versus patterns less frequently represented or not exemplified at all (see Pollo, Treiman, & Kessler, 2008). On language processing tasks, adults generalize linguistic patterns to novel forms if these patterns are well represented in a variety of words in their lexicons; that is, if these patterns are frequent and regular (Frisch et al., 2000; Nimmo & Roodendrys, 2002; Ohala & Ohala, 1987). Nimmo and Roodenrys (2002) found a facilitative syllable frequency effect in a NWR recall task when they examined whether recall accuracy was influenced by the frequency of monosyllabic nonwords within multisyllabic English words. Similar findings emerged from NWR rating studies, such as the implicit awareness of rime frequency by second and fourth graders and adults (Treiman, Kessler, Knewasser, Tincoff, & Bowman, 2000). Child and adult participants judged consonant–vowel–consonant (CVC) embedded, English rime constituents of different frequencies as more wordlike (e.g., -up in /rup/) or less wordlike (e.g., -uk in/ruk/). Results suggested that, regardless of age, participants gave the higher-frequency rimes higher wordlikeness ratings than the lower-frequency rimes. Similar findings emerged with the adults who also rated nonwords with high probability onset and rime constituents as more like real words than nonwords with low-probability constituents (Frisch et al., 2000).

The same frequency effect was replicated when Spanish nonwords were rated by adult Spanish–English bilinguals (Brea-Spahn & Frisch, 2006). The frequency effect was evident in ratings of nonwords that varied in terms of stress pattern, a previously uninvestigated phonotactic pattern. Adult bilinguals rated nonwords containing the most probable stress pattern (or penultimate stress) as more wordlike, suggesting a tendency to generalize about phonotactic patterns that recur across words in their language.

Summary

The previous literature attests that both children and adults use distributional information when perceiving, producing, and judging language tokens. It has been posited that from this distributional information that infants and young children induce sets of patterns, which exemplify the underlying organization of their native language. Awareness of these patterns allows for the generation of novel words, utterances, and discourse. Children are known to be sensitive to phonotactic patterns; therefore it is important to identify how mastery of the phonotactic patterns of a native language facilitates the expansion of the lexicon as new words are learned.

How Language-Specific Phonotactic Patterns Are Learned

The evidence that phonological and phonetic competence may be mediated by the type frequency of sound structures within a language (Pierrehumbert, 2001) does not mean that the relation between type frequency and the content of children's lexicons is a linear one (Fikkert & Levelt, in press). Children may make their own generalizations over their lexicons (Beckman, Munson, & Edwards, 2004; Edwards et al., 2004). At the perceptual level, for instance, infants must develop the ability to recognize a word form regardless of the voice that speaks it, the intonation used to express it, and the linguistic context in which it occurs (Beckman et al., 2004). As infants become speakers, the word-form abstraction should be mapped to its corresponding articulatory gesture.

For instance, toddlers may have acquired a vocabulary that contains several instances of forms that match in articulatory gestures yet contrast in their meanings: /gaga/ for *gato* versus /gaga/ for *agua*. When using these words in spoken language, these young speakers must reorganize established word forms to develop novel articulatory representations for each similar instance; that is, older forms are restructured as new functions (Gupta & MacWhinney, 1997). Caregivers provide the toddler with feedback in the appropriate contexts, while the distributional properties of the language interacting with memory and attentional resources are the foundation from which schemas emerge. Schemas are organizational patterns across lexical items or the use of long-term established representations in the scaffolding of new phonological forms and gestures.

Developing schemas for familiar words involve a hierarchy of different types of phonological information, which support different levels of abstraction about the words (Pierrehumbert, 2003). One premise states that schemas may be the result of two levels of encoding. Beckman et al. (2004) suggest that, when learning a new word, its *form* (i.e., phonological structure) is encoded at two different levels. First, there exists a coarse-grained level (auditory) of encoding, which is based on the similarity of a word form to other word forms in the language. Coarser grained encodings result in frequency effects in oral language tasks. For example, using this level of encoding, a child might recognize that a novel Spanish word that ends in a vowel should be stressed in the penultimate syllable. This level of encoding is considered coarse in nature because it is related to the frequency of individual words that share the pattern, which determine whether the pattern is common, uncommon, or prohibited. A second, more fine-grained level of encoding includes specific articulatory representations of a Spanish word with penultimate stress pattern. Specificity at the level of articulatory representations depends on an adequate sample of exemplars at the coarse-grained level, but also on sufficient experiences with hearing and saying (practicing) the specific instances of the word. In this scenario, schemas may be organizational patterns across lexical items or the use of long-term established representations in the scaffolding of new phonological forms and gestures.

Two Practical Advantages of Knowing about Phonotactic Patterns

Important benefits accrue from obtaining a detailed understanding of how the probabilities of a language's phonological patterns (phoneme co-occurrences, onsets, rimes, and syllables) affect language behaviors. Words in a language are generated from a finite set of phonemes. However, there are constraints on how these phonemes can be arranged within syllables. These constraints, sometimes known as *phonotactic* or *phoneme sequence constraints*, set boundaries on the number of syllables that would be theoretically possible if phonemes could be combined in an unconstrained way. Phonotactic constraints vary from language to language. For instance, no English word begins with the phoneme sequence /ml/. Similarly, no Spanish word ends in the vowel–consonant sequence /at/.

One benefit of understanding the specific phonotactic patterns of a language is determining whether the absence of certain phoneme sequences (as in the nonexistence of the sequence /np/ in word-medial position in English) is systematic (Pierrehumbert, 2001). By verifying how many English words are expected to have word-medial /np/, and comparing this *expected* likelihood to the count of the actual words that have the pattern results in determining whether its nonoccurrence in English is the result of a phonotactic constraint.

A second advantage relates to language performance. Knowing the patterns specific to English and Spanish allows the investigation of how they are manifested in any kind of language performance, including performance on NWR tasks.

THE CONSTRUCTION OF NWR MEASURES: DOES SPECIFIC-LANGUAGE EXPERIENCE MATTER?

Current Spanish NWR tasks vary in the degree to which they have focused on the manipulation of language-specific variables such as word-likeness. Some repetition tasks have been developed with attempts to factor out the influence of linguistic knowledge (Calderón & Gutierrez-Clellen, 2003), while other measures have been designed to control the variance explained by linguistic factors through their systematic manipulation in the nonwords (Girbau & Schwartz, 2007, 2008). For other measures, uncovering the purpose guiding their construction is difficult (e.g., Chiappe et al., 2002; Gottardo, 2002). The five distinct tasks used in the seven studies summarized in Table 3.2 (two in English and three in Spanish) are described below in terms of their potential applicability for the study of language-specific phonological patterns that may support word learning.

Counting Language Experience Out

Chiappe and colleagues administered the Sound Mimicry subtest from the Goldman, Fristoe, and Woodcock Sound–Symbol Test (Goldman et al., 1974). Validity of their NWR findings may be a concern, since knowledge of English phonology did not guide NWR item selection. The Sound Mimicry subtest requires that children repeat nonsense words of increasing difficulty and length; however, item construction does not conform to rules governing the permissible ordering of phonemes in English (syllable contact constraints). The outcome is nonwords that are low in wordlikeness (Gathercole, Willis, Baddeley, & Emslie, 1994). For example a nonword in the test is *bafmotbem*, which contains two consonant sequences that are infrequent in real English words (*fm* and *tb*). As a result, errors in repetition may be an artifact of including uncommon phoneme sequences in nonwords.

Similarly, the Calderón and Gutierrez-Clellen (2003) Spanish Nonword Repetition Test (SNRT) contains nonwords low in wordlikeness. Although some Spanish phonotactic patterns like stress assignment were maintained, infrequently occurring syllables (i.e., syllables that did not occur in more than 200 words in a corpus of approximately 2 million words) comprised the nonwords. Infrequently occurring syllables were selected to account for the potential effect of the transfer of phonological knowledge across Spanish and English. Because the Sound Mimicry subtest and the SNRT were intentionally designed to include only nonwords low in wordlikeness, neither measure may be suitable for examining the impact that language-specific phonological patterns may have on bilingual word learning.

Counting Language Experience In

The items from Gottardo (2002) and Gottardo et al. (2008) were created by combining and adapting several lists of nonwords already available (Dollaghan et al., 1995; Gathercole et al., 1991a; Goldman et al., 1974). The items were designed to follow English syllabic patterns and the relevant differences between the Spanish and English phonological systems. For example, in devising the nonwords, authors in both studies reported not including phonemes that were unshared between Spanish and English, such as the unvoiced /θ/ (as in *think*) and voiced /ð/ (as in *the*). However, all dialects of Spanish use the voiced fricative /ð/, as it appears intervocalically as an allophone of the phoneme /d/. Also, it is important to note that multisyllabic English nonwords (and words) with variable stress patterns inevitably include neutral vowels in their unstressed syllables. In Spanish, all vowels are tense (or long). Therefore, the nonwords in this study might have posed additional demands on the Spanish speakers by including vowel phonemes that were different between the two languages. The authors also noted that they accepted nonwords as correctly repeated, even when children substituted Spanish vowels for English vowels in their repetitions. Beyond stating that non-Spanish phonemes were not considered in item construction and adapting scoring procedures to some phonological differences between the languages, specific characteristics of the nonword items, such as the inclusion or exclusion of consonant clusters, were not disclosed.

The influences of L1 phonology were considered in the scoring. Vowel productions characteristic of the Spanish language, as in the production of "the Spanish form of the vowel 'o' that is of slightly shorter duration than the English version of the vowel" (Gottardo, 2002, p. 55), were accepted as correct. Although the effects of L1 phonology on nonword pronunciation were included, correct scores were assigned, for the most part, to exact repetitions. Responses were scored only as correct or incorrect and information about individual error patterns was not reported. Identical procedures were used in the Gottardo et al. (2008) study.

The Spanish nonword repetition task developed by Girbau and Schwartz (2007, 2008) takes into account phonotactic likelihood and includes nonwords constructed with low- and medium-frequency syllables (see Table 3.1). In addition, frequency of occurrence of individual phonemes was considered: "All the Spanish sounds were included on the task, except the /ŋ/ and /w/ [ñ, w], which occur very infrequently" (Girbau & Schwartz, 2007, p. 66). Furthermore, nonwords adhered to Spanish phonotactic regularities as 12 of the 20 items had one of the permissible clusters. In Spanish two segment onsets (or clusters) must contain a single obstruent (sounds that are constricted by airflow, such as /b/, /p/, /t/, /d/, /k/, /g/, /f/) followed by liquid consonants (sounds midway between consonants and vowels, i.e., /l/ or /r/) (Harris, 1983). Examples of these two-segment onsets occur in such Spanish words as _fresa_ (strawberry), _trabajo_ (work), and _principio_ (beginning).

A major constraint of the Girbau and Schwartz nonwords is that frequency information and the syllables used in the NWR task were acquired from corpora of Castilian Spanish words. As a result, their nonwords may include phonemes not produced by other dialects of Spanish. As just one example, the item _zo.llér_ in this measure was phonetically transcribed as /θoλéϒ/. However, the z is often produced as an /s/ in Latin American varieties of Spanish (Green, 1990). Because of this factor, these nonwords may not be appropriate to administer to children in the United States, where a variety of Spanish dialects are spoken.

The most recent measure of nonword repetition in Spanish was developed by Danahy et al. (2008). The authors systematically described their stimulus construction process and the variables manipulated. One- to five-syllable nonwords were developed, which consisted only of early acquired phonemes, excluding clusters and adjoining medial consonants. The authors indicated that their stimuli were wordlike (and easier to repeat) for three reasons: (1) use of the standard pattern of penultimate stress, (2) adherence to the most common Spanish syllable pattern (consonant–vowel), and (3) inclusion of frequently occurring Spanish consonant phonemes and exclusion of infrequent consonants in many of their nonwords. However, Danahy et al. (2008) did not obtain a measure of phonotactic probability for their nonwords' constituent syllables, onsets and rimes, or phonemes. They also did not obtain wordlikeness ratings for their stimulus items. Furthermore, the use of only penultimate stress assignment may have resulted in a narrow range of difficulty in the items.

SUMMARY: WHAT COUNTS IN THE CONSTRUCTION OF A SPANISH NWR MEASURE?

NWR measures are versatile in that they permit the manipulation of language-specific patterns when the assessment aim is to modify the level of complexity and the types of phonological knowledge to be included. Some of the language-specific features that could be manipulated in NWR measures are length in syllables, syllabification and stress assignment patterns, familiar language units (e.g., morphemes), and phonemes representing a particular probability range in a language.

To examine the impact of language experience on bilingual word learning (as defined by phonotactic likelihood and regularities), it must first be determined whether all of the currently available measures privilege language experience in the same way. Not all English and Spanish NWR measures have been developed with the intent to analyze the types of phonological knowledge that provide a basis for word learning (See Table 3.2 for a summary). There is considerable need for the systematic development of a Spanish NWR measure that meets at least three criteria:

- Develops from a corpus of real words representing a variety of Spanish dialects and registers.
- Adheres to the phonotactic regularities of Spanish.
- Manipulates language-specific phonotactic frequencies.

Such a measure is currently being designed (Brea-Spahn, 2009).

FUTURE DIRECTIONS: WHAT'S NEXT IN PAINTING A "BIG PICTURE" OF ELL WORD LEARNING

To date, neither longitudinal studies nor random assignment intervention studies have been conducted that might clarify causal relationships (Savage,

TABLE 3.2. NWR Measures: Controlling for Language Familiarity or Not?

Language-specific patterns	Variable length in syllables	Age-appropriate phoneme sequences	Phonotactic patterns	Degree of wordlikeness	Phonotactic probability
English NWR tasks					
Chiappe et al. (2002)	X				
Gottardo (2002) Gottardo et al. (2008)	X	X			
Spanish NWR tasks					
Calderón (2003)	X	X	X		X
Girbau & Schwartz (2007, 2008)	X	X	X		
Danahy et al. (2008)	X	X	X		

Lavers, & Pillay, 2007) between NWR performance and vocabulary knowledge in a particular language. Furthermore, in terms of ELLs, there is little research on the relationships between L1 and L2 vocabulary knowledge and NWR accuracy (Geva & Genesee, 2006). Finally, discussion of presumed linkages between phonological working memory and vocabulary learning rarely include how NWR measures have been constructed (Savage et al., 2007).

NWR is a complex task that requires, at a minimum, the active participation of working memory, articulatory precision, and a well-established repertoire of word forms. The challenge facing researchers, speech–language pathologists, and educators is one of extrapolation: To explain the significance of a low accuracy score and then determine its clinical or educational relevance is difficult, as measures typically confound the influence of a variety of skills on performance (Alt & Plante, 2006; Graf Estes et al., 2007). Although current English and Spanish NWR measures may be useful in identifying significant group differences between Spanish-learning children with and without LI, clinicians, educators, and researchers must "consider the nature of the [NWR] task that is used" (Graf Estes et al., 2007, p. 193)

What may be considered a methodological limitation for current NWR measures—the wordlikeness variable—could be advantageous for constructing new measures, provided that the purpose is to assess how children manage specific linguistic input. For example, NWR was recently found to correlate with word learning. Specifically, NWR performance predicted how well a group of young monolingual English-speaking children fast-mapped lexical and semantic information about novel words that varied in phonotactic probability (Alt & Plante, 2006). If this finding is repeated, then access to a large repertoire of stored lexical and phonological forms may no longer be sufficient to explain variability in NWR performance. Instead, the relationship between word knowledge and repetition accuracy might be mediated by a child's proficiency at *encoding* the phonological and lexical patterns of a particular language, the kind of talent that results from frequent experiences with complex word forms and explicit analytical instruction (Alt & Plante, 2006; Edwards et al., 2004). The Alt and Plante (2006) study suggests an interesting pathway for a new application of NWR tasks. The domain of interest is potential correlations between *stored* and *accessible language-specific linguistic properties*. In this context, *stored* means linguistic knowledge acquired through social interactional experience, while *accessible* refers to the rapid and accurate retrieval of common and uncommon phonological patterns from long-term memory. This connection might be stronger when nonword items are intentionally designed to include phonotactic characteristics in common with the vocabulary that children universally experience on a daily basis, or what are called basic vocabulary words (Beck, McKeown, & Kucan, 2002). Examples of basic English and Spanish vocabulary words would include *baby* (bebé), *chair* (silla), *dog* (perro), and *car* (carro).

NWR and ELL Vocabulary Learning

In the case of learners of English and Spanish, NWR measures could be utilized in studying how these children cope with multiple sets of distributional properties of their respective languages. To learn a new word, children must discover the appropriate sequence of phonemes and integrate this positional information with its contextually dependent connotation. To be successful oral language users and readers, children who are learners of Spanish and English must additionally negotiate between two different sets of phonological and semantic patterns. Their proficiency at learning words may primarily depend on two intertwined factors: the frequency of these patterns in *both* of their languages and the *quality* of social interactional experiences that arbitrate multiple exposures to word forms and their meanings.

To date, no study has attempted to analyze how children who are learning English and Spanish respond to shared and unshared language-specific patterns in their acquisition of new vocabulary. The systematic development of a Spanish NWR measure that allows for the analysis of language-specific patterns on performance is a crucial first step in this investigative process. For instance, in need of study are relationships among wordlikeness, phonotactic probability, and Spanish language proficiency on Spanish NWR performance (Brea-Spahn, 2009).

In summary, the robustness of vocabulary learning appears dependent on the nature and quality of experiences in the social world with the distributional properties of a language. The construction of NWR tasks that include common, uncommon, or absent phonetic sequences and/or transitions in a language could become an interesting option for examining individual differences in the phonological and lexical inferential capabilities of Spanish and English language learners. In other words, these measures may provide a richer snapshot of how routine, but quality, experiences with the distributional properties of a language scaffold the development of a bilingual lexicon.

NOTES

1. Nonword repetition is sometimes used interchangeably with pseudoword repetition. For the purposes of this chapter, we elected to use nonword repetition (NWR).
2. In the epidemiological study conducted by Catts, Fey, Zhang, and Tomblin (1999) with monolingual English-speaking kindergartners, the prevalence of oral language impairment was 7%. Gender differences in prevalence were not found.

REFERENCES

Alt, M., & Plante, E. (2006). Factors that influence lexical and semantic fast mapping of young children with specific language impairment. *Journal of Speech, Language, and Hearing Research, 49*(5), 941–954.

Archibald, L. M. D., & Gathercole, S. E. (2006). Nonword repetition: A comparison of tests. *Journal of Speech, Language, and Hearing Research, 49*(5), 970–983.

August, D., Calderón, M., Carlo, M., & Eakin, M. N. (2006). Developing literacy in English-language learners: An examination of the impact of English-only versus bilingual instruction. In P. McCardle & E. Hoff (Eds.), *Childhood bilingualism: Research on infancy through school age* (pp. 91–106). Tonawanda, NY: Multilingual Matters.

August, D., & Shanahan, T. (2006). *Developing literacy in second-language learners: Report of the National Literacy Panel on language minority children and youth.* Mahwah, NJ: Erlbaum.

August, D., Snow, C., Carlo, M., Proctor, C. P., San Francisco, A. R., Duursma, E., et al. (2006). Literacy development in elementary school second-language learners. *Topics in Language Disorders, 26*(4), 351–364.

Baddely, A., & Hitch, G. (1974). Working memory. In G. A. Bower (Ed.), *Recent advances in learning and motivation. Vol. 8* (pp. 47–90). New York: Academy Press.

Beck, I. L., McKeown, M. G., & Kucan, L. (2002). *Bringing words to life: Robust vocabulary instruction.* New York: Guilford Press.

Beckman, M. E., & Edwards, J. (2000). The ontogeny of phonological categories and the primacy of lexical learning in linguistic development. *Child Development, 71,* 240–249.

Beckman, M. E., Munson, B., & Edwards, B. J. (2004). Vocabulary growth and developmental expansion of types of phonological knowledge. *LabPhon9,* University of Illinois, Urbana-Champaign.

Bialystok, E. (2002). Acquisition of literacy in bilingual children: A framework for research. *Language Learning, 52,* 159–199.

Bowey, J. A. (2001). Nonword repetition and young children's receptive vocabulary: A longitudinal study. *Applied Psycholinguistics, 22,* 441–469.

Brea-Spahn, M. R. (2009). *Spanish-specific patterns and nonword repetition performance in English-language learners.* Unpublished Ph.D. dissertation, University of South Florida.

Brea-Spahn, M. R., & Frisch, S. (2006, November). *Wordlike, or not?: Segment probability, bilingualism, and word similarity ratings.* Paper presented at the annual convention of the American Speech–Language–Hearing Association, Miami, FL.

Bybee, J. (2001). *Phonology and language use.* Cambridge, UK: Cambridge University Press.

Calderón, J. (2003). *Working memory in Spanish–English bilinguals with language impairment.* Unpublished PhD dissertation, University of California, San Diego/San Diego State University.

Calderón, J., & Gutierrez-Clellen, V. (2003). *Nonword repetition in emerging bilingual children with language impairment.* Paper presented at the Fourth International Symposium on Bilingualism (ISB4), Phoenix, AZ.

Calderón, M., August, D., Slavin, R., Duran, D., Madden, N., & Cheung, A. (2005). Bringing words to life in classrooms with English-language learners. In E. H. Hiebert & M. L. Kamil (Eds.), *Teaching and learning vocabulary: Bringing research to practice* (pp. 115–136). Mahwah, NJ: Erlbaum.

Campbell, T., Dollaghan, C., Needleman, H., & Janosky, J. (1997). Reducing bias in language assessment: Processing-dependent measures. *Journal of Speech, Language, and Hearing Research, 40,* 519–525.

Carlo, M. S., August, D., McLaughlin, B., Snow, C. E., Dressler, C., Lippman, D. N., et al. (2004). Closing the gap: Addressing the vocabulary needs of English language learners in bilingual and mainstream classrooms. *Reading Research Quarterly, 39,* 188–215.

Catts, H. W., Fey, M. E., Zhang, X., & Tomblin, J. B. (1999). Language basis of reading and reading disabilities: Evidence from a longitudinal investigation. *Scientific Studies of Reading, 3,* 331–361.

Chiappe, P., Siegel, L. S., & Gottardo, A. (2002). Reading-related skills of kindergartners from diverse linguistic backgrounds. *Applied Psycholinguistics, 23,* 95–116.

Clahsen, H., & Felser, C. (2006). How native-like is non-native language process-ing? *Trends in Cognitive Sciences, 10*(12), 564–570.

Coady, J. F., & Aslin, R. N. (2004). Young children's sensitivity to probabilistic pho-notactics in the developing lexicon. *Journal of Experimental Child Psychology, 89*, 183–213.

Coady, J., & Evans, J. F. (2008). The uses and interpretations of nonword repetition tasks in children with and without specific language impairments. *International Journal of Language and Communication Disorders, 43*(1), 1–40.

Conti-Ramsden, G. (2003). Processing and linguistic markers in young children with specific language impairment (SLI). *Journal of Speech, Language, and Hearing Research, 46*, 1029–1037.

Danahy, K., Kalanek, J., Cordero, K. N., & Kohnert, K. (2008). Spanish nonword repetition: Stimuli development and preliminary results. *Communication Disorders Quarterly, 29*, 67–74.

Dollaghan, C. (1998). Spoken word recognition in children with and without spe-cific language impairment. *Applied Psycholinguistics, 19*, 193–207.

Dollaghan, C. A. (2007). *The handbook for evidence-based practice in communica-tion disorders.* Baltimore: Brookes.

Dollaghan, C. A., Biber, M. E., & Campbell, T. F. (1995). Lexical influences on non-word repetition. *Applied Psycholinguistics, 16*, 211–222.

Dollaghan, C., & Campbell, T. F. (1998). Nonword repetition and child language impair-ment. *Journal of Speech, Language, and Hearing Research, 41*, 1136–1146.

Duursma, E., Romero-Contreras, S., Szuber, A., Proctor, P., Snow, C., August, D., et al. (2007). The role of home literacy and language environment on bilin-guals' English and Spanish vocabulary development. *Applied Psycholinguistics, 28*(1), 171–190.

Edwards, J., Beckman, M. E., & Munson, B. (2004). The interaction between vocab-ulary size and phonotactic probability effects on children's production accuracy and fluency in nonword repetition. *Journal of Speech, Language, and Hearing Research, 47*, 421–436.

Edwards, J., & Lahey, M. (1998). Nonword repetitions in children with specific language impairment: Exploration of some explanations for their inaccuracies. *Applied Psycholinguistics, 19*, 279–309.

Ellis, N. C. (2002). Frequency effects in second language processing: A review with implications for theories of implicit and explicit language acquisition. *Studies in Second Language Acquisition, 24*(2), 143–188.

Fikkert, P., & Levelt, C. (in press). How does place fall into place? The lexicon and emergent constraints in the developing phonological grammar. In P. Avery, B. Elan Dresher, & K. Rice (Eds.), *Contrast in phonology: Perception and acquisi-tion.* Berlin: Mouton.

Francis, D. J., Lesaux, N. K., & August, D. (2006). Language of instruction. In D. August & T. Shanahan (Eds.), *Developing literacy in second-language learn-ers: Report of the National Literacy Panel on language-minority children and youth* (pp. 365–413). Mahawah, NJ: Erlbaum.

Frisch, S., Large, N. R., & Pisoni, D. B. (2000). Perception of wordlikeness: Effects of segment probability and length on processing of nonwords. *Journal of Mem-ory and Language, 42*, 481–496.

Fuste-Herrmann, B., Silliman, E. R., Bahr, R. H., Fasnacht, K. S., & Federico, J. E. (2006). Mental state verb production in the oral narratives of English- and Spanish-speaking preadolescents: An exploratory study of lexical diversity and depth. *Learning Disabilities Research and Practice, 21*(1), 44–60.

Gathercole, S. E. (1995). Is nonword repetition a test of phonological memory or long-term knowledge?: It all depends on the nonwords. *Memory and Cognition, 23*, 83–94.

Gathercole, S. E. (2006). Nonword repetition and word learning: The nature of the relationship. *Applied Psycholinguistics, 27*(4), 513–543.

Gathercole, S. E. (2007). Working memory: A system for learning. In R. K. Wagner, A. E. Muse, & K. R. Tannenbaum (Eds.), *Vocabulary acquisition: Implications for reading comprehension* (pp. 233–248). New York: Guilford Press.

Gathercole, S. E., & Adams, A. M. (1994). Children's phonological working memory: Contributions of long-term knowledge and rehearsal. *Journal of Memory and Language, 33*, 672–688.

Gathercole, S. E., & Baddeley, A. D. (1989). Evaluation of the role of phonological STM in the development of vocabulary in children: A longitudinal study. *Journal of Memory and Language, 28*, 200–213.

Gathercole, S. E., & Baddeley, A. D. (1990). The role of phonological memory in vocabulary acquisition: A study of young children learning new names. *British Journal of Psychology, 81*, 439–454.

Gathercole, S. E., Frankish, C. R., Pickering, S. J., & Peaker, S. (1999). Phonotactic influences on short-term memory. *Journal of Experimental Psychology, 25*, 84–95.

Gathercole, S. E., Service, E., Hitch, G. J., Adams, A. M., & Martin, A. J. (1999). Phonological short-term memory and vocabulary development: Further evidence on the nature of the relationship. *Applied Cognitive Psychology, 13*, 65–77.

Gathercole, S. E., Willis, C., Emslie, H., & Baddeley, A. D. (1991a). The influences of number of syllables and wordlikeness on children's repetition of nonwords. *Applied Psycholinguistics, 12*, 349–367.

Gathercole, S. E., Willis, C., Emslie, H., & Baddeley, A. D. (1991b). Nonword repetition, phonological memory, and vocabulary: A reply to Snowling, Chiat, and Hulme. *Applied Psycholinguistics, 12*, 349–367.

Gathercole, S. E., Willis, C. S., Baddeley, A. D., & Emslie, H. (1994). The children's test of nonword repetition: A test of phonological working memory. *Memory, 2*, 103–127.

Gathercole, S. E., Willis, H., Emslie, H., & Baddeley, A. D. (1992). Phonological memory and vocabulary development during the early school years: A longitudinal study. *Developmental Psychology, 28*, 887–898.

Geva, E., & Genesee, F. (2006). First-language oral proficiency and second-language literacy. In T. Shanahan & D. August (Eds.), *Developing literacy in second-language learners: Report of the National Literacy Panel on language-minority children and youth* (pp. 185–195). Mahwah, NJ: Erlbaum.

Girbau, D., & Schwartz, R. G. (2007). Nonword repetition in Spanish-speaking children with specific language impairment. *International Journal of Language and Communication Disorders, 42*(1), 59–75.

Girbau, D., & Schwartz, R. G. (2008). Phonological working memory in Spanish–English bilingual children with and without specific language impairment. *Journal of Communication Disorders, 41*(2), 124–145.

Goldman, R., Fristoe, M., & Woodcock, R. W. (1974). *Goldman–Fristoe–Woodcock Auditory Skills Battery.* Circle Pines, MN: American Guidance Service.

Goldstein, M. H., & Schwade, J. A. (2008). Social feedback to infants' babbling facilitates rapid phonological learning. *Psychological Science, 19*(5), 515–523.

Gottardo, A. (2002). The relationship between language and reading skills in bilingual Spanish–English speakers. *Topics in Language Disorders, 22*(5), 46–70.

Gottardo, A., Collins, P., Baciu, I., & Gebotys, R. I. (2008). Predictors of grade 2 word reading and vocabulary learning from grade 1 variables in Spanish-speaking children: Similarities and differences. *Learning Disabilities Research and Practice, 23*(1), 11–24.

Graf Estes., K., Evans, J. L., & Else-Quest, N. M. (2007). Differences in the nonword repetition performance of children with and without specific language impairment: A meta-analysis. *Journal of Speech, Language, and Hearing Research, 50*(1), 177–195.

Gray, S. (2006). The relationship between phonological memory, receptive vocabulary, and fast mapping in young children with specific language impairment. *Journal of Speech, Language, and Hearing Research, 49*(5), 955–969.

Green, J. N. (1990). Spanish. In B. Comrie (Ed.), *The world's major languages* (pp. 236–259). New York: Oxford University Press.

Gupta, P., & MacWhinney, B. (1997). Vocabulary acquisition and verbal short-term memory: Computational and neural bases. *Brain and Language, 59*, 267–333.

Harris, J. (1983). *Syllable structure and stress in Spanish: A nonlinear analysis.* Cambridge, MA: MIT Press.

Hollich, G., Hirsh-Pasek, K., & Golinkoff, R. (2000). Breaking the language barrier: An emergenist coalition model for the origins of word learning. *Monographs for the Society for Research in Child Development, Serial No. 262.*

Hurtado, N., Marchman, V. A., & Fernald, A. (2007). Spoken word recognition by Latino children learning Spanish as their first language. *Journal of Child Language, 34*(2), 227–249.

Jusczyk, P. W., Luce, P. A., & Charles-Luce, J. (1994). Infants' sensitivity to phonotactic patterns in the native language. *Journal of Memory and Language, 33*, 630–645.

Kohnert, K., Windsor, J., & Yim, D. (2006). Do language-based processing tasks separate children with language impairment from typical bilinguals? *Learning Disabilities Research and Practice, 21*(1), 19–29.

Manis, F. R., Lindsey, K. A., & Bailey, C. E. (2004). Development of reading in grades K–2 in Spanish-speaking English language learners. *Learning Disabilities Research and Practice, 19*(4), 214–224.

Michas, I. C., & Henry, L. A. (1994). The link between phonological memory and vocabulary acquisition. *British Journal of Developmental Psychology, 12*, 147–163.

Miller, J. F., Heilmann, J., Nockerts, A., Iglesias, A., Fabiano, L., & Francis, D. J.

(2006). Oral language and reading in bilingual children. *Learning Disabilities Research and Practice, 21*(1), 30–43.

Montgomery, J. (2002). Understanding the language difficulties of children with specific language impairments: Does verbal working memory matter? *American Journal of Speech–Language Pathology, 11,* 77–91.

Munson, B., Edwards, J., & Beckman, M. E. (2005). Phonological knowledge in typical and atypical speech and language development: Nature, assessment, and treatment. *Topics in Language Disorders, 25,* 190–206.

Munson, B., Kurtz, B., & Windsor, J. (2005). The influence of vocabulary size, phonotactic probability, and wordlikeness on nonword repetitions of children with and without specific language impairment. *Journal of Speech, Language, and Hearing Research, 48,* 1033–1047.

Nagy, W. (2007). Metalinguistic awareness and the vocabulary–comprehension connection. In R. K. Wagner, A. E. Muse, & K. R. Tannenbaum (Eds.), *Vocabulary acquisition: Implications for reading comprehension* (pp. 52–77). New York: Guilford Press.

Nation, K., Clarke, P., Marshall, C. M., & Durand, M. (2004). Hidden language impairments in children: Parallels between poor reading comprehension and specific language impairment? *Journal of Speech, Language, and Hearing Research, 47,* 199–211.

Nimmo, L. M., & Roodenrys, S. (2002). Syllable frequency effects on phonological short-term memory tasks. *Applied Psycholinguistics, 23,* 643–659.

Ohala, M., & Ohala, J. (1987). Psycholinguistics probes of native speakers' phonological knowledge. In W. U. Dressler (Ed.), *Phonologica 1984* (pp. 227–233). Cambridge, UK: Cambridge University Press.

Ordóñez, C. L., Carlo, M. S., Snow, C. E., & McLaughlin, B. (2002). Depth and breadth of vocabulary in two languages: Which vocabulary skills transfer? *Journal of Educational Psychology, 94*(4), 719–728.

Ouelette, G. P. (2006). What's meaning got to do with it: The role of vocabulary in word reading and reading comprehension. *Journal of Educational Psychology, 98*(3), 554–566.

Paez, M., & Rinaldi, C. (2006). Predicting English word reading skills for Spanish-speaking students in first grade. *Topics in Language Disorders, 26*(4), 338–350.

Papagno, C., & Vallar, G. (1995). To learn or not to learn vocabulary in foreign languages: The problem with phonological memory. In R. Campbell & M. Conway (Eds.), *Broken memories* (pp. 334–343). Oxford, UK: Blackwell.

Pearson, B. Z. (2007). Social factors in childhood bilingualism in the United States. *Applied Psycholinguistics, 28*(3), 399–410.

Pierrehumbert, J. (2001). Stochastic phonology. *GLOT International, 5*(6), 1–13.

Pierrehumbert, J. (2003). Probabilistic phonology: Discrimination and robustness. In R. Bod, J. Hay, & S. Jannedy (Eds.), *Probability theory in linguistics* (pp. 177–228). Cambridge, MA: MIT Press.

Plante, E., & Vance, R. (2004). Selection of preschool language tests: A data-based approach. *Language, Speech, and Hearing Services in Schools, 25,* 15–24.

Pollo, T. C., Treiman, R., & Kessler, B. (2008). Three perspectives on spelling development. In E. I. Grigorenko & A. J. Naples (Eds.), *Single-word reading: Behavorial and biological perspectives* (pp. 175–190). Mahwah, NJ: Erlbaum.

Proctor, C. P., August, D., Carlo, M., & Snow, C. (2006). The intriguing role of Spanish language vocabulary knowledge in predicting English reading comprehension. *Journal of Educational Psychology, 98*, 159–169.

Saffran, J. R. (2001). Words in a sea of sounds: The output of statistical learning. *Cognition, 81*, 149–169.

Saffran, J. R., & Thiessen, E. D. (2007). Domain-general learning capacities. In E. Hoff & M. Shatz (Eds.), *Blackwell handbook of language development* (pp. 68–86). Malden, MA: Blackwell.

San Francisco, A. R., Carlo, M. S., August, D., & Snow, C. E. (2006). The role of language of instruction and vocabulary in the English phonological awareness of Spanish–English bilingual children. *Applied Psycholinguistics, 27*(2), 229–246.

Savage, R., Lavers, N., & Pillay, V. (2007). Working memory and reading difficulties: What we know and what we don't know about the relationship. *Educational Psychology Review, 19*(2), 185–221.

Shanahan, T., & Beck, I. (2006). Effective literacy teaching for English-language learners. In T. Shanahan & D. August (Eds.), *Developing literacy in second-language learners: Report of the National Literacy Panel on language-minority children and youth* (pp. 415–488). Mahwah, NJ: Erlbaum.

Silliman, E. R., Wilkinson, L. C., & Brea-Spahn, M. R. (2004). Policy and practice imperatives for language and literacy learning: Who shall be left behind? *Handbook on language and literacy: Development and disorders* (pp. 97–129). New York: Guilford Press.

Snow, C. E., & & Kim, Y. (2007). Large problem spaces: The challenge of vocabulary for English language learners. In R. K. Wagner, A. E. Muse, & K. R. Tannenbaum (Eds.), *Vocabulary acquisition: Implications for reading comprehension* (pp. 123–129). New York: Guilford Press.

Snowling, M. (1981). Phonemic deficits in developmental dyslexia. *Psychological Research, 43*, 219–234.

Snowling, M., Goulandris, N., Bowlby, M., & Howell, P. (1986). Segmentation and speech perception in relation to reading skill: A developmental analysis. *Journal of Experimental Child Psychology, 41*(3), 489–507.

Stokes, S. F., Wong, A. M. Y., Fletcher, P., & Leonard, L. B. (2006). Nonword repetition and sentence repetition as clinical markers of SLI: The case of Cantonese. *Journal of Speech, Language, and Hearing Research, 49*, 219–236.

Storkel, H. L. (2001). Learning new words: Phontactic probability in language. *Journal of Speech, Language, and Hearing Research, 44*, 1321–1337.

Storkel, H. L. (2003). Learning new words II: Phontactic probability in verb language. *Journal of Speech, Language, and Hearing Research, 46*, 1312–1323.

Storkel, H. L., & Morrisette, M. L. (2002). The lexicon and phonology: Interactions in language acquisition. *Language, Speech, and Hearing Services in Schools, 33*, 24–37.

Storkel, H. L., & Rogers, M. A. (2000). The effect of probabilistic phonotactics on lexical acquisition. *Clinical Linguistics and Phonetics, 14*, 407–425.

Thorn, A. S. C., & Gathercole, S. E. (1999). Language-specific knowledge and short-term memory in bilingual and non-bilingual children. *The Quarterly Journal of Experimental Psychology, 52A*(2), 303–324.

Treiman, R., Kessler, B., Knewasser, S., Tincoff, R., & Bowman, M. (2000). English speakers' sensitivity to phonotactic patterns. In M. B. Broe & J. B. Pierrehumbert (Eds.), *Papers in laboratory phonology V: Acquisition and the lexicon* (pp. 269–282). Cambridge, UK: Cambridge University Press.

Vitevitch, M. S., & Luce, P. A. (1998). When words compete: Levels of processing in spoken word perception. *Psychological Science, 9,* 325–329.

Wagner, R. K., Francis, D. J., & Morris, R. D. (2005). Identifying English language learners with learning disabilities: Key challenges and possible approaches. *Learning Disabilities Research and Practice, 20,* 6–15.

Wagner, R. K., Muse, A. E., Stein, T. L., Cukrowicz, K. C., Harrell, E. R., Rashotte, C. A., et al. (2003). How to assess reading-related phonological abilities. In B. R. Foorman (Ed.), *Preventing and remediating reading difficulties: Bringing science to scale* (pp. 51–70). Baltimore: York Press.

Wagner, R. K., Muse, A. E., & Tannenbaum, K. R. (2007). Promising avenues for better understanding: Implications of vocabulary development for reading comprehension. In R. K. Wagner, A. E. Muse, & K. R. Tannenbaum (Eds.), *Vocabulary acquisition: Implications for reading comprehension* (pp. 276–291). New York: Guilford Press.

Wagner, R. K., Torgesen, J. K., & Rashotte, C. A. (1999). *Comprehensive test of phonological processing.* Austin, TX: PRO-ED.

Weismer, S. E. (1996). Capacity limitations in working memory: The impact on lexical and morphological learning by children with language impairment. *Topics in Language Disorders, 17,* 33–44.

Weismer, S. E., Tomblin, J. B., Zhang, X., Buckwalter, P., Chynoweth, J. G., & Jones, M. (2000). Nonword repetition performance in school-age children with and without language impairment. *Journal of Speech, Language, and Hearing Research, 43,* 865–878.

Windsor, J., & Kohnert, K. (2008). Processing measures of cognitive–linguistic interactions of children at risk for language and reading disorders. In M. Mody & E. R. Silliman (Eds.), *Brain, behavior, and learning in language disorders and reading disability* (pp. 135–160). New York: Guilford Press.

CHAPTER 4

■ ■ ■

Rapid Spoken Language Shift in Early Second-Language Learning

The Role of Peers and Effects on the First Language

D. KIMBROUGH OLLER
LINDA JARMULOWICZ
BARBARA Z. PEARSON
ALAN B. COBO-LEWIS

We review research illustrating that language shift occurs surprisingly rapidly in the first months of exposure to a second language (L2) for immigrant children entering school with immersion in the host language. The chapter includes (1) background on language shift and language preference highlighting an apparent loss of easy access to first-language (L1) vocabulary in early L2 learners; (2) a review of empirical evidence indicating that peer effects may play an especially large role in language choice and shift; (3) a review regarding specific effects on both L1 and L2 during the period of shift, especially during the first few years of exposure to L2; (4) an overview of additional research that suggests language shift is often accompanied by relative loss of access to certain L1 capabilities; and (5) a speculative characterization of mechanisms that could help explain the relative lack of access to L1 vocabulary, especially during the early period of learning of L2.

LANGUAGE SHIFT IN CHILDHOOD: BACKGROUND

Three Generations for Language Shift in the United States

Total language shift to English usually occurs rapidly in immigrant families to the United States. In the overwhelming majority of cases, across not more than three generations, the heritage language is replaced by English monolingualism (Fishman, 1966). This pattern of language shift is mirrored in results of a study by Hakuta and D'Andrea (1992) evaluating language use in high school students of Mexican origin. Language proficiency testing and a variety of questionnaires revealed that students who had either been born in the United States or who had arrived at age 10 or younger were very competent in English. Spanish proficiency was similarly high for all children born in Mexico, and even for children born in the United States if both parents had been born in Mexico. However, proficiency in Spanish dropped dramatically in children who had at least one parent born in the United States. As for language choice, if at least one parent had been born in the United States, the high school students showed very strong preference for English outside the home, and even the language use of adults inside the home shifted predominantly to English.

Such results provide perspective on the generational shift from L1 to L2 in immigrants to the United States, but provide little information about what may have happened during the shift as individuals began to be introduced to an English-speaking environment. We are conducting research on Hispanic students who enter elementary school with either exclusive or substantial Spanish-language background. We observe factors that appear to affect shifting language choice as well as patterns of language proficiency in both languages that seem to indicate shift during this early period of exposure to English. The present chapter reviews key aspects of this work, unveiling surprises about how different aspects of proficiency change during the shift, and confirms anecdotal reports from families, indicating that language preference can shift quickly, very early in life, apparently under the influence of schooling, and especially under the influence of peers in school.

Anecdotes and Other Indications of Rapid Shift

A Turkish scholar living in Miami reported that after his two sons started school in English only, they began to speak English only, even at home, where the parents spoke Turkish. When the family went to Turkey for the summer, the boys went through a period of silence, then shifted to speaking Turkish only. After returning to school in the United States, another silent period ensued, after which they began talking again, in English only, even though the parents were still speaking to them in Turkish.

The Turkish scholar also reported no obvious decrement in the boys' comprehension of Turkish or English during the periods of shifting preference for speaking one language or the other. He was surprised that the pattern of shift in spoken language preference seemed to be *reversible* within a few weeks of living in a Turkish-only environment, and then reversible again after returning to the United States. The reversibility suggested that the children's abilities for speaking each language, in some sense, were alternately latent and active, presumably depending on language environment. This and other anecdotes suggest that language preference can shift rather suddenly when young children are immersed in a new language environment.

Children who encounter a new peer language when they start school appear to shift their preference to L2 within the first 2 to 3 years (Oller & Eilers, 2002; Veltman, 1983b). Language processing measures indicate that a shift in language dominance may differ for comprehension and production measures, and that 3 years may be needed to complete the shift (Kohnert & Bates, 2002; Kohnert, Bates, & Hernández, 1999). Evidence points to a strong role for peers in language choice (Brown, 1980; De Houwer, 1990; Veltman, 1983a), but opinion in the scientific literature gives substantial weight to other social influences in language choice as well. For example, a model of parameters that affect L2 learning (Wong Fillmore, 1991) emphasizes a variety of social and individual factors that predict successful acquisition and treats teacher, caretaker, and peer effects on equal footing. In addition, reported evidence has not convinced the public that strong peer effects are to be expected. Yet in more than a decade of research on early bilingualism in Miami (Oller & Eilers, 2002), we repeatedly heard Hispanic parents report with astonishment that their elementary school children spoke English and refused to speak Spanish at home, even though the adults all spoke Spanish. The shift to L2 preference was often interpreted by these parents as an effect of peer language preference.

Notably, children showing strong preference for speaking the peer language in Miami (English) also showed substantial ability to *understand* L1 Spanish when it was spoken to them. Household conversations resulting from this pattern consisted of parents speaking to children in Spanish, and children responding in English.

Why Language Shift during Elementary School Has Not been a Major Topic in Bilingualism Research

Rapid language shift in childhood has not been described extensively in the literature on bilingualism. One reason is that relatively little large-scale research on bilingualism has actually focused on children's abilities *in both languages*. Especially in the United States, the focus has been so heavily on the acquisition of L2 English that many studies have simply not taken account of L1 skills (see e.g., Ramírez, Yuen, Ramey, & Pasta, 1991).

In the absence of evidence to the contrary, it might be expected that language shift should occur *gradually* in young children immersed in a new language. Of course, in important ways language shift *does* appear to be gradual—L2 learners gain gradually in L2 proficiency with respect to norms for monolingual speakers of L2 across elementary school (Cobo-Lewis, Pearson, Eilers, & Umbel, 2002; Collier, 1989). Indeed, it has been estimated that it takes at least 2 years to become conversant in a new language in school and 5 to 6 years to reach the point of doing abstract "context-reduced" verbal reasoning in L2 (Collier, 1989; Cummins, 1984). The idea of *subtractive bilingualism*, wherein *loss* of L1 occurs across the period of L2 learning (Lambert, 1975), might then be thought to imply gradual L1 loss to match gradual L2 gain. We examine data that run counter to this expectation. The shift in preference appears not to be simply subtractive, and its rather abrupt occurrence seems particularly influenced by peer environment.

Thus our review considers rapid language shift both (1) in terms of a common social circumstance that seems to predispose the occurrence of such shift, namely immersion with peers showing a preference for L2 in early schooling; and (2) in terms of apparently asymmetrical changes in L1 abilities that occur very early during the period of shift. The asymmetries that have been observed concern comprehension and production abilities for L1 after immersion in L2 schooling. Notably, such learners often seem to understand L1 about as well as monolingual L1 speakers, but show much poorer abilities in L1 expression.

PEER INFLUENCE: A SIGNIFICANT FORCE IN LANGUAGE PREFERENCE AMONG VERY YOUNG L2 LEARNERS

A New Input Pattern at the Onset of Schooling

Why should a child's language preference and profile of reception and production abilities in L1 shift soon after the onset of schooling in a new language? The question cannot be dismissed with a simple assertion that the "input" to the child changes, because in many cases where children learn L2 in school, the total input continues to include a great deal of L1, at least at home. One possibility to help explain the apparent suddenness of the change focuses on the apparent fact that children's linguistic interactions with peers dramatically increase at the start of school. This environmental change may redirect children's focus in accord with the widely touted role of peer relations in socialization (Borsari & Carey, 2001; Evans, Oates,

& Schwab, 1992; Harris, 1995; Simons-Morton, Haynie, Crump, Eitel, & Saylor, 2001). The idea is that there may be a biological imperative at stake, since children are destined to compete and form alliances primarily with peers, and language clearly plays a major role in how children compete for status and develop friendships and other sources of social support. So peers, even for very young children, may be an especially important focus of children's attention in language learning, and the effect of interacting in L2 may outweigh that of continued L1 exposure.

Yet it is surprising that so little empirical research has directly addressed peer influence in bilingualism and language shift. Online search of the PsycINFO database using keywords "peer influence" or "peer effect" and "bilingualism" or "second language" yielded no articles at all. Research related to peers in early schooling has largely addressed a different matter, namely, the effect of peer training or peer tutoring on learning in various settings (e.g., August, 1987). Such research *presumes* strong peer influence, but does not provide evidence effectively contrasting peer influence with adult influence in language choice. Anecdotal evidence, such as that reported by the Turkish scholar with the two sons, suggests that school effects (and especially effects of peer language in school) may swamp home effects in determining language preference. Furthermore, there is observational evidence (embedded in articles addressing a variety of influences) suggesting peer effects play a primary role in language choice among young children (Chesterfield, Chesterfield, & Chavez, 1982; Jia & Aaronson, 2003).

Miami Data on Language Usage and Possible Peer Effects

To shed additional light on both the fact of early language shift in children learning L2 in school in the United States as well as on the role of peers in inspiring that shift, we turn to a reevaluation of data from the Miami project in bilingualism, for which primary results can be found in *Language and Literacy in Bilingual Children*, hereafter LLBC (Oller & Eilers, 2002). The Miami project was designed to study effects of educational method, language at home, and socioeconomic status on language and literacy in Hispanic elementary school children. A total of 952 bilingual and monolingual children were studied in two-way and English-immersion (EI) schools (see LLBC for descriptions of specific program characteristics) in Miami in the 1990s. The children were administered both standardized and specialized evaluations. In addition, an extensive evaluation was made of language usage in the children's school environment. Classroom and hallway observations tracked the number of utterances produced in Spanish, English, or both (i.e., mixed utterances) by teachers and children (Eilers, Oller,

& Cobo-Lewis, 2002). In both EI and two-way schools, the demographic analysis showed there were 90–95% Hispanic students.

The Favored Status of L2 English

The results of LLBC strikingly indicated that children favored speaking English to one another, even in overwhelmingly Hispanic schools, and even in schools that used a two-way instructional method. The evidence suggests further that the preference for English was primarily a peer effect rather than a general schooling effect. The reasoning supporting this suggestion requires background about how the two languages were used.

Teachers in regular classes in the EI schools as well as teachers in English-designated periods in two-way schools almost always spoke English to the class as a whole and to the individual students in the classrooms. Similarly, teachers in Spanish-designated periods in two-way schools spoke Spanish overwhelmingly to classes as a whole and to individual children in the classes. These patterns of language usage by the teachers held at all grade levels observed: the first semester of kindergarten (K), the second semester of K, as well as at first, second, and fifth grades. When speaking to teachers, the children also followed the classroom rules—they spoke in English to teachers in English-designated classes, and in the two-way schools, they spoke in Spanish to teachers in Spanish-designated classes. The tendency to speak in the designated language to teachers accounted for at least 80% of observed utterances at every point of observation from early K to fifth grade (in both EI and two-way schools), and it accounted for virtually 100% of observations for English-designated classes at first, second, and fifth grade.

However, while children in two-way schools spoke overwhelmingly in Spanish to teachers in Spanish-designated classes, they switched languages in those classes and spoke in English to one another about half the time across all grade levels. In English-designated classes of both EI and two-way schools, the children spoke English to ome another 50% or more even at K and first grade, and then 80% or more at second and fifth grade; over-all, they engaged their peers much more in English than in Spanish. Fur-thermore, in hallway observations in the EI schools, children spoke English 80% or more at every grade level. In two-way schools, they spoke English to one another 65% or more at every grade level in hallway talk. These pat-terns suggest that children preferred English when they spoke to peers from very early in schooling. The results suggest further that peer effects may have substantially accounted for the shift toward English, a preference that became more pronounced across time. It appears, then, that rapid change in children's language preference occurs when they are immersed in a new peer language.

Interpretive Issues Regarding Possible Peer Effects in Language Shift

While the data reviewed above suggest a strong role for peers in rapid language shift, there is much more to be done to bring peer effects into clear focus. One gap is that studies offering quantitative data on test performance usually do not include direct data on amount of language heard and produced in each language of a bilingual student. There is great need for more extensive quantitative evaluation of the balance of usage of L1 and L2 in bilingual school settings. Similarly, direct observational data for bilingual children on amount of language heard and produced in each language at home is largely unavailable. In the past, research (including LLBC and Hakuta & D'Andrea, 1992) has tended to rely on questionnaires regarding language usage at home, but it is hard to gauge the reliability or validity of results from questionnaires. Providing data on language interaction between target children and both parents and (especially older) siblings may prove to be critical for the understanding of language choice.

In the Miami LLBC study, as indicated above, observational data on usage were acquired at the classroom level and in hallways indicating that Hispanic children in the schools studied tended systematically to speak English to each other (Eilers et al., 2002). However, the data were taken at the *group* level in both classroom and hallway circumstances. Only a subset of the children observed to determine usage data were among those who received the standardized test battery that included the receptive and expressive vocabulary evaluations. The data on usage represented the language environment in a broad sense, but it is possible that the individuals selected for testing on the standardized battery spoke less often or more quietly (perhaps because they knew less English) than other children in the classes. Furthermore, it is possible that the children with whom they tended to speak also spoke less often and more quietly—if so, the usage data may reflect other children's language preference more than those who were evaluated with the vocabulary tests. Clearly, to rule out such a possibility, data should be acquired on language usage for the *individual children being tested* and on language usage by other children who address them.

Influences Other Than Those of Peers in Language Shift

Of course, other influences must play a role in language proficiency, if not in language choice outside the home. Children do sometimes command a language even when their peers strongly prefer another one. De Houwer (2007) has presented recent data from a large study in Belgium indicating that children going to school in L2 can be expected to command L1, in spite of peer preference for L2, if one or both parents *does not understand L2*, or if one or both parents is rigorous about maintaining an L1-only environment in the home.

The work of Hakuta and D'Andrea (1992) amplifies the evidence that peer effects do not operate alone in determining language choice and language proficiency in L1 and L2. In fact, the article emphasizes that, across the students, "maintenance of proficiency in Spanish [was] principally associated with adult language practice in the home, rather than the subject's language attitude or language choice outside the home" (p. 82). At the same time, there was a strong tendency to show English preference in usage and better English proficiency among students for whom either parent had been born in the United States. The same point has also been highlighted by De Houwer (2007), who contends that while home language proficiency may be maintained in the context of strict parental adherence to use of the home language, there is no kind of language exposure that prevents children in Belgium from (also) acquiring strong capability in the language of their peers. And Hakuta and D'Andrea emphasize that Hispanic immigrants to the United States clearly adopt English as a primary language in not more than three generations. The shift results in both a preference for and a greater proficiency in English. Heritage language usage at home is progressively weakened across generations, and the pattern of weakening appears to be attributable in large measure to peer influence on language choice.

RELATIVE L1 AND L2 ABILITIES DURING LANGUAGE SHIFT AS SEEN THROUGH STUDIES IN ELEMENTARY SCHOOLS

Apparent Lack of Systematic Decline in Spanish Capability beyond K

The process of shift in language preference when children are immersed with L2 peers does not, however, typically show a simple pattern of gradual decline across the board for the various L1 abilities of learners. Expressive abilities seem to decline abruptly, but receptive (especially oral vocabulary comprehension) abilities in L1 are more robust. As the years of elementary schooling pass, the evidence suggests little or no change in the profile of L1 performance with respect to monolinguals in L1 based on standardized test comparisons of vocabulary comprehension and expression—a receptive– expressive gap (a profile effect; see Oller, Pearson, & Cobo-Lewis, 2007) generally remains in effect throughout elementary school for L2 learners. Yet the idea of subtractive bilingualism would seem to suggest that the process of shift should include systematic decline in L1 (i.e., relative subtraction of L1 from the communicative repertoire), to go along with systematic growth in abilities in L2 across the school years. Again the Miami LLBC data provide relevant evidence.

A variety of standardized tests were administered to 704 Hispanic children. Among them was: (1) a picture-naming task in English from the Woodcock Language Proficiency Battery: English Form—Revised (WJ-Eng; Woodcock, 1991); (2) a picture-pointing task for vocabulary reception (or recognition) in English (the Peabody Picture Vocabulary Test–III [PPVT]; Dunn & Dunn, 1981); (3) a picture-naming task in Spanish (the WJ-Span, normed with monolingual Spanish-speaking children; Woodcock & Muñoz-Sandoval, 1995); (4) and the TVIP (Test de Vocabulario en Imágenes Peabody), the Spanish version of the PPVT (Dunn, Padilla, Lugo, & Dunn, 1986). Hereafter we shall refer to the results of these tests as being evaluations of "receptive" and "expressive" skills—the terms are drawn from the tests themselves, and it should be understood that they refer specifically to picture-pointing and picture-naming tasks to assess vocabulary skills.

The data indicated systematic growth in English vocabulary for both receptive and expressive tests across K, second, and fifth grade. At the same time, performance in Spanish (while starting low at K and very low on expressive tests) did not decline across the same period, even though the data on usage (discussed above) suggested the children's language preference was shifting strongly to L2. The pattern was not thus simply subtractive. English performance improved substantially in both reception and production across the same period that Spanish performance did not decline.

Note that these patterns suggest not just that children maintained the Spanish they commanded during the first months of K, but that *they must have continued to learn Spanish* throughout the period. Had they not continued to learn Spanish, they would have lost ground with regard to Spanish monolinguals, and the standard scores would have decreased across grades—yet another indication that the shift is not simply subtractive with regard to L1.

Apparent Rapid Loss of L1 Vocabulary Access during Language Shift in Elementary School

The data from LLBC suggest a remarkable characteristic of children's Spanish performance. L1 expressive vocabulary scores (from the picture-naming task) were very low at all ages, averaging more than two standard deviations below the expected monolingual mean. The data show that although these low expressive scores did not decline from K to fifth grade, they were low from the first months of K, even though the children were selected as Spanish speakers, and many came from homes where parents reported only Spanish was spoken. Through the same period, the receptive vocabulary standard scores (from the picture-pointing task) were more than one and a half standard deviations better than the expressive scores. The data showed no such receptive–expressive gap in L2 English from K through fifth grade.

The receptive–expressive gap occurred at both high and low socioeconomic status at all grade levels. Children in both conditions of language spoken at home (Spanish only at home as well as English and Spanish at home) showed the receptive–expressive gap at all age levels, as did children in both two-way and EI training programs.

Memphis Data on the Receptive–Expressive Gap

Further evidence of limitations in L1 expressive vocabulary have been found in an ongoing study in Memphis focused on children of Spanish-speaking immigrants (hereafter "Hispanic" children) entering EI schooling at K and their monolingual English-speaking classmates. We have presented results for vocabulary tests on the first cohort of Memphis children at K (Oller et al., 2007) and have described the sample in that publication. Briefly, 44 children (30 Hispanic) were evaluated both early in K (during the first 3 months) and again at the end of K on receptive and expressive vocabulary.

The results, based on the same picture-pointing and picture-naming tasks, showed the same pattern as in Miami: a large receptive–expressive gap in L1 Spanish at both test points in K, but no such gap, or a much smaller one, in English. Importantly, the receptive–expressive gap in Spanish was present for both of two subgroups of the Hispanic children, one with presumably no significant exposure to English prior to entering school, and the other with approximately 1 year of preschool English exposure. The children who had greater exposure to English showed notably better English scores (about one standard deviation better) than those with less exposure to English, but their scores in Spanish were no worse than those of the children with less exposure to English.

Memphis Data on Rapid Naming Limitations

In addition to the standard vocabulary tests mentioned above, all children in Memphis were evaluated in Rapid Object Naming and Rapid Color Naming, subtests of the Comprehensive Test of Phonological Processing (CTOPP; Wagner, Torgesen, & Rashotte, 1999), and the Hispanic children were evaluated on Spanish adaptations of the same subtests by the Center for Applied Linguistics. Each child was asked to rapidly name pictures arranged on a test plate of either six common objects (English: pencil, star, fish, chair, boat, key; Spanish: lápiz, estrella, silla, barco, llave) or six colors (English: blue, red, green, black, brown, yellow; Spanish: azul, rojo, verde, negro, café, amarillo). A short pretest was administered to ensure that the children could recognize and name the pictures and colors. Alternative terms such as "bote" for "barco" or "marrón" for "café" were accepted in both pretest and test.

There was a notable performance difference between the groups. In short, approximately half the Hispanic children were unable to take the rapid color-naming tests in Spanish, either because they could not pass the pretest or because they were so slow in naming that they exceeded a test criterion requiring that the procedure be halted if the child hesitated too long on any item. The Hispanic children's ability to take the object-naming tests in Spanish was better, but still poorer than the ability of the monolingual English speakers in English. This result suggested that many of the L2 learners found it difficult to name pictures and colors rapidly in L1, even though the words required to name them were extremely common in childhood lexicons. Remarkably more of the Hispanic children were able to take the English than the Spanish rapid color-naming test. The monolingual English group was able to take both color and object naming tests in English more often than the Hispanic children could in either language.

The rapid-naming results suggested that many of the Hispanic children were limited in their ability to use Spanish vocabulary that they had been expected to command unquestionably. These results combined with those on the receptive–expressive gap provide considerable fuel for the suspicion that even in the first months of K, children immersed in L2 seem to show a rapid shift away from full command of L1, with important loss of ability to retrieve L1 vocabulary rapidly in naming.

Interpretive Issues Related to the Apparent Receptive–Expressive Gap

The receptive–expressive gap found in young L2 learners such as those in Miami and Memphis does not merely indicate that children understand more than they can say. To put the point another way, the pattern cannot be merely a manifestation of the well-known fact that the raw number of vocabulary items that can be recognized exceeds the raw number of vocabulary items that are utilized productively by any speaker—this latter phenomenon represents the difference between the ease of recognition relative to the difficulty of word recall and production.

The point here is different because the comparisons are based on *standard scores* for both receptive and expressive tests: Young children who are shifting from L1 to L2 showed a receptive–expressive gap in L1 *relative to receptive–expressive performance of monolingual children*. The data suggest that children in the process of shifting seemed to be unable (in comparison with monolinguals) to *access* (recall) L1 vocabulary when they were asked to name things in L1, even though they could perform well on receptive vocabulary with respect to monolinguals in L1. Perhaps it should be emphasized that there are no specific time requirements in the primary tasks (simple picture naming as in the WLPB, Spanish or English, and picture pointing as in the PPVT or TVIP) showing these patterns.

The Assumption of No English Exposure Prior to Schooling

The interpretation we suggest for the receptive–expressive gap in the Miami and Memphis data depends on an only partially verified assumption. The idea that language shift seems to occur within a few months of starting school in L2 depends on the assumption that at least some of the Hispanic children in the studies had been exposed to virtually no English prior to K. In support of this assumption, we have evidence that even when parents in Memphis reported that their children had no preschool experience in English, there was still a strong receptive–expressive gap in Spanish by the third month of K. In fact, it made little difference whether the children had experienced preschool as far as the receptive–expressive gap was concerned. The Miami data provide additional support for the assumption that children with little or no exposure to English prior to school were subject to a large receptive–expressive gap in Spanish, because many of the students came from (reportedly) Spanish-only homes.

Yet the results from Memphis and Miami cannot prove that *any of the children* showing the receptive–expressive gap had actually experienced *no* English exposure. Siblings, television, movies, friends met outside the home all provided potential sources of exposure to English in both Miami and Memphis.

A Problem with the Expressive Vocabulary Test?

It is also important to rule out the possibility that the apparent receptive–expressive gap could be an illusory result of a test problem. The very low scores of presumably near-monolingual Spanish speaking children on the expressive vocabulary test has inspired suspicions that have led us to include caveats in our prior publications reporting these effects (Oller, Pearson, et al., 2007; Oller, Jarmulowicz, Gibson, & Hoff, 2007). The suspicion that the norms might be inaccurate (and that consequently the receptive–expressive gap might be a test artifact) was intensified when we tested a cohort of 50 Hispanic children at K in Memphis, where the original WLPB-S was pitted against its successor, a newly normed expressive vocabulary test in Spanish produced by the same company for a new battery of language tests in Spanish. The expressive scores on the successor test were notably higher. One possibility is that children scored better on the successor test because they always received the original test first—perhaps practice in the test circumstance helped them (this possible test order effect will be checked in subsequent research). However, there is no feedback given on either version of the test, and the test items are substantially different across the two versions. Furthermore, the tests were administered on separate days, mitigating concerns about an order effect. It seems likely then that one of the two tests (either the successor or the original one) is improperly normed. In collaboration with Claude Goldenberg and Leslie Reese, authors of Chapter 1 in this volume, we have been evaluating data on the WLPB-S naming task (the original version) from first through third graders in Guadalajara, Mexico. These data, even for children at the youngest ages, do not show low scores compared with the norm expectations; in fact, the average scores exceed 100. Consequently, we proceed on the assumption that the L1 receptive–expressive gap is real, and that the original WLPB-S test yields realistic norm estimates of picture-naming abilities.

DIFFERENTIAL ACTIVATION OR SUPPRESSION AS POSSIBLE MECHANISMS OF L1 LIMITATION IN LEXICAL ACCESS AND EXPRESSIVE VOCABULARY

Why might there be a limitation of access to L1 vocabulary for production in young bilingual children? Some have suggested that there may be circumstances in bilingualism where L1 and L2 get in each other's way (Cook, 2003; Haugen, 1974; Kroll & Stewart, 1994; Stern, 1919). It has even been suggested that L1 needs to be "suppressed" in order for items in L2 to be accessed (Green, 1998; Kroll & Stewart, 1994; Levy, McVeigh, Marful, & Anderson, 2007; Meuter & Allport, 1999) especially at the beginning of L2 acquisition.

While a suppression mechanism is certainly a logical possibility, and one we have ourselves entertained (Oller, Jarmulowicz, et al., 2007), there is a simpler alternative that cannot be ruled out at this point as a way to explain the patterns of early bilingual vocabulary. It could be that *differential activation* levels of two languages in the brain during periods where different languages are being spoken can account for the empirically determined patterns without the need to invoke a specific suppression mechanism. To understand the options, we briefly review literature on adult bilingualism that provides models of lexical access and production. This research may illuminate the psycholinguistic processes underlying language shift and processes of interference, but we caution that the applicability of the adult-based models to processes of interference during language shift in children is unclear, given differences in participants and methods across studies.

The Adult Literature on Lexical Access in Bilingualism

For decades, interest in adult bilingual language representation and lexical interference from one language to another has been strong (Weinreich,

1953). In this context a distinction is drawn between language knowledge and organization and the processes and mechanisms that operate on that knowledge and within that organization (French & Jacquet, 2004; Grosjean, 2001). Lexical access, selection, and inhibition are all putative types of processes or mechanisms that act on an underlying language system (French & Jacquet, 2004).

Knowing more than one language has consequences for each language. Vocabulary diversity in L1 tends to decrease with increased exposure to L2, and L2 can alter L1 lexical–semantic associations (Laufer, 2003). Lexical access time in bilinguals tends to be slower in both L1 and L2 than lexical access in monolinguals (see reviews in Goral, 2004; Köpke, 2004). There are costs associated with switching between two languages. It is particularly difficult to switch from L2 to L1 (Costa & Santesteban, 2004; Meuter & Allport, 1999), a pattern that has been taken by some to suggest that L1 is suppressed in the context of L2 usage. Speakers proficient in two languages show fewer difficulties switching languages than speakers who are still learning a second language (Costa, 2004). There is also evidence that conceptual–semantic mappings merge in bilinguals, which is to say that bilinguals' word usage in each of their languages tends to be influenced by the meanings of related words in the other language (Ameel, Storms, Malt, & Sloman, 2005). Importantly, then, bilinguals are not "two monolinguals in one person" (Cook, 2003; Grosjean, 1989, 2001) but possess language capabilities and tendencies that interact across languages at a variety of levels, a point that is reinforced and augmented in a recent review (Kroll, Bobb, Misra, & Guo, 2008).

The phenomenon of L1 to L2 language shift and L1 attrition has been documented in children and adults in various populations including adopted children (Pollock, 2005; Roberts et al., 2005), normal aging (Gollan & Brown, 2006; Goral, 2004), and pathological conditions such as aphasia (Green, 2005). However, the literature indicates that there is a difference between true L1 loss and loss of access to a language (L1 or L2). A retrieval deficit can be induced in the laboratory. In fact, even limited exposure to L2 words affects L1 word accessibility; this effect has been shown to be particularly strong if the semantic overlap between L1 and L2 words is great and applies to word pairs across languages that bear little if any phonological similarity (Isurin & McDonald, 2001). Tip-of-the-tongue phenomena, which illustrate another type of retrieval deficit, are also noted among speakers of more than one language, and appear to occur more often on words that are familiar to an individual in both languages (Gollan & Brown, 2006).

The extant literature invoking the notions of lexical suppression or inhibition in adult bilinguals presents somewhat conflicting viewpoints on whether a specific suppression mechanism is needed to explain difficulties in access to L1 lexical items during L2 learning or use. Nevertheless, there is general consensus that (1) languages known by multilingual individuals share a single conceptual foundation (French & Jacquet, 2004; Kroll & Stewart, 1994), and (2) a convergence problem exists when more than one word (i.e., more than one phonological form) can map to a concept (La Heij, 2005). Thus convergence occurs, for example, where there is a single concept for "apple," but two possible words to choose from, one in English, *apple*, and one in Spanish, *manzana*. This sort of translation equivalence can produce lexical competition. Determining the mechanism underlying lexical choice when there is more than one possible word has been termed one of the "hard problems" in lexical access (Finkbeiner, Almeida, Janssen, & Caramazza, 2006). Some researchers suggest that in naming tasks, adult bilinguals by default access the two lexical forms (Thomas & Heuven, 2005) from which a selection is made, whereas others suggest that only one lexical system is active from the beginning of the process of access (La Heij, 2005).

A suppression mechanism, sometimes discussed as active inhibition, has been suggested at a lexical or possibly at a task level (Green, 1998; Meuter & Allport, 1999). Much of the evidence advanced by advocates of a suppression mechanism stems from two sources: tasks that require rapid shifting from one language to another and findings that it is easier to switch from L1 to L2 than from L2 to L1. Green (2005) suggests that a language schema is activated (either in L1 or L2), and this functions as both a filter to inhibit the nonpreferred language and a monitor that checks that the correct language is active. The degree of inhibition is predicted to be related to how active particular words are in the lexicon. Thus if the dominant L1 is suppressed while performing a task in L2, it will be particularly difficult to counter both the inhibitory pressure on L1 and the activation of L2 when the required response switches to L1. To switch between two languages requires efficient allocation of memory and attentional resources (Michael & Gollan, 2005). Of course, the resource allocation problem occurs at all ages, but both types of allocation are still developing in early school-age children, who may thus find language switching particularly difficult.

Other researchers have minimized the influence of an active suppression mechanism, maintaining that lexical items are marked or tagged for a given language (Costa, 2005; Costa, Miozzo, & Carromazza, 1999; Thomas & Heuven, 2005). In models advocated by these researchers, lexical selection mechanisms choose only from among the *active* words of the targeted language (Costa & Santesteban, 2004), and consequently no specific role for suppression is required.

MacNamara and McDaniel (2004) argue similarly that no specific suppression mechanism is necessary to explain laboratory results on apparent L2 interference with L1. Rather, they propose that differential levels of activation can account for the laboratory effects that have been observed. Still other models suggest that marking individual words is unparsimonious, and that language tags may be unnecessary (Li, 1998) or might be invoked at the concept stage of retrieval or in parallel with other pragmatic markers such as style and register of the preverbal message (La Heij, 2005). In addition, complaints have been raised concerning methodological problems in adult laboratory research on suppression of L1 in the context of L2 use, complaints that suggest interference effects may be due to more general cognitive mechanisms and task variables, and not to a specific suppression mechanism (Finkbeiner et al., 2006).

Laboratory research on L2 interactions with L1, then, has not yielded clear support for the need for a specific suppression mechanism to account for L1 access problems in the context of L2 use. In a recent effort, Levy et al. (2007) use naturalistic observations and take a strong stand in favor of suppression. They argue that naturalistic data show suppression of L1 vocabulary in the context of L2 learning. Travelers to foreign countries, who spend a few weeks speaking a language other than their native one, often find that they temporarily cannot access common vocabulary from their native language when asked to provide translations of individual words. This problem of access seems to disappear abruptly on return to the native speaking environment, and furthermore, no hindrance to native language *comprehension* is reported to occur at any point in time for travelers. Levy et al. provide laboratory illustrations of effects they think are related to the temporary loss of access to L1 vocabulary in the context of repetitive L2 use of translation equivalents. They also illustrate that this presumably suppressive effect on L1 applies primarily to *less proficient* speakers of L2.

The review by Levy et al. considers language learning in adults outside the laboratory during immersion in a foreign language, and consequently may have particular relevance to the language learning circumstance faced by immigrant children starting school. In both cases there can be strong pressures to adapt to the new language. However, the Levy et al. argument for a specific suppression mechanism does not seem airtight. It appears a differential activation model can also explain the outcomes reviewed: As the immersion language, L2, becomes more active in the brain, L1 access abilities may fade without any specific suppression being necessary. A differential activation model requires that relatively abrupt changes in activation levels for specific languages be possible in order to explain the relatively abrupt shifts of accessibility that seem to occur as language environments change (e.g., during international travel), but it is not clear that suppression is required in addition.

The Literature on Expressive Vocabulary Limitations in Childhood Bilingualism

A smaller body of research has addressed the possibility of differential activation or suppression effects in childhood bilingualism. Kohnert and colleagues have conducted a series of pertinent studies (Kohnert, 2002; Kohnert & Bates, 2002; Kohnert et al., 1999). The research involved two groups of 100 children, all L2 learners of English who spoke Spanish at home, even after the start of school at K. Thus, many of the children from the Kohnert work can be characterized as similar demographically to the Memphis and Miami Hispanic research participants. Still, there were many reports from parents of children in Miami *refusing* to speak Spanish at home. Consequently, there may have been differences in the degree of Spanish usage at home between the Kohnert studies and the Miami studies.

In the first of the Kohnert studies (Kohnert et al., 1999) 20 children in each of five age groups (5–7 years, 8–10, 11–13, 14–16, and young adults) engaged in a variety of picture-naming tasks that focused on familiar, early-acquired items. The measures were accuracy of naming and response time (RT). Picture stimuli were presented for naming in both English and Spanish. Sometimes the trials were *blocked*, such that all responses were expected in one language, while in the opposing condition the trials were *mixed*, so that the child was cued to alternate naming pictures in one language or the other. In the second study (Kohnert & Bates, 2002) an additional sample of 100 participants were given tasks of picture-name verification (a comprehension task), and again both accuracy and RT were monitored. In the most recent report (Kohnert, 2002), a smaller subgroup of children (mean age = 10 years) from the original study were followed up longitudinally an average of 13 months after the original cross-sectional sampling on the picture-naming tasks.

The Kohnert et al. studies differed in data focus from the ones reported in the present work. The Miami and Memphis studies used standardized tests, attempting to measure *breadth* of vocabulary knowledge in both Spanish and English. Kohnert et al. expressed considerable doubt about the validity of breadth measures of vocabulary knowledge in bilingual children, a point that cannot be dismissed. Kohnert et al. chose instead to address *processing* measures of speed and accuracy on relatively familiar (commonly occurring) words from both languages. The attention to processing as a key measure of vocabulary skills in L2 learners provided empirical follow-up to work by Mägiste (1979, 1992), who studied L1 German children learning L2 Swedish. A key finding was that L1 and L2 speed of processing for vocabulary tended to trade in time, such that L1 processing slowed down while L2 processing sped up across years of learning.

The results of the Kohnert et al. studies add to the perspective on change in L1 and L2 processing of relatively common vocabulary items across years of learning. The data showed more accuracy errors in both languages and slower RTs at younger ages. The mixed conditions tended to produce slower RTs, suggesting that competition for attentional or memory resources was highest between the two languages when both were being accessed. In the youngest age range (5–7), RTs were faster, and there were fewer naming errors in Spanish than in English. These patterns reversed at later ages, so that English processing was both more accurate and faster. The followup study with 6–14-year-olds also indicated that English appeared to show greater improvements in both speed and accuracy than Spanish from time 1 to time 2 (separated by 13 months), especially in the mixed-language conditions. Kohnert and colleagues emphasized that the cognitively demanding mixed-language processing condition showed the greatest gains across time in English. The focus of interpretation was on the growth of cognition in the control of the bilingualism tasks.

Kohnert et al. are persuasive on the point that growth in memory capacity and attention management has important effects in processing of both languages in bilinguals as development proceeds. At the same time, the data from Kohnert et al. are not incompatible with the possibility that either suppression or lowered activation of L1 vocabulary is involved in the early acquisition of L2. Two particular points are worth considering. First, the Spanish accuracy scores reported by Kohnert et al. on picture naming of presumably familiar words at ages 5–7 were very low, considering they were presumably Spanish-dominant children, 60% in blocked and only 46% in mixed conditions. Furthermore, at both 5–7 and 8–10 years, there was a statistically reliable effect of greater accuracy in Spanish in the blocked than the mixed conditions, suggesting English was interfering with Spanish access in the mixed conditions. In addition, greater differences between correct responses in mixed and blocked conditions for Spanish than for English for the two youngest age groups in Kohnert et al. suggest that L1 Spanish may have been more affected by cross-linguistic interference than L2 English.

Another body of research on children in the process of language shift is presented by Isurin (Isurin, 2000; Isurin & McDonald, 2001), who reviewed literature on language attrition and focused particularly on the phenomenon of *retroactive interference*. In short, the studies investigated retroactive interference on words in L1 when translation equivalents had been learned in L2. Isurin described a Russian 9-year-old, adopted into a monolingual English-speaking American family. Across a year, the child showed decreasing ability to name pictures in Russian. Loss of access to Russian words appeared to be particularly associated with the learning of English translation equivalents. Furthermore, words in Russian were not truly *forgotten* during the year of monitoring; instead, it appeared the child lost the ability to easily retrieve them. The effect even applied to cognates, which the child seemed unable to name in Russian after the corresponding word had entered her English repertoire. Isurin and MacDonald (2001) also conducted laboratory experiments where undergraduate students could be shown to lose the ability to name words in one language after having been exposed to learning translation equivalents in another. Reaction times were also slower for naming when the participants had been trained on translation equivalents.

The results of Isurin and MacDonald, like those of Kohnert and colleagues, are compatible with the idea of suppression or decreased activation of L1 in the context of L2 learning, but they add a wrinkle to the interpretation. Perhaps the primary focus of the change in lexical access is associated with translation equivalents and the interference that occurs between them. If so, an L2 learner should show a distributed characteristic of vocabulary knowledge (some words apparently known in one language but not the other; see Oller & Pearson, 2002) that might change with time. According to this interpretation, many L1 items may come to be inaccessible as their translation equivalents are learned in L2, but this inaccessibility may tend to attenuate as the learner becomes more proficient in L2.

CONCLUSION WITH A SKETCHY MODEL
ON RAPID LANGUAGE SHIFT IN EARLY CHILDHOOD

The research we have reviewed begins to address early childhood changes in language skill and choice that appear to constitute the critical beginnings of language shift. An ingredient that seems to make such shift practically inevitable (at least within a very few generations) is immersion in an L2 peer environment in early schooling. The changes that take place appear to be too abrupt to be predicted merely by the accumulated raw amount of input in L1 and L2. If that were the only factor determining shift, there should be gradual loss of L1, which does not appear to occur. Instead an abrupt loss of access to vocabulary items for production in L1 seems to occur,[1] but this apparent loss does not become exaggerated (in terms of expressive vocabulary relative to monolingual speakers of L1) as time passes across elementary school. Nor does comprehension ability, as reflected in receptive vocabulary scores (relative to monolingual speakers), seem to decline gradually as L2 grows. Why should early language shift have these characteristics? We reason here about the possible processes relevant to differential activation of neural resources. This reasoning may, of course, not represent the only possibility to explain the pattern of L1 change we have observed. Our proposal focuses on a differential activation mechanism—perhaps the most obvious alternative would invoke a suppression mechanism.

When attention is directed to a task, activation of the relevant neural resources can be thought to maximize the individual's ability to perform the task; of course, selective attention and activation implies that resources for other tasks become relatively inactive, and consequently those tasks become harder to perform. This conception of attention management has deep roots (see review on the evolution of attentional mechanisms in Damasio, 1999; for other background on attention see Norman & Bobrow, 1975, or Deutsch & Deutsch, 1963), implying that when a child enters an English-immersion school speaking L1 Spanish, a process of attentional shift to the task of learning L2 English begins. As the attentional focus on L2 grows, neural resources related to use and learning of English become highly activated, and related resources for L1 lose activation, not due to a specific suppression mechanism, but simply to lack of use in the near past.

To account for the receptive–expressive gap, this attention-based interpretation would be required to include the provision that differential activation have particularly strong effects on task capabilities requiring retrieval of information (in particular retrieval of words) and lesser (or no) effects on capabilities requiring recognition of information. To explain why receptive abilities, as they have been measured in the research reviewed above, might be affected relatively little by activation changes, consider the following: When an individual is presented with a word for recognition in a picture-pointing task, the presentation itself can be expected to have an activating effect on specific neural connections (i.e., meanings associated) with the word. Furthermore, the picture-pointing tasks that have been used in the research provide only four choices on each trial, instantiated as four pictures, thus offering further trial-by-trial activation of any existing connections between the word and its meaning.

The expressive task used in the research, on the other hand, would appear to entail much more diverse and less specific activation of the connections needed to succeed in the task. The expressive task constitutes an example of "confrontational naming": A picture is presented without any contextual support beyond the picture itself to help limit the possible naming options, that is, to help limit the fields of neural activation that the picture might stimulate. Any picture or scene can inspire numerous thoughts about shape, color, size, orientation, action, state of mind, and so on, a fact that has been treated extensively as the "indeterminacy" problem in the study of how word meanings are learned (Quine, 1960). The many thoughts that can be inspired by a picture may activate connections to numerous words, and the task of selecting the correct one may thus be considerably more complex than the task of recognizing words in four-choice picture pointing.

In accord with this reasoning, then, the two tasks that have yielded the data about the L1 receptive–expressive gap during early L2 learning may have very different activation effects. In picture pointing (reception), each trial appears to produce selective activation of the specific connections needed to succeed in the task, whereas in picture naming (expression), each trial stimulates a vast array of connections, and thus provides far less specific and more varied activation. Thus children learning L2 may be particularly vulnerable to failure on L1 tasks such as confrontational naming because their L1 activation level is generally low in the school setting, and the naming task requires activation of numerous resources to find a correct response. In contrast, the same learners may find L1 picture pointing much less difficult because in spite of the overall low level of L1 activation, the task itself tends to activate the neural circuits necessary for success.

We reemphasize that this reasoning represents one of several possibilities. For example a specific suppression mechanism is not invoked by the reasoning, but it could be. In addition, instead of emphasizing overall activation levels, one might focus on complexity of and number of mental processes invoked by different tasks: It might be argued, for example, that the four-choice picture-pointing task involves fewer mental steps to reach a decision and a less complex physical response than the confrontational picture-naming task. As research on language shift during early L2 learning progresses, it will be important to specify the models that guide the research.

Of course it is not just the particular tasks of picture naming and picture pointing that are relevant to an understanding of early language shift. In general, understanding a language may be less demanding than speaking a language. Indeed, many individuals understand a considerable amount in a foreign language without being able to speak it at all. And there exist individuals who possess an extensive comprehension ability for a language that was spoken to them in childhood, with little or no speaking ability of their own in that language. Further research will be needed to evaluate the possibility that the receptive–expressive gap we have seen in early L2 learners based on picture pointing and picture naming indicates the emergence of a general linguistic asymmetry, where L1 abilities are increasingly limited to the realm of comprehension.

This account is admittedly sketchy and will need much refinement as further information is acquired from a wider variety of tasks. Furthermore, we need information on the precise circumstances that are required for a significant differential activation to occur between L1 and L2 in an individual learner. Do more than half the learner's peers need to be speaking primarily in L2? More than half the time? Does the L2 learner need to be speaking in L2? More than half the time? How important is the language usage of friends as opposed to all peers? How much time is required in an immersion environment for an differential activation between L1 and L2 to occur? These questions will need quantitative answers.

A critical component of the account is the assumption that children showing low L1 expressive vocabulary do not actually forget words in L1, but merely lose access to them during L2 learning. There should then be ways to reactivate L1 expressive vocabulary that appears to be absent when the receptive–expressive gap is observed. Research should address this possibility by evaluating children whose language environment changes systematically back and forth from L1 to L2. It is not clear whether relative reactivation of L1 can be achieved in the short run (e.g., by testing children for L1 vocabulary expression in their Spanish-speaking homes) or whether more substantial and long-term changes in environment need to be made to fully reactivate L1, a matter that could be investigated, for example, by testing children at varying intervals after they are re-immersed in an L1 environment.

Empirical demonstration of rapid language shift at K will also require more information on language exposure and language usage *prior* to entry to K by children in these studies. In the absence of such information, it is impossible to quantify the rate of shift or the extent of its effect. Finally, better information on language use by children undergoing language shift both in school and at home is critical. We need to know what language individual children speak to other children as well as to teachers and parents.

As further evidence accumulates, it may be possible to substantially illuminate the processes of rapid language shift. The processes seem to hinge on an attention mechanism capable of shifting resources to new tasks as it becomes necessary to address them. The importance of the ability to shift attention would be hard to overestimate, since such a capability is a defining characteristic of adaptability.

It is surely relevant to emphasize that there are special biological needs associated with specifically being able to direct attention to learning the language of one's peers. That L1 should suffer by becoming more latent, at least during the first few years of L2 learning, could be a small price to pay for growth in the peer language, especially as long as the basic foundation of L1 is not fundamentally eroded while L2 ascends rapidly.

CONCLUDING REMARKS
ON EDUCATIONAL IMPLICATIONS

The existence of a receptive–expressive gap in L1 among young L2 learners suggests that such children may feel even more disadvantaged in early schooling than had previously been suspected. Not only are these children at a huge disadvantage with regard to competition in school with their monolingual peers in L2, but they also are apparently at a rather sudden disadvantage even in L1 with regard to monolingual speakers of that language. The present work implies that research on the emotional effects of L2 immersion on very young children is in order.

Furthermore, the existence of the receptive–expressive gap in L1 adds yet more fuel to the fire that has been burning for some time on the issue of how to determine language abilities of young L2 learners and perhaps of young bilinguals in general. We already know that bilingual children command some vocabulary in L1 that they do not command in L2 and vice versa (Oller & Eilers, 2002). Furthermore, we know that testing bilingual children for vocabulary knowledge in either language and comparing the results with norms on monolinguals in either language is misleading, because no matter which language is chosen for test, some of vocabulary the bilingual children possess is always in the other language. The receptive–expressive gap in L1 suggests yet another way that our typical test capabilities are likely to be misleading. They are likely to yield the impression that elementary school children in L2 immersion are poor or perhaps even disabled language learners, because even their command of L1 expressive vocabulary is low with respect to monolinguals in L1. So from a practical point of view, the present review suggests a challenge. How are we to assess the long-term language learning capabilities of young L2 learners? The research we have reviewed implies that the typical tools are inadequate to the task. Additional research into the facts of early language shift will clearly be needed in order even to begin to address the fundamental challenges of assessment in early L2 learners.

ACKNOWLEDGMENT

This research was supported by Grant No. 01 HD046947 from the National Institute of Child Health and Human Development, National Institutes of Health, to D. Kimbrough Oller (Principal Investigator), and by support to D. Kimbrough Oller from the Plough Foundation. The original work on the Miami project was also supported by Grant No. R01 HD30762 from the National Institute of Child Health and Human Development to D. Kimbrough Oller (Principal Investigator).

NOTE

1. Thus far, there has been no direct test for lost access to particular L1 vocabulary in the studies we have reviewed. Instead, loss of access to vocabulary in L1 has been inferred from lower than expected standard scores on expressive tests. For the future, we envision evaluations of recognition and production of the same vocabulary items, utilizing a variety of tasks beyond the four-choice picture pointing and confrontational picture-naming tasks that have so far provided the primary perspectives on relative weakness of L1 expressive vocabulary in early L2 learners.

REFERENCES

Ameel, E., Storms, G., Malt, B. C., & Sloman, S. A. (2005). How bilinguals solve the naming problem. *Journal of Memory and Language, 53*, 60–80.

August, D. L. (1987). Effects of peer tutoring on the second language acquisition of Mexican American children in elementary school. *TESOL Quarterly, 21*(4), 717–736.

Borsari, B., & Carey, K. B. (2001). Peer influences on college drinking: A review of the research. *Journal of Substance Abuse, 13*, 391–424.

Brown, H. D. (1980). *Principles of language learning and teaching.* Englewood Cliffs, NJ: Prentice Hall.

Chesterfield, K. B., Chesterfield, R. A., & Chavez, R. (1982). Peer interaction, language proficiency, and language preference in bilingual preschool classrooms. *Hispanic Journal of Behavioral Sciences, 4*, 467–486.

Cobo-Lewis, A., Pearson, B. Z., Eilers, R. E., & Umbel, V. C. (2002). Effects of bilingualism and bilingual education on oral and written English skills: A multifactor study of standardized test outcomes. In D. K. Oller & R. E. Eilers (Eds.), *Language and literacy in bilingual children* (pp. 64–97). Clevedon, UK: Multilingual Matters.

Collier, V. P. (1989). How long?: A synthesis of research on academic achievement in a second language. *TESOL Quarterly, 23*, 509–531.

Cook, V. E. (2003). *Effects of the second language on the first.* Clevedon, UK: Multilingual Matters.

Costa, A. (2004). Speech production in bilinguals. In T. Bhatia & W. Ritchie (Eds.), *Handbook of bilingualism* (pp. 201–223). New York: Blackwell.

Costa, A. (2005). Lexical access in bilingual production. In J. F. Kroll & A. M. B. de Groot (Eds.), *Handbook of bilingualism: Psycholinguistic approaches* (pp. 308–325). New York: Oxford University Press.

Costa, A., Miozzo, M., & Caramazza, A. (1999). Lexical selection in bilinguals: Do words in the bilingual's two lexicons compete for selection? *Journal of Memory and Language, 41*, 365–397.

Costa, A., & Santesteban, M. (2004). Lexical access in bilingual speech production: Evidence from language switching in highly proficient bilinguals and l2 learners. *Journal of Memory and Language, 50*, 491–511.

Cummins, J. (1984). *Bilingualism and special education: Issues in assessment and pedagogy (Vol. 6).* Clevedon, UK: Multilingual Matters.

Damasio, A. (1999). *The feeling of what happens: Body and emotion in the making of consciousness.* New York: Harcourt Brace.

De Houwer, A. (1990). *The acquisition of two languages from birth: A case study (Vol. XV).* Cambridge, UK: Cambridge University Press.

De Houwer, A. (2007). Parental language input patterns and children's bilingual use. *Applied Psycholinguistics, 28*(3), 411–424.

Deutsch, J. A., & Deutsch, D. (1963). Attention: Some theoretical considerations. *Psychological Review, 70*(1), 80–90.

Dunn, L., & Dunn, L. (1981). *Peabody Picture Vocabulary Test—Revised.* Circle Pines, MN: American Guidance Service.

Dunn, L., Padilla, E., Lugo, D., & Dunn, L. (1986). *Test de vocabulario en imágenes*

Peabody—adaptación hispanoamericana [Peabody picture vocabulary test— Latin American adaptation]. Circle Pines, MN: American Guidance Service.

Eilers, R. E., Oller, D. K., & Cobo-Lewis, A. (2002). Bilingualism and cultural assimilation in Miami Hispanic children. In D. K. Oller & R. E. Eilers (Eds.), *Language and literacy in bilingual children* (pp. 43–63). Clevedon, UK: Multilingual Matters.

Evans, W. N., Oates, W. E., & Schwab, R. M. (1992). Measuring peer group effects: A study of teenage behavior. *Journal of Political Economy, 100,* 966–991.

Finkbeiner, M., Almeida, J., Janssen, N., & Caramazza, A. (2006). Lexical selection in bilingual speech production does not involve language suppression. *Journal of Experimental Psychology: Learning, Memory, and Cognition, 32*(5), 1075–1089.

Fishman, J. (1966). *Language loyalty in the United States*. The Hague: Mouton.

French, R. M., & Jacquet, M. (2004). Understanding bilingual memory: Models and data. *Trends in Cognitive Science, 8*(2), 87–93.

Gollan, T. H., & Brown, A. S. (2006). From tip-of-the-tongue (TOT) data to theoretical implications in two steps: When more TOTs means better retrieval. *Journal of Experimental Psychology: General, 135*(3), 462–483.

Goral, M. (2004). First-language decline in healthy aging: Implications for attrition in bilingualism. *Journal of Neurolinguistics, 17,* 31–52.

Green, D. W. (1998). Mental control of the bilingual lexico-semantic system. *Bilingualism: Language and Cognition, 1,* 67–81.

Green, D. W. (2005). The neurocognition of recovery patterns in bilingual aphasics. In J. F. Kroll & A. M. B. de Groot (Eds.), *Handbook of bilingualism: Psycholinguistic approaches* (pp. 516–530). New York: Oxford University Press.

Grosjean, F. (1989). Neurolinguists beware! The bilingual is not two monolinguals in one person. *Brain and Language, 36,* 3–15.

Grosjean, F. (2001). The bilingual's language modes. In J. Nicol (Ed.), *One mind, two languages* (pp. 1–22). Oxford, UK: Blackwell.

Hakuta, K., & D'Andrea, D. (1992). Some properties of bilingual maintenance and loss in Mexican background high school students. *Applied Linguistics, 13,* 72–99.

Harris, J. R. (1995). Where is the child's environment? A group socialization theory of development. *Psychological Review, 102*(3), 458–489.

Haugen, E. (1974). Bilingualism, language contact, and immigrant languages in the US. In T. Sebeok (Ed.), *Current trends in linguistics, Vol. 10*. The Hague: Mouton.

Isurin, L. (2000). Deserted island or a child's first language forgetting. *Bilingualism: Language and Cognition, 3*(2), 151–166.

Isurin, L., & McDonald, J. L. (2001). Retroactive interference from translation equivalents: Implications for first language forgetting. *Memory and Cognition, 29*(2), 312–319.

Jia, G., & Aaronson, D. (2003). A longitudinal study of Chinese children and adolescents learning English in the US. *Applied Linguistics, 24*(1), 1–21.

Kohnert, K. J. (2002). Picture naming in early sequential bilinguals: A 1-year follow-up. *Journal of Speech, Language, and Hearing Research, 45*(4), 759–771.

Kohnert, K. J., & Bates, E. (2002). Balancing bilinguals II: Lexical comprehension and cognitive processing in children learning Spanish and English. *Journal of Speech, Language, and Hearing Research, 45*(2), 347–359.

Kohnert, K. J., Bates, E., & Hernández, A. E. (1999). Balancing bilinguals: Lexical–semantic production and cognitive processing in children learning Spanish and English. *Journal of Speech, Language, and Hearing Research, 42*(6), 1400–1413.

Köpke, B. (2004). Neurolinguistic aspects of attrition. *Journal of Neurolinguistics, 17,* 3–30.

Kroll, J. F., & Stewart, E. (1994). Category interference in translation and picture naming: Evidence for asymmetric connection between bilingual memory representations. *Journal of Memory and Language, 33*(2), 149–174.

Kroll, J. F., Bobb, S. C., Misra, M., & Guo, T. (2008). Language selection in bilingual speech: Evidence for inhibitory processes. *Acta Psychol (Amst), 128,* 416–430.

La Heij, W. (2005). Selection processes in monolingual and bilingual lexical access. In J. F. Kroll & A. M. B. de Groot (Eds.), *Handbook of bilingualism: Psycholinguistic approaches* (pp. 289–309). New York: Oxford University Press.

Lambert, W. E. (1975). Culture and language as factors in learning and education. In A. Wolfgang (Ed.), *Education of immigrant children* (pp. 55–83). Toronto: Ontario Institute for Studies in Education.

Laufer, B. (2003). The influence of L2 on L1 collocation knowledge and on L1 lexical diversity in free written expression. In V. Cook (Ed.), *Effects of the second language on the first* (pp. 19–31). Clevedon, UK: Multilingual Matters.

Levy, B. J., McVeigh, N. D., Marful, A., & Anderson, M. C. (2007). Inhibiting your native language: The role of retrieval-induced forgetting during second-language acquisition. *Psychological Science, 18*(1), 29–34.

Li, P. (1998). Mental control, language tags, and language nodes in bilingual lexical processing. *Bilingualism: Language and Cognition, 1,* 92–93.

MacNamara, D. S., & McDaniel, M. A. (2004). Suppressing irrelevant information: Knowledge activation or inhibition? *Journal of Experimental Psychology: Learning, Memory, and Cognition, 30*(2), 465–482.

Mägiste, E. (1979). The competing language systems of the multilingual: A developmental study of decoding and encoding processes. *Journal of Verbal Learning and Verbal Behavior, 18,* 79–89.

Mägiste, E. (1992). Second language learning in elementary and high school students. *European Journal of Cognitive Psychology, 4,* 355–365.

Meuter, R. F. I., & Allport, A. (1999). Bilingual language switching in naming: Asymmetrical costs of language selection. *Journal of Memory and Language, 40,* 25–40.

Michael, E. G., & Gollan, T. H. (2005). Being and becoming bilingual: Individual differences and consequences for language production. In J. F. Kroll & A. M. B. de Groot (Eds.), *Handbook of bilingualism: Psycholinguistic approaches* (pp. 389–407). Oxford, UK: Oxford University Press.

Norman, D. A., & Bobrow, D. G. (1975). On data-limited and resource-limited processes. *Cognitive Psychology, 7*(1), 44–64.

Oller, D. K., & Eilers, R. E. (2002). *Language and literacy in bilingual children.* Clevedon, UK: Multilingual Matters.

Oller, D. K., Jarmulowicz, L., Gibson, T., & Hoff, E. (2007). First language vocabulary loss in early bilinguals during language immersion: A possible role for suppression. In *Proceedings of the Boston University conference on language development* (pp. 368–386). Somerville, MA: Cascadilla Press.

Oller, D. K., & Pearson, B. Z. (2002). Assessing the effects of bilingualism: A background. In D. K. Oller & R. E. Eilers (Eds.), *Language and literacy in bilingual children* (pp. 3–21). Clevedon, UK: Multilingual Matters.

Oller, D. K., Pearson, B., & Cobo-Lewis, A. (2007). Profile effects in early bilingual language and literacy. *Applied Psycholinguistics, 28,* 191–230.

Pollock, K. E. (2005). Early language growth in children adopted from China: Preliminary normative data. *Seminars in Speech and Language, 26*(1), 22–32.

Quine, W. V. O. (1960). *Word and object.* Cambridge, MA: MIT Press.

Ramírez, J. D., Yuen, S. D., Ramey, D. R., & Pasta, D. J. (1991). *Final report: Longitudinal study of structured English immersion strategy, early-exit and late-exit transitional bilingual education programs for language-minority children (Contract No. 300–87–0156)* (Vol. I). San Mateo, CA: Aguirre International.

Roberts, J. A., Pollock, K. E., Krakow, R., Price, J., Fulmer, K., & Wang, P. (2005). Language development in preschool-age children adopted from China. *Journal of Speech, Language, and Hearing Research, 48*(1), 93–107.

Simons-Morton, B., Haynie, D. L., Crump, A. D., Eitel, P., & Saylor, K. E. (2001). Peer and parent influences on smoking and drinking among early adolescents. *Health Education and Behavior, 28,* 95–107.

Stern, W. (1919). Die erlernung und beherrschung fremder sprachen. *Zeitschrift fuer Paedagogische Psychologie, 20,* 104–108.

Thomas, M. S. C., & Heuven, W. J. B. v. (2005). Computational models of bilingual comprehension. In J. F. Kroll & A. M. B. de Groot (Eds.), *Handbook of bilingualism: Psycholinguistic approaches* (pp. 202–225). New York: Oxford University Press.

Umbel, V. M., Pearson, B. Z., Fernández, M. C., & Oller, D. K. (1992). Measuring bilingual children's receptive vocabularies. *Child Development, 63,* 1012–1020.

Veltman, C. (1983a). Anglicization in the United States: Language environment and language practice of American adolescents. *International Journal of the Sociology of Language, 44,* 99–114.

Veltman, C. (1983b). *Language shift in the united states.* Amsterdam: Mouton.

Wagner, R. K., Torgeson, J. K., & Rashotte, C. A. (1999). *CTOPP: Comprehensive test of phonological processing.* Austin, TX: PRO-ED.

Weinreich, U. (1953). *Languages in contact.* The Hague: Mouton.

Wong Fillmore, L. (1991). Second-language learning in children. In E. Bialystok (Ed.), *Language processing in bilingual children* (pp. 49–69). Cambridge, UK: Cambridge University Press.

Woodcock, R. W. (1991). *Woodcock Language Proficiency Battery: English form—revised.* Chicago: Riverside.

Woodcock, R. W., & Muñoz-Sandoval, A. F. (1995). *Batería Woodcock–Muñoz: Pruebas de Aprovechamiento—revisada.* Chicago: Riverside.

CHAPTER 5

■　■　■

Language Proficiency
and Its Implications for Monolingual
and Bilingual Children

ELLEN BIALYSTOK
XIAOJIA FENG

In the past decade, there has been a dramatic increase in the amount of research investigating the linguistic and cognitive abilities of bilingual children, especially in terms of how bilingualism may alter the path of development typically taken by their monolingual peers. This research has covered a broad range of developmental achievements, including metalinguistic development (Eviatar & Ibrahim, 2000; Francis, 2002; Galambos & Goldin-Meadow, 1990; Liow & Lau, 2006), acquisition of literacy (Barnard & Glynn, 2003; Durgunoğlu, 1997; Geva & Wade-Woolley, 1998; Swanson, Saez, & Gerber, 2006), and cognitive consequences of bilingualism (Bialystok & Martin, 2004; Bialystok & Shapero, 2005; Carlson & Meltzoff, 2008; Martin-Rhee & Bialystok, 2008). The picture emerging from these studies is a complex portrait of interactions between bilingualism and skill acquisition in which there are sometimes benefits for bilingual children, sometimes deficits, and sometimes no consequence at all. A summary of these patterns is described by Bialystok (2001).

Underlying this surge in interest is the assumption that the canonical body of developmental research that is based on monolingual children learning to speak and read in English does not represent a significant portion of children. Even in English-speaking countries, the number of children who speak non-English languages at home and in their communities is substantial, and by some estimates, will soon represent a majority of children. More important, the profile of skill development that has been obtained for children in the canonical group of monolinguals may be different in crucial respects from that of children who are developing two languages in childhood and establishing basic cognitive competencies through the mediation of two languages. This is different from the situation that has received more research attention in which children learn a second language when they enter school, as in the English language learners studied by Geva and Lafrance (Chapter 10, this volume). In the case of children who are bilingual from home, it is more difficult to designate one language as dominant when they enter school; English-language schooling quickly makes English the more dominant language, although children continue to use both languages. Therefore the empirical descriptions, theoretical models, and pedagogical implications of research conducted with monolingual children may not provide an accurate or adequate account of development for these bilingual children.

In this chapter, we explore some of the consequences of bilingualism for children's development of oral language skills and the implications of oral proficiency on other verbal abilities. We are not concerned with the process by which language is learned and two languages are established; there is a good deal of research on these processes for bilingual children. Issues examined include transfer across languages, role of constraints such as mutual exclusivity in vocabulary acquisition, and the acquisition of certain aspects of language in a particular bilingual group, for example, the acquisition of specific phonemes for Spanish–English children. Instead, we consider the consequences of language acquisition by comparing the relative proficiency of monolingual and bilingual children on several crucial linguistic achievements. In all cases, the children we describe have been raised with two languages at home and have been educated through one of them, namely, English.

Children's progress in the development of oral language abilities is important because of its involvement in other skills—metalinguistic ability and literacy being two examples. Therefore if there are systematic differences in the acquisition of oral language by monolingual and bilingual children, its impact could be broadly experienced through a range of fundamental abilities. We begin by presenting evidence to establish the finding of a delay in oral vocabulary by bilingual children and then consider two aspects of verbal development for monolingual and bilingual children in the context of those differences in initial levels of vocabulary knowledge. These verbal skills are semantic fluency and retrieval, and memory for words with interference from the semantic domain (release from proactive interference).

ACQUIRING VOCABULARY

Research examining the development of language proficiency in bilingual children and the milestones involved in mastering a spoken language has generally found that bilingual children develop vocabulary more slowly in each language than monolinguals speakers of that language (Mahon & Crutchley, 2006; Oller & Eilers, 2002). The generality of this claim, however, is exceedingly difficult to establish. First, the acquisition of vocabulary is characterized by enormous individual variation, as convincingly demonstrated in the large-scale research by Fenson and colleagues producing norms for vocabulary in the first few years (Fenson et al., 1994). This inherent variability makes a controlled study of vocabulary acquisition across *groups* of children especially perilous. A properly controlled study of the effects of bilingualism on lexical acquisition would need to compare the vocabulary of bilingual children in terms of its size, conceptual coverage, and linguistic sophistication to the vocabulary they *would have had* in each language had they been learning only one of them. Such hypothetical speculation is quite obviously untestable, so conclusions about relative vocabulary development in monolingual and bilingual children must be interpreted with great caution.

A second impediment to accurate estimates of the influence of bilingualism on vocabulary development is that the specific pairs of languages that bilingual children are learning will undoubtedly affect the acquisition of vocabulary in each of them. Children whose two languages are structurally similar and share many cognates are more likely to progress more rapidly in each of them, even though these children devote half the time to learning each language than do monolingual children. Thus children who are learning both English and Spanish from birth at home would be expected to demonstrate fewer delays in vocabulary acquisition in each language than do children who are learning English and Chinese under similar circumstances.

Measures of Vocabulary Size

Two formal measures of vocabulary size that have been used in research on language acquisition in bilingual children are the MacArthur Communicative Development Inventory (CDI; Fenson et al., 1993) for productive vocabulary and the Peabody Picture Vocabulary Test (PPVT-III; Dunn & Dunn, 1997) for receptive vocabulary. In the CDI, parents complete forms containing of a detailed list of words that normally comprise children's early vocabulary and indicate which of the words their child is able to use. In the PPVT, children are shown plates containing four pictures, the experimenter names one of the pictures, and children indicate which picture corresponds

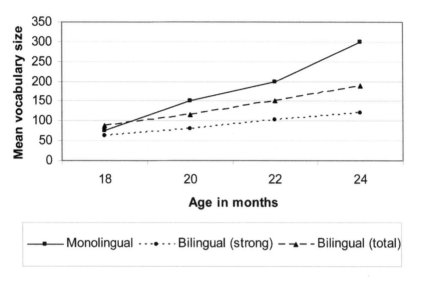

FIGURE 5.1. Vocabulary development in monolingual (data from Fenson et al., 1993) and Spanish–English bilingual (data from Pearson & Fernández, 1994) children.

but the remaining eight bilinguals were well below the 10th percentile for the monolingual norms. Considering only the vocabulary development in their *stronger* language, the bilingual children were consistently below the reported norms for monolingual children learning to speak in English.

In our ongoing research with monolingual and bilingual school-age children, we routinely administer the PPVT-III of receptive vocabulary to establish children's level of language proficiency and to compare that proficiency across the children in the two language groups. Therefore we combined the results of 16 recent studies based on 963 participants to obtain a composite picture of the language abilities of these children. The sample included 171 5-year-olds, 495 6-year-olds, 126 7-year-olds, 126 8-year-olds, and 45 9-year-olds, with approximately half of the children at each age level being bilingual. The bilingual children spoke a wide range of different languages at home, all were being educated in English, and all the children continued to use both languages every day. We examined the PPVT-III scores by age and language group. The standard scores are plotted in Figure 5.2. A two-way analysis of variance (ANOVA) for age and language group revealed a large and significant effect of language group in which monolinguals obtained higher scores than bilinguals, $F(1,953) = 141.53, p < .0001$. There was also an effect of age group, $F(4,93) = 4.48, p < .002$, because the 5-year-olds obtained higher scores than did the other children, but there was no interaction of age and language group, $F < 1$. Therefore it is clear that at

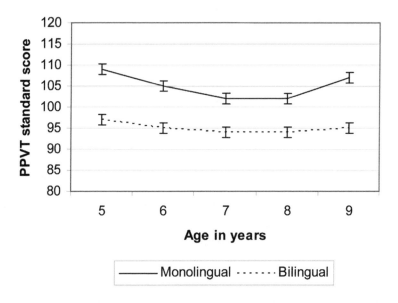

FIGURE 5.2. Mean PPVT-III standard scores and standard errors of 963 children, ages 5 to 9 years, combined from 16 studies.

all the ages included in this sample there is a substantial and persistent delay in vocabulary acquisition for the bilingual children.

The pattern obtained both by examining productive vocabulary scores of children in the first 2 years of life and receptive vocabulary scores of children in preschool and early school years is the same: There is a significant delay in the acquisition of vocabulary by bilingual children, especially when they are compared to monolingual peers who only speak that language. There is no doubt that the situation improves greatly if bilingual children are evaluated in terms of both of their languages, and it is equally certain that the communicative ability of bilingual children is at least as good as monolingual children, and possibly better because of a more varied resource of expressive options. Therefore the implication of this vocabulary deficit is not going to be found in oral speech ability or communication.

Possible Factors Influencing Reduced Vocabulary Size

Although communication is probably not impaired, the consequences of the vocabulary deficit for bilingual children may nonetheless be consequential because of the role of vocabulary in the acquisition of other verbal abilities. Many of the high-level verbal skills developed in school, notably literacy, are strongly correlated with oral proficiency and vocabulary size (review in

Stahl & Nagy, 2006). Therefore it may be that diminished vocabulary in the language of schooling places children at risk in the acquisition of literacy. At the same time, literacy also rests on prerequisites for which bilingual children have demonstrated an advantage, such as concepts of print, or at least no disadvantage, such as phonological awareness (Bialystok, 2002). Therefore the decrease in vocabulary size on its own may not adversely affect the acquisition of literacy.

We conducted a study to investigate some of the factors responsible for 6-year-old monolingual and bilingual children learning to read in first grade, where the bilingual children were learning to read in both their languages (Bialystok, Luk, & Kwan, 2005). There were three groups of bilingual children, chosen because of the different relationships between their non-English language and spoken and written English. The three groups were Spanish–English bilinguals, Hebrew–English bilinguals, and Chinese–English bilinguals. In the analysis of children's performance on a test of English nonword decoding, the Spanish–English and Hebrew–English children obtained higher scores than did the monolinguals and Chinese–English bilinguals. However, once vocabulary level, as measured by the PPVT-III standard scores, were partialled out in an analysis of covariance, all the bilingual children outperformed the monolingual children. Therefore the lower vocabulary did not necessarily hinder the bilingual children in their progress in English reading, but once vocabulary was statistically controlled to be comparable to that of monolingual speakers, the English decoding performance of the bilingual children improved.

In summary, evidence from a number of sources has demonstrated a generally slower acquisition of vocabulary for bilingual children when compared to monolingual speakers of one of their languages. There is no evidence, however, that bilingual children are incompetent communicators, and little evidence that the vocabulary deficit impairs other abilities. When vocabulary is adjusted, for example, reading acquisition proceeds at least as well for bilinguals as for monolinguals, and probably better. The real experience of the child in the classroom, however, requires dealing with that vocabulary deficit; children do not enjoy the privilege of the hypothetical situation that is offered by controlled statistical analyses. Therefore we examine two other aspects of verbal ability to determine whether bilingual children with overall lower vocabularies than monolingual children experience delays in other aspects of verbal proficiency.

SEMANTIC FLUENCY AND SHORT-TERM RECALL

Adult Bilingual Research

Research with adults has consistently shown that bilinguals perform more poorly than monolinguals on tests based on rapid lexical retrieval (Gollan

& Kroll, 2001; Michael & Gollan, 2005). Evidence for these lexical deficiencies has been found in such tasks as picture naming (Roberts, Garcia, Desrochers, & Hernandez, 2002), lexical decision (Randsell & Fischler, 1987), and tip-of-the tongue, where bilinguals experience more lapses than monolinguals (Gollan & Acenas, 2004).

The letter and category fluency task is a standardized task that is often used as part of a battery of neuropsychological tests to identify problems in cognitive functioning (Borkowski, Benton, & Spreen, 1967). Participants must generate as many words as possible in a fixed amount of time, usually 1 minute, that conform to a restriction given either by category membership (semantic fluency) or an initial letter (phonological fluency). Research with bilinguals has frequently reported bilingual deficits on both versions of this task (Gollan, Montoya, & Werner, 2002; Rosselli et al., 2000).

Studies with monolinguals have shown that performance on these fluency tests is related to language proficiency, specifically, to vocabulary size (Hedden, Lautenschlager, & Park, 2005; Salthouse, 1993), and as we have discussed above, bilinguals frequently control smaller vocabulary in each language than monolinguals. Although there is much less research comparing the vocabulary size of monolingual and bilingual adults than there is on the same question for children, it may be that bilingual children's reduced scores on fluency tests reflect smaller vocabularies rather than slower verbal processing. Therefore it is important to reexamine the fluency data from adults in terms of vocabulary level to determine whether the bilingual deficits indicate actual linguistic processing differences (fluency test scores) or simply baseline knowledge differences (vocabulary scores). In two studies with monolingual and bilingual adults, we showed that initial differences showing bilingual disadvantages in fluency tasks disappeared when vocabulary size of the two groups was matched; bilinguals performed either as well as vocabulary-matched monolinguals (Study 1) or surpassed them on the more difficult phonological fluency task (Study 2) (Bialystok, Craik, & Luk, 2008). Although such approaches do not change the fact that bilinguals usually do perform more poorly than monolinguals on these tasks, they help to isolate the reason for those differences into a specific factor that is often (but not necessarily) associated with bilingualism, namely, vocabulary size, rather than to a more general processing difference that accompanies bilingualism.

Child Bilingual Research

We are not aware of any research that has systematically examined children on these tests and determined whether fluency disadvantages also characterize the language abilities of bilingual children. It would seem that bilingual children would be more susceptible to such differences than bilingual adults because the vocabulary gap in children is more substantial relative to total vocabulary.

Some limited evidence relevant to this question can be extracted from our current research. In two studies with monolingual and bilingual children, we included a test of category fluency as part of the battery of background measures. The children in both studies were 6 years old, and each study contained 25 monolinguals and 25 bilinguals, for a total sample of 100 children. Children were asked to name as many animals as they could in 60 seconds, and the fluency score was the total number of appropriate responses produced in this time. Combining the results from the two studies, the mean number of words generated by the monolinguals was 11.32 (SD = 2.8) and by the bilinguals was 10.61 (SD = 2.3), a difference that was not significant, F (1,99) = 1.93, n.s. Separate analyses of the results of the studies individually confirmed this pattern (Study 1: t (49) = 1.7, n.s.; Study 2: $t < 1$). However, these results need to be interpreted cautiously both because of the limited amount of data and because the initial vocabulary differences between the monolingual and bilingual children in these two samples was very small, perhaps erasing potential differences in semantic fluency. Nonetheless, the results do show that in a sample of monolingual and bilingual children for whom vocabulary scores are comparable, there is no difference in performance on a semantic fluency test.

Another aspect of rapid lexical access and retrieval is indicated by the ability to hold items in memory and recite them back, as in short-term verbal memory tasks. Gathercole (2002) reports evidence for the "lexicality effect," which is the increase in short-term memory that is tied to the increase in lexical knowledge with age. Thus the ability to hold strings of words in mind in part depends on lexical representations and vocabulary knowledge. Again, bilingual children might be disadvantaged in short-term memory because they typically command smaller vocabulary and weaker lexical representations in each language than do monolingual children.

In three different experiments involving a total of 190 children, we administered a test of short-term verbal memory by asking children to recall increasingly long strings of animal names and report them back in the order in which they were heard. Testing began with strings of two animals. Children were given two trials to complete at each string length before proceeding to the longer string. Testing stopped when children failed to report the animals correctly for both trials at a given string length. The span length is the longest string for which children could complete at least one of the trials.

The mean score on the animal span task across the three studies is plotted by age group in Figure 5.3. It is clear from the graph that there is no difference between language groups, F (1,180) = 1.01, n.s. There was almost a difference in span across the ages studied, although the difference was not quite significant, F (4,180) = 2.31, p = .06, with no interaction between language and age, $F < 1$. All the children in these studies also completed the PPVT-III. Unlike the results from the animal span test, however, the difference in PPVT-III standard scores for the monolinguals (M = 101.7, SD = 10.3) and bilinguals (M = 95.0, SD = 12.6) was significant, F (1,179) =

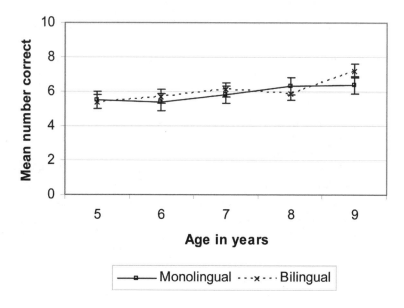

FIGURE 5.3. Mean score on animal span task and standard error by age, collapsed across three studies with 190 children.

19.37, $p < .0001$. Therefore, even with clear differences in vocabulary recognition, there was no evidence of difference in short-term verbal memory.

It seems plausible that the vocabulary deficit observed in bilingual children would translate into deficiencies of lexical access or verbal processing, but there was no evidence in the limited data examined. The results from the analysis of semantic fluency need to be treated with special caution because the sample was small and the vocabulary scores of the monolinguals and bilinguals did not differ significantly. However, the pattern showing no difference in lexical access and retrieval was replicated using the short-term test of animal span. This analysis was based on a larger number of participants, and the initial vocabulary difference between groups was robust. Therefore it appears that smaller vocabulary does not impede bilingual children's ability to rapidly access and recall lexical items.

VERBAL MEMORY AND RELEASE
FROM PROACTIVE INTERFERENCE

The Proactive Interference Paradigm

Proactive interference (PI) occurs when retrieval of recent material is impaired by the prior exposure to similar items. The continued presentation of material to be learned that shares category membership makes it difficult to keep track of which information was heard most recently and the ability to accurately recall the items on the last presented list decreases. This decrease in recall over similar lists reflects the buildup of PI. If the category membership of the items is changed on a subsequent list, recall is restored to the original level. This return to better recall indicates the release from PI.

In one major paradigm used to assess release from PI developed by Engle and colleagues (Kane & Engle, 2000), participants are given four sequential lists of words to recall. Following each list, participants engage in a filler task to prevent rehearsal and are then asked to report as many words as possible from the words just presented. The words in the first three lists are members of the same semantic category, but the words in list 4 belong to a different category. In this way, PI is built up through the first three lists and the release is shown through the change of category from list 3 to list 4. The decline in the number of words recalled in lists 2 and list 3 compared to list 1 is the index of the PI buildup and the restoration of recall in list 4 is the index of the PI release.

The PI buildup and release paradigm is used in memory research to indicate levels of controlled processing, as it is assumed that the ability to control attention to previously presented information is part of the executive function (e.g., Kane & Engle, 2000; Lustig, May, & Hasher, 2001). Therefore the PI paradigm provides a measure of executive function in a verbal task and indexes the extent to which the participant can exercise attentional control over the lists of words. Research based on this paradigm with monolingual children has indicated that PI buildup effect decreases between 4 and 13 years of age as children develop better cognitive control (Kail, 2002). This demand for cognitive control should be advantageous to bilinguals for whom these executive processes are better developed than they are in monolinguals.

In addition to assessing attentional control, however, the task also rests heavily on verbal proficiency. Therefore the bilingual deficit in vocabulary may make this task difficult for bilinguals, leading to lower performance than that found for monolinguals. Such a deficit would signal a consequence of the bilingual delay in vocabulary acquisition that might have implications for higher cognitive functioning, such as verbal memory.

The PI Paradigm Applied to Bilingual Children

We conducted a preliminary investigation of this question in a sample of 40 children who were 7 years old. Half of the children were bilingual in that they spoke a non-English language at home and attended school and community events entirely in English. There were 12 different non-English languages represented in the sample of 20 bilingual children. Children were given several background measures, including the PPVT-III and two short-term memory tests. As usual, the monolinguals (M = 105.3, SD = 9.5) had higher vocabulary scores than the bilinguals (M = 96.4, SD = 12.4), $F (1,38)$ = 6.51, $p < .01$. The first memory test required children to repeat increasingly long strings of English digits in their order of presentation, and the second required them to place the numbers into ascending order before repeating them. There were no group differences in either of these tests, both $Fs < 1$. Therefore there is no evidence that simple short-term memory in English is different for children in the two language groups.

For the PI task, children were presented with four consecutive lists of words containing five words each. The first three lists contained words from the same category and the fourth list represented a different category. The words were high-frequency words from the categories fruit, clothing, colors, and body parts (Battig & Montague, 1969). The words were presented both visually and auditorily on the computer at the rate of one word every 2 seconds and children were asked to say the word aloud when they saw each one. The presentation of the words was immediately followed by a filler task: a number randomly chosen between 14 and 29 was shown on the screen, and children counted forward from that number for 10 seconds. At the end of the 10 seconds, children were asked to recall the words from the list they just saw and were given 10 seconds to report as many of the words as they could remember. This immediately led to the next list of words.

The mean number of words recalled in each list for each language group is shown in Figure 5.4. The buildup of PI is determined by the decrease in the number of words recalled in lists 2 and 3 compared to list 1. The pattern clearly shows the standard effect of decreasing accuracy across the first three lists and recovery in list 4, $F (3,102) = 11.0$, $p < .0001$, and although the bilinguals showed a smaller decrement than the monolinguals, the difference was not significant. Performance can also be considered in terms of the difference in recall for each list relative to the participant's own baseline recall in list 1. This score, which represents the proportional change across lists, is calculated by dividing the difference between the number of words recalled on list 1 and list n by the number of words recalled on list 1. These proportional changes in recall are shown in Figure 5.5. Again, there is a strong effect of list, $F (2,68) = 6.14$, $p < .003$, and a trend for the bilinguals to show a smaller decline that is almost significant, $F (1,34) = 3.06$, $p = .08$.

Recall errors in lists 2 and 3 indicate intrusions in that they are words from the category that appeared on a previous list. The ability to monitor the lists to prevent intrusions is a function of executive control, so the relevant data are the frequency of intrusions. The mean number of intrusions by each group is shown in Figure 5.6. Bilingual children produced fewer intrusions than monolingual children, $F (1,38) = 7.00$, $p < .02$. This effect of language provides evidence for bilingual children's better executive control in the context of verbal memory task performance.

This study investigating language group differences in PI provides some

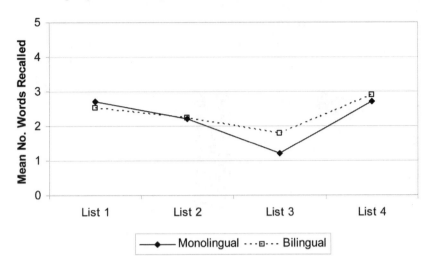

FIGURE 5.4. Mean number of words recalled in each list by monolinguals and bilinguals.

preliminary evidence that, at worst, there are no bilingual disadvantages relative to monolinguals in the ability to control attention to lists of words, and there may even be some advantages, even though the receptive vocabulary of the bilinguals in the language of testing was significantly lower than that of the monolinguals. There was a tendency for the bilinguals to experience less interference from the competing words and show less build-up of PI than did the monolinguals. These results are in line with our research with executive function tasks, such as the Simon task, in which bilingual children were less distracted by the irrelevant position of a stimulus and more successful in responding to a target feature (Martin-Rhee & Bialystok, 2008). These data provide preliminary support for the notion that the precocious ability of bilingual children to control attention when there is distracting information extends to verbal material.

CONCLUSION

It is often claimed that bilingual children experience a deficit in language proficiency relative to monolinguals. Anecdotally, parents and teachers report that bilingual children know fewer words or progress more slowly in language acquisition than do monolinguals, an impression that has been confirmed by empirical research on vocabulary size. It is not surprising that bilingual children know fewer words in each of their languages than do

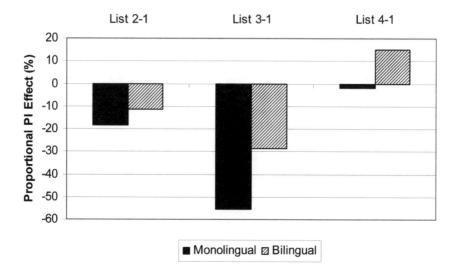

FIGURE 5.5. Mean proportional change in number of words recalled across lists by language group.

monolingual children; after all, they are building up two lexical systems to integrate into a semantic network. But does this deficiency in vocabulary size have implications for other crucial aspects of verbal ability and verbal processing that are established during childhood?

We examined evidence from short-term verbal memory (animal span) and production (fluency) tasks and verbal monitoring and memory with executive control in verbal tasks (PI buildup and release from PI) and found no evidence for bilingual deficits in the ability to process, recall, and monitor lists of words. Moreover, in tasks that included higher levels of executive control to keep track of the serial items, the bilinguals began to show an advantage over monolinguals in spite of controlling a smaller vocabulary. This divergence between groups is important because basic vocabulary size predicts performance on these memory tasks. Therefore, the bilinguals were able to not only compensate for a smaller vocabulary but also to profit from their higher executive control in performing these tasks.

This pattern of results places the verbal abilities of bilingual children in a context that takes account of both potential advantages and disadvantages that are related to their unique experience in learning two languages. Results also demonstrate that there is no evidence that bilingualism itself should be treated as a negative experience. Despite decrements in vocabulary size, bilingual children showed no significant detriments in performing

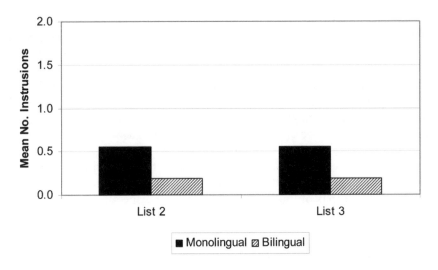

FIGURE 5.6. Mean number of intrusions in list 2 and list 3 by language group.

verbal tests, and in cases where higher control processes were involved, even showed potential advantages.

There are several salient characteristics of the bilingual children in the studies reviewed here that potentially restrict the generality of these conclusions. First, the children are bilingual in the sense that they have been learning two languages at home since birth; they are not second-language learners who are confronting school in a weak language as are the children in the studies by Geva and Lafrance and Oller et al. (Chapter 10 and Chapter 4, this volume). Consequently, it is difficult to designate the languages as first (L1) or second (L2), as is usually done in this kind of research. Nonetheless, these bilingual children were being educated entirely through English, and all the tests were conducted in English, so differences between the abilities of the bilingual and monolingual children in the language of schooling is important to determine. Second, because of the diversity in language background, we did not conduct formal assessments of children's proficiency in the home language; this information was obtained solely by responses in a parent questionnaire. Therefore we were unable to determine whether developing English proficiency resulted in weakening proficiency in the home language or, more generally, if there were trade-offs between these, as reported by Oller and colleagues (Chapter 4, this volume). However, for those children whose bilingualism emerges from an early and constant exposure to two languages, there is no reason to conclude that a reduction in the speed or depth of vocabulary acquisition in each language translates into significant costs in lexical or cognitive processing.

More than forty years ago, Macnamara (1966) warned that the verbal deficiencies of bilingual children would lead to dire consequences for their educational and cognitive development. The main evidence upon which he based those claims was that children being educated through Irish, their weaker language, performed more poorly in math classes than did children being educated through English. But his studies were uncontrolled and incomplete; research over the past several decades has replaced his pessimism with a more optimistic view of the consequences of bilingualism. The studies reviewed in the present chapter add to that positive tradition and demonstrate that basic verbal abilities in bilingual children are not compromised, even when they are accompanied by a vocabulary size that is smaller than that of monolingual children who speak only one of their languages.

ACKNOWLEDGMENTS

The research reported in this chapter was funded by Grant No. A2559 from the National Sciences and Engineering Research Council of Canada and Grant No. R01HD052523 from the National Institutes of Health to Ellen Bialystok. We thank Gigi Luk for her assistance in preparing the chapter.

REFERENCES

Barnard, R., & Glynn, T. (2003). *Bilingual children's language and literacy development*. Clevedon, UK: Multilingual Matters.

Battig, W. F., & Montague, W. E. (1969). Category norms for verbal items in 56 categories: A replication and extension of the Connecticut category norms. *Journal of Experimental Psychology, 80*, 1–46.

Bialystok, E. (2001). *Bilingualism in development: Language, literacy, and cognition*. New York: Cambridge University Press.

Bialystok, E. (2002). Acquisition of literacy in bilingual children: A framework for research. *Language Learning, 52*, 159–199.

Bialystok, E., Craik, F. I. M., & Luk, G. (2008). Lexical access in bilinguals: Effects of vocabulary size and executive control. *Journal of Neurolinguistics, 21*, 522–538.

Bialystok, E., Luk, G., & Kwan, E. (2005). Bilingualism, biliteracy, and learning to read: Interactions among languages and writing systems. *Scientific Studies of Reading, 9*, 43–61.

Bialystok, E., & Martin, M. M. (2004). Attention and inhibition in bilingual children: Evidence from the dimensional change card sort task. *Developmental Science, 7*, 325–339.

Bialystok, E., & Shapero, D. (2005). Ambiguous benefits: The effect of bilingualism on reversing ambiguous figures. *Developmental Science, 8*, 595–604.

Borkowski, J. G., Benton, A. L., & Spreen, O. (1967). Word fluency and brain damage. *Neuropsychologia, 5,* 135–140.

Carlson, S. M., & Meltzoff, A. N. (2008). Bilingual experience and executive functioning in young children. *Developmental Science, 11,* 282–298.

Dunn, L. M., & Dunn, L. M. (1997). *Peabody Picture Vocabulary Test—3rd Edition.* Circle Pines, MN: American Guidance Service.

Durgunoğlu, A. Y. (1997). Bilingual reading: Its components, development, and other issues. In A. M. B. de Groot & J. F. Kroll (Eds.), *Tutorials in bilingualism: Psycholinguistic perspectives* (pp. 255–276). Mahwah, NJ: Erlbaum.

Eviatar, Z., & Ibrahim, R. (2000). Bilingual is as bilingual does: Metalinguistic abilities of Arabic-speaking children. *Applied Psycholinguistics, 21,* 451–471.

Fenson, L., Dale, P. S., Reznick, J. S., Bates, E., Thal, D., & Pethick, S. J. (1994). Variability in early communicative development. *Monographs of the Society for Research in Child Development, 59,* v–173.

Fenson, L., Dale, P. S., Reznick, J. S., Thal, D., Bates, E., Hartung, J. P., et al. (1993). *MacArthur communicative development inventories.* San Diego, CA: Singular Publishing Group.

Francis, N. (2002). Literacy, second language learning, and the development of metalinguistic awareness: A study of bilingual children's perceptions of focus on form. *Linguistics and Education, 13,* 373–404.

Gathercole, S. E. (2002). Memory development during the childhood years. In A.D. Baddeley, M.D. Kopelman, & B. A. Wilson (Eds.), *The handbook of memory disorders* (2nd ed., pp. 475–500). West Sussex, UK: Wiley.

Galambos, S. J., & Goldin-Meadow, S. (1990). The effects of learning two languages on levels of metalinguistic awareness. *Cognition, 34,* 1–56.

Geva, E., & Wade-Woolley, L. (1998). Component processes in becoming English–Hebrew bilterate. In A. Y. Durgunoğlu & L. Verhoeven (Eds.), *Literacy development in a multilingual context: Cross-cultural perspectives* (pp. 85–110). Mahwah, NJ: Erlbaum.

Gollan, T. H., & Acenas, L.-A. R. (2004). What is a TOT?: Cognate and translation effects on tip-of-the-tongue states in Spanish–English and Tagalog–English bilinguals. *Journal of Experimental Psychology: Learning, Memory, and Cognition, 30,* 246–269.

Gollan, T. H., & Kroll, J. F. (2001). Bilingual lexical access. In B. Rapp (Ed.), *The handbook of cognitive neuropsychology: What deficits reveal about the human mind* (pp. 321–345). Philadelphia: Psychology Press.

Gollan, T. H., Montoya, R. I., & Werner, G. (2002). Semantic and letter fluency in Spanish–English bilinguals. *Neuropsychology, 16,* 562–576.

Hedden, T., Lautenschlager, G., & Park, D. (2005).Contributions of processing ability and knowledge to verbal memory tasks across the adult lifespan. *The Quarterly Journal of Experimental Psychology A, 58,* 169–190.

Kail, R. (2002). Development change in proactive interference. *Child Development, 73,* 1703–1717.

Kane, M. J., & Engle, R. W. (2000).Working-memory capacity, proactive interference, and divided attention: Limits on long-term memory retrieval. *Journal of Experimental Psychology: Learning, Memory, and Cognition, 26,* 336–358.

Liow, S. J. R., & Lau, L. H. (2006). The development of bilingual children's early spelling in English. *Journal of Educational Psychology, 98,* 868–878.

Lustig, C., May, C. P., & Hasher, L. (2001). Working memory span and the role of proactive interference. *Journal of Experimental Psychology: General, 130,* 199–207.

Macnamara, J. (1966). *Bilingualism and primary education.* Edinburgh: Edinburgh University Press.

Mahon, M., & Crutchley, A. (2006). Performance of typically developing school-age children with English as an additional language on the British Picture Vocabulary Scales II. *Child Language Teaching and Therapy, 22,* 333–351.

Martin-Rhee, M. M., & Bialystok, E. (2008). The development of two types of inhibitory control in monolingual and bilingual children. *Bilingualism: Language and Cognition, 11,* 81–93.

Michael, E. B., & Gollan, T. H. (2005). Being and becoming bilingual: Individual differences and consequences for language production. In J. F. Kroll & A. M. B. de Groot (Eds.), *Handbook of bilingualism: Psycholinguistic approaches* (pp. 389–407). New York: Oxford University Press.

Oller, D. K., & Eilers, R. E. (Eds.). (2002). *Language and literacy in bilingual children.* Clevedon, UK: Multilingual Matters.

Pearson, B. Z., & Fernández, S. C. (1994). Patterns of interaction in the lexical growth in two languages of bilingual infants and toddlers. *Language Learning, 44,* 617–653.

Pearson, B. Z., Fernández, S. C., & Oller, D. K. (1993). Lexical development in bilingual infants and toddlers: Comparison to monolingual norms. *Language Learning, 43,* 93–120.

Ransdell, S. E., & Fischler, I. (1987). Memory in a monolingual mode: When are bilinguals at a disadvantage? *Journal of Memory and Language, 26,* 392–405.

Roberts, P. M., Garcia, L. J., Desrochers, A., & Hernandez, D. (2002). English performance of proficient bilingual adults on the Boston Naming Test. *Aphasiology, 16,* 635–645.

Rosselli, M., Ardila, A., Araujo, K., Weekes, V. A., Caracciolo, V., Padilla, M., et al. (2000). Verbal fluency and verbal repetition skills in healthy older Spanish–English bilinguals. *Applied Neuropsychology, 7,* 17-24.

Salthouse, T. A. (1993). Speed and knowledge as determinants of adult age differences in verbal tasks. *Journal of Gerontology: Psychological Sciences, 48,* 29–36.

Stahl, S. A., & Nagy, W. E. (2006). *Teaching word meanings.* Mahwah, NJ: Erlbaum.

Swanson, H. L., Sáez, L., & Gerber, M. (2006). Growth in literacy and cognition in bilingual children at risk or not at risk for reading disabilities. *Journal of Educational Psychology, 98,* 247–264.

PART III

■ ■ ■

Literacy and Dual-Language Learners

CHAPTER 6

■ ■ ■

Factors Affecting the Relative Relationships between First- and Second-Language Phonological Awareness and Second-Language Reading

ALEXANDRA GOTTARDO
YAN GU
JULIE MUELLER
IULIANA BACIU
ANA LAURA PAUCHULO

This chapter examines the relationships between first-language (L1) and second-language (L2) phonological awareness and, in most cases, L2 word reading in children who are second-language learners (LL). This topic has both theoretical and practical importance. Theoretically, it is important because it will assist in building models of L2 acquisition and of relationships between L1 and L2 skills. Practically, it is important because teachers and practitioners ask for screening tools to determine which LLs are at risk for reading difficulties, whether the children are normally developing LLs or are experiencing additional difficulties, and whether assessments should be conducted in the child's L1 or L2. The chapter discusses findings from our lab and refers to research published in the area. The list of reviewed research is not exhaustive and is not meant to purposely exclude any research or researchers.

Research with monolingual English speakers examines whether phonological awareness is a unitary skill or many separate skills. At one end of the spectrum is the belief that true phonological awareness includes only phoneme-level skills and the conscious reflection on abstract representations of speech (Morais, 1991). This metalinguistic ability develops alongside general metacognitive control processes during middle childhood (Tunmer, 1991). A second definition of phonological awareness includes the awareness of all subsyllabic skills in the construct (Anthony & Lonigan, 2004). In addition, Stanovich (1992) claimed that the construct of phonological awareness should not be related to the idea of consciousness, as consciousness is hard to operationalize. Instead, he viewed phonological sensitivity as being along a continuum from a shallow sensitivity to large phonological units, to a deep sensitivity to small phonological units. In their meta-analysis, Anthony and Lonigan (2004) found that rhyme sensitivity, segmental awareness, and phonemic awareness were best characterized as manifestations of the same phonological ability in monolingual English speakers. The results of the analyses argued for a unitary construct encompassing all levels of phonological awareness, although certain tasks might be better indicators at different ages. This characterization is used in the chapter to describe phonological awareness.

Research with bilinguals examining cognitive factors related to reading only began about a decade ago (Bruck, Genesee, & Caravolas, 1997; Durgunoğlu, Nagy, & Hancin-Bhatt, 1993). In bilinguals some linguistic tasks, specifically phonological awareness, show higher L1 to L2 relationships, suggesting a language-general linguistic skill, while other skills such as vocabulary knowledge are best characterized as language specific. Language-general linguistic knowledge, such as phonological awareness, may need to be acquired only once while acquiring L1 literacy (Durgunoğlu, 2002; Sparks, Patton, Ganschow, Humbach, & Javorsky, 2008). In this case, L1 proficiency should strongly influence L2 acquisition (English, Leafstedt, Gerber, & Villaruz, 2001; Durgunoğlu, 2002; Flege, Frieda, & Nozawa, 1997). At present, no consensus exists as to whether phonological awareness in the L1 and L2 is a unitary construct or two related skills. Researchers have found that both L1 and L2 phonological awareness are related to L2 reading (see Durgunoğlu, 2002; Geva & Wang, 2001, for reviews), but that these skills are not always completely overlapping (Branum-Martin et al., 2006; Gottardo & Mueller, 2009). This chapter reviews factors that could influence relations between L1 and L2 phonological awareness and L2 reading and might explain differing results across studies.

Other than general linguistic ability, few factors mediating the relationship between phonological awareness and reading have been examined in bilinguals. However, additional contextual and child-related variables should be considered when examining the relative contributions of L1 and/or L2 phonological awareness to reading, in most cases L2 word-level reading. The factors mediating relations between L1 and L2 phonological awareness and reading discussed in this chapter include: (1) cognitive and linguistic factors, such as the characteristics of the languages being spoken and read, as well as within-child cognitive and experiential factors; (2) environmental and contextual factors; and (3) methodological issues. These factors are defined and discussed in greater detail throughout the chapter. Cognitive factors such as nonverbal reasoning and demographic variables such as parental education might mediate the relationship between phonological awareness and reading in children who are LLs. In addition, the same variables might show differential relationships to L2 reading in younger versus older LLs. Where possible, the relative contributions of L1 versus L2 phonological awareness to reading are examined in this chapter. To begin, we review two studies testing measurement models of L1 and L2 phonological awareness in bilinguals to determine whether L1 and L2 phonological awareness are unitary constructs or separate but related constructs.

MEASUREMENT MODELS

Measurement issues include the development of models to examine the relations between L1 and L2 phonological awareness. Branum-Martin et al. (2006) suggest that the measurement of phonological awareness in LLs and relations between L1 and L2 phonological awareness in bilinguals have not been fully determined. For bilinguals, measurement and definitional issues might be even more complex than measurement of phonological awareness in monolinguals (see Anthony & Longian, 2004, for a detailed discussion of assessment of phonological awareness in monolinguals).

In their study, Branum-Martin et al. (2006) tested four models examining the relationships between Spanish (L1) and English (L2) phonological awareness and L1 and L2 reading. The models included student and classroom effects and tested whether phonological awareness was a single language-independent factor at the student level and at the classroom level or two separate language-specific factors. The best-fitting model had language-specific L1 and L2 factors at the classroom and student levels, although abilities were also highly related at the student level (Branum-Martin et al., 2006). The different levels of phonological awareness in each language—specifically, blending, segmenting, and elision—were part of a single factor within each language.

We also examined a measurement model to determine whether L1 (Spanish) and L2 measures of oral language proficiency (OLP) and phonological awareness were related to L2 reading comprehension (Gottardo & Mueller, 2009). The measures included: L2 word reading, L1 and L2 vocabulary and oral cloze, L1 phoneme detection as well as rhyme, initial phoneme and final phoneme matching and L2 initial phoneme detection, phoneme deletion, and sound blending. With the exception of the standardized vocabulary measures, Peabody Picture Vocabulary Test–III (PPVT–III; Dunn & Dunn, 1997) and Test de Vocabulario en Imagenes Peabody (TVIP; Dunn, Lugo, Padilla, & Dunn, 1986), the measures were experimental tasks that had been used extensively and had excellent to good reliability.

Initially, intercorrelations that were calculated across languages suggested that the latent constructs discriminated by language. That is, the intercorrelations among English OLP measures and the Spanish OLP measures were nonsignificant (ranging from $r = -.04$ to .22). The phonological awareness correlations indicated less discrimination between languages. The Spanish phoneme detection task was significantly correlated with all three English phonological awareness measures (ranging from $r = .33$ to .44). The English phoneme detection task was also significantly correlated with the Spanish initial phoneme task ($r = .45$). The English phoneme deletion task was significantly correlated with the Spanish rhyming task ($r = .31$). The significant correlations across the languages suggested that phonological awareness might be related across languages.

A measurement model was tested using a confirmatory factor analysis to determine whether the observed variables served as adequate indicators of the latent variables. Initially, a three-factor measurement model was tested based on the assumption that phonological awareness, oral language, and word reading were three unique yet correlated latent constructs. This model included three factors: (1) L1 and L2 phonological awareness, (2) L1 and L2 oral language proficiency, and (3) L2 word-level reading. This measurement model tested the hypothesis that tasks in both English and Spanish were measuring the same construct; that is, English phonological awareness tasks and Spanish phonological awareness tasks both measured the same construct of phonological awareness. Three widely used indices of goodness of fit were utilized in analysis of the model: the chi-square statistic, the comparative fit index (CFI), and the root mean square of approximation (RMSEA).

The fit of the three-factor model was not good. The three goodness of fit indices were not within the desired range, $\chi^2 = 148.98$, $df = 62$, $p = .001$; CFI = .81; RMSEA = .10 (Kline, 1998). In addition, although only one observed variable had a nonsignificant factor loading (TVIP on OLP), several factor loadings were lower than .60. The lack of fit and the low factor loadings suggested that the observed variables were not strong indicators of the latent constructs. The lower factor loadings for the Spanish measures suggested that the constructs could be split according to language. The nonsignificant intercorrelations between Spanish and English measures also support a measurement model that splits constructs according to language.

A second confirmatory factor analysis was then conducted in which the latent constructs of phonological awareness and OLP were split according to language, resulting in five factors: (1) English phonological awareness, (2) Spanish phonological awareness, (3) English OLP, (4) Spanish OLP, and

(5) English word reading. The fit for this model was much better. All three fit indices were within the desired range, χ^2 = 67.73, df = 55, p = .116; CFI = .97; RMSEA = .04. All of the factor loadings from the observed variables to the latent constructs were significant, although some remained relatively low (Spanish rhyming task on Spanish PA = .45; Spanish picture vocabulary on Spanish OLP = .57) (see Figure 6.1).

To examine phonological awareness alone, a two-factor confirmatory factor analysis was conducted with only L1 phonological awareness and L2 phonological awareness. This analysis resulted in a good fitting model and moderate factor loadings. Although the chi square was significant (χ^2 = 24.28, df = 13, p = .029), the CFI and RMSEA were both within the acceptable range (CFI = .952 and RMSEA = .08). The factor loadings, with the exception of the Spanish rhyming task, were all above .60 for each construct (ranging from .63 to .91).

The results of the measurement model were consistent with the results of Branum-Martin et al.'s study (2006) that showed that L1 and L2 phonological awareness were two separate but highly related factors. It is likely that the relationship between L1 and L2 phonological awareness is influenced by multiple contextual, child-related, and task-related variables. As a result of these findings regarding the distinctive yet interrelated nature of L1 and L2 phonological awareness, the remaining sections of this chapter explore potential variables that influence relations among L1 and L2 phonological awareness and reading.

COGNITIVE AND LINGUISTIC FACTORS AND CONTEXTUAL AND INDIVIDUAL-DIFFERENCE VARIABLES

L1 and L2 Language and Script

With the exception of one study with adults, the research described in this chapter deals with children whose L1 is Spanish, Portuguese, or Chinese, and whose L2 is English. These languages were chosen due to the characteristics of their oral language and their script and due to differences in the demographic characteristics of their speakers. Demographic differences are discussed in greater detail below under environmental and contextual factors.

Orthography

Characteristics of the L1 orthography, specifically the size and consistency of speech units represented, affect the strategies readers use in reading their L1 and possibly their L2 (Frost, 1994; Ziegler & Goswami, 2005). The similarity of the L1 orthography to English can influence reading acquisition in English (Geva & Siegel, 2000; Mumtaz & Humphreys, 2001). Similarity can be

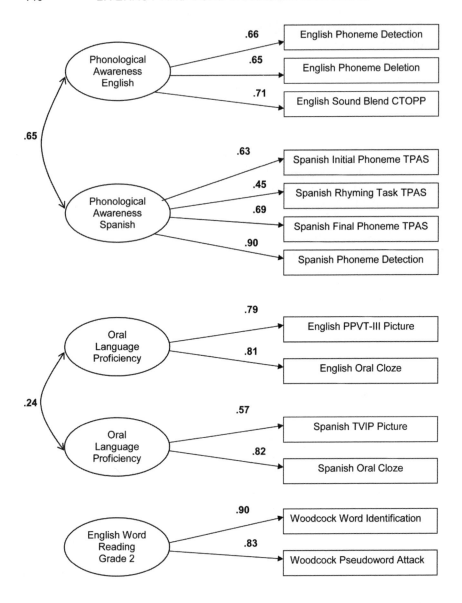

FIGURE 6.1. Measurement model with factor loadings for observed variables from latent constructs of phonological awareness and oral language proficiency in English and Spanish and word reading in English.

measured in terms of the type of script being used (English vs. Hebrew), similarity in the degree of consistency with which speech units are represented (English vs. Spanish) and similarity in the size of the orthographic unit being represented (English vs. Japanese) (see Ziegler & Goswami, 2005, for a discussion on how *grain size* influences L1 reading). One of these components, orthographic depth, refers to the regularity and consistency of the letter–sound correspondences in a language (Frost, 1994; Frost & Katz, 1992). A shallow orthography has regular and consistent letter–sound (grapheme–phoneme) mappings. The grapheme–phoneme correspondences in a deep orthography are less regular and consistent and might even map onto units larger than a phoneme. The current studies examine the impact of L1 script on learning to read English, which is a deep alphabetic orthography. English reading skills were compared in groups with "shallow" L1 orthographies (Spanish and Portuguese), and from a group with a "deep" (morphosyllabic) L1 orthography (Chinese) Ziegler and Goswami (2005) found that L1 reading strategies differ for Spanish and Portuguese speakers who learn to read regular and consistent scripts compared to English speakers for whom larger units such as rimes are consistent. Characteristics of Chinese script lead readers to use and access phonology from Chinese script in different ways (Perfetti & Liu, 2005; Perfetti, Liu, & Tan, 2005).

The Spanish writing system is a shallow or transparent orthography with regular and consistent mappings between Spanish graphemes and phonemes (Jiménez-González, 1997). Phonemic awareness and knowledge of letter–sound correspondences may be sufficient to read Spanish (Jiménez-González, 1997). Portuguese also has a shallow alphabetic orthography, although slightly less regular than Spanish, as evidenced by the greater number of phonological errors made by beginning readers (Defior, Martos, & Cary, 2002; Seymour, Aro, & Erskine, 2003). Research conducted with Portuguese–English bilinguals with reading difficulties showed that these children had lower pseudoword reading scores in both languages, suggesting a common phonological decoding deficit (DaFontoura & Siegel, 1995). In contrast, English script is characterized as a quasi-regular orthography with the regularity encoded at the level of the onset–rime (Plaut, McClelland, Seidenberg, & Patterson, 1996; Treiman, Mullennix, Bijeljac-Babic, & Richmond-Welty, 1995). On the continuum from shallow to deep orthography, English is a deep alphabetic orthography that maintains morphological relationships between root words and derived forms, at times at the cost of grapheme–phoneme correspondences (Seymour et al., 2003).

The other L1 script, Chinese, differs substantially from English script in terms of the nature of its sound–symbol relations. Chinese orthography is described as being morphosyllabic, with characters providing orthographic, morphological, and syllabic information rather than logographic information, as was previously believed (Leong & Tamaoka, 1998; Shu & Anderson, 1997). Although phonological information exists in Chinese characters, phonological awareness is more strongly related to pseudocharacter reading (Leong, Tan, Cheng, & Hau, 2005; Shu, Anderson, & Wu, 2000). Research by Perfetti and colleagues demonstrates that skilled readers of Chinese access the phonology of the characters at the same time as they identify the character (Perfetti & Liu, 2005; Perfetti et al., 2005). Therefore evidence shows that the child's specific L1 can influence strategies used in reading that language. However, relatively little research has examined the degree to which L1 reading strategies apply to L2 reading when different scripts are considered.

Phonological Typologies and Phonotactic Constraints

In addition to orthographic properties of the L1, phonological typology, phonological structure, and phonotactic constraints of the language could influence relations between phonological awareness and reading (Eckman, 2004). For the purpose of this chapter, phonological typology refers to the likelihood that specific phonemes (sounds) occur in a language. Phonotactic constraints refer to the probability that specific phoneme sequences occur or are permissible in a language. Phonological structure deals with the likelihood that native speakers of the language perceive syllables, onset–rime, or body–coda as the most salient phonological features (Alvarez, Carreiras, & Perea, 2004; Treiman et al., 1995; Yi, 1998).

Languages also differ in their relation to English in terms of the structure of lexical items. In some languages, cognates—words with similar phonological representations and meanings—could facilitate vocabulary learning. Spanish and Portuguese share some cognates with English by virtue of Latin roots common to the three languages. However, some words are false cognates, sounding similar but having different meanings. Consequently, cognates can cause both interference with language learning when the meanings differ and facilitation when the cognates have a similar pronunciation and share the same meaning (Nagy, García, Durgunoğlu, & Hancin-Bhatt, 1993). The presence of cognates and similarities in phonological typology might assist children in learning the vocabulary of English by using L1 vocabulary to acquire L2 words.

Chinese oral language differs significantly from English. Given that Chinese and English derive from different root languages, it is not surprising that the two languages do not share cognates unless the words have been imported from one language to another. Chinese words also differ from English words in terms of phonotactic constraints. They have a simpler syllabic structure than English words, with no consonant clusters (So & Dodd, 1995; Wong & Stokes, 2001). Therefore English vocabulary learning might differ for learners who must learn new root forms through paired-associate learning strategies.

Interactions between Script and Phonology

Although L1 and L2 phonological awareness are related regardless of language, differences might exist in the components of phonological awareness related to reading. These differences might arise from interrelations between L1 and L2 script and phonology mentioned previously. Studies have shown that phonological awareness skills in diverse L1s (e.g., Spanish, French, Hebrew, and Chinese) are related to reading English (Durgunoğlu et al., 1993; Geva & Siegel, 2000; Gottardo, Yan, Siegel, & Wade-Woolley, 2001; Lafrance & Gottardo, 2005; Lindsey, Manis, & Bailey, 2003; Manis, Lindsey, & Bailey, 2004). However, preliminary analyses of recent work with young children shows that slightly different components of L2 phonological awareness measured in kindergarten are related to L2 reading in first grade in bilingual Spanish–, Portuguese–, and Chinese–English speakers (Gottardo, Geva, Faroga, & Ramirez, 2006). All three groups of bilingual speakers had average to above-average reading scores in English in first grade. Predictors of first-grade L2 word reading included L2 phonological awareness as measured by syllable, onset–rime and phoneme elision tasks, L1 phonological awareness skills as measured by onset–rime-level tasks, and L2 reading in kindergarten. English onset–rime elision in kindergarten was significantly related to reading 1 year later in the Portuguese–English speakers ($n = 50$), beta = .395, $t\,(1, 49) = 3.34$, $p < .01$, even when kindergarten reading, which also had a significant beta weight, was entered in the equation, beta = .582, $t\,(1, 49) = 4.90$, $p < .001$. For the Spanish–English speakers ($n = 39$), English phoneme elision in kindergarten was significantly related to reading 1 year later, beta = .270, $t\,(1, 38) = 2.26$, $p < .05$, even when kindergarten reading, which also had a significant beta weight, was entered in the equation, beta = .676, $t\,(1, 49) = 5.90$, $p < .001$. For the Chinese–English speakers ($n = 39$) kindergarten reading was also significantly related to reading 1 year later, beta = .531, $t\,(1, 38) = 3.83$, $p < .001$. However, L2 syllable elision was the phonological awareness variable with the largest beta weight, beta = .237, $t\,(1, 38) = 1.97$, $p < .05$. None of the other phonological awareness variables approached significance for the Chinese group.

In the above sample, the specific component of L2 phonological awareness that was significantly related to L2 reading differed for each L1 group. For the Spanish–English-speaking group, phoneme awareness was most strongly related to English reading, possibly due to their shallow L1 orthography. The Portuguese–English speakers were more likely to resemble young English speakers for whom onset–rime awareness is related to beginning reading (Stuart & Coltheart, 1988). This result could be in part due to the fact that the Portuguese–English speakers showed a profile that was most similar to true simultaneous bilingualism, having the strongest English oral language skills and having been exposed to Portuguese and English at a young age. Finally, the large unit phonological awareness measure was most strongly related to English reading in the Chinese–English speaking group, despite the group's above-average mean reading scores in kindergarten and grade 1. These relationships are likely due to the large units that the children use in reading their L1, and the possibility that similar strategies are being adopted to read English.

When teaching English to speakers of different L1s, the linguistic characteristics of the L1 should be considered. For example, some learners might benefit from learning about larger orthographic units (e.g., word families) (Goswami, 1988), while other learners might benefit from small unit decoding strategies (e.g., explicit, systematic phonics). Additional research has shown that L1 phonotactic structure is related to the ease of performing specific phonological awareness tasks (Saiegh-Haddad, 2007).

Within-Child Factors

Within-child factors can mediate relations between reading and phonological awareness. These factors include but are not limited to the child's proficiency in the L2, whether the L1 or L2 is the dominant language, the child's age, as well as cognitive and linguistic factors such as speech perception skill and nonverbal reasoning ability.

Speech Perception

For monolingual English speakers, the search for factors underlying phonological awareness skill includes speech perception performance. Some researchers argue that speech perception skill is a precursor to phonological processing (Brady, 1997; McBride-Chang, 1996; Mody, Studdert-Kennedy, & Brady, 1997). Precise or differentiated phonological representations in one's L1 can enhance L1 phonological awareness (Elbro, 1998; Metsala & Walley, 1998; Walley, 1993; Walley, Metsala, & Garlock, 2003). In addition, reading acquisition could temporarily affect native and non-native speech perception (Burnham, 2003). Increases in phonological awareness and reading skills in beginning readers were related to better native language speech perception skill but also were accompanied by poorer non-native speech perception skill (Burnham, 2003). Non-native categorical perception skill decreased to a low point while native categorical perception improved at the same time that young beginning readers showed gains in phonological awareness and reading. Therefore successfully learning to read your native language might have temporary negative effects on oral learning of another language. But how does L2 categorical perception (i.e., the ability to categorize L2 phonemes in ways similar to native speakers of the language) relate to L2 phonological awareness and reading?

Research with bilingual adults found that considerable variability existed in the phonological processing and speech perception skills of L2 speakers (Flege, 1992). Sources of variability in L2 speech perception included age of acquisition and continued exposure to the L1 (Flege, 1992). Research has also shown that continued exposure to the L1 is related to L1 maintenance. For example if L1 use remains high, it is possible to maintain a foreign accent when speaking one's L2 even if the L2 was acquired prior to adolescence (Flege et al., 1997). Phoneme discrimination is also related to exposure to the L2, with beginning language learners sometimes placing novel L2 phonemes into existing L1 categories (Wade-Woolley & Geva, 2000).

Gottardo, Chiappe, Siegel, and Lafrance (2003) examined whether L2 phonological awareness is related to L2 reading in adults who are LL, and whether L2 speech perception mediates this relationship. Thirty-three LL adults were chosen from a reading assessment clinic sample. The participants were referred by accessible learning professionals at a university, community colleges, and employment and retraining services. The participants all had difficulty with the curriculum in their placements. As a result, the majority of the reading scores for the participants were in the low-average range (mean standard score = 85.3, SD = 22). The LL participants had a wide variety of L1s (e.g., Spanish n = 5, French n = 5, Farsi n = 5, Cantonese n = 5, Portuguese n = 2, Punjabi n = 4, Tagalog n = 2, and a West Coast First Nations language n = 2; and one person spoke each of the following L1s: Korean, Jamaican, and Hungarian). Due to the diversity of the languages of the participants in this sample, only L2 measures were administered. There was a wide range of ages of acquisition for the participants, with a mean age of acquisition of 9½ years. Some of the participants acquired English in early childhood, at 5 years of age. Other participants acquired English in adulthood with a maximum age of acquisition of 43 years. Key tasks included a categorical phoneme perception task in which the participants were asked to discriminate English /b/ versus /p/, and phonological awareness tasks that required the deletion of phonemes from words and pseudowords.

Hierarchical regression analyses were conducted separately for word and pseudoword reading. Predictor variables were entered in the following order: vocabulary, phoneme categorization, and phonological awareness to determine if L2 phonological awareness was related to L2 reading when control variables were entered. Only L2 phonological awareness accounted for unique variance on L2 word reading, 16.4%, beta = .453, t (1,32) = 3.40, p < .01, and pseudoword reading, 17.3%, beta = .467, t (1, 32) = 2.90, p < .01. Regression analyses that coded L1 by group, orthographically shallow (e.g., Spanish) versus orthographically deep (e.g., Chinese), or European versus Asian, revealed that L1 category was not significantly related to word and pseudoword reading scores. The relationships between L2 reading and L2 phonological awareness remained highly significant across the language groups. As with other research conducted with monolingual adults who are poor readers, phonological awareness was related to reading (Durgunoğlu & Öney, 2002; Gottardo, Siegel, & Stanovich, 1997; Öney & Durgunoğlu, 2005). However, unlike findings for monolingual children, categorical speech perception performance skill in the L2 was not related to reading in these participants.

Nonverbal Reasoning

Another variable that was examined in relation to L2 reading is nonverbal reasoning. Although it is not related to word reading in monolingual speakers (D'Angiulli & Siegel, 2003; Siegel, 1989), it should be considered in children who are LL. For example McBride-Chang (1995) examined component skills related to phonological awareness in monolingual English speakers. In addition to speech perception and verbal memory, general cognitive ability as measured by verbal and nonverbal reasoning components was uniquely related to phonological awareness. In a group of kindergarten children in Canada who were LL, nonverbal reasoning was related to L2 phonological awareness scores (Gottardo & Geva, 2005). Children from three L1 groups—Chinese, Portuguese, and Spanish—were assessed in their L1 and L2 on measures of phonological awareness and reading. Nonverbal reasoning was measured using the Matrix Analogies Test of nonverbal reasoning, a pattern completion task (Naglieri, 1989). The Chinese L1 children had above-average mean standard scores, $M = 128$, $SD = 12$. The mean standard scores for the groups of Portuguese and Spanish L1 children were in the average range, $M = 109$, $SD = 11$ and $M = 108$, $SD = 10$, respectively. Nonverbal reasoning was significantly related to L2 measures of word and pseudoword reading, syllable, onset-rime and phoneme deletion scores even when L1 category was partialed out of the correlation, $rs = .52, .47, .28, .29$, and $.25$, $p < .01$, respectively. In addition, nonverbal reasoning moderated group differences in L2 phonological awareness and reading in this mixed group of children who were LL. Analyses including the full sample showed that nonverbal reasoning was related to reading even when language category and phonological awareness were entered in the regression equation for word reading, beta $= .372$, $t(1, 118) = 5.05$, $p < .001$, and pseudoword reading, beta $= .356$, $t(1, 118) = 4.53$, $p < .001$. Phonological awareness was also uniquely related to word level reading. Bialystok (2001) found that the cognitive complexity of the phonological awareness task was related to the ease with which bilingual children completed the task. Therefore nonverbal reasoning should be measured in addition to phonological awareness and could be considered as a relevant factor in reading in children who are LL.

Age of Acquisition of L2 and Language Dominance:
Effects of Schooling

Research examining change in the neural organization of languages found that children who acquire their L2 after the preschool years, as young as 5 years of age, show differences in the organization of their L2, as compared to native speakers or to children who acquire their L2 in the preschool years (Weber-Fox & Neville, 1996). Additional research examining bilingual language acquisition suggests that true bilingualism is only found in children who acquire two L1s simultaneously at or around the age of 1 (De Houwer, 2005).

Another relevant factor in models of bilingual language acquisition is the role of language dominance (Cutler, Mehler, Norris, & Segui, 1989; Grosjean, 1988). However, the concept of language dominance is difficult to define (Grosjean, 1988). More recently, researchers have begun to classify language acquisition in children as simultaneous or sequential acquisition (Harris & Nelson, 1992, but see De Houwer, 2005, for an alternate opinion). Additional methods of describing this phenomenon include characterizing dual-language acquisition as additive versus subtractive bilingualism. Research has shown that younger children who immigrate to predominately English-speaking or diverse cultural environments will show gains in L2 skill and loss of their L1 (Jia & Aaronson, 2003), resulting in sequential, subtractive bilingualism (Valdes & Figueora, 1994). The language of reading instruction could also influence the above variables.

The age of the participants and whether they have acquired literacy in their L1 prior to or simultaneous to their L2 might affect whether L1 or L2 phonological awareness is related to L2 reading. Data collected from Chinese speakers reveals differential relationships between L1 and L2 phonological awareness and L2 reading based on the age of the child. Factors such as the child's experience in English were statistically controlled. Data from a pilot study examined the relationship between English reading and English and Chinese phonological awareness in Chinese–English-speaking children of different ages (Gottardo & Yan, 2001). All children were native speakers of Cantonese. Many had emigrated from Hong Kong after a couple of years of schooling. All of the children attended Chinese school on weekends or during summer holidays. Children were in English grades 1 to 8 at the time of testing, although some had only received part of their schooling in English. For the younger children (n = 38) in grades 1 to 4, performance on English phonological tasks was uniquely related to English reading performance. Chinese phonological awareness skill overlapped with English phonological awareness. For the older group (n = 27) in grades 5 to 8, Chinese phonological awareness accounted for unique variance on English reading, while performance on the English phonological tasks overlapped with the

Chinese measure of phonological awareness. These two groups also differed in terms of the age at which they learned English, with the older children learning English at an older age than the younger children and many of the younger children receiving all their schooling in Canada. Therefore the age of acquisition of English language and literacy might be related to whether L1 or L2 phonological awareness is predictive of L2 reading (Jackson, Chen, Goldsberry, Kim, & Vanderwerff, 1999).

An additional study was designed to directly test this hypothesis by comparing younger children in grades 1 and 2 with older children in grades 5 and 6 (Gu & Gottardo, 2004). All of the children were native Mandarin speakers. They attended Chinese school on weekends and during summer holidays. Each of the two groups had 23 participants with a mean age of 88 months (SD = 8.6 months) for the younger group and 133 months (SD = 11 months) for the older group. Several phonological awareness measures were administered in the children's L1—rhyme detection, phoneme reversal, and phoneme segmentation—as well as in the L2—rhyme detection, phoneme detection, phoneme reversal, and phoneme elision.

Preliminary data revealed that, for younger children, L2 phonological awareness as measured by phoneme elision was more strongly related to English reading than L1 phonological awareness, beta = .446, t (1, 22) = 2.31, $p < .05$. None of the L1 measures was significantly related to L2 reading. L2 phonological awareness accounted for 22.4% change in variance on L2 word reading when L1 phonological awareness had been entered. The opposite results were found for the older group. L1 phonological awareness measured using the same tasks was more strongly related to English reading than L2 phonological awareness. Chinese rhyme detection had a significant beta weight as the final step, beta = .666, t (1, 22) = 3.08, $p < .01$. Interestingly, Chinese phoneme segmentation had a significant negative relationship to English reading in this older sample, beta = −.493, t (1, 22) = −2.28, $p < .05$. L1 phonological awareness accounted for 29.6% change in variance on L2 word reading when L2 phonological awareness had been entered. Although the sample sizes are small, the results of the above studies suggest that the age of L2 acquisition and the pathway of L2 reading acquisition, sequential versus simultaneous, might be related to the relationship between phonological awareness and L2 reading.

Language dominance is another variable related to language use and exposure. In a comparison of children living in the United States and Canada, the relative dominance of L1 and L2 oral language skills influenced relations between phonological awareness and reading (Pauchulo & Gottardo, 2003). Thirty native Spanish-speaking children living in Canada and 44 native Spanish-speaking children living in the United States of America were tested in first grade. Testing revealed that Spanish was not the dominant language for all of the Canadian participants, but it was for the American sample. The Canadian sample had significantly higher scores on English measures of vocabulary and oral cloze in comparison to their scores on identical Spanish measures. No differences were noted for the L1 and L2 phonological awareness measures.

A set of hierarchical regression analyses examined relations between performance on the English word reading subtest of the Woodcock Reading Mastery Test—Revised (WRMT-R; Woodcock, 1987) and L2 oral language proficiency (OLP), L2 rapid naming (RAN), and L2 phonological awareness and L1 phonological awareness variables, separately for each group (see Table 6.1). In the Canadian group, English phonological awareness predicted 11.1% unique variance on WRMT-R word reading after Spanish phonological awareness was entered, $F(1, 28) = 8.00$, $p < .01$. Spanish phonological awareness was not significantly related to reading when entered after English phonological awareness. For the American group, English phonological awareness predicted 22.0% unique variance in English word reading when entered after Spanish phonological awareness $F(1, 42) = 15.73$, $p < .001$. Spanish phonological awareness also accounted for 8.8% unique variance on English word reading performance (WRMT-R; Woodcock, 1987) after English phonological awareness. Therefore for two groups of Spanish L1 speakers somewhat different measures of L1 and L2 phonological awareness were predictive of reading. These differences could be related to L2 experiences, such as the amount of exposure to English outside school, or L1 experiences such as socioeconomic status (SES) or

TABLE 6.1. Hierarchical Regression Analysis Predicting WRMT-R English Word Reading Performance in Canadian and American Groups with English Vocabulary, RAN, and Phonological Processing and Spanish Phonological Processing as Independent Variables

Step and variable ratio	Canadian children ($n = 30$)			American children ($n = 44$)		
	R^2	ΔR^2	F	R^2	ΔR^2	F
1. English OLP	.254	.254	9.55**	.037	.037	1.61
2. English RAN	.383	.129	5.62*	.047	.010	.45
3. English phonological processing	.664	.281	21.77***	.366	.319	20.07***
4. Spanish phonological processing	.665	.001	0.08	.454	.088	6.35*
3. Spanish phonological processing	.541	.158	8.93**	.234	.187	9.77**
4. English phonological processing	.665	.124	9.30**	.454	.220	15.73***

*$p < .05$; **$p < .01$; ***$p < .001$.

country of origin (see below for a discussion of contextual factors). The studies reviewed above show that child factors, such as nonverbal ability, the age of the child and language skill in the L1 relative to L2 should be considered when determining the strength of the relationship between L1 and L2 phonological awareness and reading.

Environmental and Contextual Factors

Contextual and demographic factors might influence whether L1 or L2 phonological awareness is related to L2 reading (Goldenberg, 2006; Reese, Garnier, Gallimore, & Goldenberg, 2000). Data collected in Canada or comparisons across Canadian and American groups can assist researchers in determining the impact of demographic factors on the relationships between phonological awareness and reading. Variables such as opportunities for L1 and L2 use, availability of L1 instruction and demographic variables such as parental education differ between groups of immigrants in the two countries (Pauchulo & Gottardo, 2003).

Most studies of L2 literacy acquisition tend to ignore SES factors. The general belief is that L2 learners can be expected to perform more poorly than L1 students because of a lack of proficiency in the L2. An implicit assumption is often made that L2 learners come from poor SES backgrounds and that low SES contributes to their poor L1 and L2 language and literacy performance (Snow, Burns, & Griffin, 1998). However, it is necessary to examine the extent to which assumptions about poor performance in the early school years are supported. Moreover, the concept of SES needs to be unpacked. In the non-immigrant population, poverty and poor home literacy go hand in hand. However, this relationship may not be the case in countries such as Canada that encourage the immigration of educated individuals. For example, factors such as educational status, professional standing, work experience and/or personal wealth, as well as knowledge of one of Canada's official languages are criteria used to evaluate potential immigrants to Canada (*www.cic.gc.ca/english/skilled*). Points are awarded to applicants in each of the above areas with higher levels within each category earning more points. Only a very small number of immigrants who are eligible to apply for refugee status are exempt from these requirements. As a result, most recent immigrants to Canada are middle-class in their native country. Due to their recent arrival in Canada, these immigrants are often underemployed and poor (Li, Gervais, & Duval, 2006), but they are literate in their L1.

Immigration policy in Canada results in a select group of new immigrants, many with relatively high levels of education. In contrast, in the United States, immigrants come from highly diverse backgrounds. A large percentage—31%—of immigrants in the United States are from Mexico (*factfinder.census.gov/servlet/GCTTable*, December 29, 2008). These people are often economic refugees with low levels of education in their L1. In addition, in the United States a larger percentage of foreign-born adults have less than ninth-grade education—23% of naturalized and 40% of not naturalized immigrants compared to 12.7% of American-born adults (*factfinder.census.gov*). Approximately equal percentages of foreign-born and American-born adults have university degrees, 15.7% and 17.5%, respectively. In Canada 6% of immigrants are from Latin America. The percentage of adults with less than ninth grade in Canada is 31.6% for non-immigrants and 25.6% for immigrants who arrived in the last 15 years (*www.12. statcan.ca/English/census01/home/index.cfm*). The difference is even greater for the percentage of adults with an undergraduate university degree, with 13.8% of Canadian-born adults and 43% of immigrants who arrived in the last 15 years having a bachelor's degree.

Parental education was one of two SES components we examined to assist in understanding individual differences in literacy achievement of young L2 learners in Canada (Gottardo & Geva, 2005). Reading, phonological awareness, and nonverbal reasoning skills were examined in this previously described group of kindergarten LL children with Chinese, Portuguese, or Spanish as an L1. Parental education, defined as whether the parents did or did not complete high school was related to L2 phonological awareness scores. The greater number of parents with a high school education was related to lower total scores on an elision task, $r = -.17$, $p < .05$, while the number of parents with a university education was positively significantly related to scores on the same measure, $r = .22$, $p < .05$. Family income, the other SES component, was not related to phonological awareness skill.

Parental education also was related to phonological awareness and reading in the previously mentioned samples of Spanish speakers from Canada and the United States. We examined the role of home demographic variables in predicting reading above and beyond L1 and L2 phonological awareness (Pauchulo & Gottardo, 2003). Phonological awareness was related to L1 and L2 reading after a home/demographic variable—consisting of maternal and paternal education, the number of times the child is read to in the home, and the country in which the family currently lives—was entered. Interestingly, in addition to phonological awareness, the home/demographic variable was also significantly related to L1 (Spanish) word reading in the complete model, beta = .271, t (1, 73) = 2.23, $p < .05$. In this study home and demographic variables, in particular parental education, were directly related to reading even when phonological awareness was entered into the equation. In other studies, parental education could be related to reading indirectly through phonological awareness. Therefore, home and demographic variables are directly and indirectly related to phonological awareness and reading in LLs. As a result, demographic factors including factors from the parents' education in their country of origin should be considered by practitioners when assessing LLs.

Methodological Issues

Although general measurement issues can be related to child and language factors, methodological factors such as the specific predictor variables being measured can affect measurement. For example, the demands of the different reading tasks can affect which L1 and L2 phonological awareness variables are more strongly related to the task. The ways in which the sample is defined and the specific prediction task, including analyses based on continuous versus categorical data, can result in different measures being more predictive. The characteristics of the participants, such as the relative number of above-average, average, and below-average readers in the sample, might also influence the relative importance of L1 and L2 phonological processing in predicting reading.

Variables and Tasks

For children reading an orthography that is not alphabetic, the specific reading task might influence the relationship between reading and phonological awareness. A group of Chinese-speaking children in Canada was tested in English, their L2, and Cantonese, their L1 (Gottardo, Chiappe, Yan, Siegel, & Gu, 2006). These children had all attended Chinese classes in Canada on weekends and for summer school, although their Chinese reading levels were lower than would be expected if they were educated in China. The children were tested on a number of measures including L1 and L2 reading, words and characters, and pseudowords and pseudocharacters.

Multiple regression analyses were conducted to examine within-language relationships between RAN, phonological awareness, phoneme categorization and oral cloze performance, and reading performance in English and Chinese. English phonological awareness was measured by a rhyme detection task and a phoneme deletion task. Chinese phonological awareness was measured by a rhyme detection task and a tone detection task. The English measures were entered as predictors of English reading. English phonological awareness performance was significantly related to English word reading, beta = 2.56, t (1, 40) = 2.66, $p < .05$, and English pseudoword reading, beta = 2.95, t (1, 40) = 4.43, $p < .001$.

Multiple regression analyses were conducted to determine which Chinese language variables were related to reading performance on four Chinese reading tasks: a simple character list, a complex character list, a similar character disambiguation task, and the number of phonetic responses for the pseudocharacter reading task. For this sample, phonological aware-ness was not related to reading for the three character reading tasks (i.e., simple character reading, complex character reading, and similar character disambiguation). However, phonological awareness was related to Chinese pseudocharacter reading, beta = 1.035, t (1, 40) = 2.44, p < .05. Although reading pseudocharacters is related to character reading performance in Chinese, additional processes such as phonological strategies are required. This finding indicates that phonological information is used for this Chinese reading task where other strategies are not effective (Gottardo et al., 2006) and replicates relationships between pseudocharacter reading and phono-logical awareness in children in China (Leong et al., 2005). Therefore, the reading measures being used in specific studies can have a differential impact on predictive relations among variables.

Sample Composition

A study examined L1 and L2 predictors of L2 word and pseudoword read-ing across time, grade 1 to grade 2, in Spanish speakers educated in English. Children were placed into one of three categories based on English reading skills: (1) consistently average readers in grade 1 and grade 2 (avg/avg), (2) poor readers in grade 1 but average readers in grade 2 (poor/avg), and (3) consistently poor readers in grade 1 and grade 2 (poor/poor). Slightly dif-ferent measures of phonological awareness differentiated the groups when compared to each other, Group 1 versus Group 2 and Group 1 versus Group 3 (Gottardo, Collins, Baciu, & Gebotys, 2008).

Four binary logistic regression models were used to predict member-ship in the avg/avg group versus the poor/poor group, and poor/avg group (switchers) versus the poor/poor group based on word reading and pseudo-word reading. These analyses were used to determine which variables were most highly related to group membership. The statistically significant read-ing models (p < 0.01) were fit with L1 and L2 phonological awareness and rapid naming, and L1 reading as predictor variables using the forward Wald criteria in SPSS. The analyses calculated the odds multiplier for each predic-tor variable, plus the discriminant power of the overall model (percent of cases correctly classified using the derived model).

Correct classification as belonging to the avg/avg group versus the poor/poor group on word reading had two significant predictor variables, namely English and Spanish phonological awareness with odds multipliers of 1.18 and 1.07, p = .01, respectively. Higher scores on English phonologi-cal awareness increased the odds by 1.18 (over one time) of being classified in the average category. The model had moderate discriminant power since 77% of the data was correctly classified using the above model. In the case of the model predicting pseudoword reading, the L1 and L2 phonological awareness predictor variables were significant and increased the odds at 1.19 and 1.23, respectively, of being classified in the average group. The model had good discriminant power, with 87% of the cases correctly classified.

Predictors of reading were examined for the poor/avg group, in contrast to the poor/poor group. For word and pseudoword reading, only English phonological awareness increased the odds of being in the poor/avg group versus poor/poor group, odds multipliers of 1.13 and 1.14, respectively. The discriminant power overall for the word and pseudoword reading variables for switchers versus poor groups was 65% and 78%, respectively. The percentages were moderate and indicated reasonable to slightly lower classification rates.

Therefore, although L1 and L2 phonological awareness discriminated between children who were consistently average readers and children who were consistently poor readers, only L2 phonological awareness discriminated between children who remained consistently poor readers and children who were poor readers in first grade but improved to become average readers in second grade. Spanish (L1) measures featured more prominently in the analyses comparing average children to children who remain low. These analyses were consistent with the findings of another study that showed that strong Spanish skills were more likely in children who begin school with average L2 (English) reading (Rolla San Francisco, Mo, Carlo, August, & Snow, 2006). Children who showed gains in reading from first to second grade acquired phonological awareness skills at school in their L2, the language of instruction. The children with consistently low reading did not come to school with strong L1 or L2 skills, nor did they acquire these skills in the first year of reading instruction.

The above results can help address why some studies have found that L1 and L2 phonological awareness predicted word reading, while other studies have only found phonological awareness in one language was predictive. The distribution of the sample, containing either a large number of consistent readers, or a large number of children with improved reading scores, could result in different phonological awareness measures being related to word reading.

Concurrent or Longitudinal Predictors

Whether factors related to the child's reading were examined in a concurrent or longitudinal way can result in different predictors in the same sample. For example, evidence for relationships between L1 and L2 phonological awareness was found in young Spanish speakers in the United States. Children in this sample were low-SES native Spanish speakers. Data collected from 85 children in first grade revealed that both L1 and L2 phonological awareness contribute variance to L2 reading in a stepwise regression (Gottardo, 2002). English phoneme deletion, Spanish phoneme detection, and Spanish reading and English oral vocabulary were related to concurrent measures of English reading. English phoneme deletion performance was most highly related to word reading performance accounting for 35% of the variance as the second step after the variable "months in school" was entered (F [1, 84] = 49.47, $p < .001$). The other three variables were statistically significant when they were entered after the phoneme deletion task, although each accounted for less than 10% of the variance after phoneme deletion was entered. Spanish phoneme detection performance was related to English word reading skill, F (1, 84) = 9.92, $p < .01$. Spanish word reading was significantly related to English reading even after the two phonological processing measures were entered, F (1, 84) = 7.14, $p < .01$. These results replicate the research of Durgunoğlu and colleagues (Durgunoğlu, 1998; Durgunoğlu et al., 1993).

Additional data were collected subsequently from 77 of the children in grade 2. L2 but not L1 phonological awareness in grade 1 predicted unique variance in L2 reading in grade 2 and had a significant beta weight as the last step, beta = .266, t (1, 76) = 2.07, $p < .05$. Similar results were found for pseudoword reading, beta = .332, t (1, 76) = 2.71, $p < .01$. These results suggest that the best longitudinal predictor is phonological awareness in the same language that is being read, usually the language of instruction.

Although kindergarten and early first grade phonological awareness in Spanish were more strongly related to English reading (Lindsey et al., 2003), English phonological awareness in first grade was more strongly related to second-grade reading (Manis et al., 2004). The children in these studies by Lindsey and Manis transitioned from English to Spanish reading at this time. Therefore, the studies reviewed in this section show that the variables being measured and classification techniques used in the study can affect the relationship between L1 and L2 phonological awareness and reading.

SUMMARY

The results of the analyses determining the measurement models suggest that L1 and L2 phonological awareness are highly related skills but can be separated in some samples based on variables discussed above. Relationships between L1 and L2 phonological awareness and reading are mediated or moderated by contextual variables, demographic variables such as parental education, and child-related variables such as nonverbal reasoning and the age of acquisition and amount or type of L2 experience of the participants. The relationships between L1 and L2 phonological awareness and reading can also be related to the measures used and classifications that are being conducted. These findings suggest that multiple factors, including the nature of the L1, child factors, and contextual and demographic factors all contribute to the relationships between phonological awareness and reading in LLs.

The factors discussed in this paper can be used to reconcile discrepant findings about whether L1 or L2 phonological awareness is related to reading. Although L1 and L2 phonological awareness is highly related across languages, contextual and child-related variables influence the degree of overlap between L1 and L2 phonological processing. These factors should be considered in deciding whether L1 or L2 phonological awareness skill is assessed in determining potential reading performance in LLs. The overlapping nature of L1 and L2 phonological awareness suggests that either L1 or L2 phonological awareness can be used as gross indicators of phonological awareness. However, for some cases discussed above, either L1 or L2 phonological awareness might be the more sensitive indicator of potential reading achievement. The multiple variables discussed in this chapter should be considered when making decisions about optimal assessment of LLs.

REFERENCES

Alvarez, C. J., Carreiras, M., & Perea, M. (2004). Are syllables phonological units in visual word recognition? *Language and Cognitive Processes, 19,* 427–452.

Anthony, J., & Lonigan, C. (2004). The nature of phonological awareness: Converging evidence from four studies of preschool and early grade school children. *Journal of Educational Psychology, 96,* 43–55.

Bialystok, E. (2001). *Bilingualism in development: Language, literacy and cognition.* Cambridge, UK: Cambridge University Press.

Brady, S. A. (1997). Ability to encode phonological representations: An underlying difficulty of poor readers. In B. Blachman (Ed.), *Foundations of reading acquisition and dyslexia: Implications for early intervention* (pp. 21–47). Mahwah, NJ: Erlbaum.

Branum-Martin, L., Mehta, P. D., Fletcher, J. M., Carlson, C. D., Ortiz, A., Carlo, M., et al. (2006). Bilingual phonological awareness: Multilevel construct validation among Spanish-speaking kindergarteners in transitional bilingual education classrooms. *Journal of Educational Psychology, 98,* 170–181.

Bruck, M., Genesee, F., & Caravolas, M. (1997). A cross-linguistic study of early literacy acquisition. In B. Blachman (Ed.). *Foundations of reading acquisition and dyslexia: Implications for early intervention* (pp. 145–162). Mahwah, NJ: Erlbaum.

Burnham, D. (2003). Language specific speech perception and the onset of reading. *Reading and Writing, 16,* 573–609.

Cutler, A., Mehler, J., Norris, D., & Segui, J. (1989). Limits on bilingualism. *Nature, 340,* 229–230.

DaFontoura, H. A., & Siegel, L. S. (1995). Reading, syntactic, and working memory skills of bilingual Portuguese–English Canadian children. *Reading and Writing: An Interdisciplinary Journal, 7,* 139–153.

D'Angiulli, A., & Siegel, L. S. (2003). Cognitive functioning as measured by the WISC-R: Do children with learning disabilities have distinctive patterns of performance? *Journal of Learning Disabilities, 36,* 48–58.

Defior, S., Martos, F., & Cary, L. (2002). Differences in reading acquisition development in two shallow orthographies: Portuguese and Spanish. *Applied Psycholinguistics, 23,* 135–148.

De Houwer, A. (2005). Early bilingual acquisition: Focus on morphosyntax and the separate development hypothesis. In J. F. Kroll & A. M. B. de Groot (Eds.), *Handbook of bilingualism: Psycholinguistic approaches* (pp. 30–48). New York: Oxford University Press.

Dunn, L. M., & Dunn, L. M. (1997). *Peabody Picture Vocabulary Test* (3rd ed.). Circle Pines, MN: American Guidance Service.

Dunn, L. M., Lugo, D. E., Padilla, E. R., & Dunn, L. M. (1986). *Test de Vocabulario en Imagenes Peabody.* Circle Pines, MN: American Guidance Service.

Durgunoğlu, A. Y. (1998). Acquiring literacy in English and Spanish in the United States. In A. Y. Durgunoğlu & L. Verhoeven (Eds.), *Literacy in a multilingual context: Cross-cultural perspectives* (pp. 135–145). Mahwah, NJ: Erlbaum.

Durgunoğlu, A. Y. (2002). Cross-linguistic transfer in literacy development and implications for language learners. *Annals of Dyslexia, 52,* 189–204.

Durgunoğlu, A. Y., Nagy, W. E., & Hancin-Bhatt, B. J. (1993). Cross-language transfer of phonological awareness. *Journal of Educational Psychology, 85,* 453–465.

Durgunoğlu, A. Y., & Öney, B. (2002). Phonological awareness in literacy acquisition: It's not only for children. *Scientific Studies of Reading, 6,* 245–266.

Eckman, F. R. (2004). From phonemic differences to constraint rankings: Research on second language phonology. *Studies in Second Language Acquisition, 26,* 513–549.

Elbro, C. (1998). When reading is "readn" or somthn": "Distinctnes" of phonological representations of lexical items in normal and disabled readers. *Scandinavian Journal of Psychology, 39,* 149–153.

English, J. P., Leafstedt, J., Gerber, M. M., & Villaruz, J. (2001, April 10–14). *Individual differences in phonological skills for Spanish speaking kindergartners learning English: Relationship between English and Spanish phonological measures.* Paper presented at the Annual Meeting of the American Educational Research Association, Seattle, WA.

Flege, J. E. (1992). Speech learning in a second language. In C. Ferguson, L. Menn, & C. Stoel-Gammon (Eds.), *Phonological development: Models, research, and implications* (pp. 565–604). Timonium, MD: York.

Flege, J. E., Frieda, E. M., & Nozawa, T. (1997). Amount of native-language use (L1) affects pronunciation of an L2. *Journal of Phonetics, 25,* 169–186.

Frost, R. (1994). Prelexical and postlexical strategies in reading: Evidence from a deep and a shallow orthography. *Journal of Experimental Psychology: Learning, Memory, and Cognition, 20,* 116–129.

Frost, R., & Katz, L. (1992). *Orthography, phonology, morphology, and meaning: Advances in psychology, 94.* Oxford, UK: North-Holland.

Geva, E., & Siegel, L. S. (2000). Orthographic and cognitive factors in the concurrent development of basic reading skills in two languages. *Reading and Writing: An Interdisciplinary Journal, 12*(1–2), 1–30.

Geva, E., & Wang, M. (2001). The development of basic reading skills in children: A cross-language perspective. *Annual Review of Applied Linguistics, 21*, 182–204.

Goldenberg, C. N. (2001b). Improving achievement for English-learners: What the research tells us. *Education Week, 25*, 34–36.

Goswami, U. (1988). Orthographic analogies and reading development. *The Quarterly Journal of Experimental Psychology, 40*, 239–268.

Gottardo, A. (2002). Language and reading skills in bilingual Spanish–English speakers. *Topics in Language Disorders, 23*, 42–66.

Gottardo, A., Chiappe, P., Siegel, L. S., & Lafrance A. (2003, June). *A comparison of phoneme categorization performance in ESL and native English-speaking adults.* Paper presented at the 10th Annual Meeting of the Society for Scientific Studies in Reading, Boulder, CO.

Gottardo, A., Chiappe, P., Yan, B., Siegel, L. S., & Gu, Y. (2006). Relationships between first and second language phonological processing skills and reading in Chinese–English speakers living in English-speaking contexts. *Educational Psychology, 26*, 367–393.

Gottardo, A., Collins, P., Baciu, I., & Gebotys, R. (2008). Predictors of grade 2 word reading, listening comprehension and reading comprehension from grade 1 variables in Spanish-speaking children: Similarities and differences. *Learning Disabilities: Research and Practice, 23*, 11–24.

Gottardo, A., & Geva, E. (2005, January). *Factors related to reading in ESL children. What is the role of SES and nonverbal reasoning?* Paper presented at the University of California Linguistic Minority Research Institute: Biliteracy Development Research Forum, Santa Barbara, CA.

Gottardo, A., Geva, E., Faroga, I., & Ramirez, G. (2006, July). *The influence of first language (L1) category on the development of second language reading: A longitudinal perspective.* Paper presented at the 13th annual meeting of the Society for Scientific Studies in Reading Annual Meeting, Vancouver, BC.

Gottardo, A., & Mueller, J. (2009). Are first and second language factors related in predicting L2 reading comprehension?: A study of Spanish-speaking children acquiring English as a second language from first to second grade. *Journal of Educational Psychology, 101*, 330–344.

Gottardo, A., Siegel, L. S., & Stanovich, K. E. (1997). The assessment of adults with reading disabilities. What can we learn from experimental tasks? *Journal of Research in Reading, 20*, 42–54.

Gottardo, A., & Yan, B. (2001, April). *Age-related differences in the relationship between first and second language phonological processing and second language reading.* Poster presented at the biennial meeting of the Society for Research in Child Development, Minneapolis, MN.

Gottardo, A., Yan, B., Siegel, L. S., & Wade-Woolley, L. (2001). Factors related to English reading performance in children with Chinese as a first language: More evidence of cross-language transfer of phonological processing. *Journal of Educational Psychology, 93*, 530–542.

Grosjean, F. (1988). Exploring the recognition of guest words in bilingual speech. *Language and Cognitive Processes, 3,* 233–274.

Gu, Y., & Gottardo, A. (2004, April). *Investigating age factors in cross-language transfer of phonological processing across English and Chinese languages.* Poster presented at the Conference on Human Development, Washington, DC.

Harris, R. J., & Nelson, E. M. (1992). Bilingualism: Not the exception any more. In R. J. Harris (Ed.), *Cognitive processing in bilinguals* (pp. 1–14). Amsterdam, North-Holland: Elsevier Science.

Jackson, N. E., Chen, H., Goldsberry, L., Kim, A., & Vanderweff, C. (1999). Effects of variations in orthographic information on Asian and American readers' English text reading. *Reading and Writing, 11,* 345–379.

Jia, J., & Aaronson, D. (2003). A longitudinal study of Chinese children and adolescents learning English in the United States. *Applied Psycholinguistics, 24*(1), 131–161.

Jiménez-González, J. E. (1997). A reading-level match study of phonemic processes underlying reading disabilities in a transparent orthography. *Reading and Writing: An Interdisciplinary Journal, 9,* 23–40.

Kline, R. B. (1998). *Principles and practice of structural equation modeling.* New York: Guilford Press.

Lafrance, A., & Gottardo, A. (2005). A longitudinal study of phonological processing skills and reading in bilingual children. *Applied Psycholinguistics, 26,* 559–578.

Leong, C. K., & Tamaoka, K. (1998). Cognitive processing of Chinese characters, words, sentences and Japanese kanji and kana: An introduction. *Reading and Writing: An Interdisciplinary Journal, 10,* 155–164.

Leong, C. K., Tan, L. H., Cheng, P. W., & Hau, K. T. (2005). Learning to read and spell English words by Chinese students, *Scientific Studies in Reading, 9,* 63–84.

Li, C., Gervais, G., & Duval, A. (2006). *The dynamics of overqualification: Canada's underemployed university graduates.* Ottawa, ON: Statistics Canada.

Lindsey, K. A., Manis, F. R., & Bailey, C. E. (2003). Prediction of first-grade reading in Spanish-speaking English-language learners. *Journal of Educational Psychology, 95,* 482–494.

Manis, F. R., Lindsey, K. A., & Bailey, C. E. (2004). Development of reading in grades K–2 Spanish-speaking English-language learners. *Learning Disabilities Research and Practice, 19,* 214–224.

McBride-Chang, C. (1995). What is phonological awareness? *Journal of Educational Psychology, 87,* 179–192.

McBride-Chang, C. (1996). Models of speech perception and phonological processing in reading. *Child Development, 67,* 1836–1856.

Metsala, J. L., & Walley, A. C. (1998). Spoken vocabulary growth and the segmental restructuring of lexical representations: precursors to phonemic awareness and early reading ability. In J. L. Metsala & L. C. Ehri (Eds.), *Word recognition in beginning literacy* (pp. 89–120). Mahwah, NJ: Erlbaum.

Mody, M., Studdert-Kennedy, M., & Brady, S. (1997). Speech perception deficits in poor readers: Auditory processing or phonological coding? *Journal of Experimental Child Psychology, 64,* 199–231.

Morais, J. (1991). Constraints on the developmental of phonological awareness. In S. A. Brady & D. P. Shankweiler (Eds.), *Phonological processes in literacy* (pp. 5–27). Hillsdale, NJ: Erlbaum.

Mumtaz, S., & Humphreys, G. W. (2001). The effects of bilingualism on learning to read English: Evidence from the contrast between Urdu–English bilingual and English monolingual children. *Journal of Research in Reading, 24,* 113–134.

Naglieri, J. (1989). *Matrix Analogies Test.* New York: The Psychological Corporation, Harcourt Brace Jovanovich.

Nagy, W. E., García, G. E., Durgunoğlu, A. Y., & Hancin-Bhatt, B. (1993). Spanish–English bilingual students' use of cognates in English reading. *Journal of Reading Behavior, 25,* 241–259.

Öney, B., & Durgunoğlu, A. Y. (2005). Research and theory informing instruction in adult literacy. In T. Trabasso, J. Sabatini, D. W. Massaro, & R. C. Calfee (Eds.), *From orthography to pedagogy: Essays in honor of Richard L. Venezky* (pp. 127–147). Mahwah, NJ: Erlbaum.

Pauchulo, A. L., & Gottardo, A. (2003, June). *Understanding reading development in second-language learners in Canada and the USA.* Poster presented at the 10th Annual Meeting of the Society for Scientific Studies in Reading, Boulder, CO.

Perfetti, C. A., & Liu, Y. (2005). Orthography to phonology and meaning: Comparisons across and within writing systems. *Reading and Writing, 18,* 193–210.

Perfetti, C. A., Liu, Y., & Tan, L. H. (2005). The lexical constituency model: Some implications of research on Chinese for general theories of reading. *Psychological Review, 112,* 43–59.

Plaut, D., McClelland, J., Seidenberg, M., & Patterson, K. (1996). Understanding normal and impaired word reading: Computational principles in quasi-regular domains. *Psychology Review, 103,* 56–115.

Reese, L., Garnier, H., Gallimore, R., & Goldenberg, C. (2000). Longitudinal analysis of the antecedents of emergent Spanish literacy and middle-school English reading achievement of Spanish-speaking students. *American Educational Research Journal, 37,* 633–662.

Rolla San Francisco, A., Mo, E., Carlo, M., August, D., & Snow, C. (2006). The influences of language of literacy instruction and vocabulary on the spelling of Spanish–English bilinguals. *Reading and Writing, 19,* 627–642.

Saiegh-Haddad, E. (2007). Linguistic constraints on children's ability to isolate phonemes in Arabic. *Applied Psycholingusitics, 28,* 607–625.

Seymour, P. H. K., Aro, M., & Erskine, J. M. (2003). Foundation literacy acquisition in European orthographies. *British Journal of Psychology, 94,* 143–174.

Shu, H., Anderson, R. C., & Wu, N. (2000). Phonetic awareness: Knowledge of orthography–phonology relationships in the character acquisition of Chinese children. *Journal of Educational Psychology, 92,* 57–62.

Shu, H., & Anderson, R.C. (1997). The role of radical awareness in the character and word acquisition of Chinese children. *Reading Research Quarterly, 32,* 78–89.

Siegel, L. S. (1989). IQ is irrelevant to the definition of learning disabilities? *Journal of Learning Disabilities, 22,* 469–478.

Snow, C. E., Burns, S., & Griffin, P. (1998). *Preventing reading difficulties in young children*. Washington, DC: National Academy Press.

Sparks, R. L., Patton, J., Ganschow, L., Humbach, N., & Javorsky, J. (2008). Early first-language reading and spelling skills predict later second-language reading and spelling skills. *Journal of Educational Psychology, 100,* 162–174.

So, L. K. H., & Dodd, B. J. (1995). The acquisition of phonology by Cantonese-speaking children. *Journal of Child Language, 22,* 473–495.

Stanovich, K. E. (1992). Speculations on the causes and consequences of individual differences in early reading acquisition. In P. G. Gough, L. C. Ehri, & R. Treiman (Eds.), *Reading acquisition* (pp. 307–342). Hillsdale, NJ: Erlbaum.

Stuart, M., & Coltheart, M. (1988). Does reading develop in a sequence of stages? *Cognition, 30,* 139–181.

Treiman, R., Mullennix, J., Bijeljac-Babic, R., & Richmond-Welty, D. (1995). The special role of rimes in the description, use, and acquisition of English orthography. *Journal of Experimental Psychology, 124*(2), 107–136.

Tunmer, W. E. (1991). Phonological awareness and literacy acquisition. In L. Rieben & C. A. Perfetti (Eds.), *Learning to read: Basic research and its implications* (pp. 105–119). Mahwah, NJ: Erlbaum.

Valdes, G., & Figueroa, R. A. (1994). *Bilingualism and testing: A special case of bias*. Norwood, NJ: Ablex.

Wade-Woolley, L., & Geva, E. (2000). Processing novel phonemic contrasts in the acquisition of L2 word reading. *Scientific Studies of Reading, 4,* 295–311.

Walley, A. C. (1993). The role of vocabulary development in children's spoken word recognition and segmentation ability. *Developmental Review, 13,* 286–350.

Walley, A., Metsala, J. L., & Garlock, V. M. (2003). Spoken vocabulary growth: Its role in the development of phoneme awareness and early reading ability. *Reading and Writing: An Interdisciplinary Journal, 16,* 5–20.

Weber-Fox, C. M., & Neville, H. J. (1996). Maturational constraints on functional specializations for language processing: ERP and behavioral evidence in bilingual speakers. *Journal of Cognitive Neuroscience, 8,* 231–256.

Wong, W. Y., & Stokes, S. F. (2001). Cantonese consonantal development: Toward a nonlinear account. *Journal of Child Language, 28,* 195–212.

Woodcock, R. W. (1987). *Woodcock Reading Mastery Test—Revised*. Circle Pines, MN: American Guidance Services.

Yi, K. (1998). The internal structure of Korean syllables: Rhyme or body? *Korean Journal of Experimental and Cognitive Psychology, 10,* 67–83.

Ziegler, J. C., & Goswami, U. (2005). Reading acquisition, developmental dyslexia, and skilled reading across languages: A psycholinguistic grain size theory. *Psychological Bulletin, 131,* 3–29.

CHAPTER 7

■   ■   ■

Learning a Nonalphabetic Script and Its Impact on the Later Development of English as a Second Language

HIM CHEUNG
CATHERINE McBRIDE-CHANG
XIULI TONG

The process of mapping a speech unit onto a functional writing unit is fundamental to learning to read (Snow, Burns, & Griffin, 1998). This process may vary greatly across languages and orthographies: Whereas in some languages only speech units as large as the syllable are represented in writing, in others writing and spelling are based on symbols encoding speech at the phoneme level. Such variation in the degree of phonological detail represented in writing has been shown to affect the user's phonological awareness, which refers to her explicit analysis of speech (Bertelson, de Gelder, Tfouni, & Morais, 1989; Lukatela, Carello, Shankweiler, & Liberman, 1995; Morais, Bertelson, Cary, & Alegria, 1986). In turn, phonological awareness predicts reading performance (de Jong & van der Leij, 1999; Elbro, Borstrom, & Peterson, 1998; Lundberg, Olofsson, & Wall, 1980; Manis & Freedman, 2001; Muter, Hulme, Snowling, & Taylor, 1998; Sprenger-Charolles, Siegel, & Bechennec, 1998; Wagner, Torgesen, & Rashotte, 1994). What would the interplay between reading experience, phonological awareness, and reading performance be like if an individual reads multiple orthographies differing in the size of the most basic phonological unit that is represented in writing?

In this chapter we examine how phonological awareness at different levels, nature of orthography, and reading instruction method jointly affect reading performance from a cross-linguistic transfer perspective. Specifically we are interested in the effect of learning to read Chinese and Korean on the later acquisition of alphabetic English as a second script. The syllable is a prominent phonological unit in spoken Chinese and Korean, corresponding to the lexical morpheme, which is the most basic semantic constituent. Such syllable prominence naturally biases the speaker's attention to segmenting speech into syllable-sized units. How may this first-language experience affect Chinese and Korean speakers' English reading, which is accomplished with an alphabet coding phonemes?

We begin with a summary of some salient features of Chinese and Korean that make them theoretically interesting in understanding universals and specifics in reading acquisition in relation to phonological awareness. We then overview reading instruction in both Chinese and Korean, as well as how English is taught as a second language to Chinese- and Korean-speaking children. Finally, we consider the broad issue of phonological transfer and how it relates specifically to learning to read English as a second language for Chinese and Korean speakers. We conclude by highlighting nature of orthography and instruction method as critical factors behind cross-language transfer of phonological awareness and reading.

NONALPHABETIC ORTHOGRAPHIES

An Overview of Chinese

The basic orthographic unit in Chinese is the character. Chinese characters are composed of unpronounceable strokes; each character corresponds to a syllable and a lexical morpheme. The morphosyllable is an indivisible functional unit. Syllables are normally equally stressed in natural speech. Because each syllable is stressed and has a rather complete meaning by itself, syllables are salient in terms of both perception and processing, compared to words. Words in modern Chinese are by and large multisyllabic and thus written as strings of characters. Because only characters are spatially marked in written Chinese, much in the same way as words are spatially marked in written English, even native Chinese users tend to disagree a lot on what a word is (Chen, 1992, 1996). This contrasts with the very salient identity of the character, having clear orthographic, phonological, and semantic boundaries.

Tone, an important element of spoken Chinese, is obligatory and used contrastively. For example, the Cantonese monosyllable /fu/ may be interpreted as any one of the following six lexical morphemes, depending on the tone it takes. The possibilities are /fu1/ 夫 (husband), /fu2/ 虎 (tiger), /fu3/ 褲

(trousers), /fu4/ 符 (symbol), /fu5/ 婦 (woman), /fu6/ 父 (father).[1] Note that tones are not represented in Chinese writing. There are four and six tones in Mandarin and Cantonese, respectively. Tones are realized as different pitch contours signifying the meaning of morphemes (Suen, 1982; Wang, 1973).

Chinese has a simple syllable structure compared to English. For example, Cantonese syllables only take the following forms in terms of consonant–vowel (CV) arrangement: V, as in 傲(pride)/ou6/; CV, as in 媽 (mother)/maa1/; CVC, as in 風 (wind)/fung1/; VC, as in 昂 (look up)/ong4/. There are no consonant clusters, which are common in English syllables, and approximately 98% of Cantonese lexical syllables are of either a CVC or CV structure (Wong, 1984). Moreover, a relatively small set of legal onsets and rimes constrains the number of syllables that can be formed. For instance, there are only 22 onsets and 37 rimes possible in Mandarin Chinese (Li & Thompson, 1981), and only about 1,200 distinct syllables exist with tone considered (Suen, 1979). Nevertheless, there are approximately 7,000 commonly used lexical syllables in Mandarin (Li, Anderson, Nagy, & Zhang, 2002), underscoring the large number of homophones. On average, hence, more than five lexical morphemes share one syllable.

As shown in Figure 7.1, written Chinese and English represent sound in very different ways. In Chinese there is little systematic correspondence between orthography and subsyllabic phonology. In this example, although the characters share a stroke pattern (in this case, the shared radical 青/qing1/), they are read very differently. There is no consistent correspondence between the pronunciation of the radical 青 and those of the four characters containing it. In contrast, English orthographic rimes represent sound in a relatively consistent way (Treiman, 1985; Treiman, Mullennix, Bijeljac-Babic, & Richmond-Welty, 1995; Treiman & Zukowski, 1996), as in the words *nice* /nais/, *rice* /rais/, *vice* /vais/, and *dice* /dais/, which contain the same orthographic rime *ice* contributing rather consistently to word pronunciation. Regarding pronunciation cueing through phonetic radicals in written Chinese, Zhou (1978) estimates that only about 39% of compound characters contain reliable sound cues. Furthermore, the actual sound and meaning relations between a compound and its components vary from situation to situation, and are often impossible to predict. For instance, a Chinese phonetic radical may represent only the segments of a certain host compound but may share both the segments and tone with another host (i.e., homophonic with it). There is no way that a child could understand such variation unless he or she already knows the pronunciations of the host compounds in question. One can thus hardly take advantage of Chinese radical cueing in beginning reading instruction. Such characteristics underscore the utility of reading Chinese characters as unique syllables, as opposed to breaking them into subsyllabic segments.

To summarize, Chinese characters represent speech at a syllable level,

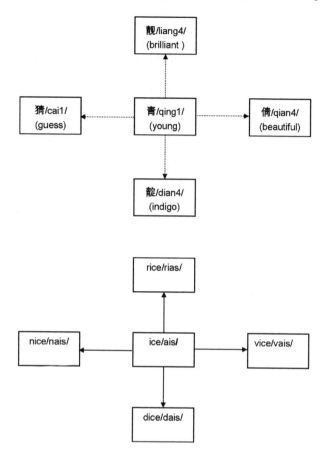

FIGURE 7.1. Phonological representation in written Chinese and English.

which fits well with the fact that Chinese syllables constitute the most important functional phonological units. Hence the accessibility of syllables facilitates young Chinese children's readiness to make use of syllable knowledge in reading words, which are composed of characters (lexical morphemes). In contrast, Korean emphasizes both syllable- and phoneme-level psycholinguistic units.

Korean Hangul

Korean Hangul is a non-Roman alphabetic script consisting of 24 letters. Of these, 14 are consonants and 10 are vowels. Each letter consistently maps onto one sound and only a limited number of combinations are possible among letters. Letters are structured in square-like blocks and were designed in part to mirror place of articulation in the vocal tract. One or more consonants are usually combined with a vowel to form a syllable, such as VC, CV, CVC, and CVCC (Taylor & Taylor, 1983). Thus both phonemes and syllables are salient in Korean. In terms of orthography, Korean is characterized as an alphabetic syllabary (Kim & Davis, 2006) because it represents phonemes organized together into separate syllable blocks, thus simultaneously highlighting phonemic and syllabic units in visual presentation.

READING INSTRUCTION ACROSS CONTEXTS

The Process of Learning to Read

Unlike speaking and listening, which come to the child spontaneously in a natural speech environment, reading is an effortful activity that requires focused instruction over and above mere availability of written materials (Bertelson, 1986). This renders method of instruction a significant factor to consider in examining reading development. One basic question is whether fundamental features of the script in question are reflected in the instructional method used. This includes the extent to which instruction effectively pinpoints how speech is represented in the script. If the learner is dealing with multiple writing systems differing in how speech is coded, the additional consideration is whether instruction is consistent across scripts.

Therefore, to evaluate the impact of reading instruction and learning environment, one must first consider the spoken language to be represented in writing. Spoken Chinese, and to a lesser extent Korean, possesses certain peculiar characteristics that are not shared by English. For example, the syllable is a primary unit of sound and meaning, corresponding to the morpheme. There is a rather clear-cut one-to-one relation between syllables and morphemes: A complete syllable is always a complete morpheme, and a complete morpheme is always a complete syllable (it must be noted, however, that Korean is less so in this regard).

Syllable salience in spoken Chinese and Korean is reinforced in the respective writings. As discussed, for instance, each Chinese character or Korean orthographic syllable (eumjeol) is a spatially marked written unit corresponding to a syllable in speech, often with a rather complete meaning in the semantic space (i.e., a lexical morpheme). Hence what we see is an interesting overlap in salient unit of analysis between speech (syllable), writing (character/eumjeol), and meaning (lexical morpheme). How is early literacy taught to Chinese or Korean children, given these characteristics, and how do these children then learn English as a second language?

Learning to Read Chinese (L1) and English (L2)

Given the phonological and orthographic salience of the syllable, one can imagine that a sensible thing to do in considering reading instruction in Chinese, therefore, is to treat the character as the primary unit of teaching and learning, without placing much emphasis on subcharacter components in the case of compound characters. This approach is known as the "look-and-say" method, in which the child is expected to memorize the pronunciations of characters as unanalyzed wholes. In this case, given that cueing provided by character components is rather limited and would not be of much help in deriving character meaning and pronunciation, analyzing compound characters into smaller components is not required.

The look-and-say method, now widely practiced in Hong Kong (Cheung & Ng, 2003), appears to match the basic properties of Chinese speech and may therefore be educationally sound. This approach highlights the holistic and unique nature of characters, each of which represents a prominent phonological (stressed syllable) and semantic unit (lexical morpheme) in speech. Nevertheless, considering the fact that alphabetic English is to be learned as a second language, the traditional look-and-say method in Chinese instruction may sometimes bewilder the child. Because characters are associated with and taught as whole syllables, English letters may as well be treated as symbols for syllables, so that, for example, the letter *b* is learned as symbol for the /bi/ syllable (i.e., the name of the letter) rather than the /b/ phoneme. One can thus imagine the following: When presented with the letter *b* the child naturally calls it /bi/; but when presented with the letter string *bat* the corresponding syllable /bæt/ still has to be learned as an unanalyzed whole, because the knowledge that *b* = /bi/, rather than *b* = /b/, does not really contribute to an analytic (phonic) way of pronouncing the *b-a-t* string. This analytic way of letter string reading is actually the whole point of adopting the phonics approach.

What is described above could give rise to a kind of English learning that is rather Chinese-like, especially in a society where children start learning the written forms of the two languages early and simultaneously, which contributes to a low degree of differentiation between the languages (e.g., Hong Kong). Because both letters and letter strings are treated as syllable-level symbols, knowledge about the former would not contribute analytically to recognizing the latter. Rather, what may happen, at most, is a cueing effect similar to how Chinese phonetic radicals may provide syllable-level cueing for character pronunciation: Because *b* has a /bi/ pronunciation, therefore the string *bat*, which contains *b*, should be read as a syllable similar to /bi/. Exactly how and in what way /bi/ and the target syllable (/bæt/) are related, the child would not know. This mimics Chinese readers' use of phonetic radicals in making "educated guesses" about character pronunciations.

In addition, if letters represent syllables, then the string *bat* would be read, analytically, as /bi/-/ei/-/ti/, which actually fulfills the requirement of a spelling rather than a reading task. This is not unlike Chinese word reading: You simply combine the syllables represented by individual component characters and you get at the pronunciation of the host compound word. This may explain why spelling is so heavily emphasized as a critical indicator of English proficiency in many Chinese societies, especially in Hong Kong, where Chinese is taught through the look-and-say method. When children, and many adults as well, are so used to combining syllables to form syllable strings (as opposed to combining phonemes to form syllables, which itself is a very "foreign" idea), spelling English words out loud (i.e., uttering monosyllabic letter names) would make much more sense than reading English words by discovering and combining the component phonemes.

In summary, "Chinese-like" learning/processing of written English is a result of three factors, namely, syllable prominence of Chinese speech, the morphosyllabic basis of the character, and a look-and-say unanalytic approach to Chinese reading instruction. It must be emphasized that the look-and-say approach actually matches the nature of Chinese speech and is thus educationally sound; it is only when English learning is considered that problems with such a method arise. Because the imaginable (negative?) effect on learning to read English (L2) is due to how the child habitually processes Chinese (L1), one may consider the effect an example of cross-language transfer. According to our analysis, part of this transfer effect is attributable to how reading is taught.

According to Cheung and Ng (2003), Hong Kong is the only major Cantonese-speaking society relying on the look-and-say method for Chinese reading instruction. We therefore speculate that the kind of transfer described above would be most easily observable there. The alternative is to represent Chinese speech at subsyllabic levels by auxiliary symbols that function as reading aids. Auxiliary symbols are needed because Chinese writing by nature does not code subsyllabic sound segments. Currently this method takes two forms. First, in Taiwan, schoolchildren are introduced to Zhuyin Fuhao, which is a transcription system representing Mandarin onsets and rimes. Within the rime, the vowel and coda are not separately coded. Children familiar with this system could thus construct character pronunciation in an analytic fashion, by recalling the right onset and rime symbols and combining the corresponding sound segments. The system is not alphabetic because sound is not represented at a phoneme level; yet the principle is very different from phonetic cueing naturally found in compound characters because it involves subsyllabic representation and assembly of speech. Second, in Singapore and mainland China, Mandarin speech is officially romanized through a system known as pinyin, which is truly alphabetic. School children are introduced to the Roman alphabet in the first grade, before any characters are formally taught. They then learn to associate the letters and patterns of letters with segments of Mandarin speech. Children familiar with the system are able to construct character pronunciation by combining phonemes represented by Pinyin letters. The two methods of Chinese reading instruction used in Taiwan, Singapore, and mainland China are analogous to the phonics approach to English reading, because of their analytical nature.

Two points are notable with the use of these phonics methods. First, the speech segments highlighted by the auxiliary symbols do not correspond to units of meaning, nor do they fit into the syllable-timed nature of Chinese speech rhythm. As discussed, Chinese syllables are both phonologically (metrically) and semantically salient. Hence, looking from this angle, highlighting subsyllabic segments in writing may not be more efficient than using unanalyzed characters to represent unanalyzed syllables. Second, perhaps more important, the child would eventually need to link zhuyin or pinyin symbols to characters. After all, children are learning to read Chinese, which is character-based, not the transcription symbols. Hence there remains a problem of how the symbols are to be paired with the corresponding characters. One could think of no way but to do the pairing by rote. Note that a more direct way to achieve the same result is simply to learn character pronunciation by rote, in a look-and-say fashion.

Nevertheless, if learning English as a second language is also considered, using an alphabet to code Chinese may make the whole learning experience more consistent. The phonics approach to Chinese learning lays the foundation for the fundamental understanding that syllables can be divided into smaller segments, each of which corresponds to a written symbol. Many of these segments are nonsyllabic; combining them may or may not result in a syllable. This habit is consistent with and thus may facilitate reading English through phonological assembly. Therefore what was described previously in a consideration of Hong Kong as Chinese-like English learning may not occur; reading and spelling may be more easily separable and less mixed up in mainland China, Singapore, or Taiwan as a consequence.

Learning to Read Korean (L1) and English (L2)

In Korean, children's earliest reading instruction generally involves rote memorization of a standard CV syllable chart. Only later are children taught to analyze these syllables into component consonants and vowels, and then to recombine consonants and vowels to construct new words (Lee, Park, & Kim, 2000). Such a focus may promote children's sensitivity to both syllables and phonemes. One study on young Korean children has demonstrated that both phonemic awareness and syllable-level awareness are unique correlates of Hangul word recognition (Cho & McBride-Chang, 2005a), underscoring the importance of both psycholinguistic units for early Korean reading acquisition.

In contrast, given that fluent word recognition in English specifically requires phonemic representation, with syllables being ultimately less reliably represented by orthographic units than phonemes (e.g., Ziegler & Goswami, 2005), mastering phonemic awareness for English word recognition is essential. Korean schools typically begin teaching English in early primary grades. The focus on English instruction includes both oral language and reading and writing. However, a phonics approach to literacy instruction in either English or Korean is rarely used in school, though a phonics approach may be used outside of school. Regardless, a phonics approach to literacy teaching has not been systematically adopted in Korean.

Nevertheless, compared with Chinese, Korean Hangul may share more in common with English in terms of subsyllabic representation of speech in writing. Each Hangul letter maps onto a phoneme-sized sound unit; letters are combined into square blocks representing syllables following specific rules. This is similar to written English, in which letters are combined to form words (Seidenberg & McClelland, 1989). There has been some evidence that Korean adult learners of English generally perform better in analyzing the internal structure of English words than Chinese learners. However, some other evidence shows that this sensitivity affects only how words are decoded, not ultimate reading or recognition performance (Koda, 1999), suggesting that Chinese and Korean learners may master English word recognition at about the same level. Nevertheless, the latter tend to rely more on analytical phonological recoding, whereas the former rely more on holistic orthographic strategies

IMPLICATIONS FOR PHONOLOGICAL TRANSFER

Differences between Korean and Chinese learners in English reading bring up more fundamental questions surrounding the extent to which phonological transfer occurs across languages, and how it occurs. Some metalinguistic skills may apply universally to all children learning to read (e.g., Hancin-Bhatt & Nagy, 1994; Koda, 1998). Therefore an emerging consensus on cross-language studies is that similar component processes are involved in reading acquisition for diverse languages and orthographies (Chiappe, Siegel, & Wade-Wooley, 2002). On the other hand, there also exists variation for certain component processes (Koda, 2000). A systematic examination of phonological awareness in Chinese or Korean as L1 in relation to English as L2 may be particularly useful in refining our understanding of phonological transfer.

A number of studies have explored the issue of phonological transfer across languages and orthographies. Comeau, Cormier, Grandmaison, and Lacroix (1999), in one of the most comprehensive studies on the topic, demonstrated such transfer across English and French. In this study, English-speaking children in grades 1, 3, and 5, who were educated in a French immersion school, were tested on a variety of phonological awareness and word recognition skills longitudinally in both English and French. Phonological awareness in both French and English explained unique variance in subsequent literacy in each language. Several other studies, mostly focusing on phonological awareness at the phoneme level, have demonstrated similar phenomena. Many of these have demonstrated relatively strong correlations of L1 phonological awareness to L2 phonological awareness. Perhaps the majority of these studies have focused on phonological awareness in languages that share the same alphabet, such as English and French (e.g., Bruck & Genesee, 1995; Comeau et al., 1999) or English and Spanish (e.g., Cisero & Royer, 1995; Durgunoğlu, Nagy, & Hancin-Bhatt, 1993; Lindsey, Manis, & Bailey, 2003). Some of these studies have also indicated that phonological skills in the native language were strongly associated with word recognition in both the L1 and L2 (e.g., Comeau et al., 1999; Durgunoğlu et al., 1993; Lindsey et al., 2003). Indeed, Comeau et al. (1999) additionally demonstrated that second-language phonological awareness distinguished reading in both the L1 and L2 orthographies equally well in their longitudinal study. In all of these studies, however, the phonological units were represented by an alphabet that is basically similar across Indo-European languages. In the alphabets of French, Spanish, and English, phonemic awareness is also ultimately important for reading words because of the alphabetic principle, the idea that letters of the alphabet represent individual speech sounds, either individually (e.g., *b* makes a single sound) or in groups (e.g., *s* and *h* together form a single fricative speech sound, represented by the *sh* found in *short* or *shave*).

Based on evidence primarily from Indo-European languages, models of phonological awareness development have proposed that awareness of phonological units progresses from whole words to syllables through onset–rimes to phonemes (e.g., Ziegler & Goswami, 2005). Thus, children's metalinguistic knowledge of phonology progresses from broad speech units (words or syllables) to individual phonemes. What is most useful in this context is phonemes because they map directly onto individual letters or letter combinations. Implicit in this description is the additional notion that the narrower units of individual phonemes are actually more useful than the broader units of syllables for facilitating word recognition skills themselves. This is clearly sensible when only Indo-European languages are considered because such languages tend to be relatively phonologically reliable. Even in English, a relatively unreliable alphabetic orthography in terms of grapheme–phoneme mapping, most letters represent phonologically meaningful units the majority of the time. Thus efficient reading of English and some other Indo-European languages relies primarily on phonological knowledge, particularly in beginning readers for whom orthographic knowledge has not yet fully developed.

Chinese poses somewhat of a challenge to this model, however, because Chinese characters do not map in any way to individual phonemes. Because each character represents a morphosyllable, the smallest unit of phonological information actively required for word recognition in Chinese is at the syllable level. At the same time, however, the extent to which phoneme awareness, particularly phoneme onset awareness, is associated with Chinese character recognition has been addressed in several studies. Part of the impetus for such studies is that some techniques for teaching reading of Chinese, such as zhuyin fuhao or pinyin, are successful and may facilitate children's reading success in Chinese (Chen, Shu, Wu, & Anderson, 2003; Shu, Anderson, & Wu, 2000; Siok & Fletcher, 2001). In addition, some Chinese children may be taught to use phoneme onsets to look up characters in a dictionary (e.g., Siok & Fletcher 2001). Given the use of some phonological coding tools as an aid to Chinese character recognition across several Chinese societies, it may not be surprising that phoneme awareness has been linked to Chinese character recognition in some studies. For example, Huang and Hanley (1995) demonstrated that a task of Chinese phoneme deletion was significantly associated with Chinese character recognition.

Another reason that phoneme awareness, typically phoneme onset awareness, may be positively associated with Chinese character recognition is that phoneme awareness is typically a fairly difficult skill to master. Among young primary schoolchildren, it may be the case that those who are adept in any given cognitive skill may also tend to be better readers because general cognitive ability may partially account for differences in both phonological awareness (McBride-Chang, 1995) and word recognition (Stanovich, 2000). However, even if general reasoning skill can account for the correlations between phonological awareness and word recognition in Chinese, such an association does not necessarily imply that awareness of phoneme-level units is causally associated with Chinese character recognition. The extent to which phoneme awareness is important for Chinese character recognition, as well as Korean, has been an issue we have pursued in some recent work.

As described above, the facilitating effect of phonological awareness on reading depends on the level at which learning and processing take place. Given the importance of the syllable unit, both psycholinguistically and orthographically for Chinese and Korean, one might expect that the syllable unit of phonological awareness would be important in early reading acquisition. In contrast, for English as a native language or even as an L2, phonemes are naturally represented in writing, and thus it is important to fine-tune phonological sensitivity down to the phoneme level in order to read well. In this simple scenario, one would expect very limited transfer of reading proficiency, due to transfer of phonological awareness, between a nonalphabetic L1 and an alphabetic L2, because good reading requires different phonological abilities in the respective languages.

Nevertheless, the situation can be modified through using alternative methods of instruction. Even if we set aside the important issues of the nature of a script or a given spoken language, we might still expect the following results of L1–L2 transfer:

- L1: look-and-say; L2: look-and-say; result: significant transfer
- L1: phonics; L2: phonics; result: significant transfer
- L1: look-and-say; L2: phonics; result: limited transfer
- L1: phonics; L2: look-and-say; result: limited transfer

What happens in reality depends on the interplay between nature of script, nature of spoken language, and method of instruction (e.g., Bialystok, McBride-Chang, & Luk, 2005).

We tested some of these ideas in some studies on Chinese and Korean readers, many of whom were beginning readers of English as well (Cho & McBride-Chang, 2005a, 2005b; McBride-Chang, Bialystok, Chong, & Li, 2004; McBride-Chang, Cheung, Chow, Chow, & Choi, 2006; McBride-Chang & Ho, 2005). For all of the studies we review below, the methodology involved large-scale (typically involving 90 children or more) correlational studies. Our focus was on determining the extent to which particular psycholinguistic units were associated with reading and/or vocabulary learning among children who were in the relatively early stages of literacy acquisition of both their L1 and L2. Most tests of phonological awareness and other reading-related skills were created in our laboratory, and all of those reported had good internal consistency reliabilities as well as face validities.

In our first study of kindergarten and second-grade Korean children learning to read Korean Hangul, apart from age, we included measures of vocabulary knowledge, speed of processing, speeded naming, and two phonological awareness tasks to explain concurrently measured Hangul recognition for each grade level separately. Results were strikingly similar across grade levels (Cho & McBride-Chang, 2005a). For both groups, only phoneme and syllable awareness tasks were unique correlates of Korean word recognition with all other variables controlled. These results were in line with those of Aidinis and Nunes (2001), who found that phonological awareness at the levels of both the phoneme and syllable were independently associated with word spelling and reading among Greek children ages 5 to 7 years.

In a follow-up study using similar predictors (vocabulary knowledge, speeded naming, and phonological awareness measures) examining children's growth in reading skills from second to third grade, we demonstrated the primacy of syllable-level awareness for reading Korean Hangul even into third grade. For that study, we included measures of both Korean and English word recognition at third grade (no measures of English word recognition were available in second grade because the children had only just been introduced to learning English at that grade level). Results demonstrated that, even with Korean Hangul in second grade statistically controlled, Time 1 syllable deletion was a unique longitudinal predictor of Korean Hangul at Time 2 (the only other significant predictor was Time 1 Hangul recognition). In contrast, apart from age, the only significant predictor of English word recognition at Time 2 was phoneme onset deletion at Time 1.

Results from this longitudinal study (Cho & McBride-Chang, 2005b) are theoretically interesting for two reasons. First, results demonstrate clearly the primacy of the phoneme for reading English, as found in numerous previous studies, even for second-language learners, and these results contrast dramatically with results for reading of Hangul, *even among the same children, who were reading both orthographies.* Second, our findings underscore the importance of the syllable for reading Korean Hangul. Indeed, they suggest a somewhat different developmental trajectory for reading of Korean than that specified by Ziegler and Goswami (2005). Rather than centering on the importance of increasingly smaller units of phonological awareness with age and reading experience as proposed by the psycholinguistic grain size theory (Ziegler & Goswami, 2005), this particular study demonstrated that a larger unit of phonological awareness was superior to that of a smaller unit of phonological awareness in explaining word recognition in Korean longitudinally.

A correlational study (McBride-Chang et al., 2004) of word recognition in Chinese and English among kindergartners and first graders in three cultures, Xian (China), Hong Kong, and Toronto, demonstrated similar results to those found in the Korean study. This study contrasted Chinese children whose experiences in learning Chinese differed. Of particular relevance for a focus on phonological awareness is the fact that the children in Xian were systematically taught pinyin as an aid to reading Chinese, whereas those in Hong Kong received no phonological coding instruction in learning to read Chinese. Given this difference, one might anticipate that sensitivity to phonological awareness at the phoneme level could be more strongly related to reading in Xian than in Hong Kong. However, across these cultures the syllable deletion task explained Chinese character recognition better than did the phoneme deletion task. Although the syllable task was also significantly associated with English word recognition in Hong Kong and Toronto, the phoneme task was more strongly associated with English word recognition than was the syllable task in both Xian and Toronto. Although these results are somewhat less straightforward than the ones on Korean, they again underscore the importance of the syllable level of awareness relative to that of the phoneme for reading of Chinese. In addition, awareness of the phoneme tends to be important for learning to read English, even as a second language.

In some related work (McBride-Chang & Ho, 2005), we examined phonological processing skills in both Chinese and English in relation to word reading in both scripts among young Hong Kong Chinese readers. We found that phonological processing in English as a second language was not useful in explaining English word recognition, although native Chinese phonological processing skills explained unique variance in both Chinese and English word recognition. Thus, unlike findings from Indo-European languages (e.g., Comeau et al., 1999), phonological transfer was not equal in this study. There was, however, one exception to this result: Phoneme sensitivity as measured using a scaled score English invented spelling measure was strongly and uniquely associated with English, but not Chinese, word recognition. Again, these results highlight the importance of phoneme-level awareness for English but not Chinese; syllable awareness in Chinese tends to be more strongly associated with Chinese reading than other phonological awareness measures, at least among beginning readers.

We even obtained similar results when examining awareness of the units of phonemes and syllables in relation to oral vocabulary knowledge, rather than word recognition, of Chinese and English in Hong Kong kindergartners (McBride-Chang et al., 2006). In that study, children were tested on receptive vocabulary knowledge in both Cantonese (L1) and English (L2). With age, nonverbal reasoning, and word recognition skills in both English and Chinese statistically controlled, syllable awareness in Chinese was the strongest correlate of Cantonese receptive vocabulary knowledge in a regression equation; Chinese phoneme onset awareness was not associated with Chinese vocabulary knowledge. In contrast, only the phoneme awareness measure, but not the syllable awareness measure, was significantly associated with English vocabulary knowledge in these Chinese children.

Again, these results do not fit perfectly with some theories of language or literacy development developed primarily based on Indo-European languages. For example, according to the lexical restructuring hypothesis (Metsala, 1999), children's sensitivity to finer phonological discriminations develops in concert with vocabulary knowledge across languages. From this theory, one might have anticipated that in both Chinese (L1) and English (L2) in this study, phoneme awareness would explain variations in vocabulary knowledge, whereas syllable awareness, which is a larger and less fine-grained unit, would not. In contrast, our results echo some of those obtained from studies of word recognition in both Korean and Chinese: The larger syllable unit of phonological awareness tends to discriminate variability in vocabulary knowledge of Chinese as it does for word recognition skill in Chinese. In contrast, even among second-language learners, the phoneme unit of awareness tends to discriminate variations in performance on both measures of reading and vocabulary knowledge for English, as found previously for children learning English as their first language (e.g., Adams, 1990).

IMPLICATIONS FOR FURTHER RESEARCH AND PRACTITIONERS

Further Research

The foregoing discussion suggests that reading proficiency is a joint result of orthographic characteristics and instructional methods. In a multilingual context, the emphasis on reading instruction makes it necessary for us to consider sociolinguistic factors such as language prestige and speaker identification, which necessarily affects how we choose to implement language education at a societal level. In addition, the interplay between multiple orthographies in the form of learning transfer is also worth serious examination. Having this big picture in mind, we think the following questions may guide future research on reading development in a multilingual environment.

How much of poor reading is actually explainable by a "mismatch" between orthographic characteristics and instructional methods? For instance, how may the amount of use of pinyin, which represents Chinese speech in phonemic terms, affect the reading of syllable-based Chinese characters? In English reading instruction, how may a "whole-word" approach, which biases the child toward whole-word and whole-syllable processing, affect reading the phoneme-based Roman alphabet?

Two follow-up questions are derived. First, is it always beneficial to start with a script that is phonologically as fine-tuned as possible? If the child's first-learned script is alphabetic, such learning may get transferred to facilitate reading a second script that may or may not be alphabetic. If the first-learned script is nonalphabetic, one may consider starting the child with an auxiliary system that is phoneme based to aid learning the first script. Second, how may the notion of a match between orthography and instructional method apply to helping dyslexic children? If the main difficulty for the dyslexic child is deficient mapping between speech and print, then emphasizing the natural correspondence (match) between the two representations and also bringing out incidents of noncorrespondence (mismatch) may enhance such mapping.

Finally, if reading comprehension instead of reading aloud is measured as the outcome variable, what role would the representation of morphemes in writing play on top of phonological representation? How may morphological and phonological representation interact in determining reading efficiently for speech and meaning? In Chinese, for instance, the natural correspondence between speech (syllable), meaning (lexical morpheme), and writing (character) may have some interesting implications for how reading aloud and reading comprehension are accomplished, compared to alphabetic English.

Practitioners

A clear message that is brought out by the foregoing discussion is that the reading instructor should pay some attention to what the orthography *is meant* to convey, and design her teaching program accordingly. For example, Chinese characters as the primary unit of writing are visually very distinct; they naturally represent syllables and lexical morphemes. In Chinese reading instruction, therefore, one may put more emphasis on learning syllable (instead of phoneme) pronunciation and also how higher-level meaning is derived from combining morphemes. On the contrary, in phonologically more (e.g., Italian) or less (e.g., English) transparent alphabetic systems one may focus on phoneme pronunciation and meaning derivation at the word level.

From an assessment point of view it may be worth looking at a variety of measures on top of conventional reading so as to arrive at a more comprehensive estimate of the child's abilities that support reading. One important auxiliary measure could be phonological awareness, which reflects children's ability analyze speech into smaller units, like onsets and phonemes. Because phonological awareness has been shown many times to correlate with and predict reading aloud, it may provide valuable information about the child's future reading performance. Fast mapping ability can be measured by tasks mimicking the rapid (digit) naming test, tapping children's ability to accurately and quickly come up with verbal labels for familiar things (and digits). This, too, is an important predictor of reading aloud. Last but not least, morphological awareness can also be assessed to examine the child's ability to combine morphemes productively. Information about these cognitive correlates that have been shown to be associated with reading is valuable in profiling the child's reading achievement.

In this chapter we examined the effect of learning to read Chinese and Korean on the later acquisition of alphabetic English as a second script. Reading in Chinese and Korean is syllable-based because the smallest phonological unit that is represented in these two orthographies is the syllable. If a look-and-say unanalytic method is used for early Chinese and Korean reading instruction, syllable-level phonological information is further emphasized and brought out as corresponding to units of writing. The resultant syllable-level phonological awareness facilitates Chinese and Korean reading because syllables are saliently represented in these writings as spatially marked square-like blocks. Nevertheless, syllable-level phonological awareness does not facilitate reading English as a second script, which because of its alphabetic nature requires assembling phoneme-sized segments into words, somehow bypassing the syllable level of organization (i.e., orthographic syllables are not always perceptually distinct). In contrast, if subsyllabic or phoneme-level phonological information is emphasized in Chinese and Korean learning through the use of an auxiliary alphabet on top of characters to transcribe Chinese speech or an emphasis on the letters embedded in Korean eumjeols, the resultant phoneme-level phonological awareness would probably transfer to and facilitate English reading.

CONCLUSION

Reading is a function of how orthography represents speech and what instructional method is employed to address the problem of reading. These two factors jointly determine the kind of phonological awareness the young reader is likely to possess, which affects reading performance. A universal theory of reading must take into consideration these parameters. In biscriptal children more communication, or transfer, is expected to occur between the two scripts if they are comparable in these parameter values. Hence, in our example situation, alphabetic English reading is cross-linguistically facilitated only if written Chinese or Korean is taught in an alphabetic way, so that phoneme-level phonological awareness is promoted.

NOTE

1. Cantonese is transcribed in Jyutping, a romanization scheme developed by the Lingusitic Society of Hong Kong in 1993. In this system the six tones are represented by numbers.

REFERENCES

Adams, M. J. (1990). *Beginning to Read: Thinking and Learning about Print*. Cambridge, MA: MIT Press.

Aidinis, A., & Nunes, T. (2001). The role of different levels of phonological awareness in the development of reading and spelling in Greek. *Reading and Writing: An Interdisciplinary Journal, 14*, 145–177.

Bertelson, P. (1986). The onset of literacy: Liminal remarks. *Cognition, 24*, 1–30.

Bertelson, P., de Gelder, B., Tfouni, L. V., & Morais, J. (1989). Metaphonological abilities of adult illiterates: New evidence of heterogeneity. *European Journal of Cognitive Psychology, 1*(3), 239–250.

Bialystok, E., McBride-Chang, C., & Luk, G. (2005). Bilingualism, language proficiency, and learning to read in two writing systems. *Journal of Educational Psychology, 97,* 580–590.

Bruck, M., & Genesee, F. (1995). Phonological awareness in young second language learners. *Journal of Child Language, 22,* 307–324.

Chen, H.-C. (1992). Reading comprehension in Chinese: Implications from character reading times. In H.-C. Chen & O. J. L. Tzeng (Eds.), *Language processing in Chinese* (pp. 175–205). Amsterdam: Elsevier.

Chen, H.-C. (1996). Chinese reading and comprehension: A cognitive psychology perspectives. In M. H. Bond (Ed.), *The handbook of Chinese psychology* (pp.43–62). Hong Kong: Oxford University Press.

Chen, X., Shu, H., Wu, N., & Anderson, R. C. (2003). Stages in learning to pronounce Chinese characters. *Psychology in the Schools, 40,* 115–124.

Cheung, H., & Ng., L. K. H. (2003). Chinese reading development in some major Chinese societies: An introduction. In C. McBride-Chang & H.-C. Chen (Eds.), *Reading development in Chinese children* (pp. 1–17). Westport, CT: Greenwood Press.

Chiappe, P., Siegel, L. S., & Wade-Wooley, L. (2002). Linguistic diversity and the development of reading skills: A longitudinal study. *Scientific Studies of Reading, 6,* 369–400.

Cho, J.-R., & McBride-Chang, C. (2005a). Correlates of Korean Hangul Acquisition among kindergartners and second graders. *Scientific Studies of Reading, 9,* 3–16.

Cho, J. R., & McBride-Chang, C. (2005b). Levels of phonological awareness in Korean and English: A 1-year longitudinal study. *Journal of Educational Psychology, 97,* 564–571.

Cisero, C. A., & Royer, J. M. (1995). The development and cross-language transfer of phonological awareness. *Contemporary Educational Psychology, 20,* 275–303.

Comeau, L., Cormier, P., Grandmaison, E., & Lacroix, D. (1999). A longitudinal study of phonological processing skills in children learning to read in a second language. *Journal of Educational Psychology, 91,* 29–43.

de Jong, P. F., & van der Leij, A. (1999). Specific contributions of phonological abilities to early reading acquisition: Results from a Dutch latent variable longitudinal study. *Journal of Educational Psychology, 91,* 450–476.

Durgunoğlu, A. Y., Nagy, W. E., & Hancin-Bhatt, B. J. (1993). Cross-language transfer of phonological awareness. *Journal of Educational Psychology, 85,* 453–465.

Elbro, C., Borstrom, I., & Peterson, D. K. (1998). Predicting dyslexia from kindergarten: The importance of distinctness of phonological representations of lexical items. *Reading Research Quarterly, 33,* 36–60.

Hancin-Bhatt, B., & Nagy, W. E. (1994). Lexical transfer and second-language morphological development. *Applied Psycholinguistics, 15,* 289–310.

Huang, H.-S., & Hanley, J. R. (1995). Phonological awareness and visual skills in learning to read Chinese and English. *Cognition, 54,* 73–98.

Kim, J., & Davis, C. (2006). Literacy acquisition in Korean Hangul. In R. M. Joshi & P. G. Aaron (Eds.), *Handbook of orthography and literacy* (pp. 377–387). Mahwah, NJ: Erlbaum.

Koda, K. (1998). The role of phonemic awareness in L2 reading. *Second Language Research, 14,* 194–215.

Koda, K. (1999). Development of L2 intraword orthographic sensitivity and decoding skills. *The Modern Language Journal, 83,* 51–64

Koda, K. (2000). Cross-linguistic variations in L2 morphological awareness. *Applied Psycholinguistics, 21,* 297–320.

Lee, J., Park, W., & Kim, H. (2000). Literacy education Korea: A sociocultural perspective. *Childhood Education, 76,* 347–351.

Li, C. N., & Thompson, S. A. (1981). *Mandarin Chinese: A functional reference grammar.* Berkeley: University of California Press.

Li, W., Anderson, R. C., Nagy, W., & Zhang, H. (2002). Facets of metalinguistic awareness that contribute to Chinese literacy. In W. Li. J. S. Gaffney, & J. L. Packard (Eds.), *Chinese children's reading acquisition: Theoretical and pedagogical issues* (pp. 87–106). Boston: Kluwer Academic.

Lindsey, K., Manis, F., & Bailey, C. (2003). Prediction of first-grade reading in Spanish-speaking English-language learners. *Journal of Educational Psychology, 95,* 482–494.

Lukatela, K., Carello, C., Shankweiler, D., & Liberman, I. Y. (1995). Phonological awareness in illiterates: Observations from Serbo-Croatian. *Applied Psycholinguistics, 16*(4), 463–487.

Lundberg, I., Olofsson, A., & Wall, S. (1980). Reading and spelling skills in the first school years predicted from phonemic awareness skills in kindergarten. *Scandinavian Journal of Psychology, 21,* 159–173.

Manis, F. R., & Freedman, L. (2001). The relationship of naming speed to multiple reading measures in disabled and normal readers. In M. Wolf (Ed.), *Dyslexia, fluency, and the brain* (pp. 65–92). Timonium, MD: York Press.

McBride-Chang, C. (1995). Phonological processing, speech perception, and reading disability: An integrative review. *Educational Psychologist, 30,* 109–121.

McBride-Chang C., Bialystok E., Chong K.-K. Y., & Li, Y. (2004). Levels of phonological awareness in three cultures. *Journal of Experimental Child Psychology, 89,* 93–111.

McBride-Chang, C., Cheung, H., Chow, B. Y., Chow, C. L., & Choi, L. L. (2006). Metalinguistic skills and vocabulary knowledge in Chinese (L1) and English (L2). *Reading and Writing, 19,* 695–716.

McBride-Chang, C., & Ho, C. S.-H. (2005). Predictors of beginning reading in Chinese and English: A 2-year longitudinal study of Chinese kindergartners. *Scientific Studies of Reading, 9,* 117–144.

Metsala, J. L. (1999). Young children's phonological awareness and nonword repetition as a function of vocabulary development. *Journal of Educational Psychology, 91,* 3–19.

Morais, J., Bertelson, P., Cary, L., & Alegria, J. (1986). Literacy training and speech segmentation. *Cognition, 24,* 45–64.

Muter, V., Hulme, C., Snowling, M., & Taylor, S. (1998). Segmentation, not rhyming, predicts early progress in learning to read. *Journal of Experimental Child Psychology, 71,* 3–27.

Seidenberg, M. S., & McClelland, J. L. (1989). A distributed, developmental model of word recognition and naming. *Psychological Review, 96,* 523–568.

Shu, H., Anderson, R. C., & Wu, N. (2000). Phonetic awareness: Knowledge of orthography–phonology relationships in the character acquisition by Chinese children. *Journal of Educational Psychology, 92,* 56–62.

Siok, W., & Fletcher, P. (2001). The role of phonological awareness and visual orthographic skills in Chinese reading acquisition. *Developmental Psychology, 37,* 886–899.

Snow, C. E., Burns, M. S., & Griffin, P. (1998). The process of learning to read. In E. C. Snow, M. S. B. Burns, & P. Griffin (Eds.), *Preventing reading difficulties in children* (pp. 41–84). Washington, DC: National Research Council Press.

Sprenger-Charolles, L., Siegel, L. S., & Bechennec, D. (1998). Phonological mediation and semantic and orthographic factors in silent reading in French. *Scientific Studies in Reading, 2,* 3–29.

Stanovich, K. E. (2000). *Progress in understanding reading.* New York: Guilford Press.

Suen, Y. C. (1979). *N*-gram statistics for natural language understanding and text processing. *IEE Transactions on Pattern Analysis and Machine Intelligence, 1,* 164–172.

Suen, Y. C. (1982). Computational analysis of Mandarin sounds with reference to the English language. In J. Hoecky (Ed.), *Coling* (pp. 371–376). Prague: North-Holland.

Taylor, I., & Taylor, M. M. (1983). *The psychology of reading.* New York: Academic Press.

Treiman, R. (1985). Onsets and rimes as units of spoken syllables: Evidence from children. *Journal of Experimental Child Psychology, 39,* 161–181.

Treiman, R., Mullennix, J., Bijeljac-Babic, R., & Richmond-Welty, E. D. (1995). The special role of rimes in the description, use and acquisition of English orthography. *Journal of Experimental Psychology: General, 124,* 107–136

Treiman, R., & Zukowski, A. (1996). Children's sensitivity to syllable, onsets, rimes, and phonemes. *Journal of Experimental Child Psychology, 161,* 193–215.

Wagner, R. K., Torgesen, J. K., & Rashotte, C. A. (1994). Development of reading-related phonological processing abilities: New evidence of bidirectional causality from a latent variable longitudinal study. *Developmental Psychology, 30,* 73–87.

Wang, W. S.-Y. (1973). The Chinese language. *Scientific American, 228,* 50–60.

Wong, S. L. (1984). *A Chinese syllabary pronounced according to the dialect of Canton.* Hong Kong: Chung Hwa Books.

Zhou, Y. G. (1978). To what degree are the phonetic radicals' of present-day Chinese characters still phonetic radicals? *Zhongguo Yuwen [Chinese Language Journal] 146,* 172–177.

Ziegler, J. C., & Goswami, U. (2005). Reading acquisition, developmental dyslexia, and skilled reading across languages: A psycholinguistic grain size theory. *Psychological Bulletin, 131,* 3–29.

CHAPTER 8

■ ■ ■

Chinese Language Learners of English Use More Orthographic– Lexical Than Phonological Strategies in English Word Recognition and Spelling

CHE KAN LEONG

Following Durgunoğlu (2002), we use the term *language learners* (LLs) to refer to students learning their home and community language or first language (L1) while at the same time developing literacy in the school language as a second language (L2). The term LLs is used mainly in this paper even though the usual expression, bilinguals, may also apply.

The term LLs may be appropriate for the school population in Hong Kong, a special administration region of China since 1997. It is official government policy that the nearly 1 million preschool, primary, and secondary students should be trilingual in the spoken languages of Cantonese (home and community language), the lingua franca Putongua (literally, speech of the common people), and English. They must also be biliterate in both their native L1 Chinese and L2 English. This notion of becoming trilingual and biliterate in Cantonese-speaking Chinese children differs from that of the bilingual, biliterate, and bicultural issues discussed by Snow and Kang (2006). Their context was immigrant children in the United States, with the L2 learners trying to catch up in literacy skills and a second culture with

188

their American monolinguals. The students in Hong Kong are mostly indigenous to the territory and do not have the added challenge of accommodating a second culture. We agree with Snow and Kang (2006), however, that literacy learning and particularly reading should be the focus of becoming bi- or trilingual and biliterate.

The purpose of this chapter is to emphasize the role of orthographic–lexical factors in 9- to 12-year-old Cantonese-speaking Chinese students learning to read and spell words in English as a second language (L2). We first define operationally the term *orthographic knowledge* as it applies to alphabetic English and morphosyllabic Chinese. We sketch some of the factors affecting these language learners in learning reading and spelling in their L2. We then discuss the issue of possible linguistic transfer and constraints from L1 to L2. The argument is that prevailing approaches to the learning and teaching of Chinese characters and words as L1 and also English as L2 in Hong Kong elementary schools may explain why Chinese students use more orthographic–lexical strategies than phonological processing strategies, at least in this age group, in their reading and spelling English words. We buttress our argument with an exploratory study and two studies of cohorts of Chinese children acquiring literacy in English.

ORTHOGRAPHIC KNOWLEDGE
OPERATIONALLY DEFINED

Orthographic knowledge is explained by Barker, Torgesen, and Wagner (1992) as "[involving] memory of specific visual-spelling patterns that identify individual words, or word parts, on the printed page" (pp. 335–336). The orthographic form of a word is generally regarded as a sequence of letters relating in a systematic way to the phonological properties of the word (Ehri, 1980, 1997; Goswami, 1990). The sequence of letters must specify letter identities comprising the spelling of a word and also the order among the graphemes, which specify abstract letter identity (Venezky, 1970). Orthographic and phonological processes might be separable but equal, and the latter process might be reinforced by the former, as argued by Foorman (1994, 1995). Alternatively, orthography and phonology are "integral" to one each other, even though it is difficult to devise "pure" measures of orthographic processing, just as it is difficult to devise "pure" measures of phonological processing (Wagner & Barker, 1994).

Typical Assessment of English Orthographic Knowledge

Typically, orthographic knowledge is assessed by such tasks as print exposure, orthographic choice of homophonic heterographs (e.g., gawn–*gone*), homophonic choice involving meaning categorization (e.g., *rose–rows* for the name of a flower), and the like. Barker et al. (1992) showed that the orthographic and homophonic tasks made a significant contribution independent of the level of phonological skills to five different types of reading measures, including timed and untimed isolated word recognition. Castles, Holmes, Neath, and Kinoshita (2003, Experiment 2) found a homophone judgment task to be a good predictor of word-specific orthographic knowledge with minimum phonological involvement. In this task 22 eleven-year-old children were given a spoken definition, such as "a green vegetable," and had to select the correct choice of two written words that were phonologically homophonic ("been–*bean*"). Castles et al. found that the use of orthographic knowledge provided added influence on phonemic awareness tasks. There is also some evidence (Castles et al., 2003, Experiment 3) that, for adult language learners, orthographic influences on metalinguistic tasks may be automatic and not just strategic.

Orthographic Knowledge of Chinese Characters

Orthographic Knowledge

Orthographic knowledge in Chinese differs from that in English. In the first place, a distinction must be made between a Chinese character (zi) as a basic orthographic unit or graphic symbol and a word (ci) consisting usually of two or more characters. The basis of character compositionality is the corpus of about 560 foundational *bujians*, which subsume about 212 *radicals* with constituent phonetic and semantic cues as aids in reading/spelling and in accessing dictionaries (Zhong guo guo jia yu wei, 1998). A character almost always corresponds to a morpheme (not a phoneme) in the spoken language, whereas a word is the smallest independent unit of meaning and is polymorphemic (Leong, 1997).

Take as an example, the English word "swimming, to swim." In Chinese, this word consists of two graphic units or characters (zi) to denote "to play in the water" 游泳 with both characters having the semantic radical in the left half of the character to denote water or hydro. The right half of the character or the phonetic radical indicates the speech sound or most likely pronunciation. The phonetic radical has two sense-discriminative functions. It discriminates the composite character from others with similar components and denotes a morpheme or a character.

Orthographic knowledge in Chinese thus refers to the sensitivity of intracharacter or zi units of the phonetic and semantic radicals. These may provide some clues to the pronunciation and meaning of a character even though the mapping from phonetic and semantic radicals to pronunciation and meaning is not isomorphic or invariant.

Morphological Knowledge

Orthographic knowledge in Chinese is distinguished from morphological knowledge. Morphological knowledge refers to intercharacter relatedness with prefixing and suffixing a constituent form to a base form to produce new two-, three-, or even four-character words (see Chao, 1968, and Packard, 2000, for discussion of linguistic and cognitive aspects). As another example, the character ice 冰 (note the semantic radical on the left meaning hydro) can be followed by such characters as "water, cold" to mean "icy water, icy cold" or can be preceded by "thin, break" to mean "thin ice, ice breaking. The *analytic* process of intracharacter radicals is part of the productivity of orthographic knowledge, which helps Chinese language learners to be more sensitive to the functional aspects of intracharacter relationships. The *synthetic* process of intercharacter morphological knowledge relates to the productivity of Chinese words. Morphological awareness and processing are the subjects of increasing investigation in relation to early reading (e.g., McBride-Chang et al., 2005), reading disorders (e.g., Shu, McBride-Chang, Wu, & Liu, 2006), and in Chinese reading comprehension and its difficulties at the secondary level (Leong & Ho, 2008). In this chapter, the focus is on the orthographic rather than morphologic processing of Chinese characters.

Chinese children have some awareness of the relationship between phonetic and meaning radicals, and the better readers are those with greater radical awareness (Shu & Anderson, 1997). Chinese children may be able to use their partial orthographic knowledge in reading Chinese characters (Anderson, Li, Ku, Shu, & Wu, 2003). Furthermore, in their detailed study of the writing samples of 1,200 Chinese children and the written spellings from 300 children, Shen and Bear (2000) showed that their spelling errors were not random. Rather, these spelling errors demonstrated a developmental trend with more graphemic and semantic errors as compared with phonological errors from grades 1 to 6. This pattern also indicated that older children were more aware of the configuration of characters, the principles of the phonetic and semantic radicals, and the lexical features of characters and words.

TRANSFER AND CONSTRAINTS FROM L1 TO L2

Researchers in L2 learning (e.g., Bialystok, 1991, 2001; Sharwood Smith, 1991) have proposed a theory of interlanguage to explain how linguistic transfer and constraints work. The general idea is that a successive reorganization of psychological and linguistic processes (i.e., a series of systematic "interlanguages") is acquired among L2 learners to approximate the skills of native language users in the mastery of the target L2. Both Bialystok and Sharwood Smith emphasize the interaction of knowledge systems and control processes as the crux of interlanguage or cross-linguistic influences on L2 learning.

Acquisition of Interlanguages

How do L2 learners acquire a series of systematic interlanguages to achieve competence? In what way does the native language help or constrain their learning of L2? We would not agree with the dictum that bilingualism refers to native-like control of two languages (Bloomfield, 1933/1962). Following MacNamara (1967), we operationally define bilinguals or LLs learning a second language broadly as individuals with a minimum competence in one or more of these four language domains: listening, speaking, reading, or writing in a language other than their mother tongue. The term *competence* is used not in the formal abstract linguistic sense, but in terms of actual language performance (MacWhinney, 1987). The aim of competence in L2 learning should be "near-nativeness" (Sorace, 2003). In what way and to what extent do some of the research findings of L1 learning apply to L2 learning?

The broad answer from the literature suggests that theories and research findings in L1 learning may be transferred and adapted to L2 language learning under certain circumstances. The possible transfer from morpho-syllabic Chinese to alphabetic English differs from the transfer between two alphabetic language and writing systems. A good example is in the realm of speaking. Since reading in both L1 and L2 is built on listening and speaking, it may be appropriate to digress briefly into this domain of oral language learning as a precursor to literacy acquisition.

Impact of L1 Chinese on L2 English: Speech Production and Speech Perception

Experimentally, there is evidence of cross-linguistic constraints on Chinese learners of English from psychoacoustic studies by Flege, McCutcheon, and Smith (1987). Flege et al. examined the acoustic, temporal, and aerodynamic parameters distinguishing the production of /p/ and /b/ in English word final positions, the duration of labial closure, the duration of voicing, and the peak oral air pressure in native Chinese children and adults (Putonghua or Mandarin speaking) as compared with native English children and adults. One of the main findings of the Flege et al. study was that the duration of voicing in the closure interval of /b/ was in the predicted direction: of English adults performing better than English children, who in turn were better than Chinese children, followed by Chinese adults. Flege et al. suggested that because Putonghua Chinese lacks voiced stops in word final positions, the Chinese adults were perceived to devoice the stop consonants /b/, /d/, and /g/. The Chinese adults might be implicitly aware of the voicing difference between /p/ and /b/ but might not be able to access the implicit knowledge to bring it to the explicit level. Compared with the Chinese children in the study, the Chinese adults made less effective use of perceptual inputs associated with stop consonants, perhaps because they did not enlarge sufficiently the supraglottal cavity to sustain voicing or had not learned to do so. Flege et al. pointed to the need for experience in listening to and uttering English stops, and they also emphasized the need for high-quality language training in general (see also Flege & Fletcher, 1992).

Impact of L1 Chinese on L2 English: Phonological and Orthographic Knowledge

The speech perception constraints imposed on the explicit learning of Chinese children and adults in perceiving English final stop consonants (Flege et al., 1987) raise the question of the impact of Chinese as L1 on other aspects of English as L2. The literature is equivocal as to whether phonology, orthography, morphology, or syntax is affected more.

In their study of 46 Putonghua-speaking Chinese immigrant children (mean age 8 years) in the Washington, DC, area, Wang, Perfetti, and Liu (2005) found a certain level of phonological transfer from Chinese lexical tone-processing skill (i.e., tone matching by segmenting mismatched rime structure) to English pseudoword reading, even after taking English phoneme skill into account. Their results showed that pinyin naming (a phonetic system to aid the reading of characters) was highly correlated with English pseudoword reading. This outcome suggested that awareness of phonological structure is not specific to one language. However, Wang et al. (2005) also hinted at "orthographic transfer [using orthographic choice of character/noncharacter in Chinese and orthographic choice such as *ffeb, beff* in English, where the double consonant *ff* is in an illegal position] across two writing systems [Chinese and English] is less likely ... " (p. 83).

This tentative statement should be read in the context of an earlier study by Wang, Koda, and Perfetti (2003). The researchers compared 21 native Korean and 20 native Chinese adult readers learning English as L2 on English tasks, such as a semantic category judgment task (e.g., whether *rows* is "a flower"). The Chinese participants were found to rely more on orthographic than phonological information and made more incorrect phonological errors, as compared with the Korean participants with similar literacy background. In a second experiment, these researchers gave their Chinese ESL and Korean ESL participants a phoneme deletion task with phonemes existing in both Chinese and Korean. The participants were asked to delete the designated speech sound, say aloud the new word, and write down this new word, which should show a different spelling from the original item (e.g., in *might*, the new word was *my* after deleting the /t/ sound). In this challenging phoneme deletion task, the adult learners were required to manipulate the individual phonemes in the word and also to access their spelling knowledge of the newly formed word. The Chinese participants were found to produce more phonological errors but orthographically plausible written responses (e.g., the production of *may* or *me* in the above item was coded as phonologically incorrect but orthographically plausible or acceptable). The Korean participants were significantly better than their Chinese counterparts in deleting the designated phonemes orally, presumably because of the alphabetic nature of the Korean Hangul syllables.

There is corroborative evidence from a study by Wang and Geva (2003) of 30 Cantonese-speaking Chinese children learning English as a second language in the Toronto area, compared with 33 native English-speaking children. In a confrontation spelling task of orthographically legal letter strings (CCVC, such as *thop* or CVCC, such as *poth*) and illegal letter strings (e.g., *stkv*), the Chinese children performed significantly better on the illegal unpronounceable letter strings. In this task individual children were shown one of the 12 items at a time for 2 seconds, then were asked to pay very close attention to the item and to write down the name of the item. Wang and Geva (2003) attributed this better performance of the Chinese children to their persistent practice to acquire the requisite orthographic–lexical skills essential to learning Chinese characters and words. They suggested these results as showing some positive orthographic–lexical transfer to spelling the type of English legal and illegal letter strings, although they also found negative transfer in a pseudoword spelling-to-dictation task in which the Chinese children performed more poorly than their L1 controls.

Possible Effects of Teaching Approaches

The Wang and Geva (2003) and Wang et al. (2003) studies provide the basic framework of the present chapter that Cantonese-speaking Chinese children between the ages of 9 and 12 may rely more on orthographic–lexical skills than phonological skills in reading and spelling regular and exception English words. This is usually explained as being due to the characteristics of Chinese. However, one other factor that should be taken into account in L2 learning is the teaching approaches in both L1 and L2. The influence of teaching methods was also emphasized by Seymour and Evans (1994) in learning English as a first language, and by Rickard Liow and Poon (1998) in reading and spelling English words in multilingual Singaporean Chinese children. That language learning, especially for learners using one language at home and another language in school, should take into account the social milieu of the environment is emphasized by Bialystok (2007) and MacWhinney (2001).

When it comes to Chinese (L1) teaching, Shu, Chen, Anderson, Wu, and Xuan (2003) found that little of the logic and principles of formation of Chinese characters was taught to Chinese children, even though they might have some implicit awareness of the orthography to phonology and semantic relationships necessary for the encoding and decoding of characters and words. However, Anderson et al. (2003) showed that Chinese children could use partial information in pronouncing tone-different characters provided that they were exposed repeatedly to the pronunciation of tone-different characters and had some level of metalinguistic awareness.

To summarize this part of the discussion, there is some evidence that in reading and spelling English words, Chinese children draw on their orthographic–lexical knowledge from their L1. They are taught in a more holistic manner. The question is how the teaching approaches and the strategies taught to children reflect on their approaches to English word recognition and spelling. In the following sections we report on an exploratory study to test indirectly the possible effects of instruction. We then summarize two studies showing the structural relationship of orthographical and phonological processing in reading and spelling English regular and exception words by Chinese learners of English.

An Exploratory Study

English is taught in Hong Kong from kindergarten onward in a rather holistic manner, beginning with the recitation of letter names, progressing to word and sentence reading, all the while emphasizing meaning more than the alphabetic principle. The typical teaching from grade 1 onward is to stress listening and speaking with progressive introduction of sentence patterns and grammatical structures. Children are taught to use contracted forms such as *it's*, *I've*, *when's*, *what's*, and similar contractions to approximate the act of face-to-face verbal communication. Moreover, a great deal of formal grammar is taught such as present continuous tense, past tense, and the like. From this observation and the study of curriculum materials it was reasoned that Chinese grade school children would find it relatively easy to use correct inflected forms of English words.

This expectation contrasts with findings of Bryant, Nunes, and their colleagues in their series of studies of the role of "grammar" (morphology and syntax) in children learning to spell (Bryant, Devine, Ledward, & Nunes, 1997; Bryant, Nunes, & Bindman, 2000; Kemp & Bryant, 2003; Nunes, Bryant, & Bindman, 1997a, 1997b). Nunes et al. (1997a) found from their longitudinal study of 363 children in grades 2, 3, and 4 a developmental sequence in moving from phonetic to inflectional morphological spelling strategies, at least in the analogic use of the inflected morphological form /-ed/ to form past regular verbs. Proficient spellers should also be sensitive to the phonotactics (i.e., arrangement of phonemes in their phonological environment) of the allomorphic bound morpheme /-ed/ that affects the surface phonetic renderings of such words as *ask-ed*, *wait-ed*, and *show-ed*.

Bryant et al. (1997, 2000) focused on children's learning about apostrophes and the grammatical status of words containing them to further understand the relation between spelling and grammar. The Bryant et al. (1997) study showed that British children between the ages of 9 and 11 years had "striking difficulties" with the use of apostrophes to signify possessive nouns, but their use of apostrophes could also be improved with short training. The Bryant et al. (2000) study further found that morphosyntactic awareness predicted children's use of the apostrophe even after controlling for phonological sensitivity and that such awareness promoted the learning of conventional spelling for morphemes. These results indicate that a deeper understanding of the morphological structure led to better spelling performance in native English-speaking children. Given the observation of the mandated and predominant teaching of contracted forms of English words to elementary school children in Hong Kong, it could be hypothesized that they might not show the same developmental pattern and experience the kind of difficulties shown in the Bryant and Nunes studies.

Participants, Task, and Procedure

The participants in this exploratory study were 156 Cantonese-speaking 10- to 12-year-old Chinese children in grades 4, 5, and 6 in three "average" and fairly representative schools in Hong Kong. There were 44 children (17 boys and 27 girls) in grade 4, 76 children (40 boys and 36 girls) in grade 5, and 36 children (14 boys and 22 girls) in grade 6. The mean ages and standard deviations in years for these three grades were, respectively: 9.88 (0.43), 10.85 (0.41), and 11.86 (0.44). The mean age and standard deviation for the total group of 156 children was 10.81 (0.83) years.

The research question was the role of contracted forms in the children's English word reading and spelling. It was hypothesized that since English contracted forms are taught and practiced extensively in these and other Hong Kong schools the children might find them fairly easy, contrary to the findings of Bryant et al. (1997, 2000).

Accordingly, a contracted form task with 10 items and three choices each was devised in a multiple-choice format for the children to underline the correct contracted forms embedded in short sentence frames on the printed page. Some sample items were: "The two (boy's *boys'* boys) uncle is tall." "(*Hank's* Hanks Hanks') good at music." "The (childrens *children's* childrens') dog was happy." Care was taken to ensure that the words used were within the vocabulary of the children as verified from curriculum materials, and all sentences were simple, declarative, and in active voice. Cronbach's alpha reliability coefficient of the 10-item task based on 156 children was .599.

The multiple-choice task was administered to groups of children in three schools. In addition, a 42-item specially constructed decontextualized individual English word-reading task was administered to the children. Following Bradley and Bryant (1979), the same words embedded in short sentence frames were used as a group spelling task. There were 30 regular words such as *tell*, *beach*, *season*, and *borrow*, and 12 exception words such as *ache*, *break*, *lose*, and *island*. None of the exception words were of the "strange" kind such as *yacht*, *aisle*, or *pint*. Cronbach's alpha coefficient based on the 156 children for word reading was .935 and for spelling was .955. The spelling task was given first as a group task and, after 6 to 8 weeks, the same task with the decontextualized words was administered as an individual word-reading task. The 60-item Hong Kong version of the Standard Raven's Progressive Matrices (Raven, Court, & Raven, 1983) was used as a control task for general learning ability in schools.

Results and Discussion

The mean performance on the 10-item contracted form task of the three grades was 7.55 (1.90) for the 44 fourth-grade children, 7.47 (1.79) for the 76 fifth-grade children, 6.81 (1.69) for the 36 sixth-grade children, and 7.34 (1.81) for the total group of 156 children. In a one-way analysis of covariance (ANCOVA) with Raven's as the covariate, there was an overall significant difference among grades, $F(2, 152) = 3.421$, $p = .035$. Pairwise comparison showed significant differences between grades 4 and 6 ($p = .015$) in favor of grade 4, and grades 5 and 6 ($p = .027$) in favor of grade 5, but not between grades 4 and 5.

The results suggested that the contracted form task was relatively easy for the 156 Cantonese-speaking children in grades 4, 5, and 6 learning English as a second language, as shown by the average performance of between 68% correct (grade 6) and 76% correct (grade 4). It was not exactly clear why the grade 6 children performed lower than those children in grades 4 and 5. A plausible explanation was that in grades 5 and 6 the children were taught more by using full forms of words in sentences and fewer contracted forms, as compared with the grade 4 children.

This pattern of results seems to be at variance with at least one aspect of the Bryant et al. (1997, 2000) results of British children finding apostrophes quite difficult. The nonsignificant correlations of the contracted form task with any of the reading and spelling tasks could be due to the single and narrow focus of the task (use of contracted forms), the small number of items (10), and the moderate reliability coefficient (.599). The results, however, provide some evidence to support the findings of Bryant et al. that with massive teaching, apostrophes and grammar could be taught and learned as shown by the relatively good performance of the Hong Kong Chinese children after fairly regular drills in the use of contracted forms in the classrooms.

TWO-YEAR STUDIES
OF 10- TO 12-YEAR-OLD CHINESE STUDENTS

The exploratory study outlined above at best gives some indirect evidence to the effect of instruction and learning aspects of English words by 10- to 12-year-old Chinese students in Hong Kong. A more direct test of the contribution of orthographic factors to reading and spelling English words is needed. Outlined below are two studies directly comparing the impact of the orthographic and the phonological constructs on the reading and spelling of English words. The participants for the first study (Leong, Tan, Cheng, & Hau, 2005) were the same students in the exploratory study and for the second study (Leong, Hau, Cheng, & Tan, 2005) the 2-year cohort of 108 students from the same group.

Study 1 (Leong, Tan, et al., 2005)

Three tasks each subserving the orthographic construct and the phonological sensitivity construct were used to study individual differences in English word reading and spelling and to model literacy acquisition. The same decontextualized word reading task (both regular and exception words) and a written spelling task used in the exploratory study were also given to the children. The three paper-and-pencil orthographic knowledge tasks were all administered to groups and took about 8 minutes each (about 25 to 30 minutes in total); the three phonological sensitivity tasks were given individually and took a total of about 30 minutes per child. The written spelling tasks were given to groups of children and took just over 20 minutes each, while the individual isolated word-reading task took about 8 minutes per child. The phonological sensitivity tasks were: (1) pig Latin, (2) phoneme deletion, and (3) Spoonerism. In pig Latin the child listened to a spoken word with either one or two syllables and was asked to remove the first speech segment to the end of the word, add /ay/, and say the new word (e.g., "day" would become "ayday"). In phoneme deletion the child was asked to delete the initial, medial, or final phoneme of a heard pseudoword and to say the new word without the elicited speech sound (e.g., *bice*). In Spoonerism the child was asked to listen to two sets of two word pairs or item pairs and to report them orally in such a way that their first sounds were reversed (e.g., *gold-sheep* would become *shold-geep*). The orthographic knowledge tasks are outlined below.

Past Tense

The aim of this group task was to tap word-specific knowledge and to capitalize on the massive teaching of English "grammar" and the tendency for Hong Kong Chinese students to memorize the words. The task was an open-ended completion task with irregular verbs of the type: "Do not **fall** again; you *fell* yesterday." and "They **sing** beautifully now. Last week they *sang* poorly." The target verbs were shown in the sentence frame in bold type on the printed sheet. The children were asked to read each sentence frame silently and carefully and to write down the past-tense verb derived from the base present tense. In the practice examples, the experimenters took great care to explain that the to-be-spelled irregular verbs would generally sound different from the present-tense base forms (e.g., see–*saw*; hear–*heard*). This careful explanation with examples should minimize the possibility of the children simply writing down the regular *-ed* form for the to-be-spelled past-tense verbs. Twenty of the original 24 items in the tryout were found to be most discriminating, and Cronbach's alpha coefficient was .854.

Orthographic Choice

In this paper-and-pencil group task the children were asked to underline the real word in a pair of lexical items consisting of one real English word and one homophonic pseudoword with similar word shape. Examples were: *soap*, sope; gawn, *gone*; and *shoe*, shew. The original concept was from Olson, Kliegl, Davidson, and Foltz (1985). The present items were adapted from Manis, Seidenberg, Doi, McBride-Chang, and Petersen (1996) to suit the vocabulary level of the Hong Kong English learners. We agree with Manis et al. (1996, p. 170) that this task cannot be considered a pure or unconfounded orthographic task, but we also agree with them that the task assesses "something distinct from phonological decoding skills." Twenty item pairs were selected from the original 36 pairs after item analysis, and the alpha coefficient was .573.

Orthographic/Phonemic Choice

In this paper-and-pencil group task the children were asked to read each of the 15 short sentences embedding five orthographically and phonemically similar monosyllabic words or pseudowords and to underline the one correct word that completed the meaning of the sentence. Some examples were: "Please go fast; you are too (sloe slew *slow* slou sloo)." "The boats (*sail* sale soil sayl soyl) down the river." By using error substitutions, which were real words homophonous with the target word (e.g., "sale" for *sail*), compatible pseudohomophones (e.g., "sloe" for *slow*), and incompatible pseudohomophones (e.g., "soyl" for *sail*) it was reasoned that the children would use orthographic comparison to carry out the match-to-target task in a sentential context. The present task with five plausible choices embedded in a sentence context was a variant form and an improvement over the two-choice task (e.g., "What can you do with a needle and thread? so, *sew*") used by Barker et al. (1992). The 15 sentences were selected from the original 20 sentences after item analysis, and Cronbach's alpha coefficient was .653.

The main question of interest was the relative contribution of the two latent constructs of orthographic knowledge (assessed by three tasks) and phonological sensitivity (assessed by three tasks) to the latent dependent construct of literacy (i.e., reading and spelling of regular and exception English words). The latent independent components of orthographic knowledge and phonological sensitivity were found to relate to the latent dependent component of literacy (reading and spelling words) by the structural coefficients of gammas (.83 and .20, respectively, for the orthographic–lexical construct and the phonological sensitivity construct) as shown in linear structural equation modeling (Jöreskog & Sörbom, 1996–2001).

The main result of direct interest from the Leong, Tan, et al. (2005) study was the high predictive power of orthographic and lexical knowledge (gamma of .83) as compared with the substantially lower predictive power of the phonological sensitivity construct (gamma of .20) in relation to reading and spelling English regular and exception words. Would these relationships hold in a follow-up study of the same cohort of students?

Study 2 (Leong, Hau, et al., 2005)

In this two-wave study Leong, Hau, et al. (2005) further examined the component processes of English word reading and spelling in a cohort of the same 10- to 11-year-old Chinese children (now numbered 108 because of the promotion of grade 6 children to secondary schools and hence lost to the cohort study). The same tasks were administered to this second-year cohort of students. The results showed that Chinese children in Hong Kong relied on orthographic knowledge in distinguishing such word specific patterns as munk–*monk* and heterographic homophones such as "The color of the polar (bare beer bair beir *bear*) is white" to read and spell regular and exception English words. What might be the reasons for the pattern of structural relation of word-specific knowledge to the construct of word identification? We would again attribute findings in this two-wave study to the possible effect from L1 language background and the entrenched teaching for meaning as plausible explanations.

Results of the two-wave structural equation analyses provided evidence that for modal 10- to 11-year-old Chinese children word identification in Time 2 was best predicted by the same construct in Time 1. Orthographic knowledge and phonological sensitivity in Time 1 did not seem to add much to the predicative efficacy. These results were more fine-grained that those found in the structural analysis of just the Time 1 group of 156 children (Leong, Tan, et al., 2005), where it was shown that orthographic knowledge played a considerable role in reading and spelling regular and exception words. It was also noted that Time 1 word identification affected Time 2 orthographic knowledge much more than Time 2 phonological sensitivity. The greater variation in orthographical knowledge might also reflect greater demand made on this construct as children progressed from year to year while phonological sensitivity at the 10- to 11-year-old level tended to stabilize more beyond the early years.

It is likely that the 1-year time span was too short for growth in the constructs of orthographic knowledge, phonological sensitivity, and word identification. Future studies with more than two time points will permit the use of more sophisticated techniques such as growth curve modeling to assess the differential word reading and spelling growth. It will also be beneficial to try out more diversified and sensitive orthographic and phonological tasks to tap and examine the small growth in language competence within the comparatively short durations studied in typical empirical research. However, the results of the effects of orthographic knowledge and phonological sensitivity on English word reading and spelling generally support the findings of studies of reading related skills in children from different linguistic backgrounds, especially Chinese learning English as L2 (Bialystok, 2007; Bialystok, Majumder, & Martin, 2003; Chiappe, Siegel, & Wade-Wooley, 2002; Gottardo, Yan, Siegel, & Wade-Wooley, 2001; McBride-Chang & Kail, 2002, Wang & Geva, 2003).

Spelling Errors

Perusal of the Chinese children's writing to dictation of English regular words and exception words in the Leong, Hau, et al. (2005) and Leong, Tan, et al. (2005) cohort studies has provided some insight into the difficulties these Chinese students had in spelling English words. They generally did not show a good understanding of the interaction between graphotactics (arrangement of graphemes in their graphemic environment) and phonotactics (arrangement of phonemes in their phonological environment). Graphemes and phonemes have a probabilistic relationship in that graphemes can assume different forms in different orthographic environments in much the same way that phonemes can have different phonetic renderings in varying phonological environments.

Take as an example the case of graphemic variation: The phoneme /k/ can be represented as <c>, in *cap*; as <k>, in *king*; or as <ch>, in *chord*. Sensitivity to the graphotactics and phonotactics of words provides readers and spellers the insight into where the letter *c* is lax (soft) or tense (hard), or the spelling of *disstress* or *mispell* is ill-formed. While phonological knowledge affects children's spelling, their knowledge of letter patterns is also important. Even young children showed awareness of simple orthographic patterns such as allowable doublets (e.g., *yill*) as more word-like than nonwords with initial doublets (e.g., *hhenis*), as found by Cassar and Treiman (1997) in several experiments. Knowledge of the relationship between orthography and phonology is particularly critical when words have weak orthographic representation but are phonetically plausible such as the misspelled *mispell* or *disstress* (Fischer, Shankweiler, & Liberman, 1985; Katz & Frost, 2001; Leong, 1998). The speller needs to form an internal orthographic representation to remember orthographic information of the correct word form.

Neurocognitive Basis of Transfer and Constraints of Chinese as L1

The Leong, Tan, et al. (2005) finding of a fairly strong orthographic effect in relation to phonological sensitivity on Chinese children learning to read and spell English words and the further finding of the same effect, though slightly reduced in strength, in the Leong, Hau, et al.'s (2005) two-cohort study of the same children, support the general tenet of the roles of home language and school instruction. These results are in accord with the findings of strong involvement of orthographic information in addition to phonological information in adult Chinese learners' reading (Wang et al., 2003) and young Chinese readers' spelling of English words (Wang & Geva, 2003). A study by Rickard Liow and Lau (2006), using a forced-choice flaps spelling task in English (e.g., /t/ or /d/ in *water*), also confirmed the role of orthographic awareness in addition to phonological awareness in young bilingual Singaporean children from different home backgrounds.

The implication from the behavioral studies discussed above is that L1 learning experiences affect reading strategies. There is some neurocognitive evidence in this regard from a neuroimaging study by Tan et al. (2003). These researchers carried out a functional magnetic resonance imaging (fMRI) study to visualize the brain activities of Chinese–English bilinguals in processing morphosyllabic Chinese and alphabetic English. Tan et al. (2003) found their bilingual Chinese subjects applied their L1 learning strategy to their L2 English reading. This implies their participants were less able to use grapheme-to-phoneme rules to read English words. Difficulties in reading

Chinese were associated with both orthography–phonology and orthography–meaning mappings (Siok, Perfetti, Jin, & Tan, 2004). Moreover, Tan, Laird, Li, and Fox (2005) showed in a meta-analysis high concordance of cortical activities across multiple studies in Chinese and English writing systems and also significant differences in neural circuits between languages. These fMRI studies provide a possible neurocognitive explanation for our behavioral finding of the considerable involvement of lexical–orthographic knowledge in Chinese children reading and spelling English words (Leong, Hau, et al., 2005; Leong, Tan, et al., 2005).

CONCLUSION

Theoretically, learning two languages should facilitate the development of sensitivity to the structures of these languages at certain levels. Practically, it is only with sustained and systematic instruction that both L1 and L2 English language learners will progress from a meaning-based perspective to one of form and function and the gradual conscious access to the formal characteristics of these languages.

We began this paper with the in-class observation that Cantonese-speaking Chinese children in Hong Kong between the ages of 9 and 12 years are not well taught in the logic and analytic aspects of the internal structure of Chinese characters. They rely on their implicit and partial knowledge of the constituent phonetic and semantic radicals to address the phonology of the character and to deduce its meaning. This approach to teaching and learning may have an effect on these children's reading and spelling of English regular and exception words. The exploratory study of 156 grades 4, 5, and 6 Chinese children (mean age of 10.81 years) provides some evidence of the effect of the "communicative approach" to teaching English on their learning of the contracted forms of English. The Chinese children found this to be easy, as compared with similar groups of British children who found learning inflected forms of words to be difficult.

A more direct test of the construct of orthographic knowledge, compared with that of phonological sensitivity, in a 1-year and a two-wave study of the same cohort of Chinese children (Leong, Hau, et al., 2005; Leong, Tan, et al., 2005) shows that orthographic processing had more influence on English word reading and spelling, at least in the first-year study. In the two-wave study the effect of the construct of lexical knowledge in Year 1 had greater impact on word learning in Year 2, and the direct influence of orthographic processing on word reading and spelling was somewhat reduced. Examination of the children's protocols in the written spelling of both regular and exception words further points to the intricate relationship between graphotactics and phonotactics in reading and spelling English words.

Proper teaching methods emphasizing the analysis and synthesis of components of Chinese characters should help children gain insight into the formation of characters and words. This insight might be utilized in their reading and spelling of English words. Children draw on their lexical memory of analogous spelling patterns (for reading) and analogous pronunciations (for spelling) in reading and spelling familiar English words. They utilize knowledge of letter patterns and morphographs, sensitivity to speech sounds, and sensitivity to grapheme–phoneme units in reading and phoneme–grapheme units in spelling unfamiliar English words. From their first contact with print, children acquiring Chinese and English should be helped to learn about the orthographic and phonological characteristics of characters and words.

From the teaching and learning perspective, interlanguage error analyses may shed light on how Chinese-language learners of English as L2 might think in Chinese first before writing in English. Using self-reports, translation, and grammaticality judgment, Chan (2004) showed that 710 Hong Kong Chinese L2 learners at both university and upper secondary forms tended to use surface structures of their L1 (Chinese) in writing interlanguage strings in their L2 (English). Their writing errors in English were found to represent systematic deviations from the accepted forms of the target language. Some typical errors consisted of omission of the English copula in sentences with modal verbs, incorrect use of the verb *to be*, and the inappropriate use of *very* to intensify the meaning of the sentence. These qualitative analyses of verbal reports as data add to group findings in many of the studies discussed in this chapter.

While much of the current research on LLs learning their second language is concentrated on the effect of L1 on L2, the possibility of backward transfer of L2 to L1 and the further possibility of using some combined or amalgamated strategies in processing L1 and L2 need to be investigated (Cook, 2003). This integration continuum is particularly relevant to Chinese students learning English in the international city of Hong Kong. In their qualitative analyses of the "Anglicized" Chinese writing errors among teachers in Hong Kong, Tse, Shum, Miao, and Ki (2001) noted backward or negative transfers from English to Chinese. The categories of errors include inappropriate use of the articles *a*, *an*, and *the*, mandatory in English but redundant in Chinese (e.g., "I have *one* father"); excessive or redundant use of possessive (e.g., in Chinese "I do my homework" does not need the possessive *my*); the wrong use of the passive form *bei* 被, which is meant to express unexpected or unhappy events in Chinese (e.g., 我們被人打了。 [We are/were beaten by others]) but not the negation (e.g., *我們被人不打了。 [We are/were not beaten by others]); inappropriate transfer of function words; unacceptable order of causative and conditional clauses in Chinese and other linguistic aspects. These analyses of written errors suggest that the effect of

L1 on L2 and L2 on L1 go further than the phonological, orthographic, and morphological aspects and provide insight into interlanguage error types in simple sentence structures.

ACKNOWLEDGMENTS

The studies summarized were supported with a research grant from the Social Sciences and Humanities Research Council of Canada. This assistance is gratefully acknowledged. I also thank the editors for their helpful comments.

REFERENCES

Anderson, R. C., Li, W., Ku, Y.-M., Shu, H., & Wu, N. (2003). Use of partial information in learning to read Chinese characters. *Journal of Educational Psychology, 95,* 52–57.

Barker, T. A., Torgesen, J. K., & Wagner, R. K. (1992). The role of orthographic processing skills on five different reading tasks. *Reading Research Quarterly, 27,* 334–345.

Bialystok, E. (1991). Achieving proficiency in a second language: A processing description. In R. Phillipson, E. Kellerman, L. Selinker, M. Sharwood Smith, & M. Swain (Eds.), *Foreign/second language pedagogy research* (pp. 63–78). Clevedon, UK: Multilingual Matters.

Bialystok, E. (2001). *Bilingualism in development.* Cambridge, UK: Cambridge University Press.

Bialystok, E. (2007). Language acquisition and bilingualism: Consequences for a multilingual society. *Applied Psycholinguistics, 28,* 393–397.

Bialystok, E., Majumder, S., & Martin, M. M. (2003). Developing phonological awareness: Is there a bilingual advantage? *Applied Psycholinguistics, 24,* 27–44.

Bloomfield, L. (1962). *Language.* London: George Allen & Unwin. (Original work published 1933)

Bradley, L., & Bryant, P. (1979). The interdependence of reading and spelling in backward and normal readers. *Developmental Medicine and Child Neurology, 21,* 27–44.

Bryant, P., Devine, M., Ledward, A., & Nunes, T. (1997). Spelling with apostrophes and understanding possessives. *British Journal of Educational Psychology, 67,* 91–110.

Bryant, P., Nunes, T., & Bindman, M. (2000). The relations between children's linguistic awareness and spelling: The case of the apostrophe. *Reading and Writing: An Interdisciplinary Journal, 12,* 253–276.

Cassar, M., & Treiman, R. (1997). The beginnings of orthographic knowledge: Children's knowledge of double letters in words. *Journal of Educational Psychology, 89,* 631–644.

Castles, A., Holmes, V. M., Neath, J., & Kinoshita, S. (2003). How does orthographic knowledge influence performance on phonological awareness tasks? *The Quarterly Journal of Experimental Psychology, 56A*(3), 445–467.

Chan, A. Y. W. (2004). Syntactic transfer: Evidence from the interlanguage of Hong Kong Chinese ESL learners. *The Modern Language Journal, 88*, 56–74.

Chao, Y. R. (1968). *A grammar of spoken Chinese.* Berkeley: University of California Press.

Chiappe, P., Siegel, L. S., & Wade-Wooley, L. (2002). Linguistic diversity and the development of reading skills: A longitudinal study. *Scientific Studies of Reading, 6*, 369 400.

Cook, V. (Ed.). (2003). *Effects of the second language on the first.* Clevedon, UK: Multilingual Matters.

Durgunoğlu, A. Y. (2002). Cross-linguistic transfer in literacy development and implications for language learners. *Annals of Dyslexia, 52*, 189–204.

Ehri, L. C. (1980). The development of orthographic image. In U. Frith (Ed.), *Cognitive processes in spelling* (pp. 311–338). London: Academic Press.

Ehri, L. C. (1997). Learning to read and learning to spell are one and the same, almost. In C. A. Perfetti, L. Rieben, & M. Fayol (Eds.), *Learning to spell: Research, theory, and practice across languages* (pp. 237–269). Mahwah, NJ: Erlbaum.

Fischer, F. W., Shankweiler, D., & Liberman, I. Y. (1985). Spelling proficiency and sensitivity to word structure. *Journal of Memory and Language, 24*, 423–441.

Flege, J. E., & Fletcher, K. L. (1992). Talker and listener effects on degree of perceived foreign accents. *Journal of the Acoustic Society of America, 91*, 370–389.

Flege, J. E., McCutcheon, M. J., & Smith, S. C. (1987). The development of skill in producing word-final English stops. *Journal of the Acoustical Society of America, 82*, 433–447.

Foorman, B. R. (1994). Phonological and orthographic processing: Separate but equal? In V. W. Berninger (Ed.), *The varieties of orthographic knowledge. I: Theoretical and developmental issues* (pp. 321–357). Dordrecht, The Netherlands: Kluwer.

Foorman, B. R. (1995). Practical connections of orthographic and phonological processing. In V. W. Berninger (Ed.), *The varieties of orthographic knowledge. II: Relations to phonology, reading, and writing* (pp. 377–419). Dordrecht, The Netherlands: Kluwer.

Goswami, U. (1990). Phonological priming and orthographic analogies in reading. *Journal of Experimental Child Psychology, 49*, 323–340.

Gottardo, A., Yan, B., Siegel, L. S., & Wade-Wooley, L. (2001). Factors related to English reading performance in children with Chinese as a first language: More evidence of cross-language transfer of phonological processing. *Journal of Educational Psychology, 93*, 530–542.

Jöreskog, K., & Sörbom, D. (1996–2001). *LISREL 8: User's reference guide.* Lincolnwood, IL: Scientific Software.

Katz, L., & Frost, S. J. (2001). Phonology constrains the internal orthographic representation. *Reading and Writing: An Interdisciplinary Journal, 14*, 297–332.

Kemp, N., & Bryant, P. (2003). Do beez buzz? Rule-based and frequency-based knowledge in learning to spell plural -s. *Child Development, 74*, 63–74.

Leong, C. K. (1997). Paradigmatic analysis of Chinese word reading: Research findings and classroom practices. In C. K. Leong & R. M. Joshi (Eds.), *Cross-language studies of learning to read and spell: Phonologic and orthographic processing* (pp. 379–417). Dordrecht, The Netherlands: Kluwer.

Leong, C. K. (1998). Strategies used by 9– to 12–year-old children in written spelling. In C. Hulme & R. M. Joshi (Eds.), *Reading and spelling: Development and disorders* (pp. 421–432). Mahwah, NJ: Erlbaum.

Leong, C. K., Hau, K. T., Cheng, P. W., & Tan, L. H. (2005). Exploring two-wave reciprocal structural relations among orthographic knowledge, phonological sensitivity, and reading and spelling of English words by Chinese students. *Journal of Educational Psychology, 97*, 591–600.

Leong, C. K., & Ho, M. K. (2008). The role of lexical knowledge and related linguistic components in typical and poor language comprehenders of Chinese. *Reading and Writing: An Interdisciplinary Journal, 21*, 559–586.

Leong, C. K., Tan, L. H., Cheng, P. W., & Hau, K. T. (2005). Learning to read and spell English words by Chinese students. *Scientific Studies of Reading, 9*, 63–84.

MacNamara, J. (1967). The bilingual's linguistic performance. *Journal of Social Issues, 23*, 58–77.

MacWhinney, B. (1987). Applying the competition model to bilingualism. *Applied Psycholinguistics, 8*, 315–327.

MacWhinney, B. (2001). The competition model: The input, the context, and the brain. In P. Robinson (Ed.), *Cognition and second language instruction* (pp. 69–90). Cambridge, UK: Cambridge University Press.

Manis, F. R., Seidenberg, M. S., Doi, L. M., McBride-Chang, C., & Petersen, A. (1996). On the bases of two subtypes of developmental dyslexia. *Cognition, 58*, 157–195.

McBride-Chang, C., Cho, J.-R., Liu, H., Wagner, R. K., Shu, H., Zhou, A., et al. (2005). Changing models across cultures: Associations of phonological awareness and morphological structure awareness with vocabulary and word recognition in second graders from Beijing, Hong Kong, Korea, and the United States. *Journal of Experimental Child Psychology, 92*, 140–160.

McBride-Chang, C., & Kail, R. V. (2002). Cross-cultural similarities in the predictors of reading acquisition. *Child Development, 73*, 1392–1407.

Nunes, T., Bryant, P., & Bindman, M. (1997a). Morphological spelling strategies: Developmental stages and processes. *Developmental Psychology, 33*, 637–649.

Nunes, T., Bryant, P., & Bindman, M. (1997b). Spelling and grammar: The necsed move. In C. A. Perfetti, L. Rieben, & M. Fayol (Eds.), *Learning to spell: Research, theory, and practice* (pp. 151–170). Mahwah, NJ: Erlbaum.

Olson, R. K., Kliegl, R., Davidson, B., & Foltz, G. (1985). Individual and developmental differences in reading disability. In T. Waller (Ed.), *Reading research: Advances in theory and practice* (Vol. 4, pp. 1–64). London: Academic Press.

Packard, J. L. (2000). *The morphology of Chinese: A linguistic and cognitive approach*. Cambridge, UK: Cambridge University Press.

Raven, J. C., Court, J. H., & Raven, C. (1983). *Manual for Raven's Progressive Matrices and Vocabulary Scales*. London: Lewis.

Rickard Liow, S. J., & Lau, L. H.-S. (2006). The development of bilingual children's early spelling in English. *Journal of Educational Psychology, 98*, 868–878.

Rickard Liow, S. J. R., & Poon, K. K.-L. (1998). Phonological awareness in multilingual Chinese children. *Applied Psycholinguistics, 19*, 339–362.

Seymour, P. H. K., & Evans, H. M. (1994). Levels of phonological awareness and learning to read. *Reading and Writing: An Interdisciplinary Journal, 6*, 221–250.

Sharwood Smith, M. (1991). Language modules and bilingual processing. In E. Bialystok (Ed.), *Language processing in bilingual children* (pp. 10–24). New York: Cambridge University Press.

Shen, H. H., & Bear, D. R. (2000). Development of orthographic skills in Chinese children. *Reading and Writing: An Interdisciplinary Journal, 13*, 197–236.

Shu, H., & Anderson, R. C. (1997). Role of radical awareness in the character and word acquisition of Chinese children. *Reading Research Quarterly, 32*, 78–89.

Shu, H., Chen, X., Anderson, R. C., Wu, N., & Xuan, Y. (2003). Properties of school Chinese: Implications for learning to read. *Child Development, 74*, 27–47.

Shu, H., McBride-Chang, C., Wu, S., & Liu, H. (2006). Understanding Chinese developmental dyslexia: Morphological awareness as a core cognitive construct. *Journal of Educational Psychology, 98*, 122–133.

Siok, W. T., Perfetti, C. A., Jin, Z., & Tan, L. H. (2004). Biological abnormality of impaired reading is constrained by culture. *Nature, 431*, 71–76.

Snow, C. E., & Kang, J. Y. (2006). Becoming bilingual, biliterate, and bicultural. In K. A. Renninger & I. E. Siegel (Eds.), *Handbook of child psychology, Vol. 4: Child psychology in practice* (pp. 75–102). Hoboken, NJ: Wiley.

Sorace, A. (2003). Near-nativeness. In C. J. Doughty & M. H. Long (Eds.), *Handbook of second language acquisition* (pp. 130–151). Oxford, UK: Blackwell.

Tan, L. H., Laird, A. G., Li, K., & Fox, P. T. (2005). Neuroanatomical correlates of phonological processing of Chinese characters and alphabetic words: A meta-analysis. *Human Brain Mapping, 25*, 83–91.

Tan, L. H., Spinks, J. A., Feng, C.-M., Siok, W. T., Perfetti, C. A., Xiong, J., et al. (2003). Neural systems of second language reading are shaped by native language. *Human Brain Mapping, 18*, 159–166.

Tse, S. K., Shum, S. K., Miao, K. O., & Ki, W. W. (2001). *Errors in mapping out essay topics and language expressions.* Hong Kong: Hong Kong University Press.

Venezky, R. L. (1970). *The structure of English orthography.* The Hague: Mouton.

Wagner, R. K., & Barker, T. A. (1994). The development of orthographic processing ability. In V. W. Berninger (Ed.), *The varieties of orthographic knowledge I: Theoretical developmental issues* (pp. 243–276). Dordrecht, The Netherlands: Kluwer.

Wang, M., & Geva, E. (2003). Spelling performance of Chinese children using English as a second language: Lexical and visual–orthographic processes. *Applied Psycholinguistics, 24*, 1–25.

Wang, M., Koda, K., & Perfetti, C. A. (2003). Alphabetic and nonalphabetic L1 effects in English word identification: A comparison of Korean and Chinese English L2 learners. *Cognition, 87*, 129–149.

Wang, M., Perfetti, C. A., & Liu, Y. (2005). Chinese–English biliteracy acquisition: Cross-language and writing system transfer. *Cognition, 97,* 67–88.

Zhong guo guo jia yu wei [Chinese National Language Committee]. (1998). *Xun xi chu li yong GB13000. 1 zi fu ji: Hanzi bu jian gui fan* [Information processing using GB13000. 1 character symbol anthology: Hanzi bujian analyses]. Beijing: Beijing Language Institute Press.

CHAPTER 9

■ ■ ■

Writing Acquisition among English Language Learners in U.S. Schools

LAURA MÉNDEZ BARLETTA
JANETTE K. KLINGNER
MICHAEL J. OROSCO

In 2000, 32.8 million Latinos resided in the United States, representing 12% of the population. According to the U.S. Census Bureau (2003), the percentage of the school-age children who did not speak English at home was well over 20% in states such as Arizona, Florida, Nevada, New Jersey, New Mexico, New York, and Rhode Island. In California and Texas these percentages are much higher (42.6% in California and 32.4% in Texas); however, they do not point to an isolated phenomenon, but rather part of a national trend. As Zehler et al. (2003) have indicated, nearly all of the nation's school districts include English language learners.[1] According to the U.S. Department of Education, in 2003 43% of all teachers in the United States had at least one ELL in their classroom. States not typically associated with non-English speakers—Indiana, North Carolina, South Carolina, and Tennessee—each saw an increase in the ELL population of at least 300% between 1994–1995 and 2004–2005 (NCELA, 2008). Furthermore, recent data indicate that between 1979 and 2004 the population of school-age children in the United States increased by 18% (Fry, 2006). Along these lines, according to the U.S. Department of Education (2008), between 1979 and 2006 the number of school-age children (5–17 years old) who spoke a language other than English at home increased from 3.8 to 10.8 million (or from 9% to 20%). In addition, the percentage of children (5–17 years old) who spoke English with difficulty increased from 3% to 6% between 1979 and 2000 (this percentage remained between 5% and 6% between 2000 and 2006).

Minority groups are the majority in some of the nation's largest school districts (Gutiérrez, 1993). Due to the large number of language-minority students, the schooling of these children has become increasingly problematic for an educational system that is essentially unprepared and reluctant to ensure the success of this student population (Gutiérrez, 1993). Gutiérrez argued that schools have difficulty understanding and dealing with the wide range of cultural and social experiences these children bring to the school setting and are unprepared to deal with different linguistic experiences and abilities of this student population.

As the U.S. population has become more diverse, educators' concerns about English as a second language (ESL) literacy have also increased (Fitzgerald, 1995). Along these lines, Echiburu Berzins and López (2001) stated that meeting the needs of the growing number of ethnically and linguistically diverse students continues to be one of the major challenges for today's teachers and other school professional staff, who continue to be primarily white, middle-class, monolingual English speakers.

Historically, analyses of literacy in education and other social sciences have focused to an overwhelming extent on reading while dealing with writing on only rare occasions (Duranti & Ochs, 1998; Street, 1984). What has been overlooked in many cases is that for children from linguistically and culturally diverse backgrounds, writing instruction is a powerful means to acquire the forms of language use that most consistently lead to success in American schools. Lee (2004) argues that although writing ability is one of the most important elements that determines students' success in an academic setting, ELLs in U.S. public elementary schools have difficulty writing in English due to an insufficient amount of vocabulary, a lack of grammatical knowledge, an unfamiliarity with appropriate rhetorical styles in English, and sometimes a lack of experiences to write about. Therefore, Lee maintains, one of the important roles for the teachers of these young language learners is helping them to improve their English writing ability so that they can succeed academically in their mainstream classrooms. Kaplan and Grabe (1997) state that "all second language learners need to attain some proficiency in writing, and all second language teachers need to know how to teach a writing class in the L2" (p. 183).

With its focus on writing acquisition, the present chapter is especially important, given that recent assessments have established that all too many ELLs are not acquiring the range of writing proficiencies needed for advanced academic tasks (Hernández, 2001). The purpose of this chapter is to review the research on writing and to describe the current state of the research base.

In this chapter, we document the studies that have been conducted on writing and summarize their findings in the following two sections: (1) research on ELL writing; and (2) educational contexts. The following three subsections are included in the first section: first- and second-language (L1 and L2) writing development; language of instruction and effects on biliteracy; and comparing L1 and L2 writing and the possibilities of transfer. The following five subsections are included in the second section: teachers' perceptions of ELL students' writing; classroom and community approaches to writing; ELL writing instruction in U.S. classrooms; assessment of students' writing samples; and language difference or learning disability. We conclude with recommendations for future writing research and educational implications.

RESEARCH ON ELL WRITING

L1 and L2 Writing Development

Moll, Sáez, and Dworin (2001) identify some of the dynamics of early biliteracy and how biliteracy, through classroom instruction, may become a powerful intellectual asset for students. The authors present two case examples as illustrations—one of incipient biliteracy, obtained in a bilingual kindergarten classroom, and another of instructed biliteracy, obtained in a third-grade classroom. In both examples, Moll et al. highlight how children use the social processes and cultural resources to develop their literate competencies in Spanish and English.

In the first case study example, the authors focus on how two kindergartners produce bilingual text, even before coming to control the conventions of alphabetic literacy in either language (i.e., English and Spanish). In the second case study example, gathered in a bilingual third-grade classroom, the authors concentrate on "literate thinking"; that is, how writing in two languages is used as a tool for thinking.

Gort (2006) investigated the writing processes of eight emergent bilingual children (four English-dominant students and four Spanish-dominant students) as they composed stories in two languages in a 45- to 60-minute writing workshop context. Gort's study took place in two first-grade classrooms in a Spanish–English two-way bilingual education program in the northeastern United States. For 6 months, researchers observed students during Spanish and English writing workshops, interviewed students about their writing behaviors and understandings, and collected samples from all stages of the writing process.

Findings from Gort's study reveal similarities and differences in students' cross-linguistic skills, as well as patterns of transfer. Patterns of bilingual writing related to strategic code switching, positive literacy transfer, and interliteracy led to the development of a preliminary model of bilingual writing development for English-dominant and Spanish-dominant bilingual learners. More specifically, Gort found that most Spanish-dominant children code switched in both L1 and L2 contexts, while one Spanish-dominant child code-switched in the L1 context only. On the other hand, English-dominant children only code-switched in the L2 context. Furthermore, Gort found that bilingual writers used their L1 while writing in the L2 to monitor their writing and to ask questions during writing. Results indicate that when children began writing in both languages, they employed the majority of their writing-related behaviors and skills cross-linguistically and bidirectionally. They were developing two written language systems by applying what they knew about writing in one language to the other language. Gort indicates that children applied specific hypotheses, more general strategies, and abstract knowledge about language and literacy to both languages.

Lesaux, Geva, Koda, Siegel, and Shanahan (2008) review research focused on the development of reading and writing skills among language-minority students, the predictors of their development, and the profiles of these students with literacy difficulties. According to Lesaux et al., the bulk of the studies reviewed used correlational designs to examine a relationship between L2 skills and reading/writing skills in the second language.

In terms of differences and similarities between language-minority and native speakers in the development of writing skills, Lesaux et al. (2008) found that studies varied in the way writing was assessed and examined (e.g., students were asked to write a narrative on a short prompt or write in response to a picture or short film). All studies scored students' writing on overall quality, linguistic and syntactic complexity, lexical variety, genre-specific features, semantics, productivity, and spelling. Lesaux et al. indicate that they could not draw substantive conclusions about the writing development of language-minority students due to the studies being highly diverse in the tasks and assessment criteria employed.

Lesaux et al. (2008) also examined for factors that have an impact on the writing development of language-minority children and youth. The authors argue that writing (like reading) is a multidimensional process involving word-level skills, cognitive abilities, and higher-order skills. They go on to argue that "just as effective reading comprehension is dependent, in part, on fluent, automatic decoding, effective writing development depends, in part, on automatization of low-level transcription skills" (p. 32). The authors also indicate that writing is influenced by sociocultural practices (specifically discourse styles). They emphasize that when creating written text, students must generate discourse in the absence of the social context of oral communication (thus adding a challenge to language-minority students).

Finally, Lesaux et al. (2008) found that few writing studies have examined the relationship between English oral language proficiency and English writing. They found that studies of elementary and middle school English-language learners suggest that well-developed oral language skills in English are associated with better writing skills in English. Lesaux et al. also point out that there are aspects of oral language proficiency that are important for proficient writing in English as a second language, including decontextualized language skills, grammatical skills, and knowledge of cohesive devices such as anaphora, relativization, temporal reference, and conjunctions. In addition, the acquisition of proficient writing skills entails good spelling skills, metacognitive skills (e.g., audience awareness), and familiarity with and opportunities to practice writing different text genres.

Reese, Linan Thompson, and Goldenberg (2008) examined the activities involving the use of text and the cultural values, attitudes, feelings, and relationships that shape and give meaning to those events. According to the authors, the focus of the study is on understanding the relationships between community and family variations in Spanish-speaking children's language and literacy experiences and the role of the school as a moderator of that relationship. The study consisted of 632 Spanish-speaking students in grades K–2 across 14 schools (seven in urban Texas, four in border Texas, and three in urban Southern California), and their surrounding communities.

Results of Reese et al.'s study indicate that communities offered varying opportunities for children to hear, see, and use both English and Spanish for a variety of purposes. They indicate, for example, language use in the community and the home, literacy opportunities in the community, frequency of literacy use in the home, and the types or domains of functional literacy uses in which children participate or have an opportunity to observe. Furthermore, in the community, differences in exposure to reading and writing opportunities were noted in the availability of environmental print and texts in English and Spanish. However, community differences had only a weak association with child literacy opportunities, such as books or reading in the home. The authors found that access to reading material was limited overall, especially for families living in the lower-income areas where few books and magazines were available for purchase in local stores.

Edelsky's (1986) longitudinal study investigated the writing development of 27 first-, second-, and third-grade students who attended a bilingual program in Phoenix, Arizona. More than 500 written pieces were analyzed from the three different classrooms for code switching, invented spelling, nonspelling conventions (punctuation, segmentation), stylistic devices, structural features (e.g., beginnings, endings, links between clauses), and quality of content. Findings from the study show that bilingual children had many language strengths, that their bilingualism was not a barrier to displays of written language competence, and that they could account for audience needs and text demands. In both their genuine writing and their simulations of writing, even first graders used advanced vocabulary (e.g., *encerrado*, isolated; *se emborrachó*, he/she got drunk; *en ese instante*, in that instant). Edelsky noted that complex tenses such as subjunctives and conditionals also appeared in students' writing.

Edelsky (1986) also found that students seemed better able to access a schema for a genre when the genre was one that was familiar, rather than school-created. With the opportunity to decide genre and content, students used a greater variety of genres and became more involved with the text. Edelsky noted that, when writing in a second language, writers call on what they know about writing in their first language. She found that fundamental L1 composing processes were applied to L2 composition.

Hudelson (1989) observed two native Spanish-speaking children (enrolled in second grade) in order to understand their ESL writing development. Hudelson worked individually with these two students once or twice a month, for one school year. Outside the classroom (with Hudelson), the children were allowed to draw whatever they wanted (since they would write only after drawing), talk about what they had drawn, and were asked to write something about their drawing.

Hudelson (1989) stated that initially both children viewed writing as copying, reproducing workbook material, or using spelling words to construct sentences. Over time, each child responded to an environment quite different from that of the classroom. This environment allowed them to produce English texts while still learning the language. Hudelson indicated that although both children made progress, one of them made more progress than the other (probably due to her being more willing to guess at answers, to use what she knew at a particular time, to make mistakes, and to ask for information). It is important to mention that progress was determined by the author closely observing the children as they drew and produced narratives.

Through a series of longitudinal case studies, Serna and Hudelson (1993) investigated the literacy acquisition of Spanish-speaking children enrolled in a bilingual program in Phoenix, Arizona. They analyzed specific, discrete aspects of children's Spanish writing, such as invented spelling, segmentation, code switching, stylistic devices, and topic choice. The researchers were also interested in how students responded to the writing environments in their classrooms in order to become writers and how and why they began to add English to their writing.

Focusing their attention on one female student (Lilia), Serna and Hudelson (1993) followed her classroom writing activities in the first, second, and third grades. The researchers indicate that Lilia's writing narratives became longer, more complete and complex, and included dialogues among the characters. Serna and Hudelson indicated that because Lilia received no formal literacy instruction in English, she used what she knew about writing in Spanish to express herself in her second language. In other words, her journal entries began to demonstrate the influences of both Spanish and English.

Riojas Clark (1995) describes a supportive cultural and linguistic environment where Mexican American kindergarten students (identified as limited English proficient) were naturally learning a second language. The focus of the study was to view the process of L1 and L2 development in the classroom. Riojas Clark found that the children, who were writing letters in a computer lab, were writing phonetically in Spanish (i.e., they were writing what they were saying). She states that children were sounding out the words and searching for the letter on the keyboard that they felt approximated the relationship between sound and literal symbol.

Results of Riojas Clark's (1995) study also found that students were learning to read by writing (i.e., students were connecting print to meaning). Riojas Clark indicates that students were learning to read and write because the teacher encouraged them to write on the computer on a daily basis and also because the teacher encouraged inventive spelling and thinking aloud as they wrote. By the end of the year, children were writing extensively in Spanish.

McClure, Mir, and Cadierno (1993) compared the types of information included in the narratives written by fourth- and ninth-grade monolingual American students, the English narratives written by bilingual Mexican students, and the Spanish narratives written by monolingual Mexican students. Data consisted of English and Spanish written narratives elicited with a silent animated film of the animal fable genre. The film lasted slightly over 4 minutes and was shown to all students twice. Students were then asked to write the story they had seen as if they were writing an animal fable to be read by a child who had not seen the film. The task was administered in a 60-minute class period.

The researchers analyzed the data by dividing the stories into three categories: the orientation or setting, six episodes, and the resolution. The researchers then counted the number of propositions devoted to each category in each story, normalizing these numbers by dividing by the total number of propositions in the story. The following five analytic categories were included to assess the effect of age on the narratives: (1) causal links; (2) details for setting and actions; (3) physical descriptions of characters; (4) descriptions of characters' personal traits; and (5) descriptions of characters' emotional states.

Findings indicated that although the general English narrative structure did not differ for bilingual Mexicans and Americans, Mexicans provided more information about emotional states and personal traits. Furthermore, in general, younger writers tended to include fewer physical and action details than did older writers and to provide fewer causal links between actions and states. Younger writers also provided less information about the emotional states of characters and about their physical and personal traits. McClure et al. (1993) found that bilinguals showed a developmental lag in their second language with respect to inclusion of information about setting and action details. Regarding story structure categories, the authors found that grade level did not play a role or did so "very little." On the other hand, there were notable age differences in terms of describing protagonists in the stories. The authors concluded by stating that although fourth-grade bilinguals showed a clear lag, at ninth grade they were equivalent to English monolinguals.

One final study that deserves mentioning is Fitzgerald's (2006) synthesis of preschool through 12th grade multilingual research conducted from 1988 through 2003. In order for studies to be included in her synthesis, Fitzgerald indicates that the research question had to be stated or easily inferred; data on writing had to have been collected; participants had to be of preschool through 12th-grade age; the study had to have undergone editorial or peer review and been "published"; and she had to be able to identify the work as fitting her definition of multilingual writing (i.e., "ability or competency in process or product, to whatever extent, in writing in two or more languages," p. 337).

Fitzgerald found that of the 56 studies included in the synthesis, too few were alike with regard to contextual situations (e.g., studies within a particular country, with participants of the same native language background learning the same new language under similar circumstances) to draw many generalizations. Therefore, Fitzgerald presents three assertions about students' multilingual writing done over 15 years. First, Fitzgerald indicates that for young children, features of early ESL writing may develop in ways that are quite similar to certain features of early writing development of native English children. She indicates that this assertion is reminiscent of that made by some researchers studying young children's multilingual reading development. That is, how some young children's capabilities for making strong progress in developing early reading strategies in ESL can be as compared to that of typically developing native English children. Second, Fitzgerald asserts that for primary- and intermediate-grade students, knowledge/skill can transfer between L1 and L2 writing. She refers to the meaning of transfer as developing knowledge or skills in one language and then using these in another language. Finally, Fitzgerald points out that for secondary- and/or intermediate-level bilingual students or students learning English as a foreign language, selected composing processes may be highly similar across native and second-language writing, although differences may also exist. That is, that unskilled L2 writers' processes are similar to those of L1 unskilled writers and that skilled L2 writers processes are similar to those of L1 skilled writers.

The studies listed in this subsection emphasized the importance of biliteracy; that is, the studies indicate that learning to write in the first language does not negatively affect the process of learning to write in the second language. These studies suggest further that students call on what they know about writing in their first language when writing in the second language. In the section that follows, we include studies that examine the acquisition of literacy among students who were taught in Spanish or English.

Language of Instruction and Effects on Biliteracy

Gale, McClay, Christie, and Harris (1981) examined a group of adolescent students who learned to write in their L1 prior to learning to write in their L2. Their study compares the writing of 15 bilingual program students and 12 submersion program students in a primary school serving an Aboriginal community on Milingimbi (an island off the Northern territory of Australia). During the years that the 15 students attended the bilingual program, they received nearly half of their entire schooling through their native language, Gupapuyngu. Furthermore, the bilingual students learned to read and write in Gupapuyngu before receiving instruction in English. In contrast, the 12 students in the submersion program received all of their education in English and did not develop literacy skills in their L1 (Gupapuyngu).

When the bilingual and submersion students reached their last year of schooling, Gale et al. (1981) tested the students on their writing ability in English by having them first watch a filmstrip and listen to a tape on "Ferdinand the Bull." After viewing the film, the students wrote a narrative on the film, and then all papers were rated on a 0 to 10 scale (0 = no ability to communicate through written English; 10 = fluent writer of English). Results indicated that the papers written by the bilingual students rated significantly higher than those written by the submersion students. Interestingly, the quality of the papers written by both groups was distinctly below the national average. Unfortunately, Gale et al. did not provide any indication on the amount of class time devoted to the instruction of writing in the native language or English. Therefore, it is not known why both groups of students were writing below the national average.

Ferris and Politzer (1981) examined the writing proficiency of seventh- and eighth-grade students writing in their L2. Study participants included two groups of students enrolled in a junior high school in Santa Paula, California. Participants in the first group (Group A) were born in Mexico and received elementary schooling at least through the third grade in Mexico. Participants in the second group (Group B) were born in the United States and received their entire elementary education in the United States and had not achieved literacy in Spanish. These students had, however, acquired oral ability in Spanish. A total of 30 students per group participated in the study. Furthermore, the study consisted of an experimental (Group A) and control (Group B) group. The variables for distinguishing between both groups were place of birth, location of early elementary schooling, and language of instruction.

The researchers examined the writing proficiency of both groups of students by having them provide a writing sample by watching a 15-minute film and then writing about its contents (within a 40-minute time period). Teams of raters then evaluated the essays on the following (Ferris & Politzer, 1981): (1) three measures of holistic scores: paragraph development, sentence boundaries, and verb inflections; (2) three objective measures of syntactic maturity: the length of T-unit; and (3) six measures of error frequency: fused sentences, period faults, verb tense, pronoun agreement, article agreement, and possessives.

The major hypotheses of the study tested the prediction that there would not be any differences between Groups A and B in proficiency in English composition. Ferris and Politzer (1981) revealed that there was an insignificant difference between Group A and B in either paragraph development or in the skill of organizing sentence boundaries. Chi square tests revealed that differences for five out of six error categories were not statistically significant at the .05 scale (Ferris & Politzer, 1981). The only category with a clear significant difference between the groups was verb tense. Ferris and Politzer concluded that Group A students were able to function as though they had begun U.S. public instruction from the very first year of primary education, and that they did not possess demonstrably lower English skills than Group B students. This was interpreted as indicating that these students' early foundation in Spanish was not a detriment to their later acquisition of English. Ferris and Politzer also emphasized that Group A students had more positive attitudes toward school and school achievement and seemed more highly motivated. They argue that this may have been related to a cultural background where school achievement and teachers are highly valued.

Carlisle (1989) investigated the writing of Hispanic students in a bilingual program and compared their writing with that of Hispanic students in a submersion program and with native English speakers in a regular program. The study consisted of 64 students in the fourth and sixth grades in which the following variables were examined: rhetorical effectiveness, overall quality of writing, productivity, syntactic maturity, and error frequency. In addition, socioeconomic status and amount of English used in the home were examined to determine the quality of writing of the two Hispanic groups.

According to Carlisle (1989), monolingual English speaking students were given two packets of writing tasks that were to be completed in 75 minutes or less. The first packet consisted of four writing tasks in English: "Kangaroo," "Rainy Day," "Fireflies," and "Loss." The second packet consisted of the other three writing tasks in English ("Describe Something," "Letter to Principal," and "Puppy"). Finally, the third packet was given only to the bilingual and submersion program students. This packet of two essays ("Describe Algo" ["Describe something"] and "Pececito Dorado" ["Goldfish"]) required the students to write in Spanish and included a questionnaire on the amount of English used at the home. It is important to point out that the genres included in the Spanish packet did not differ from those in English packets.

Carlisle's (1989) study revealed that bilingual students (fourth and sixth grade) had significantly lower scores than those in the regular program in terms of rhetorical effectiveness, overall quality of writing, and error frequency. Carlisle also found that bilingual students did as well as the native English speakers on two of the five dependent variables, and as well on error frequency in the sixth grade. Carlisle argued that given this, the bilingual students were developing rhetorical skills in English and could be expected with time to reach academic norms. Furthermore, results indicated that when the essays were analyzed individually, the bilingual students did as well as the native English speakers on five of the seven variables (indicating that group data showed a different pattern than did the individual data).

Carlisle and Beeman (2000) investigated the acquisition of literacy of Hispanic children who were taught to read and write in either Spanish or in English. They followed the progress of a group of children for 2 years. In the first year, first graders were taught literacy in English for 80% of the day; in the second year, the students were taught literacy in Spanish for 80% of the day. The question was whether instruction in Spanish would lead to different achievement levels than instruction in English in the initial year of literacy acquisition.

There were two successive first-grade classes at the same school that participated in the study: a total of 17 children taught in English for the first grade, and 19 children taught in Spanish for the first grade. Children's text comprehension was assessed by measures of listening and reading comprehension in Spanish and English. In addition, writing samples were collected and scored for productivity, linguistic complexity, spelling, and discourse.

Results of the study show different patterns of literacy achievement for the two groups. One important finding was that the Spanish class was as strong as the English class on measures of English reading and writing but was significantly stronger on measures of Spanish reading and writing. Children who received instruction in Spanish benefited noticeably in their performance on the standardized test in Spanish reading comprehension and were not put at a disadvantage in terms of performance in English reading comprehension. Furthermore, instruction in Spanish made a significant contribution to the development of Spanish reading comprehension, above and beyond the students' Spanish vocabulary or listening comprehension.

As for writing proficiency, the Spanish class wrote longer main clauses (with greater use of modifiers) and wrote more elaborate stories in Spanish. Given the results of Carlisle and Beeman's (2000) study, more studies are needed to determine whether Latino children taught initial literacy skills in Spanish show an advantage in bilingual literacy achievement; if so, it will be important to determine whether the advantage is maintained as they advance in grade level.

The studies reviewed in this subsection indicate that students who learn to write in their L1 (e.g., Spanish) before learning to write in their L2 (e.g., English) will write just as effectively in their L2 as those students who learn to write only in their L2. Along these lines, these studies indicate that the writing skills of strong L2 writers are indistinguishable from those of strong L1 students. In addition, participating in bilingual programs is a factor in helping Spanish-speaking students learn to write in Spanish and meet state content writing standards. Results of the previously presented writing studies also indicate that stronger L1 development is associated with better literacy achievement. In other words, having good verbal ability in one's native language might underlie the development of both oral and written language skills. In the next section, we focus on the ability to transfer literacy skills from one language to another.

Comparing L1 and L2 Writing and the Possibilities of Transfer

A great deal of research has been published on literacy transfer. Results show that becoming literate in one's L1 helps with literacy development in the L2. Genesee, Geva, Dressler, and Kamil (2008), for example, review research that addresses relationships across languages in the development of literacy skills in children and adolescents who are learning to read and write English as a second language. In this study, Genesee et al. review and summarize theories related to language and literacy development (specifically, frameworks that deal with transfer, target language influences, interlanguage theories, underlying cognitive abilities, and moderator variables). The authors provide research evidence that certain aspects of L2 literacy development are related to performance on similar constructs in the L1, suggesting that common underlying abilities play a significant role in both L1 and L2 development. Furthermore, their research suggests that certain error types can be understood in terms of differences between L1 and L2, and that well-developed literacy skills in the L1 can facilitate L2 development.

Support for transfer of skills is also demonstrated in Goldenberg's (2008) summary of two major reviews of the research on educating English learners. The two reviews that Goldenberg highlights were completed in 2006 by the National Literacy Panel (NLP) and the Center for Research on Education, Diversity, and Excellence (CREDE). In his article, Goldenberg indicates that the NLP and CREDE concluded that learning to read in the home language promotes reading achievement in the second language. With respect to English learners, a substantial body of research reviewed by both NLP and CREDE researchers suggests that literacy and other skills and knowledge transfer across languages.

A number of other studies have indicated that writers will transfer writing abilities and strategies (whether good or inefficient) from their L1 to their L2 (e.g., Friedlander, 1990). Mohan and Lo (1985), for example, indicate that students who lack L1 strategies display a similar lack of strategies for writing in their L2 and suggest that this type of inefficient strategy use might be developmental. Mohan and Lo found that students who have not developed good strategies for writing in their L1 will not have appropriate strategies to transfer to their L2. They also emphasize, however, that there are other explanations for weaker writing performances among ELLs such as: inadequate knowledge and English skills for expressing complex and abstract ideas; unfamiliarity with the cultural components of a topic; a heavier focus on morphology and syntax level than on the communication of meaning or ideas; and unfamiliarity with the cultural conventions of expository writing in the target or native language.

The strongest case for transfer of language skills has been made by Cummins (1981), who proposed the interdependence hypothesis, which states:

> To the extent that instruction in Lx [i.e., Language x] is effective in promoting proficiency in Lx, transfer of this proficiency to Ly [i.e., Language y] will occur provided there is adequate exposure to Ly (either in school or environment) and adequate motivation to learn Ly. (p. 29)

The interdependence hypothesis holds that a common set of proficiencies underlies both the first and second languages (Fitzgerald, 1995, 2003). What is learned in one language will transfer to another language. Also, Fitzgerald (1995) speculates that using a skill or strategy in one language is nearly the same process as in another. It is important to point out, however, that other research has indicated that universal knowledge bases coexist *with* language-specific strategies.

Given the theory behind the hypothesis, some researchers (e.g., Wong Fillmore & Valdez, 1986) argue that it would seem more sensible to teach complex academic content to students in their native language first so that they can understand and discuss challenging material without the added demand of constantly translating or expressing ideas in a second language. This, however, may be somewhat unlikely, given current political realities.

Cobo-Lewis, Eilers, Pearson, and Umbel (2002) report that for second- and fifth-grade ESL students who speak Spanish as a first language, performance on tests involving reading and writing is highly intercorrelated, regardless of the language of the test. Performance on tests involving oral language (verbal analogies, oral vocabulary), however, intercorrelates only with other oral tests given in the same language.

Evidence that an L1 may assist writers can also be found in some studies of ESL adults. Chelala (1981) and Lay (1982), for example, found that when students switched to their L1, it aided them in retrieval of topic information. Another example is a study by Friedlander (1990) with 28 Chinese-speaking university students who responded to two letters, one in their native language, the other in English. Friedlander found that positive transfer of L1-related content was enhanced when writers wrote using the language in which their information was acquired. It seemed that L2 writers planned for their writing more effectively, wrote better texts containing more content, and created more effective texts when they were able to plan in the language related to their acquisition of topic knowledge in the area.

In a study that reports the relationships among communities, families, and Spanish-speaking children's language and literacy development (in both English and Spanish) in kindergarten and grade 1, Reese and Goldenberg (2008) looked at how the language characteristics of the communities influenced patterns of home language and literacy use, and paid particular attention to access to oral and written language in children's L1 and L2 in different types of communities. The question that Reese and Goldenberg addressed is to what extent community sociodemographics and community language and literacy resources and opportunities facilitated or constrained family literacy practices. Reese and Goldenberg's study was carried out in 35 schools and communities in urban California and urban and border Texas. Methods of data collection included surveying parents (through a questionnaire), interviewing families on three separate occasions, interviewing school principals, having teacher focus groups, and administering the Woodcock Language Proficiency Battery—Revised in English and Spanish.

Reese and Goldenberg (2008) indicate that they were not surprised to find that community characteristics (e.g., ethnicity, education levels, and income) were associated with literacy and language resources in the community. They were surprised to find, however, that there was no association between literacy resources in the community and literacy practices in families (i.e., that families in "high-literacy communities" did not report more literacy in the home than did families in "low-literacy communities"). Reese and Goldenberg point out that patterns of language use in the community appeared to be a greater influence on home reading practices. They observed that patterns of relationships revealed the importance of considering what language is being used in the community and in which language texts were available.

Reese and Goldenberg also found that home literacy practices appeared to have language-specific effects on early literacy development. The authors argue that for children of immigrants growing up bilingually, it is not enough to examine the quantity of materials or frequency of literacy activities in general but rather take into account the language in which these occur. The reason why language needs to be taken into account is due to the language influencing home language and literacy practices, which in turn influence children's literacy development (Reese & Goldenberg, 2008). Finally, Reese and Goldenberg reveal that the families they studied varied considerably in the literacy opportunities they provided their children. They point out that this variability is the result of the agency at both the family level and the school level (e.g., what parents, children, and teachers do and the decisions they make), and that this agency influences children's performance in school.

In a similar study, Reese, Goldenberg, and Saunders (2006) sought to understand the influences of Spanish and English literacy attainment among Spanish-speaking children living in Texas and California. The study consisted of 183 Spanish-speaking students in kindergarten through second grade in three schools with instructional programs for English learners. In the study, Reese et al. examined how community characteristics affected families' language use and experiences in both their first and second languages in ways that might also have influenced children's academic performance. The authors documented characteristics (e.g., socioeconomic status, ethnic heterogeneity, language use, availability of literacy materials) of the three communities and examined how family language and literacy use varied in these settings. Reese et al. hypothesized that prominent use and visibility of one language (L1 or L2) in the community would support children's literacy development in that language, and that this support could independently influence children's literacy development in either language.

Results from Reese et al.'s study show that the schools were located in communities (including the homes of students) that offered students and families varied language-learning opportunities. Furthermore, findings indicate that literacy practices in the home (such as reading job-related materials or writing letters) were varied and not evenly distributed across communities and instructional programs. Variation in family practices were associated with different opportunities available in the surrounding community (e.g., proximity to a church offering services in Spanish) and parents' workplaces (e.g., where some parents used literacy for tasks such as filing orders or writing reports). In terms of end-of-year reading achievement, Reese et al. found that students in programs that emphasized Spanish instruction in K–2 scored higher in Spanish, and students in programs with all-English instruction scored higher in English. They point out that although it would be reasonable to attribute these results primarily to language program, the school program language was confounded with children's language learning opportunities outside school. In other words, variation among communities and families might complement and reinforce language and literacy instruction at school. Reese et al. conclude by stating that the key variable in determining English outcomes is not solely the language of instruction in school but rather the interplay between language of instruction in school and language exposure at home and in the community.

The studies reviewed in this section indicate that learning to write in the L1 aids students in learning to write in the L2. Furthermore, students who learn to write in their L1 before learning to write in their L2 will write as effectively as those who learn to write only in their L2. Studies presented in this section also indicate that a strong first language might result in stronger literacy skills (i.e., the development of oral and written language skills). Finally, it was indicated that writing well in one's first language is associated with successful acquisition of writing skills in a second language (due to the process of language transfer).

EDUCATIONAL CONTEXTS

Teachers' Perceptions of ELL Students' Writing

Despite the notion that some students cannot speak or write well in Spanish or English, Edelsky and Jilbert's (1985) year-long study found that children's bilingualism enhanced their options for making meaning, rather than reducing or limiting it. They found that students were able to maintain their writing in either Spanish or English, were not confused about which language they were using or needed to use, and code-switched for specific reasons (e.g., to indicate direct quotations and for emphasis).

In a study conducted on 110 fourth- and fifth-grade students, Escamilla (2006) examined how concepts of semilingualism (i.e., the belief that one is nonverbal in English as well as in one's native language) have been applied to students who are learning to read and write in Spanish and English in U.S. schools. The purpose of the study was to examine teachers' perceptions of the writing behaviors of students who were learning to write in both Spanish and English in an elementary school in Colorado. Escamilla found that students' Spanish and English writing samples had multiple strengths (e.g., the writing samples consisted of complex ideas).

When teachers discussed students' writing, however, many conveyed their beliefs that students were weak writers in both English and Spanish. They viewed students as "bi-illiterate," and attributed perceived writing needs in English as being caused by Spanish. Escamilla argued that rather than students being bi-illiterate, students' writing samples demonstrated signs of emerging biliteracy. Escamilla also found that, contrary to teachers' beliefs, students lacked background knowledge, students' writing samples indicated strong evidence that they had deep knowledge of the social and economic realities of their communities, and they had plenty of ideas for how to improve these conditions. Escamilla concluded that teachers' beliefs in the idea of semilingualism can be detrimental to students in that teachers may form "deficit" beliefs about linguistic minorities, and these beliefs may have a negative effect on achievement. Escamilla (2006) further argued that the deficit-based perspective has been embedded in school policy and practices. The underlying assumption is that "if the 'norm' is monolingual, then bilingual by definition is not normal" (p. 2332). Similarly, rather than considering knowing two languages to be an asset, the prevailing belief is that a child's native language (e.g., Spanish) is the root cause of his or her learning problems.

In a study conducted in Colorado, Escamilla, Chávez, and Vigil (2005) found that although teachers and policy makers largely adhered to the notion that there was an achievement gap between Spanish-speaking students and other Colorado students, the Spanish speakers in English-language acquisition/bilingual classrooms were among the highest-performing students in their schools. A major factor in helping Spanish-speaking children learn to read and write in Spanish and meet state content standards was participation in bilingual programs. In the case of Spanish-speaking students who were learning Spanish academic content and being tested in Spanish, their outcomes from the state assessment program far exceeded comparable students at their schools and in their school districts.

In another study, Hernández (2001) compared the writing proficiencies of four elementary school-age bilingual children with those of native English speakers over a 2-year period. The study consisted of four fifth-grade students (from four different classrooms) who were nominated by their teachers as either strong or weak writers. The writing events that were observed included: (1) the teachers' oral instruction; (2) the students' writing; (3) the student–student and student–teacher interactions; and (4) the views of writing voiced by the teachers, students, and parents.

Hernández (2001) indicated that all children constructed ideas in a sophisticated way, using compound and complex sentences. Her results showed that students categorized as weak L2 writers were capable of presenting a variety of ideas persuasively. For example, these students were able to write proficiently about details of a school field trip, facts they learned, results of experiments conducted on the trip, evaluation statements about the activities of the trip, and personal observations. Results also suggested that the writing skills of strong L2 writers were indistinguishable from those of strong L1 children. In terms of organization and communication, Hernández also found that students categorized as weak L2 writers did not lag significantly behind L1 writers, even when the weak writers had been in and out of mainstream and bilingual education programs. However, there were substantial differences in the legibility of students' handwriting and the mechanics of spelling and punctuation, and these factors may have been partly responsible for teacher (mis)perceptions.

Classroom and Community Approaches to Writing

Studies on children's writing show that learning to write is a socio-cultural, generative, and developmental process (Lu, 2000). Observational studies of monolingual children's writing development, for example, reveal that children's early writing is usually accompanied by talking and drawing (Bissex, 1980; Dyson, 1988).

In "The Prehistory of Written Language" (1978), Vygotsky argued that "teaching [writing] should be organized in such a way that reading and writing are necessary for something." Vygotsky went on to lament

> the contradiction that appears in the teaching of writing … namely that writing is taught as a motor skill and not as a complex cultural activity … the issue of teaching writing … necessarily entails a second requirement: writing must be "relevant to life." (1978, pp. 117–118)

While some classrooms today may be emphasizing vocabulary more than the pure mechanics of writing, Vygotsky's criticisms of writing instruction still apply in many schools, where writing continues to be taught as a set of mechanical and technical skills with the result that children's writing experience in the primary grades is often limited to worksheet exercises in handwriting and spelling (McLane, 1990). Addressing similar issues of literacy instruction as they manifested in France during the last quarter of the 20th century, Bourdieu (1973) pointed out that formal education systems (i.e., schooling in general) tend to teach and promote the learning of only the barest of rudimentary skills for communicating. Proper spelling and grammar, varied vocabulary, and topic-sentenced paragraphs are not sufficient to make cohesive, intelligent, whole narratives or expositions (Heath & Branscombe, 1985). For example, Calhoun (1970) argued that although schools teach and test students to ensure that they understand automatic responses and rule-of-thumb techniques, neither teaching nor testing helps students develop the active (even emergent) sense necessary to set up an interchange between ideas, needs, and external reality.

Classroom Approaches

The following two studies are classroom-based studies that demonstrate how a group of L2 learners improved their English writing skills and the role that their teachers played in the process. In the first study, Ammon

(1985) conducted a study in which he focused on four L2 learners in two third-grade classrooms in order to determine how their English writing improved in the course of a year. Students in the study had been identified as either limited- or non-English speakers when they first entered their school. Ammon stressed that frequent writing did not suffice to explain the gains made by the students and noted that both third-grade teachers treated writing as an act of communication about content that is important to the writer and to the reader. Furthermore, both teachers gave children the opportunity to write about events of personal interest, posted student writing on their bulletin boards, shared enthusiasm for their writing pieces, and built effectively on abilities their students already had.

In Ammon's (1985) interpretation, students' motivation to engage in writing increased not only in response to their teachers' attitudes toward writing as a communicative activity to take pleasure in, but also as an activity to work at in order to enhance both the writer's and reader's appreciation of the product. The conclusion was that success in helping children learn to write in English occurred due to teachers' use of instructional activities that were rich in opportunities for exposure to, production of, and reflection on English discourse, and that such activities included frequent writing on topics of personal interest with guidance and feedback. Ammon's analysis suggests that students can learn to write in English through a program of instruction that emphasizes doing just that, even when the children's initial efforts at English writing seem limited.

In the second classroom-based study, Urzua (1987) examined the oral and written interactions and texts of four Southeast Asian ESL students who participated in writing activities such as dialogue journal writing and peer response groups. Urzua found that when ESL students chose their own topics (i.e., when they were given more freedom and control over their writing topics), their own voices emerged more strongly. As a result, students in the study were more effective writers in terms of content, development, and grammar. Urzua found that allowing students control over topics gave them the freedom to build on their own knowledge and to share that knowledge with others.

Community Approaches

The two studies that follow are examples of after-school programs that enhanced children's writing experiences. In the first study, children playfully explored the way language looks on the page, using different colors, different kinds of handwriting, and different spatial arrangements for letters and words. In the second study, a technological approach to writing was employed. The approach promoted cognitive and social development and fostered collaboration among cross-generational and diverse group of participants.

In the first study, McLane (1990) observed how 6- to 8-year-old children (16 total) from a poor, inner-city community of Chicago used writing in an after-school program. After finding that children were doing little writing, McLane introduced a range of writing activities that would get the children interested in writing. McLane was able to get children interested in writing by scribing their dictated stories and then helping them to dramatize them. Another approach was asking children about their drawings and later asking whether they wanted labels or stories to go with them. Several children were initially hesitant and uncertain about what to write about, as well as their own writing competence. Later, McLane found that children were increasingly willing (at times, eager) to write only if they were allowed to control their own writing and if an adult would offer encouragement and support while they wrote. When the above conditions were met, children used writing in a variety of playful and social ways not generally encountered or encouraged in school writing programs. Furthermore, children expanded their use of writing to communicate their ideas, sometimes creating products in which drawing and writing was evenly distributed and equally important in conveying meaning.

In the second study, Gutiérrez, Baquedano-López, Alvarez, and Ming Chiu (1999) organized an after-school computer lab ("Las Redes") in which elementary children and university undergraduate students participated in educational activities that brought play and learning together. The children at Las Redes came from an elementary school in Los Angeles that served mainly Latino, African American, and Tongan students. In the computer lab, participants drew from their own as well as each other's linguistic and sociocultural resources to collaborate in problem-solving activities, creating rich zones of development that became the tools for mediating literacy learning (Gutiérrez et al., 1999; Gutiérrez, Badequano-López, & Alvarez, 2001). "El Maga" is an entity in cyberspace that helps sustain the culture of collaboration and promotes participation, socialization to the culture of the setting, and affiliation among participants through ongoing and personalized dialogue (Gutiérrez et al., 2001). Children are asked to tell El Maga about how they accomplish the various computer-learning tasks, how they solve problems, and to describe any difficulties encountered while playing the games. From this, the children and El Maga engage in problem-solving exchanges in which they pose questions to one another, hoping to achieve their own individual and shared goals.

Although Gutiérrez et al. (1999) do not include evaluation data in their article, they found that the collaborative literacy learning at Las Redes stimulated joint participation and learning for all learners (experts and novices). Furthermore, the literacy event helped children reflect on the day's activities by narrating and thus externalizing their thoughts in writing (Gutiérrez et al., 2001). Participants also received explicit and implicit instruction about literacy, including the nuances of language use, spelling, vocabulary, sentence structure, and language play, and learned how to write a letter and how to request assistance.

Despite these positive examples of writing activities, what is found in U.S. classrooms can be different from what was described above. The section that follows provides an overview of students' writing outcomes, what writing activities consist of in U.S. classrooms, and the teacher's role in the process.

ELL Writing Instruction in U.S. Classrooms

Research suggests that students from language-minority backgrounds in the United States do poorly in school because they do not acquire the specific forms of English necessary for reading and writing academic papers and discussing academic issues (Wong Fillmore & Snow, 1999). Carlisle and Beeman (2000) argue that in terms of bilingual writing development, the results of many studies suggest that progress depends on the language of instruction and on exposure to literacy activities in both students' native language and English. Other studies, however, suggest that stronger native-language writing development is associated with better literacy achievement in English (Carlisle & Beeman, 2000; Carlo & Royer, 1999).

According to Edelsky (1986) and Gutiérrez (1993), writing is a rare event in bilingual and ESL programs. Johnson (1989) states that teachers in most ESL classes do not treat writing as a social activity focused on purposeful and meaningful communication with others. Johnson argues that writing assignments are usually limited to a common form of student–teacher interaction: the teacher initiates a topic, the students respond with a piece of writing, and the teacher responds to content and form. The teacher assumes the role of expert in content and language use, and the child remains in a subordinate role (Johnson, 1989).

Similar to Johnson, McLane (1990) states that this "traditional" writing instruction is usually a one-shot affair in which the child is told to write something, which is then corrected for handwriting, spelling, and grammar, and then graded and forgotten. Teachers using this traditional approach to writing often focus on the technical aspects of writing and pay little attention to the writer's communicative purposes with the result that, for many children, writing becomes an exercise in formal mechanics divorced from personal content and intentions (McLane, 1990).

In many U.S. public schools, ELLs in mainstream classrooms are required to perform a wide variety of writing activities, including writing short answers, descriptions of historical events, book summaries, reports on experiments in a science class, and long essays (Lee, 2004). In some ESL classrooms, however, writing activities are limited to simple writing tasks. When describing the writing practices of children, Edelsky (1989) distinguished between "authentic writing" and "writing simulations." She argued that much of children's writing is not authentic writing but simulations of writing and pointed out that a student is "likely to be simulating writing when he or she is filling in blanks on a worksheet, finishing a story starter, or producing a story that includes the week's spelling words" (Edelsky, 1989, p. 167). In contrast, in authentic writing the language is used to make meaning for some purposes.

Significantly, Heath (1986) argued that in order to promote development in second language literacy, educators need to expand, not limit, students' ways of using written language. Furthermore, writing research recommends that teachers create contexts for writers that are grounded in meaningful classroom experiences, connecting students to the school environment as well as to their home cultures. A few researchers (e.g., Au, 1993; Dyson, 1989) have suggested that effective classroom practices, which validate students' experiences, provide interaction among students and place writing in a larger context, allowing students to develop written proficiency in their L1 and L2. Meaningful classroom experiences include allowing students to retell their home and school experiences during classroom discussions through personal narratives (Hudelson, 1994). It is believed that once students have experienced language orally, it will be easier for them to represent their language in print.

As a result of the type of writing opportunities in U.S. classrooms, many students from diverse backgrounds leave school without acquiring skills in written academic discourse. Mexican American students, in particular, seem to be affected by this trend, as they fall far behind their white peers in literacy acquisition assessments and experience much higher dropout rates. Educational implications are discussed in a later section.

Assessment of Students' Writing Samples

Although it can be difficult to assess students, assessment is an important practice, largely because it can provide periodic feedback on how students are progressing. García (2005) described the professional planning and development component of the Authentic Literacy Assessment System (ALAS), a collaborative project of the San Francisco Unified School District, university researchers, and teachers in two urban, linguistically diverse elementary schools. Since 1997, teachers at the two elementary schools, a literacy coach, and university researchers have worked together to develop and implement research-based ways of teaching and assessing writing with diverse students.

ALAS is designed to provide teachers with a meaningful and periodic writing assessment of their students. ALAS allows students to explore writing as a process in the context of the language arts curriculum in bilingual and English language development classrooms. At the two participating schools, ALAS is administered three times a year, giving teachers regular indicators of students' writing strengths and needs. The writing produced by students is a response to a writing prompt, which is thematically related to reading and writing activities (García, 2005).

In both schools, students' writings were examined by teachers using the same holistic and analytic writing rubrics. The holistic rubrics described general features of student writing at different levels of proficiency (e.g., word choice and syntax), while analytic rubrics studied different elements of writing in relation to each other (e.g., topic, organization, style/voice, conventions). At both schools, the teachers began by developing English rubrics as a whole staff. Later, bilingual teachers developed rubrics in Spanish and in Chinese.

Similar findings were achieved at both elementary schools. For example, students demonstrated the ability to expand on the topic of the writing, communicate the main idea, and better understand the various spelling strategies to orthographic patterns, contractions, compounds, and the role of correct punctuation. García (2005) also found improvement in the organization of students' writing (i.e., a topic sentence and concluding sentence, and presentation of ideas), and that students acquired English writing proficiency at grade levels, while at the same time developing and maintaining proficiency in their native language. In addition, students' English and first language writing scores equaled or were slightly above grade-level writing benchmarks.

Language Difference or Learning Disability?

Just as with oral language, features of writing in a second language for students in the process of becoming bilingual can mimic the writing of students with learning disabilities. Students with learning disabilities as well as English language learners may struggle with written expression, grammar, spelling, and vocabulary (Haager & Klingner, 2005). Thus it can be difficult to distinguish between difference and disability.

Barrera (2003, 2006) examined the writing of secondary-level ELLs with and without school-identified learning disabilities in an attempt to determine the characteristics of writing that distinguished between typical language development and disability. Barrera (2006) asked 38 teachers from general and special education to assess 114 writing samples from three groups of Mexican American students: (1) second-language learners identified with learning disabilities; (2) second-language learning peers not in special education; and (3) peers considered normal- to high-achieving bilingual or English proficient. When scoring the writing samples, the teachers had no idea to which of these groups each student author belonged. Barrera found that ELLs with learning disabilities could be differentiated from the other groups, and that differentiation was clearest with quantitative measures (e.g., words and letters written, percentage of words spelled correctly, number of complete sentences). Although the implications from this study suggest that writing samples might be a useful authentic assessment tool in identifying disabilities, it is crucial to note that the ELLs in this study had been identified by their schools as having learning disabilities, and it is quite possible, and even likely, that some students were identified not because they truly had learning disabilities but because they were experiencing some confusion while acquiring English proficiency.

This section primarily focused on teachers' perceptions of students' writing, classroom and community approaches to writing, and writing instruction in U.S. classrooms. Studies on teachers' perceptions of ELL students' writing indicate that teachers tended to believe that students were weak writers in both English and Spanish (Escamilla, 2006). Results of students' writing samples, however, demonstrated signs of emerging biliteracy and strong evidence that students had deep knowledge of the social and economic realities of their communities. In a similar study, Escamilla et al. (2005) found that Spanish-speaking students in English-language acquisition/bilingual classrooms were among the highest performing students in their schools. In the case of Spanish-speaking students who were learning Spanish academic content and being tested in Spanish, their outcomes from state assessment program far exceeded comparable students at their schools and in their school districts. In another study, Hernández (2001) found that students categorized as weak L2 writers were capable of presenting a variety of ideas persuasively, that their writing skills were indistinguishable from those of strong L1 children, and that they did not lag significantly behind L1 writers, even when the weak writers had been in and out of mainstream and bilingual education programs.

Studies on classroom approaches to writing demonstrate that teachers played a role in L2 learners' acquisition of writing skills (Ammon, 1985). That is, gains made by students were attributed to teachers having frequent writing with guidance and feedback, giving students the opportunity to write about events of personal interest, sharing enthusiasm for their writing pieces, and building effectively on abilities their students already had. In another study, Urzua (1987) found that ESL students were more effective writers (i.e., in terms of content, development, and grammar) when they chose their own topics and when they were given the freedom to build on their own knowledge and share that knowledge with others.

Similarly, studies on community approaches to writing show that children demonstrated an interest in writing when they playfully explored the way language looks on the page, using different colors, different kinds of handwriting, and different spatial arrangements for letters and words (McLane, 1990). In addition, students were interested in writing when they scribed their dictated stories and later dramatized them. In another study, an after-school computer lab was organized in which children participated in educational activities that brought play and learning together (Gutiérrez et al., 1999). The approach promoted cognitive and social development and fostered collaboration among a diverse group of students by means of indicating how they accomplished the various computer-learning tasks, how they solved problems, and how they described difficulties encountered while playing the games.

Research on ELL writing instruction in U.S. classroom state that teachers do not treat writing as a social activity focused on purposeful and meaningful communication with others (e.g., Johnson, 1989; McLane, 1990). This is largely due to the teacher initiating a topic, the students responding with a piece of writing, and the teacher responding to content and form. As a result, writing tends to become an exercise in formal mechanics divorced from personal content and intentions (McLane, 1990). In order to improve writing skills, writing research indicates that educators need to expand students' ways of using written language, create contexts for writers that are grounded in meaningful classroom experiences, validate students' experiences, and place writing in a larger context that allows students to develop written proficiency in their first and second languages.

CONCLUSION

Pertinent Findings

Results of the reviewed writing studies are suggestive in a variety of ways. The most general conclusion is that repeated writing activities—such as activities from worksheets, finishing a story starter, or writing from an assigned prompt—do not lead to frequent writing or improved writing from students. In fact, these studies found that frequency of writing and student writing outcomes tend to improve if teachers allow students to write about something of personal interest as well as offer them support and encouragement during writing activities. In turn, students' motivation is likely to increase, their own voices can come through more strongly in their written narratives; they can build on their own knowledge; and they can become more effective writers in terms of content, development, and grammar. Students are also more likely to explore, play, and experiment with written language when they choose their own topics.

The studies presented in this chapter also found that students who learn to write in their L1 (e.g., Spanish) before learning to write in their L2 (e.g., English) will write just as effectively or better in their L2 as those students who learn to write only in their L2. Along these lines, the writing skills of strong L2 writers are indistinguishable from those of strong L1 students. In addition, participating in bilingual programs helps Spanish-speaking students learn to write in Spanish and meet state content writing standards.

Recommendations for Future Research

After reviewing the research on ELLs and writing, we conclude that more studies are needed comparing the writing of students who learned to write in their L1 before learning to write in their L2 with that of students who learned to write only in their L2. Along these lines, little research has been conducted on elementary school-age children learning to write in English as their second language. When examining children's writing development in English, important factors that should be considered include their English language proficiency, prior knowledge and experiences, and primary language literacy. Not only do we need to know more about the writing development of English learners of different ages and backgrounds, but we also need to learn more about effective instruction for particular groups of ELLs.

Because there is ample research that supports the interdependence hypothesis, finding ways to facilitate and accelerate the transfer of information across languages may be a promising approach for helping ethnically and linguistically diverse students become successful writers. Unfortunately, there is little research on instructional practices that promote this transfer. Such research would be useful in helping to design instruction to improve bilingual students' writing outcomes. In addition, further studies are needed to determine whether ethnically and linguistically diverse students taught initial literacy skills in their L1 (e.g., Spanish) show an advantage in bilingual literacy achievement. It would also be significant to determine whether an observed advantage is maintained as students advance to higher grade levels.

We also lack research focused on the writing practices of ethnically and linguistically diverse primary school students across different settings outside the classroom (e.g., their home and community). Studies that address the different writing practices in which students engage across settings may help us understand not only how written language is learned but also to recognize the importance of context and the nature of interactions within those contexts in the language learning process. Finally, more research is needed to determine whether ELLs' early writing is accompanied by talk, drawing, and play (as has been shown with monolingual English speakers).

Educational Implications

The school environment plays an important role in helping ELLs develop their writing proficiencies in English. The writing experiences they encounter in school have a significant impact on how they approach writing and affect their success as English writers. There are numerous implications from the research we have reviewed in this chapter for how teachers can go about promoting students' writing development.

The first and perhaps most important implication is that it is far more beneficial to view ELLs from a positive rather than a deficit perspective. For example, if a student who is developing skills in two languages knows how to write 10 words in her/his first language and a different 10 words in English, s/he knows more, not fewer, words than the student who can write 15 words in English only (cf. Oller & Pearson, 2002). We encourage practitioners to follow Escamilla's (2006) suggestion of viewing such students as "emerging biliterates" rather than as "semilinguals."

Teachers should engage with students and teach them according to their individual needs by providing direct and explicit instruction that is at their language level and giving them time to process the new instruction. In addition, teachers need to recognize the diverse ways that their students make sense of the world and approach learning. This recognition allows teachers to realize that learning is deeply influenced by factors such as race/ethnicity, social class, and the process of language acquisition. This critical understanding enables teachers to provide instruction that develops bridges for their ELLs. ELLs benefit from writing instruction that is based on their unique needs. Although there are similarities, becoming biliterate or proficient in English as a second language is not the exact same process as becoming literate in a first language. Students may need more time, and explicit instruction, in how their first and second languages are the similar and different, especially with vocabulary and syntax.

ELLs need sufficient time to think, talk, read, and write in order to become successful writers. How and what students read affects what and how they write. Sharing their writing with others promotes interest and motivation. Instructional activities should not be limited to discrete tasks and skill practice, but should also include opportunities for students to engage in meaningful tasks that are motivating and engaging. Students benefit from ample time for authentic practice.

Similarly, instructional practices should build on students' prior knowledge and help them make connections between what they already know, their lived experiences, and new knowledge. Practices that incorporate the funds of knowledge (cf. González, Moll, & Amanti, 2005) in students' homes and communities are more likely to help them understand the importance of writing in everyday lives. An instructional goal should be to produce competent writers who view themselves as authors and experience joy in the writing process.

Given that proficiency in one's L1 promotes proficiency in an L2, writing in an L1 should be fostered whenever possible (although this may not be feasible in states that prohibit bilingual education). Providing students with explicit instruction in ways in which the two languages are similar can promote the transfer of knowledge (e.g., such as cognates, or words that mean the same thing in both languages). Although some students figure out on their own the ways that strategies they use in one language can apply in another, other students benefit from having this pointed out to them.

Finally, rather than giving writing instruction second class status or considering it of less importance than reading instruction, teachers and administrators should make sure that opportunities for writing are integrated into instructional routines throughout the school-day, across the curriculum. Reading and writing are reciprocal processes, each reinforcing the other. Writing in the content areas promotes the acquisition of content knowledge as well as the development of writing skills in different genres.

NOTE

1. The term *English language learner* (ELL), as used in this chapter, indicates a person who is in the process of acquiring English and has a first language other than English. In the field of education, the term has been defined as a student who speaks one or more languages other than English and is developing proficiency in English. Other terms commonly found in the literature include language-minority students, limited English proficient (LEP), English as a second language (ESL), and culturally and linguistically diverse (CLD).

REFERENCES

Ammon, P. (1985). Helping children learn to write in English as a second language: Some observations and some hypotheses. In S. W. Freedman (Ed.), *The acquisition of written language: Response and revision* (pp. 65–84). Norwood, NJ: Ablex.

Au, K. H. (1993). *Literacy instruction in multicultural settings.* Forth Worth, TX: Harcourt Brace Jovanovich College Publishers.

Barrera, M. (2003). Curriculum-based dynamic assessment for new- or second-language learners with learning disabilities in secondary education settings. *Assessment for Effective Intervention, 29*(1), 69–84.

Barrera, M. (2006). Roles of definitional and assessment models in the identification of new- or second-language learners of English for special education. *Journal of Learning Disabilities, 39*(2), 142–156.

Bissex, G. L. (1980). *GNYS AT WRK: A child learns to read and write.* Cambridge, MA: Harvard University Press.

Bourdieu, P. (1973). Cultural reproduction and social reproduction. In R. Brown (Ed.), *Knowledge, education and cultural change: Papers in the sociology of education* (pp. 71–112). London: Tavistock.

Calhoun, D. (1970). *The intelligence of a people.* Princeton, NJ: Princeton University Press.

Carlisle, R. S. (1989). The writing of Anglo and Hispanic elementary school students in bilingual, submersion, and regular programs. *Studies in Second Language Acquisition, 11,* 257–280.

Carlisle, J. F., & Beeman, M. M. (2000). The effects of language instruction on the reading and writing achievement of first-grade Hispanic children. *Scientific Studies of Reading, 4*(4), 331–353.

Carlo, M. S., & Royer, J. M. (1999). Cross-language transfer of reading skills. In D. A. Wagner, R. L. Venezky, and B. Street (Eds.), *Literacy: An international handbook* (pp. 148–154). Boulder, CO: Westview Press.

Chelala, S. (1981). *The composing process of two Spanish speakers and the coherence of their texts: A case study.* Unpublished doctoral dissertation, New York University.

Cobo-Lewis, A., Eilers, R., Pearson, B., & Umbel, V. (2002). Interdependence of Spanish and English knowledge. In D. K. Oller & R. E. Eilers (Eds.), *Language and literacy in bilingual children* (pp. 118–132). Clevedon, UK: Multilingual Matters.

Cummins, J. (1981). The role of primary language development in promoting educational success for language minority students. In California State Department of Education (Ed.), *Schooling and language minority students: A theoretical framework* (pp. 3–49). Los Angeles: National Dissemination and Assessment Center.

Duranti, A. and Ochs, E. (1998). Syncretic literacy. In L. B. Resnick, R. Saljo, C. Pontecorvo, & B. Burge (Eds.), *Discourse tools, and reasoning: Essays on situated cognition* (pp. 169–202). Berlin: Springer.

Dyson, A. H. (1988). Unintentional helping in the primary grades: Writing in the children's world. In B. A. Rafoth & D. L. Rubin (Eds.), *The social construction of written communication* (pp. 218–248). Norwood, NJ: Ablex.

Dyson, A. H. (1989). *Multiple worlds of child writers: Friends learning to write.* New York: Teachers College Press.

Echiburu Berzins, M., & López, A. E. (2001). Starting off right: Planting the seeds for biliteracy. In M. Reyes & J. J. Halcón (Eds.), *The best for our children: Critical perspectives on literacy for Latino students* (pp. 81–95). New York: Teachers College Press.

Edelsky, C. (1986). *Writing in a bilingual program: Había una vez.* Norwoood, NJ: Ablex.

Edelsky, C. (1989). Bilingual children's writing: Fact and fiction. In D. Johnson & D. Roen (Eds.), *Richness in writing: Empowering ESL students* (pp. 165–176). New York: Longman.

Edelsky, C., & Jilbert, K. (1985). Bilingual children and writing: Lessons for all of us. *The Volta Review, 87*(5), 57–72.

Escamilla, K. (2006). Semilingualism applied to the literacy behaviors of Spanish-speaking emerging bilinguals: Bi-illiteracy or emerging biliteracy? *Teachers College Record, 108*(11), 2329–2353.

Escamilla, K., Chávez, L. & Vigil, P. (2005). Rethinking the "Gap": High-stakes testing and Spanish-speaking students in Colorado. *Journal of Teacher Education, 56*(2), 132–144.

Ferris, M. R., & Politzer, R. L. (1981). Effects of early and delayed second language acquisition: English composition skills of Spanish speaking junior high school students. *TESOL Quarterly, 15,* 263–274.

Fitzgerald, J. (1995). English-as-a-second-language learners' cognitive reading processes: A review of research in the United States. *Review of Educational Research, 65*(2), 145–190.

Fitzgerald, J. (2003). Multilingual reading theory. *Reading Research Quarterly, 38,* 118–122.

Fitzgerald, J. (2006). Multilingual writing in preschool through 12th grade: The last 15 years. In C. A. MacArthur, S. Graham, & J. Fitzgerald (Eds.), *Handbook of writing research* (pp. 337–354). New York: Guilford Press.

Friedlander, A. (1990). Composing in English: Effects of a first language on writing in English as a second language. In B. Kroll (Ed.), *Second-language writing: Research insights for the classroom* (pp. 109–125). Cambridge, UK: Cambridge University Press.

Fry, R. (2006). The changing landscape of American public education: New students, new schools. Pew Hispanic Center research report. Retrieved November 12, 2008, from *pewhispanic.org/files/reports/72.pdf.*

Gale, K., McClay, D., Christie, M., & Harris, S. (1981). Academic achievement in the Milingimbi bilingual program. *TESOL Quarterly, 15,* 297–314.

García, E. E. (2005). *Teaching and learning in two languages: Bilingualism and schooling in the United States.* New York: Teachers College Press.

Genesee, F., Geva, E., Dressler, C., & Kamil, M. L. (2008). Cross-linguistic relationships in second language learners. In D. August & T. Shanahan (Eds.), *Developing reading and writing in second-language learners* (pp. 61–93). New York: Routledge.

Goldenberg, C. (2008). Teaching English language learners: What the research does—and does not—say. *American Educator,* Summer 2008, 8–44. Retrieved December 2, 2008, from *www.aft.org/pubs-reports/american_educator/issues/summer08/ goldenberg.pdf.*

González, N., Moll, L. C., & Amanti, C. (2005). *Funds of knowledge: Theorizing practices in households and classrooms.* Hillsdale, NJ: Erlbaum.

Gort, M. (2006). Strategic codeswitching, interliteracy, and other phenomena of emergent bilingual writing: Lessons from first grade dual language classrooms. *Journal of Early Childhood Literacy, 6*(3), 323–354.

Gutiérrez, K. D. (1993). Biliteracy and the language-minority child. In B. Spodek and O. N. Saracho (Eds.), *Language and literacy in early childhood education* (pp. 82–101). New York: Teachers College Press.

Gutiérrez, K. D., Baquedano-López, P., & Alvarez, H. H. (2001). Literacy as hybridity: Moving beyond bilingualism in urban classrooms. In M. Reyes & J. J. Halcón (Eds.), *The best for our children: Critical perspectives on literacy for Latino students* (pp. 122–141). New York: Teachers College Press.

Gutiérrez, K. D., Baquedano-López, P., Alvarez, H. H., & Ming Chiu, M. (1999). Building a culture of collaboration through hybrid languages and practices. *Theory into Practice, 38*(2), 87–93.

Haager, D., & Klingner, J. K. (2005). *Differentiating instruction in inclusive classrooms: The special educators' guide.* Boston: Allyn & Bacon.

Heath, S. B. (1986). Sociocultural contexts of language development. In California

State Department of Education (Ed.), *Beyond language: Social and cultural factors in schooling language-minority students* (pp. 143–186). Los Angeles: Evaluation, Dissemination and Assessment Center, California State University.

Heath, S. B., & Branscombe, A. (1985). "Intelligent writing" in an audience community: Teacher, students, and researcher. In S. W. Freedman (Ed.), *The acquisition of written language: Response and revision* (pp. 3–32). Norwood, NJ: Ablex.

Hernández, A. C. (2001). The expected and unexpected literacy outcomes of bilingual students. *Bilingual Research Journal, 25*(3), 251–276.

Hudelson, S. (1989). A tale of two children: Individual differences in ESL children's writing. In D. M. Johnson & D. H. Roen (Eds.), *Richness in writing: Empowering ESL students* (pp. 84–99). New York: Longman.

Hudelson, S. (1994). Literacy development of second-language children. In F. Genesee (Ed.), *Educating second-language children: The whole child, the whole curriculum, the whole community* (pp. 129–157). Cambridge, UK: Cambridge University Press.

Johnson, D. M. (1989). Enriching task contexts for second-language writing: Power through interpersonal roles. In D. M. Johnson & D. H. Roen, (Eds.). *Richness in writing: Empowering ESL students* (pp. 39–54). New York: Longman.

Kaplan, R., & Grabe, B. (1997). The writing course. In K. Bardovi-Harlig & B. Hartford (Eds.), *Beyond methods* (pp. 172–197). New York: McGraw-Hill.

Lay, N. D. (1982). Composing processes of adult ESL learners. *TESOL Quarterly,* 16, 406.

Lee, C. (2004). *Another tale of two children: The writing development of two ESL learners.* Retrieved January 6, 2006, from *www.midtesol.org/Newsletter/20040210LeeArticle.htm.*

Lesaux, N. K., Geva, E., Koda, K., Siegel, L. S., & Shanahan, T. (2008). Development of literacy in second-language learners. In D. August and T. Shanahan (Eds.), *Developing reading and writing in second-language learners* (pp. 27–59). New York: Routledge.

Lu, M. (2000). *Writing development* (ERIC Clearinghouse on Reading, English, and Communication Digest #159). Retrieved January 6, 2006, from *reading.indiana.edu.ieo.digests.d159.htm.*

McClure, E., Mir, M., & Cadierno, T. (1993). What do you include in a narrative?: A comparison of the written narratives of Mexican and American fourth and ninth graders. *Pragmatics and Language Learning, 4*, 209–224.

McLane, J. B. (1990). Writing as a social process. In L. C. Moll (Ed.), *Vygotsky and education: Instructional implications and applications of sociohistorical psychology* (pp. 304–318). New York: Cambridge University Press.

Mohan, B. A., & Lo, W. A. (1985). Academic writing and Chinese students: Transfer and developmental factors. *TESOL Quarterly, 19*(3), 515–534.

Moll, L. C., Sáez, R., & Dworin, J. (2001). Exploring biliteracy: Two student case examples of writing as a social practice. *The Elementary School Journal, 101*(4), 435–449.

NCELA. *ELL Demographics by State.* Washington, DC: NCELA. Retrieved November 18, 2008, from *www.ncela.gwu.edu/stats/3_bystate.htm.*

Oller, D. K., & Pearson, B. Z. (2002). Assessing the effects of bilingualism: A background. In D. K. Oller & R. E. Eilers (Eds.), *Language and literacy in bilingual children* (pp. 3–21). Clevedon, UK: Multilingual Matters.

Reese, L., & Goldenberg, C. (2008). Parental involvement and the academic achievement of Hispanic students: Community literacy resources and home literacy practices among immigrant Latino families. *Marriage and Family Review, 43*(1/2), 109–139.

Reese, L., Goldenberg, C., & Saunders, W. (2006). Variations in reading achievement among Spanish-speaking children in different language programs: Explanations and confounds. *The Elementary School Journal, 106*(4), 363–386.

Reese, L., Linan Thompson, S., & Goldenberg, C. (2008). Variability in community characteristics and Spanish-speaking children's home language and literacy opportunities. *Journal of Multilingual and Multicultural Development, 29*(4), 271–290.

Riojas Clark, E. (1995). "How did you learn to write in English when you haven't been taught English?": The language experience approach in a dual-language program. *The Bilingual Research Journal, 19*(3 & 4), 611–627.

Serna, I., & Hudelson, S. (1993). Becoming a writer of Spanish and English. *The Quarterly of the National Writing Project and The Center for the Study of Writing and Literacy, 15*(1), 1–5.

Street, B. V. (1984). *Literacy in theory and practice.* Cambridge, UK: Cambridge University Press.

Urzua, C. (1987). "You stopped too soon": Second-language children composing and revising. *TESOL Quarterly, 21*(2), 279–304.

U.S. Census Bureau. (2003). Retrieved December 28, 2005, from *quickfacts.census. gov.*

U.S. Department of Education. (2003, June). *Key indicators of Hispanic student achievement: National goals and benchmarks for the next decade.* Retrieved October 17, 2004, from *www.ed.gov/pubs/hispanicindicators.*

U.S. Department of Education. (2008). *National Center for Education Statistics, Condition of Education 2000–2008.* Retrieved March 5, 2009, from *nces. ed.gov/programs/coe/2008/section1/indicator07.asp#info.*

Vygotsky, L. S. (1978). *Mind in society: The development of higher psychological processes.* Cambridge, MA: Harvard University Press.

Wong Fillmore, L., & Snow, C. E. (1999). What educators—especially teachers—need to know about language: The bare minimum. Retrieved January 14, 2006, from *www.cal.org/ericcll/teachers/teachers.pdf.*

Wong Fillmore, L., & Valdez, C. (1986). Teaching bilingual learners. In M. C. Wittrock (Ed.), *Handbook of research on teaching* (pp. 648–685). New York: Macmillan.

Zehler, A., Fleischman, H., Hopstock, P., Stephenson, T., Pendzick, M., & Sapru, S. (2003). *Policy report: Summary of findings related to LEP and SPED-LEP students.* Submitted by Development Associates, Inc., to U.S. Department of Education, Office of English Language Acquisition, Language Enhancement, and Academic Achievement of Limited English-Proficient Students.

PART IV

. . .

Assessment and Diagnosis

CHAPTER 10

■   ■   ■

Linguistic and Cognitive Processes in the Development of Spelling in English Language Learners

First-Language Transfer, Language Proficiency, or Cognitive Processes?

ESTHER GEVA
ADÈLE LAFRANCE

Although learning to read and learning to spell are related, they are considered to be separate processes (Holmes & Castles, 2001). In alphabetic languages, word reading and spelling skills depend on knowledge of the alphabet and letter–sound correspondences, and familiarity with the orthographic conventions of the language at hand. However, reading words involves the pronunciation of a letter string, whereas spelling requires the writing of letters in a particular sequence (Ehri, 1997). Compared to the volume of research on reading, there are fewer studies examining the development of first-language (L1) spelling in school children.

One area that has received even less attention in the research community is the development of spelling skills in a second language (L2). Little research is available on the development of spelling in English language learners (ELLs) and the role of language proficiency and cognitive processes in understanding the spelling performance of ELLs (Geva, 2006a). This void

245

in the literature is problematic given that a significant number of well-intentioned educators and practitioners believe that low levels of L2 oral language proficiency are at the root of literacy-based difficulties in ELLs whose L2 is English (Geva, 2000; Limbos & Geva, 2001). According to Geva (2006a), these trends lead to both the overdiagnosis of learning disabilities (LDs) (by interpreting poor language and literacy skills as LD) and the underdiagnosis of L2 learners who might actually have a LD. For example, Limbos and Geva (2001) have found that whereas classroom teachers were accurate in identifying L1 schoolchildren who may be at risk for reading disability, they interpret similar warning signs in ELLs as reflecting their L2 status.

Delaying assessments of ELL students who may have difficulties in developing adequate spelling skills is a problem for a variety of reasons. First, in the early grades, spelling ability makes significant contributions to writing ability (Juel, Griffith, & Gough, 1986), a skill crucial for academic and occupational success. Moreover, according to Wagner, Francis, and Morris (2005), at least in the case of reading disabilities, the longer the problems exist without adequate intervention, the more difficult they are to remediate. In addition, poor spelling is often negatively perceived by readers (Figueredo & Varnhagen, 2006; Kreiner, Schnakenberg, Green, Costello, & McClin, 2002). Figueredo and Varnhagen (2006) asked undergraduates to read a cover letter for a job application and then rate both the applicant and the cover letter. A manipulation of the presence of spelling errors revealed that participants' ratings of the applicant's abilities decreased when the letter contained spelling errors, suggesting that perceptions of a job applicant's abilities are negatively affected by spelling errors.

A handful of Canadian studies that examined the development of spelling to dictation of older ELLs in elementary school have found similar profiles to those of monolingual children (e.g., Chiappe & Siegel, 1999; Da Fontoura & Siegel, 1995; Limbos & Geva, 2001; Wade-Woolley & Siegel, 1997). However, in a cross-sectional study, Fashola, Drum, Mayer, and Kang (1996), who examined spelling in ELLs with Spanish as the L1, found that they made more errors than the English-as-L1 (EL1) students. In that study fifth- and sixth-grade students made fewer errors than third- and fourth-grade students. Relatedly, research has revealed that ELL and monolingual EL1 readers who are good readers and spellers have similar cognitive profiles. Likewise, poor ELL and monolingual EL1 readers and spellers have similar cognitive profiles (DaFontoura & Siegel, 1995; Chiappe, Siegel, & Wade-Woolley, 2002; Everatt, Smythe, Adams, & Ocampo, 2000; Wade-Woolley & Siegel, 1997).

Even less is known about the development of spelling skills of ELLs over time. Moreover, to date no studies examined the impact of cognitive processing factors on spelling development both concurrently and longitudinally. There is no doubt that differences in proficiency in the societal language (the L2) and in L2 spelling skills exist when ELLs enter school. As such, it is imperative that well-designed longitudinal studies be conducted in order to contribute to the body of knowledge in the area of literacy development of linguistically diverse populations. To fill this void, the current chapter focuses on a comparison of the spelling abilities of ELL and EL1 children over time, the influence of intraindividual variables such as nonverbal reasoning, vocabulary, phonological awareness, and naming speed on later spelling abilities in both EL1 and ELL children, as well as a comparison of the development of spelling, cognitive, and linguistic processes of ELL and EL1 learners of varying spelling ability.

FACTORS RELATED TO SPELLING SKILLS IN L2 LEARNERS

Various cognitive–linguistic factors have been studied in the research on the development of spelling skills. These factors include vocabulary knowledge, naming speed, and phonological awareness.

Vocabulary

L2 language proficiency is demonstrated by a child's ability to understand and communicate effectively in the L2. Component skills of L2 proficiency include vocabulary, grammatical skills, discourse, and pragmatics (Roberts & Neal, 2004). There is ample evidence in the literature that there is a significant delay in the acquisition of vocabulary by bilingual children, especially when they are compared to monolingual peers who only speak that language (Bialystok & Feng, Chapter 5, this volume). Some ELLs' performance in areas of English literacy is lower than their EL1 counterparts. These difficulties are often attributed to low levels of English oral language. For example, well-intentioned educators often assume that the vocabulary levels of ELL children affect their basic literacy skills (Limbos & Geva, 2001).

With regard to word-level reading skills of ELL children, a recent meta-analysis suggests that the impact of vocabulary knowledge is not robust (for a review see Geva, 2006a), and that factors such as phonemic awareness and rapid automatized naming explain a larger proportion of the variance on word and pseudoword reading tasks in ELLs. The relationship between vocabulary and spelling is not as well documented in ELL samples, and the results are somewhat mixed; however, some research suggests that vocabulary does not play a major role in explaining individual differences in spelling skills of ELLs (Arab-Moghaddam & Sénéchal, 2001; Everatt et al., 2000; Geva, 2006a, 2006b; Lesaux & Siegel, 2003; Wade-Woolley & Siegel, 1997; Wang & Geva, 2003). For example in one Canadian study, Lesaux and Siegel (2003) tracked the patterns of reading and spelling development of a large sample of EL1 and ELL children from kindergarten to grade 2. All children received phonological awareness instruction in kindergarten and phonics instruction in grade 1. Although the ELL children entered kindergarten with little or no English, by grade 2 they were able to attain a level of achievement in the areas of reading and spelling comparable to that of their EL1 peers. Wang and Geva (2003) reported similar results in their longitudinal study comparing the spelling development of Cantonese-speaking primary level ELLs with that of English controls. Specifically, although the Cantonese-speaking children had lower vocabulary scores at each testing time, their spelling development trajectory was quite similar to that of the monolingual English group. These results suggest that ELLs may be able to perform phoneme to grapheme matching in spite of their less-than-perfect oral proficiency, and that the impact of vocabulary on word-level skills may not be as strong as some would believe.

There is some evidence (e.g., Arab-Moghaddam & Sénéchal, 2001; Proctor, August, Carlo, & Snow, 2006) that vocabulary skills in English may be correlated with the spelling skills of ELLs. For example, Arab-Moghaddam and Sénéchal (2001) studied the spelling skills of grade 2 and 3 Farsi–English speakers living in Canada. They found a positive and moderate correlation between children's English vocabulary scores and English spelling. However, the correlation between spelling and phonological skills was very high, and regression analyses revealed that English vocabulary explained 17% of the variance, whereas phonological processing skills in English, entered after vocabulary, explained an additional 40% of the variance in spelling English words.

Phonological Awareness

Phonological awareness refers to the awareness of the sound structure of the language (McBride-Chang, 1995). The importance of phonological awareness in word-reading skills has been documented amply with L1 learners (e.g., Dreyer, Luke, & Melican, 1995; National Reading Panel, 2000; MacDonald & Cornwall, 1995; Siegel & Ryan 1989; Stage & Wagner, 1992; Stanovich, Cunningham, & Freeman, 1984). Phonological awareness has also been consistently linked to the development of spelling skills in EL1 populations (Bruck & Treiman, 1990; Griffith, 1991; Juel et al., 1986; Read, 1986; Stuart & Masterson, 1992; Treiman, 1993). In essence, children who are aware of the phonological structure of the spoken word use this awareness in their early spelling attempts to segment the sounds in words and try to represent these smaller units of sounds with corresponding letters. For example, a young child may segment the phonemes in *cat* as /k/, /ae/, and /t/, and represent each with the corresponding graphemes *k, a, t*. Children with weaknesses in this area are not equipped with the tools necessary for success in reading and spelling.

Phonological awareness has also been found to be related to spelling skills in ELLs (e.g., Arab-Moghaddam & Sénéchal, 2001; Stuart, 1999; Wade-Woolley & Siegel, 1997). For example, Arab-Moghaddam and Sénéchal (2001) examined the development of English spelling skills in ELL children living in Canada. Iranian Canadian ELLs whose home language was Persian were assessed on reading, spelling, and phonological processing skills, including phonological awareness. The authors found that English phonological awareness skills were highly correlated with, and uniquely predictive of, English spelling abilities. Results of a U.K.-based study by Everatt et al. (2000) are consistent with these studies. They found that children from Sylheti-speaking homes with poor spelling skills had significantly lower phonological skills (e.g., rhyme detection and nonword repetition) than children with the same L1 background matched on a nonverbal ability who did not have literacy difficulties. Moreover, there were no group differences between the ELLs and EL1s who were poor spellers on rhyme detection, nonword repetition, and a phoneme-detection task.

Naming Speed

Naming speed is another phonological processing skill shown to predict later spelling abilities in L1 children (Bear & Barone, 1991; Strattman & Hodson, 2005; Uhry, 2002). This construct is considered by some researchers to be associated with speed of lexical access (Chiappe, Stringer, Siegel, & Stanovich, 2002; Wagner, Torgesen, & Rashotte, 1994), while others believe it to include a broader construct involving speed of access to information in any form (Bowers & Wolf, 1993; Breznitz, 2006). The relationship between spelling and naming speed is hypothesized by some to result from its relationship to orthographic knowledge (Sunseth & Bowers, 2002). Specifically, the speed of activating letter names in a word is critical for the acquisition of orthographic knowledge (Bowers & Ishaik, 2003; Wolf & Bowers, 1999). Knowledge about orthography is especially important when learning to spell in a language such as English due to its allophonic variations of vowels and inconsistent word patterns. Accurate spelling cannot be derived on the sole basis of phonics and is thought to be acquired, at least in part, through exposure to print as children develop spelling-to-sound knowledge (Stanovich, 1992; Treiman & Bourassa, 2000).

For this reason, it is possible that the importance of naming speed in the development of spelling abilities increases in the later grades, when reliance on memorization of irregular letter patterns is necessary (Manis, Seidenberg, & Doi, 1999) and with increased exposure to print. One would then expect that the strength of the predictive relationship of phonological awareness on spelling would remain stable over time, while that of naming speed should increase. However, it should be noted that Juel et al. (1986) found that spelling–sound correspondences could not be acquired in a sample of young learners until a sufficient level of phonological awareness skills had been reached, and that exposure to print without this skill had little influence on subsequent development of basic word skills.

Two recent studies show that, in fact, both phonological awareness and naming speed predict spelling skills of EL1 beginning readers. Strattman and Hodson (2005) examined the decoding and spelling scores of 75 beginning readers in relation to their performance on tasks of phonological awareness, verbal memory, naming speed, multisyllable word naming, receptive vocabulary, and nonverbal intelligence. Analyses revealed that both phonological awareness and naming speed contributed significantly to the prediction of spelling abilities. In a similar vein, Uhry (2002) examined the spelling abilities of children from senior kindergarten to grade 2. She found that both early phonological awareness and naming speed made significant and unique contributions to grade 2 spelling measures, even when controlling for early word reading and vocabulary.

According to Cummins's interdependence hypothesis (1984, 1991, 2000), the development of L1 literacy skills can facilitate L2 development. Cummins maintains that L1 and L2 higher-order academic language skills are developmentally linked through common underlying proficiencies. He states that "academic proficiency transfers across languages such that students who have developed literacy in their first language will tend to make stronger progress in acquiring literacy in their second language" (1984, p. 173).

While the interdependence hypothesis framework tends to focus on higher-order academic skills that may be related cross-linguistically, the central processing framework highlights underlying cognitive processing commonalities across languages (Geva & Ryan, 1993). Cummins (1984) maintained that this process can take place provided that a certain linguistic competence in the L2 has been attained. However, evidence for positive L1–L2 relationships that can be attributed to common requirements for various cognitive resources has been demonstrated in numerous studies relating to the development of basic literacy components involving word-level skills of different L2 populations, including ELLs and learners of other L2s (e.g., Durgunoğlu, Nagy, & Hancin-Bhatt, 1993; Cisero & Royer, 1995; Comeau,

Cormier, Grandmaison, & Lacroix, 1999; Gottardo, Yan, Siegel, & Wade-Woolley, 2001). A similar argument has been made by Bialystok with regard to children who acquire literacy skills in two languages (Bialystok & Feng, Chapter 5, this volume).

Of relevance in the current context is the fact that phonological awareness and naming speed have been found to be uniquely related to EL1 and ELL spelling. This suggests that these skills might be at the core of difficulties with word-based skills regardless of language status. As such, children who are at risk for reading or spelling problems, as indicated by their difficulties on phonological processing skills, will experience difficulties developing literacy skills in their L1 as well as their L2, despite differences in their language status or typological differences in the nature of their L1 and/or L2 (Brown & Hulme, 1992; Durgunoğlu et al., 1993; Geva & Ryan 1993; Geva & Siegel, 2000; Geva & Wade-Woolley, 2004; Geva & Wang, 2001; Geva, Yaghoub-Zadeh, & Schuster, 2000; Lesaux & Siegel, 2003; Wade-Woolley & Siegel, 1997). Therefore it is likely that ELLs from different language backgrounds who are considered to be at risk, on the basis of phonological awareness and naming speed skills, would display the same developmental trends in spelling as EL1 learners with similar deficits. To illustrate, Wade-Woolley and Siegel (1997) compared the spelling abilities of 79 ELL and EL1 learners in grade 2 on the basis of their reading performance, either average or poor. Their results revealed that the processing profiles of L2 speakers and native speakers were very similar, and that ELLs and EL1s who displayed phonological deficits diverged from the common patterns. Similarly, Lipka, Siegel, and Vukovic (2005) reviewed published studies of the English literacy of ELL children in Canada and concluded that ELLs with reading disabilities experienced difficulties similar to those of EL1 students with the same profile.

L1 Influences

A handful of studies involving young L2 learners point also to the fact that children learning to read and spell in L2 process novel phonological units according to the categories of their native language until they have mastered the new language. This evidence comes from studies involving native speakers of English acquiring literacy skills in Hebrew as L2 (e.g., Geva, Wade-Woolley, & Shany, 1993; Wade-Woolley & Geva, 2000), ELLs who are native speakers of Chinese (e.g., Wang & Geva, 2003), and children whose home language is Spanish (e.g., Fashola et al., 1996). For example, in their instructional study of young Latino children, San Francisco, Mo, Carlo, August, and Snow (2006) report that children who received Spanish literacy instruction exhibited Spanish-influenced spelling in their English spelling patterns, whereas children who received literacy instruction in English did not display such L1-related spelling patterns.

In summary, vocabulary skills in English may be correlated with the spelling skills of ELLs. However, over and above the potential role of vocabulary, there is consistent evidence that phonological processing skills play a substantial role in understanding individual differences in the spelling skills of ELLs. There is also consistent research support indicating that, like their EL1 counterparts, L2 learners in general and ELLs in particular who are poor spellers have similar cognitive–linguistic and spelling profiles. This appears to hold even though the L2 and L1 learners differ in their command of the target language. The lack of consistency in research on the role of vocabulary in spelling of L2 learners may be explained to some extent in terms of restrictions in the range of young children's oral proficiency scores and "floor effects." At the same time, more basic aspects of linguistic knowledge such as phonological awareness may be less dependent on language proficiency yet sensitive enough to capture individual differences in basic processes in ELLs and EL1 alike (Geva, 2006a). A similar point is being made by Bialystok and Feng (Chapter 5, this volume). Their chapter demonstrates that bilingual children's have more limited vocabulary knowledge does not impede them on tasks that focus on basic underlying cognitive processes such as rapid naming and memory.

THE PRESENT STUDY

This chapter focuses on the development of spelling in ELLs and EL1s over time, with a particular focus on the predictors of spelling skills. The utility of these predictors in explaining EL1 and ELL spelling skills concurrently and longitudinally is examined, as well as their interrelationships from grades 1 through 3. We then turn to an examination of the profiles of good and poor spellers. On the basis of the available literature and consistent with previous research, no differences were expected between EL1 and ELL spelling, although vocabulary levels were expected to be lower for the ELL group. Phonological awareness was expected to be the strongest predictor for both language status groups, and despite lower levels of language proficiency, the cognitive profiles of ELL good and poor spellers were expected to be similar to those of EL1 good and poor spellers, respectively.

Procedure

As part of a larger longitudinal project, children from four school boards in a large, multiethnic metropolis in Canada, were recruited at various time points between grade 1 to 3 ($n = 168$). The ELL children were recruited from 12 different schools, and the EL1 children were recruited from 8 of these schools. Consent forms in English and the family's home language were distributed, and only those children with parental consent participated in the project. At the first time of testing (grade 1), children had spent .5 to 1 year in schools where English was the language of instruction (i.e., senior kindergarten). The children were administered a series of tests (in small groups or on an individual basis) by trained examiners, measuring a variety of cognitive, linguistic, and literacy skills starting in grade 1. The battery was administered yearly over a 3-year period (i.e., Time 1 of testing was in the fall term of grade 1, Time 2 of testing was in the fall of grade 2, and Time 3 testing took place in the winter of grade 3). Tests within the battery were administered according to a fixed order, and certain measures were administered at specific time points such as the Matrix Analogies Test (MAT; Naglieri, 1989),[1] a test of nonverbal intelligence. Because there were more ELL than EL1 children in the study, for the purpose of this chapter, equal samples of ELL and EL1 boys and girls were randomly selected for a total of 35 girls and 15 boys in each language status group. In addition, the cognitive and linguistic profiles of at-risk spellers irrespective of language status were explored using spelling scores in grade 1. Specifically, children at or below the 25th percentile were categorized as poor spellers, while those at or above the 50th percentile were categorized as good spellers. Those children whose scores fell between the 25th and 50th percentiles were excluded from the dataset, resulting in a total of 26 poor spellers and 50 good spellers.

Participants

Although detailed information about home literacy or patterns of language use for individual participants was not available, the children's language status was determined through multiple sources. For example, language status information from children's student records were compared with parent responses included in the consent forms. This information was subsequently validated during interviews with classroom teachers. Only children whose student records and teacher interviews indicated an ELL status were considered as such. ELL status was determined based on the criteria that children spoke a language other than English at home before learning English. Some children were born in Canada to immigrant parents, and others were born abroad, but to be included in the study, children born outside of Canada must have arrived by the age of 6 years (or younger) in addition to having been schooled in Canada as of grade 1. On the basis of this method, 50

EL1 participants were recruited and 50 ELL participants were randomly selected from the total sample of 118 for equal sample sizes. The following native language groups were represented in the ELL sample (total n = 50): Punjabi (n = 18; 36%), Portuguese (n = 11; 22%), Cantonese (n = 9; 18%), Tamil (n = 9; 18%), and Hindi (n = 3; 6%). An equal sample of EL1 participants were also included (n = 50).

In English-speaking Canada, school-age children who are recent arrivals from a non-English-speaking country typically attend school-based ESL classes for up to 2 years. In the school districts where the research was conducted, ELL instruction was provided on a withdrawal basis in daily 30- to 40-minute sessions with small groups of children. In these small groups, children typically have similar levels of English language proficiency but not necessarily the same L1. Teachers with ESL training conduct these classes, which focus on the development of spoken English and readiness for English literacy. Anecdotal reports revealed that some of the ELL children were also attending heritage language classes at the time of testing, or had attended such classes in the recent past. Otherwise, except for withdrawal for small-group ELL tutoring, the ELL children were completely integrated into the regular classroom.[2]

Missing Data

Missing values are inevitable in large longitudinal studies (especially in school settings), and incomplete datasets make the statistical analysis very difficult, as many standard statistical procedures were devised for complete datasets (Peugh & Enders, 2005). To address this problem, researchers have opted for various methods to handle missing data, including deleting cases with missing data or imputing missing values based on different mathematical algorithms (Peugh & Enders, 2005). Patterns of missing data on the different spelling measures from grades 1 to 3 were analyzed to evaluate the assumption that the values were missing completely at random using Little's Missing Completely at Random (MCAR) test from the Statistical Package of the Social Sciences (SPSS, 2004). Results suggested that spelling data for the complete sample were MCAR from grades 1 to 3 (χ^2 [7] = 13.57, p = .060). On the basis of these results, data imputations using the expectation-maximization (EM) method were generated using Missing Values Analysis in SPSS 13 (SPSS, 2004). To ensure the values generated by EM were unbiased, estimated EM means for the spelling measures of the subset were compared with means estimated by alternative methods (all available raw data for spelling from grades 1 to 3 and regression-based imputations of the subset using Missing Values Analysis in SPSS). No significant differences were found among these methods.

Measures

Nonverbal Reasoning

Children completed the MAT (Naglieri, 1989) to assess nonverbal reasoning. The test has 64 abstract designs (divided into four subtests) of the standard progressive matrix type. The child was presented with an illustration of an incomplete visual–spatial matrix and asked to complete it by locating the missing piece among five or six patterned segments. Testing within each subtest was discontinued after four consecutive errors. Results are reported in standard scores (with a mean of 100 and a standard deviation of 15).

Vocabulary

Vocabulary knowledge was estimated using the Peabody Picture Vocabulary Test—Third Edition (PPVT-III; Dunn & Dunn, 1981). The experimenter read a vocabulary word aloud and presented the child with four pictures. The child was required to identify the picture that corresponded to the target. If the child made eight errors within a set of 12 items, the administration of the test stopped. The total number of correct responses corresponded to the child's score, with a possible range of scores from 0 to 204.

Phonological Awareness

Phonological awareness was measured with a task adapted from the Auditory Analysis Task developed by Rosner and Simon (1971). Methodological considerations guided the adaptation of the task to the ELL population in order to minimize the possible confound of language proficiency. Specifically, the items on the adapted task were all high-frequency words, as were the resultant words (e.g., "Say *leg*. Now say it without the /l/"). The first four items of the task involved syllable deletion while the remainder required phoneme deletion in word initial, word final, or word medial position. Some items required the deletion of a phoneme in a consonant cluster. Four practice items preceded the administration of the test items. Administration was discontinued after five consecutive errors, and the total number of correct responses corresponds to the child's score, with a possible range of scores from 0 to 20 in grade 1 and 0 to 25 in grades 2 and 3. The total correct responses are reported. The Cronbach alpha is .92.

Naming Speed

The RAN (rapid automatized naming) task, developed by Denckla and Rudel (1974), was used to measure speed of rapid serial naming. In this continuous naming task, children were asked to name, from left to right, a series of five letters, appearing 10 times in random order.[3] All response times were recorded with a stopwatch, and the child was encouraged to name the stimuli as quickly and as carefully as possible. Reliability coefficients for the RAN were not possible to determine because of the administration and scoring methods used. However, Wagner et al. (1994) administered a similar task with digits and obtained a split-half reliability coefficient of .91 after Spearman–Brown correction. The number of items children named per second was used as the naming speed measure, with a higher score indicating faster speed of naming.

Spelling

The dependent variable was an experimental spelling task, used to assess emergent spelling in English from grades 1 to 3. This task consisted of high-frequency words that, we hypothesized, would be familiar to ELLs. We felt that such a task would be better suited to evaluate in a detailed manner the development of spelling skills of ELL children in the lower grades. This task comprised an experimental list of 16 words administered in group format by trained examiners. The list reflected simple and highly frequent words included on the basis of orthographic considerations (e.g., digraphs, as in the word *stick*) and the presence of phonological (and orthographic) patterns (e.g., the soft /th/, as in *thick* and *teeth*), and the doubling of consonants (e.g., *happy*). After hearing each word in isolation, in sentence context, and in isolation again, the child was prompted to spell the word.

SCORING

Assigning a score of 0 or 1 to the spelling of each word does not reveal much information about how close the spelling of a word is to its conventional spelling. This latter consideration is important, however, especially in the early school years, when the ability to spell is emerging (Bruck & Treiman, 1990). Indeed, this traditional method of scoring spelling provides an insensitive picture of individual and developmental differences in spelling acquisition. As such, it was necessary to develop a fine-grained analysis, given that many children were not able to correctly spell many of the words in the early grades, but were nevertheless able to represent with varying degrees of accuracy phonemes in words. To this end, a scoring procedure based on Tangel and Blachman (1992) was developed to rate the spelling of 10 dictated words. The objective was to score incorrect word spellings developmentally, capturing the phonetic and/or orthographic structure of word spelling approximations. The revision was necessary, as the original scoring offered in the Tangel and Blachman (1992) scheme was developed for specific words, and it did not give credit for lower-level responses. The scoring scheme consisted of a 9-point scale (0–8) applied to each word. It

Score	Criteria	Example
0	No response	
1	A drawing	(☺)
2	Random letter string	(fsos)
3	Related or correct letter use (initial or final position)	(cd)
4	Consonant use only (related/correct)	(cts)
5	At least 1 correct consonant and includes use of a vowel in its correct position	(can)
6	Related/correct number of phonemes and every phoneme/letter is represented	(cots)
7	Transposition error and/or additional letters in otherwise conventional spelling	(calt)
8	Conventional spelling	(cats)

FIGURE 10.1. Early spelling scoring scheme.

took into consideration the number of phonemes represented and the level of orthographic representation (use of phonetically and orthographically related or correct letter sequences). Ten words for each of the participants from grades 1 to 3 were scored according to this 9-point scale. Figure 10.1 presents an example of the scoring scheme applied to the word *cats*. The total spelling score ranged from 0 to 80 (Cronbach's alpha = .93 in grade 1, .89 in grade 2, and .90 in grade 3).

To examine interrater reliability, the percentage of agreement between the two scorers for the total responses (excluding those used to train the researchers on the scoring criteria) was calculated for each word at each time. Using this method, the percentage of agreement ranged from 81.6% to 94.2% in grade 1 (overall agreement: 89.7%); 83.4% to 99.3% in grade 2 (overall agreement: 94.2%); and 98.8% to 100% in grade 3 (overall agreement: 99.5%). In instances of disagreement, differences centered around unclear letter formation produced by the children and the improper use of the scoring criteria as developed. Thus it was determined that the scale developed for scoring the experimental spelling task was highly reliable.

Results

Language Status

DESCRIPTIVE ANALYSES

The means and standard deviations for the various measures are presented in Table 10.1 for both EL1 and ELL children. A multivariate analysis of

TABLE 10.1. Descriptive Statistics for EL1 and ELL Children

Variables	Status	Grade 1 mean (SD)	F(Sig.)	Grade 2 mean (SD)	F(Sig.)	Grade 3 mean (SD)	F(Sig.)
Spelling	EL1	54.09 (14.00)	0.10 (.78)	69.40 (5.89)	2.02 (0.16)	77.77 (2.49)	0.10 (0.32)
	ELL	53.28 (11.97)		71.16 (6.48)		77.04 (4.48)	
Nonverbal reasoning	EL1	101.50 (9.16)	0.61 (.435)	100.21 (10.85)	1.72 (.193)	101.87 (10.19)	0.00 (.988)
	ELL	99.87 (11.52)		97.28 (11.47)		101.84 (7.88)	
Vocabulary	EL1	66.79 (17.73)	32.12 (.000)	80.39 (14.19)	25.07 (.000)	94.16 (13.61)	23.04 (.000)
	ELL	48.24 (14.88)		65.53 (15.45)		81.15 (13.49)	
Phonological awareness	EL1	7.76 (3.33)	0.09 (.761)	10.71 (4.97)	1.70 (.195)	17.84 (5.84)	1.30 (.267)
	ELL	7.97 (3.60)		12.26 (5.73)		19.18 (5.91)	
Naming speed	EL1	1.20 (0.40)	0.98 (.325)	1.52 (0.42)	2.93 (.09)	1.93 (0.42)	1.96 (.165)
(items per second)	ELL	1.28 (0.37)		1.65 (0.37)		2.05 (0.43)	

Note. n = 50 for EL1; *n* = 50 for ELL.

258

variance revealed significant group differences favoring the EL1 group on English vocabulary at each grade level: grade 1—$F(1,98) = 32.12, p < .001$; grade 2—$F(1,98) = 25.07, p < .001$; grade 3—$F(1,98) = 23.04, p < .001$. Consistent with our predictions, no significant group differences were found for the remaining variables, indicating that, overall, EL1 and ELL children are performing at the same level on nonverbal ability, phonological awareness, naming speed and spelling measures from grades 1 to 3, despite clear differences in their levels of English vocabulary.[4]

CORRELATIONAL ANALYSES

Correlational analyses were conducted to determine the degrees of association among the variables for both the EL1 and ELL groups (Table 10.2). ELL correlations are reported above the diagonal, while EL1 correlations are below the diagonal. For both language status groups, significant correlations were found between the phonological awareness measure assessed in each grade, and spelling in grades 1 to 3. This pattern of relationships was also evident among the naming speed measures and spelling over time, although it was more consistent for the ELL group than for the EL1 group. Vocabulary and spelling were correlated positively and significantly concurrently and across times for the ELL group; however, this was not consistently true for the EL1 group, whose spelling scores correlated with vocabulary only in grade 1. Intercorrelations among the spelling scores across time for each of the language status groups were also positive and significant, ranging from high to moderate associations.

REGRESSION ANALYSES

Three sets of separate regression analyses examined the longitudinal relationships between predictors in grade 1, grade 2, and grade 3, and spelling in grade 3 for both EL1 and ELL groups. In other words, parallel analyses for both ELL and EL1 groups were conducted by entering in separate multiple regression analyses scores on nonverbal reasoning, vocabulary, phonological awareness, and naming speed for each grade separately. In each of these analyses grade 3 spelling was the dependent variable.

Within each of the language status groups, the first regression model included nonverbal reasoning; the second model included nonverbal reasoning as Step 1 followed by vocabulary; the third model included nonverbal reasoning as Step 1, vocabulary as Step 2, and phonological awareness as Step 3; the fourth and final model included nonverbal reasoning as Step 1, vocabulary as Step 2, phonological awareness as Step 3, and naming speed as Step 4. This order was chosen to determine whether phonological awareness and naming speed would be significant predictors of spelling in grade 3,

TABLE 10.2. Bivariate Correlations among the Variables of Interest by Language Status

EL1 versus ELL	1	2	3	4	5	6	7	8	9	10	11	12	13	14	15
1. Spelling grade 1		.73	.62	.27	.36	.22	.40	.48	.60	.49	.51	.55	.59	.42	.34
2. Spelling grade 2	.65		.71	.27	.29	.07	.31	.41	.49	.47	.59	.62	.57	.51	.52
3. Spelling grade 3	.35	.41		.13	.27	.09	.31	.33	.45	.51	.57	.62	.48	.41	.51
4. Nonverbal Reasoning grade 1	.04	.03	.08		.66	.40	.31	.21	.38	.10	.07	.13	.25	.21	.14
5. Nonverbal Reasoning grade 2	.28	.12	.17	.60		.56	.24	.23	.39	.41	.34	.24	.30	.24	.17
6. Nonverbal Reasoning grade 3	.37	.42	.26	.54	.58		.07	-.00	.25	.31	.12	.42	.12	.07	-.01
7. Vocabulary grade 1	.26	.13	-.04	.15	.35	.29		.82	.69	.42	.34	.31	.42	.20	.33
8. Vocabulary grade 2	.29	.07	-.01	.22	.39	.32	.81		.65	.34	.29	.28	.32	.15	.21
9. Vocabulary grade 3	.31	.22	.17	.19	.38	.42	.66	.73		.49	.40	.55	.50	.32	.38
10. Phonological Awareness grade 1	.45	.56	.30	.05	.17	.45	.17	.20	.31		.69	.63	.42	.18	.30
11. Phonological Awareness grade 2	.49	.60	.27	.31	.36	.47	.26	.32	.48	.57		.63	.38	.20	.41
12. Phonological Awareness grade 3	.47	.60	.32	.01	.15	.31	.30	.24	.28	.54	.57		.39	.28	.36
13. Naming Speed grade 1	.60	.65	.36	-.17	-.08	.09	.01	.05	.12	.46	.38	.50		.81	.77
14. Naming Speed grade 2	.37	.67	.35	-.07	-.07	.19	-.06	-.10	-.00	.47	.39	.53	.80		.81
15. Naming Speed grade 3	.22	.54	.27	-.21	-.20	-.02	-.05	-.07	.05	.46	.31	.43	.70	.79	

Note. Correlations greater than .29 correspond to *p* values at the .05 level, and correlations greater than .35 correspond to a *p* value at the .01 level.

260

after the potential contribution of nonverbal ability and vocabulary knowledge was taken into account.

RELATIONSHIPS BETWEEN GRADE 1 PREDICTORS AND SPELLING IN GRADE 3

Results of multiple regression analyses pertaining to the relationship between grade 1 predictors and grade 3 spelling are presented in Table 10.3. The results of the third model for the EL1 group revealed that spelling performance in Grade 3 was related to phonological awareness in grade 1, explaining 10% of the variance, beta = .32, t (49) = 2.26, p = .03. However, once naming speed was added to the model, phonological awareness lost its significance, and naming speed was the sole significant Grade 1 predictor, beta = .31, t (49) = 1.99, p = .05, of grade 3 spelling. The final model accounted for 18% of the variance in grade 3 spelling, with grade 1 naming speed accounting for 7% of the variance. Neither nonverbal ability nor vocabulary was significantly related to grade 3 spelling for the EL1 group at any stage.

For the ELL group, the results of the final model indicated that spelling performance in grade 3 was related to grade 1 phonological awareness, beta = .37, t (49) = 2.63, p = .01, and naming speed, beta = .31, t (49) = 2.21, p = .03 . This model accounted for 34% of the variance in grade 3 spelling, with grade 1 phonological awareness and naming speed accounting for more than half of the variance explained (25%). Although vocabulary was

TABLE 10.3. R^2, R^2 Change, and Beta Weights for Longitudinal Regression Models Predicting Grade 3 Spelling Performance with Grade 1 Variables by Language Status Groups

Model	Total R^2	R^2 change	Nonverbal reasoning (beta)	Vocabulary (beta)	Phonological awareness (beta)	Naming speed (beta)
EL1						
1	.00	.00	.08			
2	.01	.00	.08	−.06		
3	.11	.10*	.08	−.11	.32*	
4	.18	.07	.13	−.10	.17	.31*
ELL						
1	.02	.02	.13			
2	.10	.08*	.04	.30*		
3	.27	.18**	.05	.09	.46**	
4	.34	.07*	.01	.02	.37**	.31*

Note. ** < .01; * < .05.

a significant predictor for the ELL group when entered in the second model following nonverbal reasoning, beta = .30, t (49) = 2.02, p = .05 (explaining 8% of the variance), it was no longer significant once the phonological awareness variable was entered. Nonverbal reasoning was not related to ELL grade 3 spelling at any step.

RELATIONSHIPS BETWEEN GRADE 2 PREDICTORS AND SPELLING IN GRADE 3

The second set of multiple regression analyses determined whether the predictors in grade 2 were statistically predictive of spelling performance in grade 3 (Table 10.4). The results for the EL1 group showed that spelling performance in grade 3 was marginally related to grade 2 naming speed only, beta = .30, t (49) = 1.92, p = .06. The final model accounted for 16% of the variance in grade 3 spelling, with grade 2 naming speed accounting for 7% of the total variance explained. Neither nonverbal ability nor vocabulary was significantly related to later spelling for the EL1 group at any stage in this analysis.

For the ELL group, the results of the regression analyses indicated that spelling performance in grade 3 was related to grade 2 phonological awareness, beta = .47, t (49) = 3.78, p < .001, and naming speed, beta = .29, t (49) = 2.48, p = .02. The final model accounted for 44% of the variance in grade 3 spelling, with grade 2 phonological awareness and naming speed accounting for more than half of the variance explained (29%). Similar to the grade

TABLE 10.4. R^2, R^2 **Change, and Beta Weights for Longitudinal Regression Models Predicting Grade 3 Spelling Performance with Grade 2 Variables by Language Status Groups**

Model	Total R^2	R^2 change	Nonverbal reasoning (beta)	Vocabulary (beta)	Phonological awareness (beta)	Naming speed (beta)
EL1						
1	.03	.03	.16			
2	.03	.01	.19	−.08		
3	.08	.05	.13	−.14	.25	
4	.16	.07	.20	−.09	.10	.30
ELL						
1	.07	.07⁺	.27⁺			
2	.15	.08*	.20	.29*		
3	.36	.21**	.05	.18	.50**	
4	.44	.08*	.00	.15	.47**	.29*

Note. ** <.01; * <.05; ⁺ < .06.

1 results, when entered prior to phonological awareness and naming speed, vocabulary was significantly related to grade 3 spelling for the ELL group, beta = .29, t (49) = 2.07, p = .04 (explaining 8% of the variance). However, vocabulary was not significant once phonological awareness and naming speed were included in the equation. Again, nonverbal ability was not a significant predictor at any stage.

RELATIONSHIPS BETWEEN GRADE 3 PREDICTORS AND SPELLING IN GRADE 3

Table 10.5 presents the third and final set of multiple regression analyses examining which of the variables in grade 3 were related to spelling performance in the same year. For the EL1 sample, the results showed that the strongest beta weight for the final model was for naming speed, although it did not reach significance. The final model accounted for 16% of the variance in grade 3 spelling, with grade 3 naming speed accounting for 3% of the total variance explained. For the ELL group, the results of the regression analyses indicated that grade 3 vocabulary was a significant predictor of grade 3 spelling skills in the second model, beta = .45, t (49) = 3.34, p < .01 (explaining 19% of the variance), but once the phonological awareness variable was entered in Step 3, it was no longer related to grade 3 spelling. Instead, the final model revealed that spelling performance in grade 3 was related to grade 3 phonological awareness, beta = .53, t (49) = 3.84, p < .001, and naming speed, beta = .29, t (49) = 2.42, p = .02 in grade 3. The

TABLE 10.5. R^2, R^2 Change, and Beta Weights for Concurrent Regression Models Predicting Grade 3 Spelling Performance with Grade 3 Variables by Language Status Groups

Model	Total R^2	R^2 change	Nonverbal reasoning (beta)	Vocabulary (beta)	Phonological awareness (beta)	Naming speed (beta)
EL1						
1	.07	.07[+]	.26[+]			
2	.07	.00	.23	.07		
3	.13	.06	.17	.03	.26	
4	.16	.03	.21	.03	.16	.20
ELL						
1	.01	.01	.09			
2	.20	.19**	−.02	.45**		
3	.43	.24**	−.21	.16	.62**	
4	.50	.07*	−.15	.08	.53**	.29*

Note. ** < .01; * < .05; + < .06.

final model accounted for 50% of the variance in grade 3 spelling, with grade 3 phonological awareness and naming speed accounting for more than half of the variance explained (31%). Nonverbal ability was not a significant predictor at any stage.

SUMMARY OF LANGUAGE STATUS GROUP RESULTS

In summary, it is clear that there are both similarities and differences in terms of the predictors of spelling ability between language groups. In both groups, nonverbal ability is not related to spelling skills. In addition, vocabulary is not a good predictor of spelling for the EL1 group. In fact, only naming speed assessed in grade 1 predicted grade 3 spelling. In the case of ELLs, when entered after nonverbal reasoning, vocabulary in grades 1 to 3 was related to spelling in grade 3. However, its influence was surpassed by that of phonological awareness and naming speed, which significantly predicted grade 3 spelling both longitudinally and concurrently. As such, the results of these analyses provide only partial support for the hypothesis that both phonological awareness and naming speed would be strong predictors of spelling dictation for both ELL and EL1 groups.

Good and Poor EL1 and ELL Spellers

To further explore the development of spelling, cognitive and linguistic abilities of ELL and EL1 learners of different levels of spelling ability, children at or below the 25th percentile on the spelling task in grade 1 were categorized as poor spellers, while those at or above the 50th percentile were categorized as good spellers. Those children whose scores fell between the 25th and 50th percentiles were excluded from the dataset, resulting in a total of 26 poor spellers and 50 good spellers. This systematic method of classification was carried out irrespective of language status and yielded similar numbers of good and poor spellers in each of the ELL and EL1 group (25 good spellers and 14 poor spellers, and 25 good spellers and 12 poor spellers, respectively). A chi-square test yielded nonsignificant results, indicating that the percentage of participants classified as good and poor spellers did not differ by language status, $\chi^2(1) = 0.10$, $p = .75$.

ANALYSES

A series of four separate repeated measures analyses of variance were conducted to compare the development of spelling, vocabulary, phonological awareness, and naming speed according to language status (ELL and EL1) and spelling ability (good and poor) from grades 1 to 3. Specifically, the first repeated measures multivariate analysis of variance was conducted with

TABLE 10.6. Descriptive Statistics for Good and Poor Spellers

Variables	ELL/EL1	Good spellers			Poor spellers		
		Grade 1 mean (SD)	Grade 2 mean (SD)	Grade 3 mean (SD)	Grade 1 mean (SD)	Grade 2 mean (SD)	Grade 3 mean (SD)
Spelling	EL1	64.74 (5.39)	72.96 (4.62)	78.44 (2.18)	35.60 (11.45)	64.75 (4.39)	77.17 (2.66)
	ELL	62.90 (5.44)	75.17 (3.66)	79.30 (1.36)	37.75 (6.30)	64.54 (6.47)	72.89 (6.29)
Nonverbal reasoning	EL1	102.17 (9.92)	101.72 (13.06)	104.60 (10.03)	101.42 (9.24)	98.92 (8.50)	98.00 (7.75)
	ELL	103.72 (9.81)	101.74 (9.70)	102.62 (7.40)	98.55 (11.58)	95.46 (11.14)	100.48 (9.53)
Vocabulary	EL1	71.08 (13.11)	83.56 (12.39)	96.68 (11.27)	64.24 (16.32)	75.83 (13.84)	93.17 (15.53)
	ELL	53.50 (16.46)	71.74 (16.55)	87.54 (9.81)	41.51 (12.22)	58.30 (14.66)	70.94 (15.03)
Phonological awareness	EL1	9.07 (3.39)	13.08 (5.64)	20.64 (4.79)	6.07 (2.56)	8.50 (2.65)	15.08 (5.85)
	ELL	9.53 (3.53)	15.04 (5.11)	20.94 (4.42)	5.78 (3.22)	8.20 (4.47)	14.26 (7.09)
Naming speed (items per second)	EL1	1.42 (0.41)	1.66 (0.49)	2.04 (0.50)	0.91 (0.24)	1.32 (0.29)	1.83 (0.32)
	ELL	1.46 (0.33)	1.76 (0.38)	2.19 (0.38)	0.99 (0.33)	1.47 (0.33)	1.81 (0.43)

grade (grades 1 to 3), language status (EL1/ELL), and spelling level (good/poor), with spelling as the dependent variable in order to compare the spelling growth of ELLs and EL1s according to their spelling ability (good and poor) from grades 1 to 3. The subsequent analyses examined the growth trajectories of both good and poor ELL and EL1 spellers on measures of vocabulary, phonological awareness, and naming speed. Table 10.6 presents the means and standard deviations for all measures according to language status (ELL and EL1) for both good and poor spellers.

SPELLING DEVELOPMENT BY LANGUAGE STATUS AND SPELLING ABILITY

In terms of spelling ability, results revealed a significant within-subjects main effect for grade, indicating that, overall, spelling scores improved over time, $F(2,144) = 660.72$, $p < .001$. Within-subjects contrasts revealed that this growth was significant from both grades 1 to 2, $F(1, 72) = 482.30$, $p < .001$, and from grades 2 to 3, $F(1, 72) = 482.30$, $p < .001$). A significant two-way interaction between grade and spelling ability was also noted, $F(2,144) = 129.17$, $p < .001$, suggesting that poor spellers experienced steeper growth than the good spellers. Within-subjects contrasts indicated that, again, this growth was significantly steeper from both grades 1 to 3, $F(1, 72) = 103.68$, $p < .001$, and from grades 2 to 3, $F(1, 72) = 26.04$, $p < .001$.[5] A significant three-way interaction was also noted for grade, language status, and spelling ability, $F(2,144) = 4.80$, $p = .01$, suggesting that this steeper pattern of growth for the poor spellers was more marked for the EL1 group, but within-subjects contrast revealed a marginal effect from grades 1 and 2 $F(2,144) = 3.41$, $p = .07$, only. No significant interactions were noted for grade and language status, $F(2,144) = 1.68$, $p = .19$; however, within-subjects contrasts revealed a significant difference in growth from grades 2 to 3, favoring the EL1 group, $F(2,144) = 6.14$, $p = .02$. The results are presented in Figure 10.2.

A significant between-subjects main effect was noted for spelling ability, $F(1, 72) = 230.33$, $p < .001$, suggesting that good spellers outperformed poor spellers. This result is not surprising, given the classification method used to form the groups. The between-subjects main effect for language status and the interaction between language status and spelling ability did not reach significance, $F(1, 72) = 0.04$, $p = .84$, and $F(1, 72) = 0.45$, $p = .51$, respectively.

VOCABULARY DEVELOPMENT BY LANGUAGE STATUS AND SPELLING ABILITY

A second repeated measures multivariate analysis of variance was conducted with grade (grades 1 to 3), language status (EL1/ELL), and spelling level (good/poor), with vocabulary as the dependent variable. Results revealed a significant within-subjects main effect for grade, indicating that, overall,

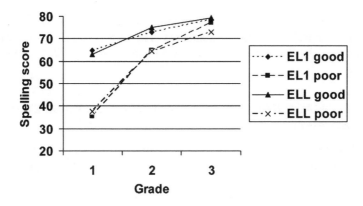

FIGURE 10.2. Spelling scores by language status and spelling ability.

vocabulary scores improved over time, $F(2,144) = 247.29$, $p < .001$. Within-subjects contrasts revealed that this growth was significant from both grades 1 to 2, $F(1, 72) = 162.23$, $p < .001$, and from grades 2 to 3, $F(1, 72) = 118.10$, $p < .001$. Interactions for grade and language status, grade and spelling ability, and grade, language status, and spelling ability did not reach significance, $F(2,144) = 2.41$, $p = .09$; $F(2,144) = 0.10$, $p = .91$; $F(2,144) = 1.40$, $p = .25$, respectively. However, within-subjects contrasts revealed steeper growth for the ELL group from grades 1 to 2 compared to their EL1 counterparts, $F(1,72) = 5.57$, $p = .02$. These results are presented in Figure 10.3.

Significant between-subjects main effects were noted for language status, $F(1, 72) = 31.66$, $p < .001$, favoring the EL1 group, and spelling ability,

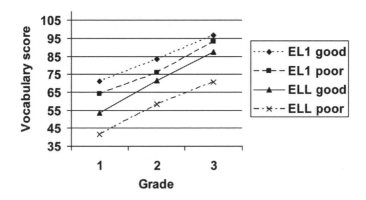

FIGURE 10.3. Vocabulary scores by language status and spelling ability.

$F(1, 72) = 11.21$, $p = .001$, suggesting that, overall, poor spellers had lower vocabulary scores than did good spellers. The between-subjects interaction between grade and spelling ability did not reach significance $F(1, 72) = 1.78$, $p = .19$.

PHONOLOGICAL AWARENESS DEVELOPMENT BY LANGUAGE STATUS AND SPELLING ABILITY

A third repeated measures multivariate analysis of variance was conducted with grade (grades 1 to 3), language status (EL1/ELL) and spelling level (good/poor), with phonological awareness as the dependent variable. Results revealed a significant within-subjects main effect for grade, indicating that overall, phonological awareness scores improved over time, $F(2,144) = 169.71$, $p < .001$. Within-subjects contrasts revealed that this growth was significant from both grades 1 to 2, $F(1, 72) = 51.44$, $p < .001$, and from grades 2 to 3, $F(1, 72) = 114.70$, $p < .001$. A significant within-subjects interaction between grade and spelling ability was also noted, $F(2,144) = 3.53$, $p = .03$. Within-subjects contrasts revealed that good spellers experienced steeper growth from grades 1 to 2 on the phonological awareness measure than did poor spellers, $F(2,144) = 5.41$, $p = .02$. Interactions between grade and language status, and grade, language status, and spelling ability did not reach significance, $F(2,144) = 0.51$, $p = .60$, and $F(2,144) = 0.25$, $p = .78$, respectively. The results are presented in Figure 10.4.

A significant between-subjects main effect was noted for spelling ability, $F(1, 72) = 31.10$, $p < .001$, favoring the good spellers. The between-subjects main effect for language status, and the interaction between grade and spelling ability did not reach significance, $F(1, 72) = 0.06$, $p = .81$, and $F(1, 72) = 0.57$, $p = .45$, respectively.

NAMING SPEED DEVELOPMENT BY LANGUAGE STATUS AND SPELLING ABILITY

A fourth and final repeated measures multivariate analysis of variance was conducted with grade (grades 1 to 3), language status (EL1/ELL) and spelling level (good/poor), with naming speed as the dependent variable. Results revealed a significant within-subjects main effect for grade, indicating that overall, naming speed improved over time, $F(2,144) = 280.50$, $p < .001$. Within-subjects contrasts revealed that this growth was significant from both grades 1 to 2, $F(1, 72) = 151.29$, $p < .001$, and from grades 2 to 3, $F(1, 72) = 164.44$, $p < .001$. A significant within-subjects interaction between grade and spelling ability was also noted, $F(2,144) = 5.25$, $p = .03$. Within-subjects contrasts revealed that poor spellers experienced steeper growth on the naming speed measure from grades 1 to 2 only $F(2,144) = 8.82$, $p <$

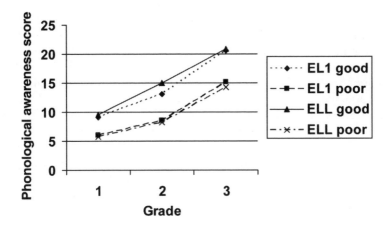

FIGURE 10.4. Phonological awareness scores by language status and spelling ability.

.01. Interactions for grade and language status, and grade, language status, and spelling ability did not reach significance, $F(2,144) = 0.67$, $p = .50$, and $F(2,144) = 1.64$, $p = .20$, respectively. These results are presented in Figure 10.5.

Between-subjects main effects were noted for spelling ability, $F(1, 72) = 17.76$, $p < .001$, favoring the good spellers. The between-subjects main effect for language status, and the interaction between grade and spelling ability did not reach significance, $F(1, 72) = 0.98$, $p = .33$, and $F(1, 72) = 0.03$, $p = .88$, respectively.

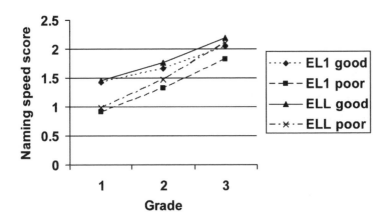

FIGURE 10.5. Naming speed scores by language status and spelling ability.

In summary, both similarities and differences are evident when comparing the development of spelling, cognitive, and linguistic skills of good and poor ELL and EL1 learners. Significant growth over time was noted for all measures, regardless of language status or spelling ability. However, poor spellers from either language status group were distinguished from good spellers on the basis of weaknesses in vocabulary, phonological awareness, and naming speed. In fact, despite steeper growth rates for the poor spellers in regards to spelling ability and naming speed, the gap between the two groups remained significant over time. Similarly, and consistent with previous analyses, the vocabulary scores of the EL1 group were consistently higher than those of the ELL group despite the fact that the ELLs experienced steeper growth on this measure from grades 1 to 2. Taken together, these results suggest that the poor spellers who are also ELLs are at the greatest disadvantage with respect to vocabulary development.

Discussion

Despite consistent differences on oral language abilities between ELL and EL1 children across time, the results reported in this chapter reiterate the fact that language status alone is not a satisfactory mechanism for understanding spelling development of EL1 and ELLs in the first three years of elementary school. Moreover, no differences were found between ELL and EL1 groups on any of the cognitive measures. This means that ELLs are able to perform phoneme to grapheme matching of high-frequency words, even when their oral proficiency is still emerging. This result echoes the results reported by Bialystok and Feng (Chapter 5, this volume) with regard to bilingual children. The current results also replicate those reported by Wang and Geva (2003), who found that the spelling trajectory of a group of ELLs with Chinese as the L1 was similar to that of the monolingual English as L1 group. The findings extend these conclusions to a more diverse group of L2 learners over a longer period of time, and suggest that the impact of schooling and the quality of instruction on the acquisition of basic spelling skills may help those from linguistically diverse backgrounds to catch up to (or surpass) their monolingual English peers on word-level skills as early as grade 1.

Vocabulary knowledge was a significant, albeit weak, predictor of spelling skills, and in the presence of phonemic awareness and rapid naming measures it lost its significance. These phonological processing measures were significant predictors of spelling development over time, providing evidence in support of the central processing hypothesis, which suggests that children who are poor spellers are likely to be at risk due to phonological processing skills deficits, regardless of their home language (Brown & Hulme 1992; Durgunoğlu et al. 1993; Everatt et al., 2000; Geva & Siegel, 2000; Geva et al., 2000; Wade-Woolley & Siegel, 1997). This result echoes the results of Wade-Woolley and Siegel (1997), who found that the profiles of EL1 and ELL children in grade 2 were similar for spelling real words, with only those displaying deficits in phonological processing diverging from the pattern. The results reported here indicate that ELL children lag behind their EL1 counterparts on vocabulary knowledge of the societal and school language. Yet despite poorer command of English vocabulary, the spelling skills of ELL and EL1 groups are highly similar. In both groups there is improvement over time, and the ELLs do not lag behind EL1 in their ability to spell high-frequency words. In addition, in contrast to the cross-sectional study of Wade-Woolley and Siegel's (1997) findings, it appears that ELL children were not disadvantaged on phonological awareness skills. At the same time, deficits on naming speed and phonological awareness were related to poor spelling in both language groups, although this result was more consistent in the ELL group.

Indeed, differences were noted in terms of the predictors for both language status groups. Phonological awareness and naming speed measured in grade 1 contributed unique variance to the prediction of later spelling in the ELL group. In contrast, EL1 spelling was only predicted by naming speed, and the influence of naming speed decreased steadily over time. This result can be explained on the basis of different processes occurring in the development of spelling for the EL1 and ELL groups. ELL children must draw upon all of their cognitive and linguistic resources when spelling in a language with which they are less familiar. Perhaps L2 learners whose familiarity with the structure of words and their meaning is less automatized seem to be faced with a more demanding cognitive task. Both phonological awareness and naming speed are correlated with spelling in both EL1 and ELL groups. Compared with vocabulary skills, individual differences in cognitive processes involving phonological awareness and naming speed abilities are better aligned with individual differences in spelling in the case of L2 learners, because they are less susceptible to language proficiency. Stated differently, in the case of young ELLs, phonological awareness and rapid naming are more reliable and valid measures of individual differences in processes that underlie spelling skills. The possibility that the scenario may be different for ELLs with higher levels of proficiency in the L2 needs to be examined in future studies.

When the profiles of good and poor spellers were compared across the three grade levels it became evident that, regardless of EL1–ELL status, the cognitive and linguistic profiles of poor spellers are highly similar, as are the profiles of good spellers. However, one important difference was noted for the ELL poor spellers. Whereas all poor spellers, irrespective of language status, differed from good spellers on the measures of phonological awareness and naming speed, ELL poor spellers were the worst off in terms of their vocabulary skills.

Taken together, these results underscore the fact that ELL children are able to spell highly frequent words as successfully as their monolingual peers. However, monolingual and ELL learners appear to rely on somewhat different sets of skills to achieve the same outcome.

Despite these differences, the profiles of good and poor spellers on cognitive and phonological processing measures are quite similar. EL1 and ELL poor spellers alike experience weaknesses on phonological awareness and naming speed measures. However, in addition to these weaknesses, the risk profile of ELL children who have difficulty spelling also includes more serious difficulties in developing receptive vocabulary than their EL1 and ELL peers who are good spellers. Moreover, an examination of the profiles of the different groups suggest that even though spelling skills of EL1 poor spellers are similar to the spelling skills of ELL children who are poor spellers at the onset, EL1 poor spellers eventually are able to spell high-frequency words with similar accuracy to that noted for the EL1 children who are good spellers. Indeed, an examination of the profiles suggests that, by grade 3, the EL1 poor spellers reach the level of spelling accuracy noted a year earlier in the case of the EL1 good spellers. However, even in grade 3 the ELL poor spellers continue to be challenged by the spelling of high-frequency words and have not reached yet the level of their counterparts. In summary, the profile of the ELL poor spellers is characterized by slower rate of acquisition of vocabulary as well as lower phonological processing skills. The profile of the EL1 spellers does not display the same pattern with regard to vocabulary skills, although their phonological processing skills are similar to those of their ELL counterparts who are poor spellers.

Earlier it was suggested that individual differences in phonological awareness and naming speed abilities are better aligned with individual differences in spelling in the case of L2 learners because they are less susceptible to differences in language proficiency. The literature on the cognitive underpinnings of vocabulary development suggests that individual differences in phonological processing skills may drive vocabulary development in EL1 and ELLs (Dickinson, McCabe, Anastasopoulos, Peisner-Feinberg, & Poe, 2003; Farnia & Geva, 2010; Muter, Hulme, Snowling, & Stevenson, 2004). Thus it may not be surprising that ELLs who have poor phonological processing skills suffer from a "triple whammy": they are ELLs, their vocabulary develops more slowly, and they take longer to develop literacy skills.

Educational and Clinical Implications

The results of this longitudinal study are relevant for professionals who are concerned with the education of second language learners in the schools. For example, despite some variability across EL1–ELL language status groups, the importance of phonological awareness and naming speed surpasses the influence that nonverbal reasoning and English vocabulary may exert on the normal development of spelling skills in school-age children. Consequently, the same instructional methods can be used to teach children from different language backgrounds. By identifying how individual differences in underlying cognitive processes distinguish successful and delayed ELL spellers, educators should also be better equipped to identify accurately and intervene in a timely manner when ELLs experience spelling difficulties in the primary grades. The results of this research can also inform clinicians assessing ELL children with respect to signs indicating an underlying learning difficulty by providing empirical support needed for the development of spelling assessment measures for at-risk ELLs whose L2 proficiency is still developing. This is essential given the recent trend toward withholding resource help from children learning English as a second language (Bruck, 1985; Geva, 2000; Limbos & Geva, 2001). In addition, these results have important policy implications by helping to inform the provision of appropriate services for ELL and EL1 children who do have learning disabilities that affect their spelling abilities.

CONCLUSION

The findings reported in this chapter support a framework that conceptualizes spelling skills in EL1 and ELLs as involving the ability to segment words into units and retrieve specific letter patterns from memory, and, therefore, both phonological awareness and naming speed are important to assess in order to understand a child's spelling ability, particularly for children whose home language is not English. Early identification and appropriate interventions are essential because "language and literacy are the foundation of social, academic, and occupational success. Canadian adults with low literacy skills cannot share in that lifetime of success and in most cases, these difficulties can be traced back to early childhood" (Canadian Language and Literacy Research Network, 2001).

ACKNOWLEDGMENTS

The research reported on in this chapter was partially funded by the Social Sciences and Humanities Research Council of Canada, The Ontario Ministry of Education, and the University of Toronto (OISE).

NOTES

1. The Matrix Analogies Test (MAT) was administered in the spring of grade 1 and 2 as well as in the fall of grade 3.
2. In addition, children who had not lived in an English-speaking country for at least 4 months at the onset of grade 1 were not included in the study to ensure some exposure to language instruction.
3. Prior to administering the RAN task, the child was asked to name each of the five letters in order to ascertain familiarity with the letters. The RAN measure was not administered to those children who could not correctly name all five letters.
4. It is worth noting that similar analyses were conducted comparing the different language groups with their monolingual peers within a larger sample. The analyses revealed that although the Punjabi and Portuguese children had significantly lower scores than the EL1 group in grades 1 and 2, these differences were no longer discernible in grade 3 and beyond.
5. This result is very likely the result of a ceiling effect on this measure.

REFERENCES

Arab-Moghaddam, N., & Sénéchal, M. (2001). Orthographic and phonological processing skills in reading and spelling in Persian/English bilinguals. *International Journal of Behavioral Development, 25*, 140–147.

Bear, D. R., & Barone, D. (1991). The relationship between rapid automatized naming and orthographic knowledge. *National Reading Conference Yearbook, 40*, 179–184.

Bowers, P. G., & Ishaik, G. (2003). RAN's contribution to understanding reading disabilities. In H. L. Swanson, K. R. Harris, & S. Graham (Eds.), *Handbook of learning disabilities* (pp. 140–157). New York: Guilford Press.

Bowers, P. B., & Wolf, M. (1993). Theoretical links among naming speed, precise timing mechanisms and orthographic skill in dyslexia. *Reading and Writing, 5*, 69–85.

Breznitz, Z. (2006). *Fluency in reading: Synchronization of processes*. Mahwah, NJ: Erlbaum.

Brown, G. D. A., & Hulme, C. (1992). Cognitive psychology and second-language processing: The role of short-term memory. In R. J. Harris (Ed.), *Cognitive processing in bilinguals* (pp. 105–121). Oxford, UK: North-Holland.

Bruck, M. (1985).Consequences of transfer out of early French immersion programs. *Applied Psycholinguistics, 6,* 101–119.

Bruck, M., & Treiman, R. (1990). Phonological awareness and spelling in normal children and dyslexics: The case of initial consonant clusters. *Journal of Experimental Child Psychology, 50,* 156–178.

Canadian Language and Literacy Research Network. (2001). Retrieved August 8, 2001, from *www.cllrnet.ca.*

Chiappe, P., & Siegel, L. S. (1999). Phonological awareness and reading acquisition in English- and Punjabi-speaking Canadian children. *Journal of Educational Psychology, 9,* 20–28.

Chiappe, P., Siegel, L. S., & Wade-Woolley, L. (2002). Linguistic diversity and the development of reading skills: A longitudinal study. *Scientific Studies of Reading, 6,* 369–400.

Chiappe, P., Stringer, R., Siegel, L. S., & Stanovich, K. E. (2002). Why the timing deficit hypothesis does not explain reading disability in adults. *Reading and Writing, 15,* 73–107.

Comeau, L., Cormier, P., Grandmaison, É., & Lacroix, D. (1999). A longitudinal study of phonological processing skills in children learning to read in a second language. *Journal of Educational Psychology, 91,* 29–43.

Cummins, J. (1984). *Bilingualism and special education: Issues in assessment and pedagogy.* Clevedon, UK: Multilingual Matters.

Cummins, J. (1991). Interdependence of first- and second-language proficiency in bilingual children. In E. Bialystok (Ed.), *Language processing in bilingual children* (pp. 70–89). New York: Cambridge University Press.

Cummins, J. (2000). *Language, power, and pedagogy: Bilingual children in the crossfire.* Clevedon, UK: Multilingual Matters.

DaFontoura, H. A., & Siegel, L. S. (1995). Reading, syntactic and working memory skills of bilingual Portuguese–English bilingual children. *Reading and Writing, 7,* 139–153.

Denckla, M. B., & Rudel, R. G. (1974). Rapid automatic naming of pictured objects, colors, letters and numbers by normal children. *Cortex, 1,* 186–202.

Dickinson, D., McCabe, A., Anastasopoulos, L., Peisner-Feinberg, E. & Poe, M. P. (2003). The comprehensive language approach to early literacy: The interrelationships among vocabulary, phonological sensitivity, and print knowledge among preschool-age children. *Journal of Educational Psychology, 95*(3), 465–481.

Dreyer, L. G., Luke, S. D., & Melican, E. (1995). Children's acquisition and retention of word spellings. In V. W. Berninger (Ed.), *The varieties of orthographic knowledge: II. Relationships to phonology, reading, and writing* (pp. 291–320). Dordrecht, The Netherlands: Kluwer.

Dunn, L. M., & Dunn, L. M. (1981). *Peabody Picture Vocabulary Test—Revised.* Circle Pines, MN: American Guidance Service.

Durgunoğlu, A. Y., Nagy, W. E., & Hancin-Bhatt, B. J. (1993). Cross-language transfer of phonological awareness. *Journal of Educational Psychology, 85,* 453–465.

Ehri, L. (1997). Learning to read and learning to spell are one and the same, almost. In C. A. Perfetti, L. Rieben, & M. Fayol (Eds.), *Learning to spell: Research, theory, and practice across languages* (pp. 237–270). Mahwah, NJ: Erlbaum.

Everatt J., Smythe, I., Adams, E., & Ocampo, D. (2000). Dyslexia screening measures and bilingualism. *Dyslexia, 6,* 42–56.

Farnia, F., & Geva, E. (2010). Cognitive correlates of vocabulary growth in English language learners. *Applied Psycholinguistics.*

Fashola, O. S., Drum, P. A., Mayer, R. E., & Kang, S. J. (1996). A cognitive theory of orthographic transitioning: Predictable errors in how Spanish-speaking children spell English words. *American Educational Research Journal, 33,* 825–843.

Figueredo, L., & Varnhagen, C. K. (2006, July). *Effects of spelling errors on readers' judgments about job applicants.* Paper presented at the meeting of the Society for Scientific Studies of Reading, Vancouver.

Geva, E. (2000). Issues in the assessment of reading disabilities in L2 children: Beliefs and research evidence. *Dyslexia, 6,* 13–28.

Geva, E. (2006a). Second-language oral proficiency and second-language literacy. In D. August & T. Shanahan (Eds.), *Developing literacy in second-language learners: A report of the National Literacy Panel on language-minority children and youth* (pp. 153–174). Mahwah, NJ: Erlbaum.

Geva, E. (2006b). Learning to read in a second language: Research implications, and recommendations for services. In R. E. Tremblay, R. G. Barr, & R. Peters (Eds.), *Encyclopedia on early childhood development.* Montreal: Centre of Excellence for Early Childhood Development.

Geva, E., & Siegel, L. (2000). Orthographic and cognitive factors in the concurrent development of basic reading skills in two languages. *Reading and Writing: An Interdisciplinary Journal, 12,* 1–30.

Geva, E., & Ryan, E. B. (1993). Linguistic and memory correlates of academic skills in first and second languages. *Language Learning, 43,* 5–42.

Geva, E., & Wade-Woolley, L. (2004). Issues in the assessment of reading disability in second language children. In I. Smythe, J. Everatt, & R. Salter (Eds.), *The international book of dyslexia* (pp. 195–206). Chichester, UK: Wiley.

Geva, E., Wade-Woolley, L., & Shany, M. (1993). The concurrent development of spelling and decoding in two different orthographies. *Journal of Reading Behavior, 25,* 383–406.

Geva, E., & Wang, M. (2001). The role of orthography in the literacy acquisition of young L2 learners. *Annual Review of Applied Linguistics, 21,* 182–204.

Geva, E., Yaghoub-Zadeh, Z., & Schuster, B. V. (2000). Understanding individual differences in word recognition skills of ESL children. *Annals of Dyslexia, 50,* 123–154.

Gottardo A., Yan, B., Siegel, L. S., & Wade-Woolley, L. (2001). Factors related to English reading performance in children with Chinese as a first language: More evidence of cross-language transfer of phonological processing. *Journal of Educational Psychology, 93,* 530–542.

Griffith, P. L. (1991). Phonemic awareness helps first graders invent spellings and third graders remember correct spellings. *Journal of Reading Behavior, 23,* 215–233.

Holmes, V. M.., & Castles, A. (2001). Unexpectedly poor spelling in university students. *Scientific Studies in Reading, 5*, 319–350.

Juel, C., Griffith, P. L., & Gough, P. B. (1986). Acquisition of literacy: A longitudinal study of children in first and second grade. *Journal of Educational Psychology, 78*, 243–255.

Kreiner, D. S., Schnakenberg, S. D., Green, A. G., Costello, M. J., & McClin, A. F. (2002). Effects of spelling errors on the perception of writers. *Journal of General Psychology, 129*, 5–17.

Lesaux, N. K., & Siegel, L. S. (2003). The development of reading in children who speak English as a second language. *Developmental Psychology, 39*, 1005–1019.

Limbos, M., & Geva, E. (2001). Accuracy of teacher assessments of second-language students at risk for reading disability. *Journal of Learning Disabilities, 34*, 136–151.

Lipka, O., Siegel, L. S., & Vukovic, R. (2005). The literacy skills of English language learners in Canada. *Learning Disabilities Research and Practice, 20*, 39–49.

MacDonald, G. W., & Cornwall, A. (1995). The relationship between phonological awareness and reading and spelling achievement eleven years later. *Journal of Learning Disabilities, 28*, 523–527.

Manis, F. R., Seidenberg, M. S., & Doi, L. M. (1999). See Dick RAN: Rapid naming and the longitudinal prediction of reading subskills in first and second graders. *Scientific Studies of Reading, 3*, 129–157.

McBride-Chang, C. (1995). What is phonological awareness? *Journal of Educational Psychology, 87*, 179–192.

Muter, V., Hulme, C. Snowling, M., & Stevenson, J. (2004). Phonemes, rimes, vocabulary, and grammatical skills as foundations of early reading development: Evidence from a longitudinal study. *Developmental Psychology, 40*, 665–681.

Naglieri, J. (1989). *Matrix Analogies Test.* New York: Psychological Corporation.

National Reading Panel. (2000). Report of the National Reading Panel. *Teaching children to read: An evidence-based assessment of the scientific research literature on reading and its implications for reading instruction.* Washington, DC: National Institutes of Child Health and Human Development.

Peugh, J. L., & Enders, C. K. (2005). Missing data in educational research: A review of reporting practices and suggestions for improvement. *Review of Educational Research, 74*, 525–556.

Proctor, C. P., August, D., Carlo, M. S., & Snow, C. (2006). The intriguing role of Spanish language vocabulary knowledge in predicting English reading comprehension. *Journal of Educational Psychology, 98*, 159–169

Read, C. (1986). *Children's creative spelling.* Boston and London: Routledge/Kegan Paul.

Roberts, T., & Neal, H. (2004). Relationships among preschool English language learner's oral proficiency in English, instructional experience and literacy development. *Contemporary Educational Psychology, 29*, 283–311.

Rosner, J., & Simon, D. P. (1971). The Auditory Analysis Test: An initial report. *Journal of Learning Disabilities, 4*, 40–48.

San Francisco, A. R., Mo, E., Carlo, M., August, D., & Snow, C. (2006). The influences of language of literacy instruction and vocabulary on the spelling of Spanish–English bilinguals. *Reading and Writing 19*(6), 627–642.

Siegel, L. S., & Ryan, E. G. (1989). The development of working memory in normally achieving and subtypes of learning disabled children. *Child Development, 60*, 973–980.

SPSS for Windows, rel. 13.0. (2004). Chicago: Author.

Stage, S. A., & Wagner, R. K. (1992). Development of young children's phonological and orthographic knowledge as revealed by their spelling. *Developmental Psychology 28*, 287–296.

Stanovich, K. E. (1992). Speculations on the causes and consequences of individual differences in early reading acquisition. In P. B. Gough, L. C. Ehri, & R. Treiman (Eds.), *Reading acquisition* (pp. 307–342). Hillsdale, NJ: Erlbaum.

Stanovich, K. E., Cunningham, A. E., & Freeman, D. J. (1984). Intelligence, cognitive skills and early reading progress. *Reading Research Quarterly, 19*, 278–303.

Strattman, K., & Hodson, B. W. (2005). Variables that influence decoding and spelling in beginning readers. *Child Language Teaching and Therapy, 21*, 165–190.

Stuart, M. (1999). Getting ready for reading: Early phoneme awareness and phonics teaching improves reading and spelling in inner-city second language learners. *British Journal of Educational Psychology, 69*, 587–605.

Stuart, M., & Masterson, J. (1992). Patterns of reading and spelling in 10-year-old children related to prereading phonological abilities. *Journal of Experimental Child Psychology, 54*, 168–187.

Sunseth, K., & Bowers, P. G. (2002). Rapid naming and phonemic awareness: Contributions to reading, spelling, and orthographic knowledge. *Scientific Studies of Reading, 6*, 401–429.

Tangel, D. M., & Blachman, B. A. (1992). Effect of phoneme awareness instruction on kindergarten children's invented spelling. *Journal of Reading Behavior, 24*, 233–261.

Treiman, R. (1993). *Beginning to spell: A study of first-grade children.* New York: Oxford University Press.

Treiman, R., & Bourassa, D. C. (2000). The development of spelling skill. *Topics in Language Disorders, 20*, 1–18.

Uhry, J. K. (2002). Kindergarten phonological awareness and rapid serial naming as predictors of grade 2 reading and spelling. In E. Witruk, A. D. Friederici & T. Lachmann (Eds.), *Basic mechanisms of language and language disorders* (pp. 315–328). Dordrecht, The Netherlands: Kluwer Academic.

Wade-Woolley, L., & Geva, E. (2000). Processing novel phonemic contrasts in the acquisition of L2 word reading. *Scientific Studies of Reading, 4*, 295–311.

Wade-Woolley, L., & Siegel, L. S. (1997). The spelling performance of ESL and native speakers of English as a function of reading skills. *Reading and Writing: An Interdisciplinary Journal, 9*, 387–406.

Wagner, R. K., Francis, D. J., & Morris, R. D. (2005). Identifying English language learners with learning disabilities: Key challenges and possible approaches. *Learning Disabilities Research and Practice, 20,* 6–15.

Wagner, R. K., Torgesen, J. K., & Rashotte, C. A. (1994). Development of reading-related phonological processing abilities: New evidence of bidirectional causality from a latent variable longitudinal study. *Developmental Psychology, 30,* 73–87.

Wang, M., & Geva, E. (2003). Spelling performance of Chinese children using English as a second language: Lexical and visual–orthographic processes. *Applied Psycholinguistics, 24,* 1–25.

Wolf. M., & Bowers, P. G. (1999). The double-deficit hypothesis for the developmental dyslexias. *Journal of Educational Psychology, 91,* 415–438.

CHAPTER 11

■　■　■

Cognitive and Oral Language Contributors to Reading Disabilities in Spanish–English Bilinguals

FRANKLIN R. MANIS
KIM A. LINDSEY

There is now considerable evidence that basic literacy skills develop in a similar manner for monolinguals and children learning to read in a second language, including word identification and phonological processing (August, Calderon, & Carlo, 2000; Chiappe, Siegel, & Wade-Wooley, 2002; Comeau, Cormier, Grandmaison, & Lacroix, 1999; Durgonoglu, Nagy, & Hancin-Bhatt, 1993; Gottardo, 2002; Leafstedt & Gerber, 2005; Lesaux & Siegel, 2003; Lindsey, Manis, & Bailey, 2003; Manis, Lindsey, & Bailey, 2004; Swanson, Saéz, Gerber, & Leafstedt, 2004). This suggests that reading difficulties in monolinguals and second-language learners may have a similar basis. Given the preponderance of evidence indicating a phonological basis for reading difficulties in children across languages (Ziegler & Goswami, 2005), it is reasonable to propose that children at risk for reading difficulties will tend to have phonological processing problems in both languages. Wagner and Torgesen (1987) identified three aspects of phonological processing that seem to be related to early reading development: phonological awareness, phonological processing in working memory, and phonological access in lexical memory. However, there have been few direct investigations of reading disabilities in second-language learners. The purpose of the present study was to explore the developmental course and predictors of reading disabilities in Spanish-speaking children learning to read in English.

Prior studies have found that bilingual children struggling with reading in one language tend to have reading problems in the other language. This is a logical inference from theories of language interdependence (e.g., Cummins, 1979; Durgunoğlu, 2002), which propose a common core of skills across languages, such that progress in one language can lead to advances in the other. For example, DaFontoura and Siegel (1995) found a similar profile of word identification, syntactic awareness, and phonological working memory difficulties in both languages for poor readers in a Portuguese–English bilingual sample in Canada. Additional evidence was provided by a comprehensive investigation of bilingual children in Miami (cf. Oller & Eilers, 2002). Cobo-Lewis, Eilers, Pearson, and Umbrel (2002) factor analyzed a parallel set of standardized tasks in Spanish and English in a large cross-sectional sample (second and fifth grades). Controlling for socioeconomic status (SES), language exposure in the home, and instructional program, they found a language-general factor that accounted for the majority of the variability in language and literacy skills, and had relatively equal loadings of English and Spanish reading, spelling, and writing tasks. Additional variability was accounted for by oral language comprehension and vocabulary, but measures of oral language loaded on two distinct factors, one English and the other Spanish. They proposed a variation on the interdependence hypothesis of Cummins (1979), that is, that individual differences in reading and writing skills are highly related for English and Spanish, but differences in oral language skills are not. Whether English and Spanish oral language skills are related may depend on the measures. For instance, in a large cross-sectional study in grades K–3, Miller et al. (2006) reported that English measures of narrative production accounted for substantial variance in English reading comprehension, controlling for grade level, and identical Spanish measures accounted for 2% of additional variance.

It is important to investigate predictors of reading difficulties longitudinally in an ELL sample. Lindsey et al. (2003) classified the Spanish-speaking English language learners in the present longitudinal sample as good and poor readers in first grade using word-level and comprehension tasks in English and Spanish as outcome measures. Discriminant analyses revealed that letter knowledge and rapid automatic naming of objects (RAN-Objects) in Spanish at kindergarten were the two strongest predictors of reading group classification across all tasks for both languages, but that measures of phonological awareness and expressive vocabulary contributed to word-level and comprehension outcomes, respectively. Following the sample into the second grade, Manis et al. (2004) found a moderate correlation of Spanish print awareness, phonological awareness, and rapid automatic naming with parallel measures in English. However, we found that first-grade English performance on these tasks mediated the contribution of Spanish variables to later reading in English. In addition, stronger within- than cross-language associations were found for the relationship of expressive language to later reading. Manis et al. (2004) suggested that some components of developing reading skill in second-language learners of English are held in common across the two languages (i.e., word reading and phonological processing), and some may be more language-specific (vocabulary and language comprehension) (although see Miller et al., 2006).

The hypothesis that aspects of phonological processing skill may be one important source of the interdependence among reading and writing measures across languages was further explored by Swanson and colleagues. Swanson et al. (2004) classified Spanish speakers learning to read in English as at risk for reading disabilities in first grade based on low word identification or pseudoword reading and normal-range nonverbal IQ. A group of low-risk readers was also studied. They found that the groups differed in Spanish short-term memory and also to some extent in working memory measures across Spanish and English. A follow-up study by Swanson, Saéz, and Gerber (2006) reported that growth in English reading skills was predicted by growth in Spanish working memory, but not English working memory. The finding of a contribution of working memory is unique to this study and might implicate either phonological processes (e.g., the phonological loop of working memory) or executive processes (e.g., planning, inhibition, and monitoring) as contributing factors to reading difficulties in second-language learners.

In the present study, we analyzed data from an 8-year longitudinal study. The general goal of the analyses was to identify important cognitive and oral language correlates and precursors of reading difficulties in English. We had four specific questions: First, is it possible to identify children with reading disabilities in a sample of generally low-achieving English language learners? We hypothesized that these children would show phonological processing problems in both Spanish and English. Second, how stable is the reading disabled/nonreading disabled profile over time (i.e., from fifth grade to seventh grade)? Based on monolingual data on reading disabilities, a moderate degree of stability might be expected at this age (Shaywitz, Escobar, Shaywitz, Fletcher, & Makuch, 1992). Third, would we replicate Cobo-Lewis et al.'s (2002) finding of greater interdependence among reading than among oral language measures? We predicted that phonological tasks from both languages would load on the hypothesized cross-language reading factor, but that oral language measures would load on separate factors for each language. Fourth, what variables in kindergarten and first grade predict RD status in fifth grade? Our hypothesis, based on our prior work with this sample (Lindsey et al., 2003; Manis et al., 2004) was that letter knowledge, phonological awareness, and rapid automatic naming would all be important predictors, but that English measures obtained at first grade would be more important than Spanish measures obtained at kindergarten.

METHOD

Participants

The sample of children came from a population of low-income, Latino, limited English-speaking families residing in a Texas border town. All of the children participated in an early-exit bilingual literacy education program called Esperanza (Hagan, 1997) that provided extra instruction first in Spanish and then in English phonological awareness and decoding, using parallel multisensory teaching methods in both languages. They were transitioned to an English curriculum called Language Enrichment One (Neuhaus Education Center, 1997) (with supplemental Spanish instruction as needed) beginning in the latter part of first grade and continuing into the second and third grades, if necessary. See Manis et al. (2004) for further details on the characteristics of the population and the school program.

The goals of the study required us to define a reading disabled (RD) and non-RD group who were equivalent in nonverbal ability and oral language comprehension in English, but who differed in word decoding ability. We began with the full sample of children who had complete test scores in grades K, 1 and 5 (n = 243, from an original sample of 303 children in kindergarten). We screened out 28 cases that had low nonverbal ability based on scores below the 25th percentile (standard score of 90) on fifth-grade scores on the Spatial Relations subtest of the Woodcock–Johnson III (WJ-III) Tests of Achievement, leaving 215 children. Children who had fifth-grade composite scores on the Letter–Word Identification and Word Attack subtests of the WJ-III Tests of Achievement at or below the 25th percentile for the decoding composite were assigned to the group with RD (n = 45). The letter–word identification test mostly measures word reading past the kindergarten level, and the Word Attack test requires children to give reasonable pronunciations of pseudowords (such as *bim* and *narp*). All children who scored above the 25th percentile on the decoding composite were assigned to the non-RD group (n = 169). Next, we chose two cases from the non-RD group to match each case with RD on gender, age (plus or minus 6 months), and on Spatial Relations and Understanding Directions percentiles (plus or minus 10 percentile points) (n = 90).

Tasks

Most of the tests used were from standardized test batteries and are only briefly described here.

1. *Spatial Relations*. Participants view a series of increasingly complex two-dimensional shapes and have to decide which of four rotated versions matches the original. English: Woodcock–Johnson Tests of Cognitive Abilities III (WJ-III; Woodcock, McGrew, & Mather, 2001).

2. *Picture Vocabulary*. Participants view a pictured object or action and have to supply a word to go with it. English: Woodcock–Johnson Revised Tests of Cognitive Ability (WJ-R; Woodcock & Johnson, 1989—grades 1–3) and Woodcock–Johnson III Tests of Achievement (Woodcock et al., 2001—grades 5–7); Spanish: Woodcock–Muñoz Language Proficiency Battery (Woodcock & Muñoz-Sandoval, 1995).

3. *Memory for Sentences*. Participants listen to a series of words, phrases and sentences and repeat them back verbatim. English: WJ-R (Woodcock & Johnson, 1989—grade 1); Spanish: Woodcock–Muñoz Language Proficiency Battery (Woodcock & Muñoz-Sandoval, 1995).

4. *Understanding Directions*. Participants view a pictured scene (e.g., a park) and follow directions by pointing to various objects in the picture. English: Woodcock–Johnson Tests of Achievement (Woodcock et al., 2001—grades 5–7).

5. *Listening Comprehension*. Participants listen to a phrase or sentence and fill in a missing word, usually near the end of the sentence. English: WJ-III (Woodcock et al., 2001—grades 5–7); Spanish: Woodcock–Muñoz Language Proficiency Battery (Woodcock & Muñoz-Sandoval, 1995).

6. *Letter–Word Identification*. Participants name a letter or read a word out loud. English: Woodcock–Johnson Psychoeducational Battery—Revised (Woodcock & Johnson, 1989—grades 1–3; Woodcock et al., 2001—grades 5–7); Spanish: Woodcock–Muñoz Language Proficiency Battery (Woodcock & Muñoz-Sandoval, 1995).

7. *Word Attack*. Participants pronounce a nonsense word out loud. English: WJ-R (Woodcock & Johnson, 1989—grades 1–3 and 5); WJ-III (Woodcock et al., 2001—grades 6–7); Spanish: Woodcock–Muñoz Language Proficiency Battery (Woodcock & Muñoz-Sandoval, 1995).

8. *Passage Comprehension*. Participants read a phrase or passage up to two sentences in length and fill in a missing word near the end of the final sentence. English: WJ-R (Woodcock & Johnson, 1989—grades 1–3; Woodcock et al., 2001—grades 5–7; Spanish: Woodcock–Muñoz Language Proficiency Battery (Woodcock & Muñoz-Sandoval, 1995).

9. *Reading Fluency*. Participants read a series of short, simple sentences and circle whether the sentence is true or false. They complete as many as they can in 3 minutes. English: WJ-III (Woodcock et al., 2001—grades 6–7). A Spanish version was developed for the longitudinal study by the second

author, who is a native Spanish speaker, with the aid of a professional Spanish interpreter. Sentences were modeled after the English sentences on the Woodcock in terms of word frequency, sentence length, and grammatical complexity.

10. *Elision.* Participants listen to a word, followed by a single phoneme, and repeat the word with the phoneme deleted. The first three items involve syllable deletion and the remaining items single-phoneme deletion. Five of the 17 phonemic items were bisyllabic. English: Comprehensive Test of Phonological Processing (CTOPP; Wagner, Torgesen, & Rashotte, 1998). A Spanish version was developed with the same number of deletions from the beginning, middle and end of the word as the CTOPP English items. Sixteen of the 17 single-phoneme deletion items were bisyllabic (e.g., *trio*: delete /r/ to yield *tio*). All correct deletions resulted in a real word in both English and Spanish.

11. *Rapid Automatic Naming (RAN)—Digits.* Participants view a sheet with rows of printed digits and name the digits in order as fast as they can. English: CTOPP (Wagner et al., 1998).

12. *Sound Matching.* Participants view a picture and the examiner pronounces the name. They are asked to pick which of three additional named pictures has the same beginning sound (Part 1) or the same ending sound (Part 2). English: CTOPP (Wagner et al., 1998).

13. *Sound Categorization.* Participants view three pictures and are asked which three pictures rhymed. Adapted from a preliminary version of the CTOPP.

14. *Letter Knowledge and Letter Sounds.* Participants were shown all lowercase and uppercase letters used in the appropriate language and had to name the letter and provide a sound (phoneme) to with each letter in Spanish (kindergarten) and in English (first grade).

We created several Spanish-language tasks for the kindergarten test sessions to provide parallel measures to those used in English in first grade, including Sound Matching, Sound Categorization, and RAN-Objects, based on preliminary CTOPP versions of these tasks. More complete descriptions of the kindergarten and first-grade tests are provided by Lindsey et al. (2003).

Data Collection Procedures

Data used in the present analyses were collected during May of the kindergarten, first-, second-, and third-grade years (1999–2002). No data were collected in fourth grade, and testing resumed during a 2-week period in January of the fifth-, sixth-, and seventh-grade years (2004–2006).

RESULTS AND DISCUSSION

Defining RD and Non-RD groups in English (Fifth Grade)

The first issue was whether we could identify RD and non-RD groups resembling groups studied in the monolingual literature. Table 11.1 reveals that the groups were closely matched in age. Significant differences were obtained for the English measures of Letter–Word Identification, Word Attack, and Passage Comprehension, but not for Spatial Relations and Understanding Directions, the expected outcome based on the matching procedure. The RD group had slightly but significantly lower scores on English Listening Comprehension and Picture Vocabulary. Spatial Relations scores for both groups were close to the norm group mean (standard score of 100), but all language scores and the Passage Comprehension score were below average. The pattern of scores in English indicates that the RD and non-RD groups were comparable to groups studied in the monolingual literature, at least as

TABLE 11.1. Means, Standard Deviations (in Parentheses), and Group Comparisons (*t*-Test) for the Fifth-Grade English and Spanish Standardized Tasks (Standard Scores)

Variable	RD group	Non-RD group	Comparison	Partial eta^2
Age (in months)	130.2 (4.4)	129.5 (4.2)	ns	< .01
English Tasks				
Spatial Relations	99.0 (11.3)	99.9 (7.0)	ns	< .01
Letter–Word Ident.	79.1 (7.9)	101.8 (11.2)	$F(133) = 148.9^{**}$	.53
Word Attack	81.1 (11.2)	111.9 (16.6)	$F(133) = 132.9^{**}$	.52
Passage Comp.	74.2 (9.3)	85.9 (6.7)	$F(132) = 69.5^{**}$	.34
Understanding Dir.	85.3 (8.2)	87.3 (6.7)	ns	.02
Listening Comp.	73.2 (14.5)	80.5 (12.0)	$F(133) = 9.72^{*}$	.07
Picture Vocabulary	69.8 (9.6)	80.3 (9.2)	$F(133) = 37.5^{**}$	.22
Spanish tasks				
Letter–Word Ident.	89.5 (21.0)	114.5 (21.1)	$F(133) = 42.1^{**}$	.24
Word Attack	84.5 (14.0)	103.7 (16.2)	$F(133) = 61.6^{**}$	.32
Passage Comp.	77.3 (12.1)	86.2 (10.5)	$F(131) = 18.9^{**}$	.13
Memory for Sent.	76.7 (12.6)	78.7 (15.0)	ns	< .01
Listening Comp.	84.6 (13.4)	85.9 (14.5)	ns	< .01
Picture Vocabulary	84.2 (20.3)	85.1 (24.0)	ns	< .01

$^{*}p < .01; ^{**}p < .001.$

far as nonverbal ability and word-level reading skills. However, it is obvious that both groups were still struggling to master English oral language skills and reading comprehension.

It is of interest whether the general profile of performance in English would be replicated for Spanish. The groups did not differ on any of the Spanish oral language tasks (Listening Comprehension, Picture Vocabulary, and Memory for Sentences), but the RD group was significantly lower on the Letter–Word Identification, Word Attack, and Passage Comprehension tests in Spanish. The results indicate the group profiles in Spanish were similar to the profiles in English. Spanish standard scores in Table 11.1 were based on monolingual Spanish speakers predominantly from Mexico, the United States, and Puerto Rico. According to the test manual for the Woodcock–Muñoz Battery, Spanish tests were equated in difficulty to the corresponding tasks in English on the WJ-R. Hence, it is appropriate to compare the standard scores between English and Spanish. Both groups generally performed better in Spanish than in English on comparable tasks. Some of this may be due to regression to the mean (e.g., in the case of the defining variables). However, some part of the difference may be the greater ease of phonological decoding in Spanish (due to greater regularity of spelling–sound correspondences) or the fact that children were initially taught to read in Spanish and may have had more practice at this task. Higher language scores in Spanish indicate that the majority of the children were still somewhat Spanish-dominant.

The validity of the RD/non-RD group classification depends on whether predicted patterns of performance would be obtained on theoretically important tasks. The most salient differences in the monolingual literature are various aspects of phonological processing (Stanovich & Siegel, 1994; Wagner & Torgesen, 1987). Raw scores on measures of phonological awareness and lexical retrieval speed are reported in Table 11.2. It is apparent from the F-tests and effect sizes in Table 11.2 that the groups differed to a considerable extent in number correct on CTOPP Elision (a measure of phonological awareness in which a spoken word must be re-pronounced after deleting a specified sound from the beginning, middle, or end of the word). The non-RD group was also faster at naming digits (CTOPP RAN-Digits time, a measure of lexical retrieval speed). The number of errors on RAN-Digits did not differ between groups. We created a Spanish version of the elision test utilizing primarily bisyllabic Spanish words. The groups differed significantly on this task as well. Mean scores were very similar across the English and Spanish versions of the task. The standard score was available only for CTOPP Elision, and it reveals that the children in the RD group scored below average, whereas the non-RD group was close to the norm group mean (scaled score of 103.5).

TABLE 11.2. Means, Standard Deviations (in Parentheses), and Group Comparisons (t-Test) for the Fifth-Grade English and Spanish Standardized Tasks (Raw or Standard Scores)

Variable	RD group	Non-RD group	Comparison	Partial eta^2
English tasks				
CTOPP Elision (std.)	84.9 (11.6)	103.5 (11.0)	$F(133) = 79.2^{***}$	.381
CTOPP Elision (raw)	10.6 (5.1)	16.6 (3.2)	$F(133) = 68.7^{***}$	.341
RAN-Digits time (sec)	20.8 (6.4)	16.6 (3.9)	$F(133) = 22.2^{***}$	.143
RAN-Digits errors	0.2 (.2)	0.4 (2.6)	ns	< .01
Spanish task				
Elision raw score	10.4 (5.9)	15.8 (4.6)	$F(133) = 32.2^{***}$	.21

$^{***}p < .001$.

To summarize and evaluate the results thus far, the data are consistent with the picture of children with reading disability obtained from the monolingual literature. The RD–non-RD group differences seen at the fifth-grade time point replicated the major patterns seen in the monolingual literature, except, of course, that English oral language comprehension (and, as it turns out, Spanish oral language comprehension as well) were below average both for children classified here as RD and children classified as non-RD. The generally low English oral language performance was expected, given the language and SES background of the children and informal reports by teachers in this school district that the children spoke mostly Spanish with their families, and a mixture of Spanish and English with their peers. Although reading disabilities are traditionally defined in terms of relatively adequate verbal ability, we argue that the RD group in the present study can be considered reading disabled, because the non-RD group was similar in mastering English and Spanish oral language, yet was superior on tests of word reading, phonological decoding, phonological awareness, and rapid naming.

The poor performance of the RD group on Passage Comprehension (mean percentile = 7.0) would also be expected, given their difficulties in both word reading and oral language comprehension. The fact that the non-RD group was also below average on Passage Comprehension (mean percentile = 19.5) is also readily explained by their low overall command of English oral language. Oral language is thought to play a stronger role in reading comprehension as children move from early to late elementary school (e.g., Carlisle, Beeman, Davis, & Spharim, 1999; Hoover & Gough, 1990; Proctor, Carlo, August, & Snow, 2005). Our results differed somewhat from the findings of Swanson et al. (2006), who did not obtain a difference in reading comprehension between groups of RD and non-RD children defined on the basis of word and pseudoword reading. One difference between the two samples is that our sample was lower in SES and overall oral language comprehension. It makes sense that the reading comprehension of children who are still struggling to master basic English vocabulary and sentence comprehension in fifth grade and who have fewer educational opportunities in their home environment would suffer.

Subgroups of Reading Difficulty in the Two Languages

Three possible profiles of reading difficulties are likely in a bilingual context. We identified 25 cases (out of 45) that met the criteria for the RD group in both English and Spanish (composite Letter–Word Identification and Word Attack scores lower than the 25th percentile for both English and Spanish), 20 cases that met it only for English, and nine that met it only for Spanish (i.e., they were in the non-RD group based on the original definition of the group using English). The remaining 81 children were non-RD for both English and Spanish.

Standard scores and raw scores where applicable are shown for these groups in Table 11.3 for ease of comparison. Because of the large discrepancies in sample size across the four subgroups, we did not conduct statistical comparisons, so all conclusions must be tentative. However, we would like to make three general observations. First, of the three reading difficulty subgroups, the double-reading difficulty (English and Spanish) subgroup appeared to be the most impaired on both English and Spanish phonological awareness and decoding, suggesting that this group was the best match to the notion of a phonological deficit in reading disability. Second, language and nonverbal ability were comparable in the double-reading difficulty and English-only reading difficulty subgroups, suggesting that the double-reading difficulty group was not simply a generally language-delayed group (based on the limited oral language measures in this study), but also had difficulties in phonological processing and decoding. Third, the Spanish-only subgroup appeared to have weaker Spanish than English oral language comprehension and literacy. This subgroup had the numerically weakest Spanish oral language comprehension scores (average of 2nd percentile on listening comprehension and picture vocabulary) and the numerically strongest English oral language comprehension scores (average of 25th percentile on listening comprehension and picture vocabulary) of the four subgroups. Because we lacked data on children's home language and literacy experiences and detailed data on classroom experiences, we must be cautious about interpreting this pattern. Children with difficulties in only one language might

TABLE 11.3. Mean Standard Scores and Standard Deviations (in Parenthesis) for Subgroups with English and/or Spanish Reading Difficulty in Fifth Grade

Variable	Double RD (*n* = 25)	English-only (*n* = 20)	Spanish-only (*n* = 9)	Non-RD (*n* = 81)
English tasks				
Spatial Relations	98.4 (13.8)	99.8 (7.3)	98.4 (4.9)	100.0 (7.2)
Letter–Word Identification	77.6 (7.8)	81.0 (7.6)	98.8 (10.0)	102.2 (11.3)
Word Attack	77.0 (10.9)	85.6 (7.5)	103.7 (12.9)	113.2 (16.1)
Passage Comprehension	75.1 (10.1)	73.0 (8.4)	89.6 (5.0)	85.5 (6.8)
Understanding Directions	86.8 (8.2)	83.6 (8.1)	86.4 (6.7)	87.4 (6.7)
Listening Comprehension	76.4 (14.7)	69.1 (13.5)	83.4 (9.3)	80.2 (12.3)
Picture Vocabulary	72.6 (10.2)	66.4 (7.7)	91.7 (11.9)	79.0 (8.0)
Elision	81.2 (8.9)	88.9 (13.0)	101.1 (6.5)	103.8 (11.3)
Elision (raw)	8.0 (5.0)	12.9 (4.3)	16.8 (1.2)	14.6 (4.9)
Spanish tasks				
Letter–Word Identification	75.1 (13.2)	107.4 (13.5)	78.7 (10.0)	118.4 (18.1)
Word Attack	71.7 (10.4)	93.6 (6.1)	82.4 (7.3)	106.1 (15.2)
Passage Comprehension	70.6 (11.7)	85.0 (6.9)	67.8 (18.1)	88.3 (7.0)
Memory for Sentences	71.9 (10.6)	82.7 (12.5)	51.8 (15.6)	81.7 (11.7)
Listening Comprehension	81.8 (13.5)	88.1 (12.6)	60.6 (14.8)	88.7 (11.4)
Picture Vocabulary	79.9 (23.2)	89.5 (14.7)	40.6 (25.7)	90.0 (18.0)
Elision (raw)	7.0 (4.6)	14.6 (4.4)	12.4 (5.9)	16.1 (4.3)

either have a mild phonological delay or lack of sufficient exposure and/or instruction in that language.

The data indicate a moderate degree of stability in reading problems across the two languages. Based on the limited set of measures we utilized, reading difficulties primarily manifested as difficulties in phonological processing in both languages. However, differences in oral language competence also appear to be an important factor (e.g., as in the Spanish-only reading difficulty subgroup) and seemed somewhat specific to Spanish or English. This indicates that screening for reading problems in ELL children suspected of having reading disability or a delay in reading should include parallel measures of phonological decoding and oral language comprehension in both L1 and L2. It is possible that in older children (e.g., Proctor, August, Carlo, & Snow, 2006) or with different language measures, such as the storytelling production measures used by Miller et al. (2006), that oral language competence in both Spanish and English may be important to reading comprehension.

Factor Analyses of the English and Spanish Language Batteries

The validity of the reading ability groups (based on the original classification as RD/non-RD that we began with) was pursued further with factor analyses of the data. If there is a continuum of phonological processing ability that underlies reading difficulties in both languages, a factor analysis should reveal that most or all reading and phonological tasks across both languages cluster on a common factor. However, measures of oral language comprehension may be distinct in the two languages, which might result in specific factors for each language. This combination of three factors (a general reading factor for Spanish and English and separate English and Spanish oral language factors) was precisely what was found by Cobo-Lewis et al. (2002) for a generally higher SES and more English-exposed sample of children in Miami. We applied their analytic techniques to the present sample.

As a further test of the hypothesized set of relationships between variables, we included measures of phonological awareness and RAN in our factor analysis. We subjected all of the fifth-grade Spanish and English oral language comprehension, reading, and phonological processing measures (raw scores) to a principal components factor analysis with Varimax rotation. The resulting factor matrix is shown in Table 11.4. We identified three factors. Factor 1 (word decoding and phonological processing skill) accounted for 37.8% of the variance and had moderate to high loadings for all Spanish and English word and nonsense word reading and phonological awareness tasks, as well as English RAN-Digits. Factor 2 (Spanish oral language and reading comprehension) accounted for 19.9% of the variance, and Factor 3 (English oral language and reading comprehension) accounted for 12.3% of the variance, for a total of 70.1% of the variance. Memory for Sentences (given only in Spanish) requires children to repeat longer and longer sentences verbatim, which might make it appear to be at least in part a measure of phonological short-term memory. However, both in our factor analysis and in factor analyses conducted by Woodcock and colleagues (Woodcock & Johnson, 1989) it loaded more highly on an oral language, rather than a memory or phonological processing factor. The overall results of our factor analysis closely paralleled Cobo-Lewis et al. (2002), indicating that variability in word-level reading and related phonological processing skills is shared across the two languages, whereas variability in oral language comprehension is largely specific to each language. It is interesting that passage comprehension scores in the two languages loaded on both the reading/phonology factor and the language-specific factors, but more highly on the latter, indicating that reading comprehension involves both language-general word identification and phonological processing skills as well as oral language skills that are specific to a particular language.

TABLE 11.4. Factor Loadings for Principal Components Analysis of the Spanish and English Tasks at Grade 5 (Raw Score Data)

Variable	Factor 1	Factor 2	Factor 3
English tasks			
Letter–Word Identification	.867	.083	.244
Word Attack	.907	.024	.042
Passage Comprehension	.546	−.080	.662
Elision	.782	.083	.244
RAN-Digits	−.493	−.029	−.229
Understanding Directions	−.024	.196	.721
Listening Comprehension	.023	.038	.830
Picture Vocabulary	.356	−.294	.694
Spanish tasks			
Letter–Word Identification	.678	.616	−.207
Word Attack	.761	.461	−.144
Passage Comprehension	.489	.704	.073
Elision	.596	.439	−.031
Memory for Sentences	.030	.807	−.083
Listening Comprehension	.143	.873	.256
Picture Vocabulary	.030	.807	−.083

Stability of RD and Non-RD Groups over 2 Years

There is typically at least moderate stability of reading disabilities over time (Bruck, 1990; Francis, Shaywitz, Stuebing, Shaywitz, & Fletcher, 1996). However, reading disabled individuals are often able to compensate and make some progress in word identification and reading comprehension over time (Bruck, 1990). We investigated the stability and progress of the RD and non-RD groups in oral language and reading. First, we asked how stable the RD/non-RD classification was through grade 7. About 15% of the participants in each group were no longer available for testing. Inspection of the attrited group and the remaining participants revealed no obvious differences in overall score profile. Using the same criteria as in fifth grade, we found that 23 of the 39 remaining RD cases at grade 7 would still be classified RD in seventh grade (in English), and 79 of the remaining 83 non-RD cases would still be classified as non-RD in seventh grade. This indicates moderate to high stability.

Next we asked whether the same overall group performance profile would be observed in English and Spanish at grade 7 as was observed at grade 5. We used standard scores again for ease of comparison to Table

11.1. Table 11.5 reveals that despite the fact that some children had moved out of the RD category by grade 7, the overall group means continued to show the patterns of low word reading and decoding. We added Reading Fluency (WJ-III) in seventh grade, a task that requires participants to read silently a series of short, simple sentences (e.g., "A house is made of wood.") and answer true or false. They read and answer as many sentences as possible in 3 minutes. The RD group's mean standard score was 81.4 on this measure and the non-RD group's mean was 98.5, indicating the RD children were well below average and the non-RD within the average range based on test norms. Group differences in oral language and reading comprehension continued to favor the non-RD group (compare Tables 11.1 and 11.5).

Finally, we asked whether there was any tendency of the RD or non-RD groups to catch up to national norms for monolingual English or Spanish speakers. It is apparent from Table 11.5 that oral language comprehension remained at about the same level in both English and Spanish for both groups across the 2-year time span. The only tasks on which some catch-up seems to have occurred were Word Attack (up by 8.6 standard score points)

TABLE 11.5. Means and Standard Deviations (in Parentheses) for Seventh-Grade English and Spanish Standardized Tasks (Standard Scores) for Groups Defined in Fifth Grade

Variable	RD group ($n = 39$)	Non-RD ($n = 83$)	Comparison	Partial eta^2
English tasks				
Letter–Word Ident.	83.5 (12.0)	103.4 (13.0)	$F(120) = 65.6^{**}$	.35
Word Attack	89.7 (8.6)	104.6 (10.9)	$F(120) = 56.8^{**}$	.32
Passage Comp.	74.4 (14.4)	86.9 (10.8)	$F(120) = 28.7^{**}$	.19
Reading Fluency	81.4 (7.4)	98.5 (12.5)	$F(119) = 61.6^{**}$	.34
Spelling	80.2 (12.4)	101.7 (14.6)	$F(119) = 61.8^{**}$	.34
Understanding Dir.	85.7 (7.7)	89.4 (9.9)	$F(120) = 4.2^{*}$	.03
Listening Comp.	74.7 (19.3)	79.4 (13.4)	ns	.02
Picture Vocabulary	70.5 (10.5)	78.7 (9.8)	$F(120) = 17.8^{**}$	.13
Reading Fluency (raw)	37.2 (9.6)	54.2 (10.9)	$F(119) = 68.2^{**}$	.36
Spanish tasks				
Letter–Word Ident.	88.4 (22.6)	107.1 (19.2)	$F(120) = 22.3^{**}$	.16
Word Attack	85.0 (21.8)	102.6 (16.4)	$F(120) = 25.1^{**}$	.17
Passage Comp.	73.4 (16.7)	82.8 (11.0)	$F(120) = 13.8^{**}$	.10
Listening Comp.	78.0 (15.5)	81.7 (16.3)	ns	.01
Picture Vocabulary	76.7 (26.2)	82.7 (18.7)	ns	.02
Reading Fluency (raw)	22.0 (9.9)	36.2 (10.2)	$F(116) = 48.9^{**}$	.30

$^{*}p < .05$; $^{**}p < .001$.

and Letter–Word Identification (up by 4.4 points). However, as these were the defining measures in fifth grade, a large part of the change might be due to regression to the mean. Word Attack scores for the non-RD group moved down by about 7 points, which is also consistent with regression to the mean. On balance, there does not appear to have been much catch-up to the norms in our sample.

Spanish variables are also shown in Table 11.5, including a measure of reading fluency created for this study that paralleled the WJ-III measure. The same overall pattern of performance was seen at both grades 5 and 7 (smaller group differences on the oral language measures than the reading measures, the latter including Reading Fluency and Passage Comprehension.

Prediction of Reading Disabilities from Grades K–1

The final question we considered was whether reading disabilities in English could be predicted from Spanish measures at kindergarten and English measures at grade 1. Rather than examine the smaller subgroups identified earlier in the paper based on cross-linguistic comparisons, we concentrated on discriminating between RD and non-RD within English alone, in keeping with past studies. As was the case in previous studies by our group (Lindsey et al., 2003; Manis et al., 2004), we included the strongest predictor variables identified in the monolingual prediction literature (e.g., Scarborough, 1998). The performance of the RD and non-RD groups on the kindergarten Spanish measures is shown in Table 11.6 (percentile or raw scores, where applicable). The major differences appeared to involve letter and word knowledge, RAN-Objects time scores, and Sound Matching (a measure of phonological awareness adapted in Spanish for our study from the English CTOPP). No significant differences were observed on the two measures of oral language, Memory for Sentences and Picture Vocabulary, and Sound Categorization (another measure of phonological awareness adapted in Spanish for our study from the English CTOPP task).

Performance on English predictor variables in grade 1 is shown in Table 11.7 (percentile or raw scores, where applicable). Group differences were seen in almost every category of measure: print knowledge (Letter Knowledge, Letter–Word Identification, and Word Attack), phonological awareness (Sound Matching and Elision, from the CTOPP), and lexical retrieval (RAN-Objects and RAN-Digits). Both groups had very low scores on the oral language comprehension tasks, but significant group differences were not observed.

Because of the large number of variables on which the groups differed at kindergarten and first grade, and possible overlap between these measures, it is of interest which measures would account for the most independent variance in classifying the groups. A discriminant analysis using the kinder-

TABLE 11.6. Means, Standard Deviations (in Parentheses), and Comparisons on the Kindergarten Spanish Tasks (Standard or Raw Scores) for Groups Defined in Fifth Grade

Variable	RD group	Non-RD group	Comparison[a]	Partial eta^2
Letter Naming (raw)	41.7 (15.8)	49.2 (12.8)	$F(133) = 8.91^{**}$	.06
Letter Sounds (raw)	35.8 (19.9)	43.1 (17.5)	$F(116) = 4.1^{*}$	.03
Letter–Word Ident.	89.1 (14.4)	109.8 (27.9)	$t(133) = 21.9^{***}$	.14
Sound Categor. (raw)	6.9 (2.9)	6.9 (2.9)	ns	< .01
Sound Matching (raw)	14.5 (5.4)	16.4 (4.9)	$F(133) = 4.26^{*}$	.03
RAN-Objects Time (sec)	85.4 (25.9)	70.3 (20.6)	$F(132) = 13.6^{***}$	.09
Memory for Sent.	86.2 (15.3)	87.0 (13.8)	ns	< .01
Picture Vocabulary	81.6 (23.9)	88.6 (25.4)	ns	< .02

[a]df for the t-test is corrected for unequal variance.
$^{*}p < .05$; $^{**}p < .01$; $^{***}p < .001$;

garten Spanish measures (raw scores) produced a canonical correlation of 0.435, and the best-fitting function had a chi-square value of 26.95 ($df = 7$), $p < .001$. The canonical discrimination function coefficients are shown in Table 11.8 (upper panel). The three most powerful predictors (based on correlations of .5 or higher with the discriminant function) were Letter–Word Identification, RAN-Objects time, and Letter Knowledge. The phonological awareness and oral language comprehension measures were the least pow-

TABLE 11.7. Means, Standard Deviations (in Parentheses), and Group Comparisons on the First-Grade English Tasks (Standard or Raw Scores) for Groups Defined in Fifth Grade

Variable	RD group	Non-RD group	Comparison	Partial eta^2
Letter Naming (raw)	40.6 (12.7)	48.0 (9.0)	$F(133) = 15.2^{**}$	.10
Letter Sounds (raw)	39.0 (11.8)	44.0 (11.2)	$F(133) = 5.8^{*}$	.04
Letter–Word Ident.	82.8 (16.9)	103.4 (20.8)	$F(133) = 33.2^{***}$	.20
Word Attack	91.9 (12.3)	103.7 (12.5)	$F(133) = 27.3^{***}$	.17
Passage Comp.	87.1 (15.6)	99.1 (13.7)	$F(133) = 21.1^{***}$	.14
Sound Matching	91.7 (9.0)	96.4 (9.4)	$F(130) = 7.5^{**}$	.05
Sound Matching (raw)	11.9 (4.4)	14.7 (4.2)	$F(133) = 13.4^{***}$	.09
Elision (SS)	95.7 (13.0)	105.6 (15.5)	$F(116) = 11.3^{***}$	.09
RAN-Objects Time (sec)	69.6 (26.6)	51.5 (18.6)	$F(133) = 21.1^{***}$	.14
RAN-Digits Time (sec)	45.9 (24.5)	31.0 (12.2)	$F(133) = 22.5^{***}$	.14
Memory for Sent.	68.8 (11.8)	74.1 (16.1)	ns	<.04
Picture Vocabulary	47.0 (17.8)	53.9 (19.2)	ns	<.04

$^{*}p < .05$; $^{**}p < .01$; $^{***}p < .001$.

erful predictors. A stronger contribution of oral language to the prediction of reading comprehension would be expected for oral language scores at later grades, and in fact has been obtained in our own longitudinal analyses of reading comprehension data from grades 3–6 in this sample (Nakamoto, Lindsey & Manis, 2008) and also reported in cross-sectional studies of fourth-grade and older Spanish-speaking English language learners (e.g., Miller et al., 2006; Proctor et al., 2006).

A discriminant analysis was conducted using the English predictor variables (again, raw scores) at first grade to predict English RD classification at fifth grade. The canonical correlation was 0.569, and the best-fitting function had a chi-square value of 50.01 ($df = 10$), $p < .001$. Table 11.8 (lower panel) reveals that Letter–Word Identification, Word Attack, RAN-Digits, and RAN-Objects were the four most powerful variables. Loadings for the phonological awareness measures were the next strongest, and the weakest loadings were found for the oral language tasks.

In previous work (Manis et al., 2004) predicting the English reading skills of the longitudinal sample at grade 2, we utilized hierarchical regression analyses to show English variables at grade 1 superceded the predictions provided by Spanish variables at kindergarten. We now asked to what extent both English and Spanish variables contributed to the prediction of RD status at grade 5. We included two parallel sets of measures from Spanish and English in this third discriminant analysis: Letter–Word Identification, Letter Knowledge, Sound Matching, and RAN-Objects time. The best-fitting discriminant function had a canonical correlation of 0.545, with a chi-square of 45.12 ($df = 8$), $p < .001$. Four variables correlated 0.5 or higher with the discriminant function (not shown in any of the tables). Three variables were in English (Letter–Word Identification, RAN-Objects time, and Letter Knowledge), and one was in Spanish (Letter–Word Identification).

In summary, the discriminant analyses revealed that children who would later experience reading difficulties in English tended to be low in letter and word knowledge and object and digit naming speed in either English or Spanish in kindergarten and first grade. Phonological awareness and oral language skill were relatively weaker predictors of later reading status. Unlike previous analyses predicting reading achievement at second grade, English measures at first grade did not totally supplant Spanish measures at kindergarten.

CONCLUSIONS

We have reported several pieces of evidence supporting our main thesis that reading disabilities can be identified at grade 5 in English language learners with a Spanish-speaking background by testing them in English

TABLE 11.8. Correlation of Kindergarten Spanish and First-Grade English Variables with Discriminant Functions Classifying Children in Fifth-Grade Reading Disability Groups

Spanish kindergarten measure	Correlation with best-fitting function
Letter–Word Identification	.76
RAN-Objects Time	–.66
Letter Naming	.53
Sound Matching	.38
Picture Vocabulary	.26
Memory for Sentences	.04
Sound Categorization	–.01

English first-grade measure	Correlation with best-fitting function
Letter–Word Identification	.82
Word Attack	.60
RAN-Digits Time	–.59
RAN-Objects Time	–.58
Letter Naming	.49
Sound Matching	.46
Elision	.44
Letter Sounds	.30
Picture Vocabulary	.28
Memory for Sentences	.23

and carefully matching them to normally achieving readers on nonverbal and verbal ability measures. The groups differed on key measures of phonological awareness and rapid digit naming. The same basic patterns of group performance were found in Spanish at grade 5, and again in both languages 2 years later in grade 7. Factor analyses of the tasks at grade 5 revealed a common factor across both languages identifiable as a printed word/phonological processing factor. This supports earlier studies suggesting that there is language interdependence for word-level and phonological processing variables (e.g., Cobo-Lewis et al., 2002; DaFontoura & Siegel, 1995; Lindsey et al., 2003). Our finding that the RD and non-RD groups defined at fifth grade differed on both Spanish and English measures of letter–word knowledge and some measures of phonological processing skill at kindergarten and first grade supports the notion of a common core phonological processing deficit that is somewhat stable over the elementary school years. In keeping with the independence of phonological decoding and oral language comprehension skills at fifth grade, we observed that the oral language tasks at kindergarten and grade 1 did not discriminate as well between the RD and non-RD groups as the letter–word knowledge and phonological processing variables.

It is interesting that phonological awareness did not differentiate the RD and non-RD groups in grades K–1 as strongly as measures of print knowledge and rapid naming. This was true for both Spanish and English. One reason for this may be the high level of phonological decoding training the children received. We established in our prior work with this sample that the children as a group (referring to the entire sample of 303 children) performed higher in phonological decoding and word identification than would be expected based on their SES and initial English competence. For example, their English Word Attack percentile scores in English were 57, 59, 50, and 58 in grades 1, 2, 3, and 5, and their Spanish Letter–Word Identification percentile scores were even higher (77, 68, and 62 at grades 1, 3, and 5) (Lindsey & Manis, 2005). Studies of children learning highly regular orthographies such as Spanish, Dutch, and German have shown that phonological awareness is a relatively weaker predictor of later reading skills than speeded naming (e.g., van den Bos, 1998; Wimmer, 1993; Ziegler & Goswami, 2005). We hypothesize that the curriculum was successful in improving phonological decoding above a level that would be expected for this low-SES sample of English language learners. The limiting factors for acquisition of word reading skills might thus be variables beyond phonological awareness and decoding, such as fluency of access to phonological codes and amount of exposure to English and Spanish text.

It might be argued that our sample was atypical of RD samples in that the oral language comprehension of both the RD and non-RD groups was below average (one standard deviation or more below norms for both groups on picture vocabulary and listening comprehension in English as late as grade 7). This would only be a problem for our interpretation if oral language interacted with the phonological processing variables or had an independent relationship with word reading measures, apart from the contribution of the phonological variables. However, our data indicate that oral language scores have their primary impact on reading comprehension and not on word identification and decoding. As further evidence of independence, Nakamoto et al. (2008) developed structural equation models of the third- through sixth-grade longitudinal data from our sample that revealed highly stable and distinct factors of English phonological decoding and oral language processing in third and sixth grade. These factors did not interact with each other within or across grades and contributed independently to sixth-grade English reading comprehension. Taken together with the present findings, the results of these additional analyses indicate that reading disabilities in this sample can be viewed as a language-independent problem involving phonological processing and word identification (see Ziegler & Goswami, 2005, for a similar argument), and that oral language variables make language-specific contributions to reading comprehension.

Limitations

We must be cautious about characterizing all aspects of reading achievement as deriving from levels of phonological processing and oral language comprehension. Our sample was extremely low-SES and had relatively few opportunities outside the school setting to develop English language and literacy skills. One limitation of our study is that we were not able to collect data on home literacy practices and attitudes or detailed data on classroom exposure to English and Spanish. It is possible that greater progress in English reading skills is in part associated with particular literacy practices in the home; greater opportunities to speak English in the home, school, or community; or greater motivation to speak English. These practices might in turn have a reciprocal effect on phonological processing. Enhanced literacy experiences might have been a factor for the small subset of the non-RD children who were achieving at or near national norms for English literacy and language measures. Relatively enriched experiences with English may also have occurred for some children at the expense of Spanish language and literacy, as seen, for example, in the small subgroup that actually became specifically low in Spanish over the course of the study.

Another limitation of our study is that only one model of Spanish–English bilingual instruction was followed with the current sample, a transitional bilingual model, where the primary objective is to transition out of Spanish and into English as soon as possible in the elementary school years. It is possible that a stronger educational emphasis on Spanish, as occurs for example in two-way immersion programs, might prove more efficacious for these children. We are currently analyzing data from the same district for children in three different programs, transitional bilingual (the same as the current sample), English immersion, and two-way Spanish–English immersion. The English immersion or two-way immersion programs may have a greater positive impact on long-term English literacy achievement than the early-exit program.

Educational Implications

With these limitations of the current study in mind, there are several practical implications of our results. First, there is evidence that English language learners are often overlooked for remedial literacy training because teachers appear to assume that their literacy difficulties are due to lack of proficiency in the language of instruction (Limbos & Geva, 2001). Our results indicate that easy-to-administer Spanish language variables at kindergarten and English language variables in first grade can be used to identify a sample that is at risk for later reading difficulties. The at-risk pattern for reading disability emerges even among children with low oral language skill; in this case, it manifests as grade-inappropriate print knowledge and phonological processing difficulties at every step of the educational process. Second, although the prediction of later reading difficulties from these kindergarten and first-grade measures is not perfectly accurate, it does allow educators to track a group of at-risk children. By monitoring their reading skills at each grade, more accurate identification can be made (using "dynamic assessment," Durgunoğlu, 2002, and other techniques). Third, low levels of oral language skill in either of the languages being acquired by bilingual children have a high predictive accuracy for later reading comprehension problems within that specific language. Taken together, the data indicate that the greatest need for this population of children, and indeed probably for most Spanish-speaking bilingual children in the United States, is for more effective instruction in vocabulary, listening comprehension, and reading comprehension, beginning at early grades (Proctor et al., 2006). Even the attainment of high levels of Spanish vocabulary knowledge may transfer to English vocabulary only under certain circumstances. Bilingual education models will need to take into account aspects of oral language that depend more highly on specific experiences within the second language (Carlo et al., 2004; Proctor et al., 2006).

ACKNOWLEDGMENTS

The research was funded in part by grants from the National Institute of Child Health and Human Development and the Institute for Education Sciences to both Franklin R. Manis and Kim A. Lindsey. We thank the school district officials and children of the Brownsville, Texas, school district for their cooperation in this study.

REFERENCES

August, D. A., Calderon, M., & Carlo, M. (2001, March/April). The transfer of skills from Spanish to English. *NABE News, 11–12*, 42.

Bruck, M. (1990). Word recognition skills of adults with childhood diagnoses of dyslexia. *Developmental Psychology, 26*, 439–454.

Carlisle, J. F., Beeman, M. M., Davis, L. H., & Spharim, G. (1999). Relationship of metalinguistic capabilities and reading achievement for children who are becoming bilingual. *Applied Psycholinguistics, 20*, 459–478.

Carlo, M. S., August, D., McLaughlin, B., Snow, C. E., Dressler, C., Lippman, D. N., et al. (2004). Closing the gap: Addressing the vocabulary needs of English language learners in bilingual and mainstream classrooms. *Reading Research Quarterly, 39,* 188–215.

Chiappe, P., Siegel, L. S., & Wade-Wooley, L. (2002). Linguistic diversity and the development of reading skills: A longitudinal study. *Scientific Studies of Reading, 6,* 369–400.

Cobo-Lewis, A., Pearson, B. Z., Eilers, R. E., & Umbrel, V. C. (2002). Interdependence of Spanish and English knowledge in language and literacy proficiency among bilingual children. In D. K. Oller & R. E. Eilers (Eds.), *Language and literacy in bilingual children* (pp. 118–132). Clevedon, UK: Multilingual Matters.

Comeau, L., Cormier, P., Grandmaison, E., & Lacroix, D. (1999). A longitudinal study of phonological processing skills in children learning to read in a second language. *Journal of Educational Psychology, 91,* 29–43.

Cummins, J. (1979). Linguistic interdependence and the educational development of bilingual children. *Review of Educational Research, 49,* 222–251.

DaFontoura, H. A., & Siegel, L. S. (1995). Reading, syntactic, and working memory skills of bilingual Portuguese–English Canadian children. *Reading and Writing: An Interdisciplinary Journal, 7,* 139–153.

Durgunoğlu, A. Y. (2002). Cross-linguistic transfer in literacy development and implications for language learners. *Annals of Dyslexia, 52,* 189–204.

Durgunoğlu, A. Y., Nagy, W. E., & Hancin-Bhatt, B. J. (1993). Cross-language transfer of phonological awareness. *Journal of Educational Psychology, 85,* 453–465.

Francis, D. J., Shaywitz, S. E., Stuebing, K. K., Shaywitz, B. A., & Fletcher, J. A. (1996). Developmental lag versus deficit models of reading disability: A longitudinal, individual growth curves analysis. *Journal of Educational Psychology, 88,* 3–17.

Gottardo, A. (2002). The relationship between language and reading skills in bilingual Spanish–English speakers. *Topics in Language Disorders, 22,* 46–70.

Hagan, E. C. (1997). *Esperanza: A Spanish multisensory structured language program.* Unpublished program materials, Brownsville, TX.

Hoover, W. A., & Gough, P. B. (1990). The simple view of reading. *Reading and Writing: An Interdisciplinary Journal, 2,* 127–160.

Leafstedt, J. M., & Gerber, M. M. (2005). Crossover of phonological processing skills. *Remedial and Special Education, 26,* 226–235.

Lesaux, N. K., & Siegel, L. S. (2003). The development of reading in children who speak English as a second language. *Developmental Psychology, 39,* 1005–1019.

Limbos, M., & Geva, E. (2001). Accuracy of teacher assessments of ESL children at risk for reading disability. *Journal of Learning Disabilities, 34,* 136–151.

Lindsey, K. A., & Manis, F. R. (2005). Development of reading skills in Spanish-speaking English-language learners: A six-year longitudinal study. *Perspectives, 31,* 22–26.

Lindsey, K. A., Manis, F. R., & Bailey, C. E. (2003). Prediction of first-grade reading in Spanish-speaking English-language learners. *Journal of Educational Psychology, 95,* 482–494.

Manis, F. R., Lindsey, K. A., & Bailey, C. E. (2004). Development of reading in grades K–2 in Spanish-speaking English-language learners. *Learning Disabilities Research and Practice, 19,* 214–224.

Miller, K. D., Heilman, J., Nockerts, A., Iglesias, A., Fabiano, L., & Francis, D. J. (2006). Oral language and reading in bilingual children. *Learning Disabilities: Research & Practice, 21,* 30–43.

Nakamoto, J., Lindsey, K. A., & Manis, F. R. (2008). The development of English language learners' reading comprehension and the moderating effect of reading fluency. *Scientific Studies of Reading, 12,* 351–371.

Neuhaus Education Center. (1997). *Language enrichment.* Bellaire, TX: Author.

Oller, D. K., & Eilers, R. E. (2002). *Language and literacy in bilingual children.* Clevedon, UK: Multilingual Matters.

Proctor, C. P., August, D., Carlo, M. S., & Snow, C. (2006). The intriguing role of Spanish language vocabulary knowledge in predicting English reading comprehension. *Journal of Educational Psychology, 98,* 159–169.

Proctor, C. P., Carlo, M., August, D., & Snow, C. (2005). Native Spanish-speaking children reading in English: Toward a model of comprehension. *Journal of Educational Psychology, 97,* 246–256.

Scarborough, H. S. (1998). Early identification of children at risk for reading disabilities: Phonological awareness and some other promising predictors. In B. Shapiro, P. Accardo, & A. Capute, A. (Eds.), *Specific reading disability: A view of the spectrum* (pp. 77–121). Timonium, MD: York Press.

Shaywitz, S. E., Escobar, M. D., Shaywitz, B. A., Fletcher, J. M., & Makuch, R. (1992). Evidence that dyslexia may represent the lower tail of a normal distribution of reading ability. *The New England Journal of Medicine, 326,* 145–150.

Stanovich, K. E., & Siegel, L. S. (1994). The phenotypic performance profile of reading-disabled children: A regression-based test of the phonological-core variable-difference model. *Journal of Educational Psychology, 86,* 24–53.

Swanson, H. L., Saéz, L., Gerber, M., & Leafstedt, J. (2004). Literacy and cognitive functioning in bilingual and non-bilingual children at or not at risk for reading disabilities. *Journal of Educational Psychology, 96,* 3–18.

Swanson, H. L., Saéz, L., & Gerber, M. (2006). Growth in literacy and cognition in bilingual children at risk or not at risk for reading disabilities. *Journal of Educational Psychology, 98,* 247–264.

van den Bos, K. (1998). IQ, phonological awareness, and continuous naming speed related to Dutch children's poor decoding performance on two word identification tests. *Dyslexia, 4,* 73–89.

Wagner, R. K., & Torgesen, J. K. (1987). The nature of phonological processing and its causal role in the acquisition of reading skills. *Psychological Bulletin, 101,* 192–212.

Wagner, R. K., Torgesen, J. K., & Rashotte, C. A. (1998). *Comprehensive Test of Phonological Processing (CTOPP).* Austin, TX: PRO-ED.

Wimmer, H. (1993). Characteristics of developmental dyslexia in a regular writing system. *Applied Psycholinguistics, 14,* 1–33.

Woodcock, R. W., & Johnson, M. B., (1989). *Woodcock–Johnson Psycho-Educational Battery—Revised.* Chicago: Riverside.

Woodcock, R. W., McGrew, K. S., & Mather, N. (2001). *Woodcock–Johnson III.* Itasca, IL: Riverside.

Woodcock, R. W., & Muñoz-Sandoval, A. F. (1995). *Woodcock Language Proficiency Battery—Revised, Spanish Form.* Chicago: Riverside.

Ziegler, J. C., & Goswami, U. (2005). Reading acquisition, developmental dyslexia, and skilled reading across languages: A psycholinguistic grain size theory. *Psychological Bulletin, 131,* 3–29.

CHAPTER 12

■ ■ ■

Assessment of Reading Problems among English Language Learners Based on the Component Model

R. MALATESHA JOSHI
P. G. AARON

Recent reports by groups such as the National Reading Panel (2000), RAND Reading Study Group (2002), and Alliance for Excellence in Education (2003) have noted that reading achievement is a major concern of the United States. To briefly illustrate the situation, consider the fact that more than 8 million American students in grades 4–12 are not fluent readers (U.S. Department of Education, 2003). More than 3,000 students drop out of high school every school day (Alliance for Excellence in Education, 2003), poor reading and writing skills being one of the contributing factors. The Hearing on Measuring Success (2001) has called reading failure a national public health problem because lack of adequate reading skills affects individual lives as well as society at large. Interestingly, math scores have increased at both fourth- and eighth-grade levels and the gap between the performance of white students and black and Hispanic students in math is narrowing. The National Assessment of Educational Progress (NAEP) report of 2007 notes that more than one third of all students and about two thirds of minority students cannot read with clarity and fluency, again illustrating the discrepancy between white and minority students.

ENGLISH LANGUAGE LEARNERS AND READING

The number of children entering elementary schools in the United States who speak a language other than English is increasing rapidly. Approximately 11 million children and adolescents—more than 20% of the 5- to 17-year-olds enrolled in PreK to 12th grade—speak a language other than English at home; nearly half these children—5.1 million—are English language learners, or ELLs (Goldenberg & Reese, Chapter 1, this volume). Most of these children come from families where Spanish is the first language. The NAEP (2007) reports that Hispanic fourth-grade students averaged a score of 203 on reading compared to 229 for the white students—a 26-point difference. A similar gap is seen in higher grades with eighth-grade students scoring 246 points compared to 271 for whites—a 25-point difference. Although the NAEP reports a narrowing of the gap between Hispanic and whites between 2003 and 2005, the scores are not significantly different from the 1992 scores for fourth- and eighth-grade students. A similar achievement gap exists at state levels as well. For example, the State Education Indicators with a Focus on Title I (U.S. Department of Education, 2007), report that 15% of the students in Arizona are listed as ELLs; however, 35% of fourth grade ELLs are underachieving in reading and math compared to 12% of the general school population. The percentage increases 69% at the eighth-grade level for ELLs compared to 39% for the general school population. Similar discrepancies are shown in states like Texas and California as well. According to the National Center for Education Statistics (NCES, 2004) the dropout rate for ELLs is 31% compared to 10% of students whose home language is English.

In order to help these children become better readers, the source of the reading problems must be identified first so that appropriate instructional procedures can be applied. However, subjective evaluation may not be a good predictor of reading skills and can result in misidentification of the source of the reading problem of ELLs. A study by Limbos and Geva (2001) reported that teacher rating scales and teacher recommendations were less reliable for both monolingual English speakers (L1) and ELLs. According to the No Child Left Behind (NCLB) requirements, states should measure the English proficiency of ELLs in reading, writing, and listening and speaking, as well as math. Thus empirical procedures derived from a good theoretical model of reading is the rational way to assess reading skills of both monolingual English speakers and bilinguals for whom English is a second language. One such model that has received empirical support for its effectiveness in diagnosing and treating reading problems is the component model of reading (Aaron & Joshi, 1992). The model was inspired by the Simple View of Reading proposed by Gough and Tunmer (1986) and Hoover and Gough (1990), and in its current format is considerably expanded. In this chapter, we provide a brief outline of the model first and then discuss how the model is also applicable to ELLs.

A Brief Outline of the Component Model of Reading

The reading performance of children in the classroom is affected by not only cognitive factors, but also by environmental and psychological factors (cf. Berninger, Dunn, Lin, & Shimada, 2004; Dudley-Marling, 2004). The component model of reading is broadly conceptualized and takes this fact into account. In the component model, factors that have an influence on the acquisition of reading skills are organized into three domains; the components of reading are nested within each domain. The three domains are (1) the cognitive domain, (2) the psychological domain, and (3) the ecological domain. The component model provides a framework for teachers and psychologists for navigating the various assessment formats and determining remedial strategies for use in the classroom. The three domains of the component model and their constituent components are shown in Figure 12.1.[1]

The cognitive domain of the model has two components: word recognition and comprehension. The psychological domain includes components such as motivation and interest, locus of control, learned helplessness, learn-

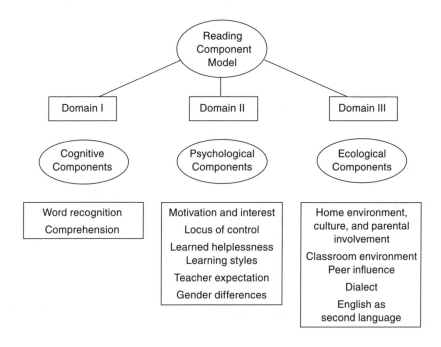

FIGURE 12.1. The component model of reading.

ing styles, teacher expectation, and gender differences. The ecological domain includes components such as home environment and culture, parental involvement, classroom environment, dialect, and English as a second language.

When applied to reading acquisition, the component model envisages that a child can fail to acquire satisfactory levels of reading skills because of deficiency in any component in any one of these three domains. In this chapter, we address assessment techniques based on the cognitive domain of the component model of reading.

THE COGNITIVE DOMAIN: WORD RECOGNITION AND COMPREHENSION

The initial idea of the componential nature of reading comes from a proposal by Gough and Tunmer (1986) in the form of a simple mathematical formula

$$RC = D \times LC$$

where RC is reading comprehension, D is decoding of the printed word, and LC is listening comprehension. This means that decoding and comprehension are two components of the cognitive module of reading.

According to Gough and Tunmer (1986), if $D = 0$, then $RC = 0$; and if $LC = 0$, $RC = 0$; that is, if children's decoding skill is zero, their reading comprehension skill is zero; when children's listening comprehension is zero, then their reading comprehension skill will also be zero. In other words, a child who cannot decode the printed word cannot read and understand; similarly, a child who cannot listen and understand also cannot read and understand. The model as used in this chapter is slightly modified from the Gough–Tunmer formula. The modified formula is

$$RC = WR \times LC$$

where RC is reading comprehension, WR is word recognition, and LC is listening comprehension. The independent nature of word recognition and comprehension is also reported by Carver and Clark (1998), Catts and Kamhi (2005, 2006), and de Jong and van der Leij (2002, 2003). Other investigators have described word recognition skill and comprehension skill as lower-level processing and higher-level processing skills, respectively (Hannon & Daneman, 2001; Pressley, 2000). The "verbal efficiency theory" (Perfetti, 1988) captures the essence of the bicomponential nature of reading by stressing the independent roles of verbal efficiency and text comprehension. According to this theory, word recognition accuracy alone is not enough for good reading comprehension, but decoding skills should be highly efficient and automatic so that the reader can devote more attention to meaning and comprehension.

Several studies have shown the predictive nature of the component model for assessment and instruction (see Aaron & Joshi 1992; Aaron, Joshi, Boulware-Gooden, et al., 2008; Aaron, Joshi, & Quotrochi, 2008; Adlof, Catts, & Little, 2006; Joshi & Aaron, 2000). Empirical evidence for theoretical support of the model derives from experimental (Levy & Carr, 1990; Palmer, McCleod, Hunt, & Davidson, 1985), developmental (Frith & Snowling, 1983; Leach, Scarborough, & Rescorla, 2003; Oakhill, Cain, & Bryant, 2003; Shankweiler et al., 1995); neuropsychological (Marshall & Newcombe, 1973); and genetic studies (DeFries, Fulker, & LaBuda, 1987; Olson, 2006). Various studies have shown different percentages of variance, ranging from 40 to 60%, contributed by decoding and comprehension depending on the type of measures used and grade levels of the students studied. In one of our studies (Aaron, Joshi, Boulware-Gooden, et al., 2008) the variance of reading achievement scores that can be explained by word recognition and listening comprehension ranged from 37 to 42% from grades 2 to 5.

The component model is applicable to other languages as well. In one of our studies (Joshi & Aaron, 2007), reading comprehension, decoding, and listening comprehension measures from Batería III Woodcock–Muñoz (Woodcock, Muñoz-Sandoval, McGrew, & Mather, 2006) were administered to 40 children in each of grades 2 and 3 whose home language was Spanish and whose instruction in school was also in Spanish. Regression analyses showed that approximately 60% of the variance in reading comprehension could be explained by decoding and listening comprehension. Furthermore, it was observed that the third graders' performance resembled that of English-speaking children in grade 4. This may be due to the transparency of Spanish orthography and the results support the Orthographic Depth Hypothesis, which states that the degree of correspondence between orthography and the phonology of the written word influences the rate and ease with which reading skills are acquired (Frost, Katz, & Bentin, 1987).

In the following sections, assessment procedures that can be used to assess reading skills of ELLs are described along with certain pitfalls that are to be avoided.

COGNITIVE DOMAIN, COMPONENT 1: WORD RECOGNITION

Phonological and Phonemic Awareness

The first component of the cognitive domain of the component model, word recognition, is also referred to by several related terms such as lexical processing, phonological decoding, and grapheme–phoneme conversion. Studies that have probed word recognition skill further suggest that phonemic awareness, which is described as awareness that spoken language is made up of separate speech sounds, complements word recognition. Phonological awareness includes phonemic awareness as well as the ability to segment words into syllables and the ability to produce rhyming words. Thus phonological awareness is a comprehensive term that includes phonemic awareness. Rhyming skill can be readily assessed by presenting a word orally and then requiring the child to produce similar-sounding words. Segmenting skill can be assessed by presenting a word orally and asking the child to indicate, by tapping on the desk or by clapping, how many syllables the word contains.

Because phonemic awareness is a strong correlate of reading skill (Ball & Blachman, 1991; Bradley & Bryant, 1985; Muter, 1998; Stahl & Murray, 1994) and a good predictor of reading and spelling skills of kindergarten children, it is often assessed first. Among the standardized tests of phonemic awareness are the Test of Phonological Awareness (TOPA; Torgesen & Bryant, 1995), and the Comprehensive Test of Phonological Processing (CTOPP; Wagner, Torgesen, & Rashotte, 1999). Tests of phonemic awareness include tasks of phoneme identification and phoneme manipulation. The phoneme identification task requires the child to indicate the number of phonemes in a spoken word by tapping on the desk. Phoneme manipulation is the ability to identify and deal with individual phonemes in a word. In one sense, all these tasks test the child's ability to deal with individual phonemes. Some researchers (Cisero & Royer; 1995; Durgunoğlu, Nagy, & Hancin-Bhatt, 1993; Quiroga, Lemos-Britton, Mostafapour, Abbott, & Berninger, 2002) have developed foreign-language equivalents of phonological measures, such as the Auditory Analysis Test (AAT; Quiroga et al., 2002). The Test of Phonological Processing in Spanish (TOPPS; August et al., 2001) is the Spanish equivalent of the CTOPP.

A word of caution is in order here. When preschool children are administered a test of phoneme awareness, it is important to make sure that these young children understand the nature of the task that is required of them. Tasks such as phoneme substitution can be difficult for some children to understand, which can lead to erroneous responses. Furthermore, while developing phonological awareness tasks for ELLs, the child's first language should be taken into consideration since some of the sounds in English may not exist in the child's first language. For instance, children whose first language is Arabic may have difficulty with the /p/ sound, and children with a background in Bengali may have difficulty with the /v/ sound. In addition, children with a first-language background in an alphabetic language, such as Spanish, German, and Italian, may perform better on phonemic awareness tasks than children whose first language is a syllabic language like Japanese

Kana or a morphosyllabic language like Chinese Kanji. Holm and Dodd (1996), for example, compared the phonemic awareness and English non-word reading skills of children from mainland China, who were exposed to pinyin (an alphabetic written form of Chinese), with children from Hong Kong who were not exposed to pinyin. They found that children from mainland China performed better at segmenting English words as well as naming English nonwords.

Another good predictor of reading skill in first grade is children's *letter knowledge* when they are in kindergarten. There is evidence that children who do not have alphabetic knowledge by the end of first grade might experience problems in reading as they progress through the grades (Adams, 1990; Juel, 1994). It is obvious that letter knowledge is a step beyond phonemic awareness. That is, letter knowledge requires the ability not only to be aware of the phonemes of the language but also to relate these sounds to the letters of the alphabet. This does not mean that phonemic awareness facilitates acquisition of letter knowledge; in fact, some researchers claim that letter knowledge leads to phonemic awareness. It is fair to say that the relationship between phonemic awareness and letter knowledge is reciprocal. This means exposure to written language can enhance awareness about phonemes; at the same time, increasing an awareness of phonemes can also increase children's knowledge about the written language. A list of uppercase and lowercase letters of the alphabet in random order can be administered to find out the letter knowledge of children in kindergarten and grade 1. Studies (Chiappe, Siegel, & Gottardo, 2002; Stage, Sheppard, Davidson, & Browning, 2001) have demonstrated that letter naming and phonological processing skills are reliable predictors of reading disability for both the native speakers of English as well as ELLs.

Many studies report that training in phonemic awareness in young children increases their reading skills when they enter the early elementary grades not only in English (Ball & Blachman, 1991; Blachman, Tangel, Ball, Black, & McGraw, 1999) but also in other languages such as Danish (Lundberg, Frost, & Petersen, 1988), French (Leybaert & Content, 1995), Spanish (Sebastian-Gallés & Vacchiano, 1995), Portuguese (Pinheiro, 1995), and Italian (Cossu, Gugliotta, & Marshall, 1995). Nevertheless, Castles and Coltheart (2004) have argued that many preschool children already come to school with a knowledge of written letters and that no study has provided unequivocal evidence of a causal link from phonological awareness to success in reading and spelling; however, there is growing evidence that phonological awareness plays a causal role in learning to read and spell not only in alphabetic languages (Caravolas, Hulme, & Snowling, 2001; Hulme, Snowling, Caravolas, & Carroll, 2005; Ziegler & Goswami, 2005) but in nonalphabetic languages as well (Cho & McBride-Chang, 2005; McBride-

Chang & Kail, 2002; So & Siegel, 1997; Wang & Geva, 2003; Ziegler & Goswami, 2005).

Decoding

Decoding skill can be assessed with the aid of a test of nonword reading and a test of spelling. Nonwords are also referred to as pseudowords; *daik* and *brane* are examples of nonwords. Nonword reading (or pseudoword reading) is a recognition task, whereas spelling is a recall task. This makes spelling a more sensitive test of decoding skill than nonword reading.

There is also a misconception regarding the nature of pseudowords in that they are all alike. This is because some nonwords can be read by analogy. For example, the nonword *dake* can be read more easily if the child is familiar with words such as *cake*, *bake*, and *take*. Thus *dake* has many neighbors, which makes it a "friendly" nonword. In contrast, a nonword such as *daik* has few neighbors and is therefore "unfriendly." Unfriendly nonwords cannot be decoded by using the analogy strategy. For this reason, it is essential that nonword lists designed to test decoding skill have a balance of both friendly and unfriendly words. Word attack subtests can be found in standardized tests such as the Woodcock Johnson Tests of Achievement (Woodcock, McGrew, & Mather, 2001) and the Woodcock Language Proficiency Battery–R (Woodcock, 1994). Bateria III: Woodcock–Muñoz (Woodcock et al., 2006) provides the word attack subtests for Spanish speakers. Since both the English and the Spanish versions are constructed by the same research group, the scores may be easy to compare.

Instant Word Recognition

We have used the term "instant word recognition" for what is traditionally called "sight-word reading." The expression "instant word recognition" is preferred because the term "sight-word reading" creates an impression that quick and accurate recognition of written words is a visual task, with phonology being relegated to a subordinate position. However, this is not entirely true. As noted earlier, instant word recognition skill is built on the foundation of phonological, morphological, and orthographic knowledge.

A fluent reader must possess good decoding skills, adequate comprehension skills, and the ability to process information at an optimal rate. In a review of 17 studies of monolingual English speakers, Compton and Carlisle (1994) found that students with weak word recognition skills are slower in naming words and nonwords, which led them to conclude that word reading speed is an important factor in differentiating individuals with reading disability from readers with normal ability. In fact, in languages such as Spanish, German, and Italian, which have almost one-to-one correspondence between spelling and pronunciation, dyslexia is diagnosed on the basis of the speed with which children read words and sentences (Joshi & Aaron, 2006).

Beyond third grade, the speed with which written words are recognized becomes an important factor. Some children who are given ample training in decoding and phonics may be able to pronounce pseudowords accurately, but they do so slowly and laboriously. Under such circumstances, if the time it takes to finish the task is not taken into account, test scores alone will give an incorrect impression that the child has adequate word recognition skills. In one study (Joshi & Aaron, 2002), 37 fifth graders were administered the Word Attack subtest from the Woodcock Language Proficiency Battery—Revised (Woodcock, 1994), which is not a timed test. When the word recognition skill of these children was evaluated by using a composite index of accuracy and time, it was found that many children who had average decoding scores obtained composite scores in the lowest quartile. These children, who were slow but accurate decoders, could escape diagnosis as poor decoders and, therefore, represent instances of false negatives. For this reason, when measuring decoding through the use of nonwords, both speed and accuracy must be considered.

A simple way to come up with a composite index that combines both decoding skill and speed of processing is to administer a timed standardized word-naming test. The Test of Word Reading Efficiency (TOWRE; Torgesen, Wagner, & Rashotte, 1999) is a good example of such a test. The TOWRE has two subtests. One subtest is sight-word efficiency, which assesses the number of printed words that can be accurately named in 45 seconds; the second measures the number of nonwords that can be decoded in 45 seconds.

There are different ways to assess reading speed. The Rapid Automatized Naming (RAN) test, developed by Denckla and Rudel (1976), requires the reader to name a series of colors, pictures of objects, and letters. The test reliably distinguishes between poor and normal readers across a broad range (Bowers & Wolf, 1993; Vellutino et al., 1996; Wolf & Bowers, 1999). In a recent study (Aaron et al., 1999), we demonstrated that children from grade 2 took longer to name a common word than to name a letter of the alphabet, the difference being statistically significant. However, children from grade 3 and up, including college students, named both letters and words at about the same rate. This indicates that by about the third grade most children have mastered decoding skills and have become instant word readers. The time it takes to name a letter of the alphabet and a common content word, therefore, could be used to assess instant word-reading skill. When a list of 20 common monosyllabic content words (nouns, verbs, and adjectives) is named as rapidly as a list of 20 letters, then it can be concluded that these words are read as sight words. Of course, the word list would vary from grade to grade. However, classroom teachers can prepare a list of words that the children have encountered many times in their classroom text and use it to assess instant word-reading skill.

While selecting the items for reading of words and nonwords to measure child's ability of decoding and word recognition skills, a knowledge of the structure of the first language is important. For instance, a child whose native language is Spanish may perform poorly on reading words and nonwords with consonant blends beginning with, for example, *st, sl, sm,* or *str,* since these blends are not permissible at the beginning of a word in Spanish.

Spelling

Spache, as early as 1940, noted that children who were poor spellers also were deficient in decoding skills. In a study that specifically examined the question of whether children use similar processes to read and spell words, Waters, Bruck, and Seidenberg (1985) found that third-grade children, regardless of their ability level, used spelling–sound correspondences for both reading and spelling. Excessive spelling errors, therefore, often indicate a weakness in phonological skill and should not be interpreted, without strong evidence, as an indication of poor visual memory (Joshi & Aaron, 1991). Several studies have shown that spelling ability predicts reading ability even after phonological skills have been controlled for not only in English but also in Spanish (Cunningham & Stanovich, 1990; Ferroli & Krajenta, 1989; Stage & Wagner, 1992). Spelling development parallels reading development. Several studies have shown that reading and spelling require common cognitive linguistic processes as well as unique orthographic processes (Berninger, Abbottt, Abbott, Graham, & Richards, 2002; Fitzgerald & Shanahan, 2000; Joshi & Aaron, 1991). Thus spelling performance should not be viewed as a purely visual memory skill. In spite of its being a good diagnostic tool, spelling is seldom utilized as a test of decoding skill.

Traditionally, spelling ability is assessed by dictating a list of words to children and then scoring their output as right or wrong. This kind of quantitative assessment has two drawbacks. First, it is quite possible that students tend to spell unfamiliar words phonetically, which often will lead to spelling errors. Under such a condition, these spelling errors do not reflect a deficit in spelling skill per se, but rather limited vocabulary knowledge. Familiarity with words, as indicated by the ability to pronounce them, must be taken into account when spelling lists are constructed. Spelling scores derived from standardized spelling tests are particularly susceptible for this type of misinterpretation. A mistake of this nature can be avoided if teachers use in their spelling tests only those words already introduced in the classroom (Joshi, 2003).

Furthermore, ability to spell words falls on a continuum. Therefore, spelling errors cannot be validly dichotomized as "right" or "wrong." Such a quantitative assessment of spelling can yield an incomplete and distorted picture of the child's spelling skill. For instance, a child who spells KAT for *cat* has better knowledge of letter–sound correspondence than a child who spells *cat* as TCA, even though both are incorrect when scored right or wrong. Furthermore, dichotomizing spelling performance as "right" or "wrong" may not give a comprehensive picture of the source of children's spelling difficulty. Quantitative assessment also does not tell the teacher how to address the child's spelling problems. A quasi-qualitative assessment procedure is provided by Tangel and Blachman (1995). Under this procedure, a score of 0 is assigned to random symbols with little or no alphabetic representation, and a score of 6 is given to correct spelling. Scores 1 through 5 are assigned depending on the degree of proximity to real spelling.

Several studies indicate that the acquisition of grapheme–phoneme conversion (GPC) skill follows a developmental course moving from a mastery of simple to complex spelling–sound relationship (Calfee, Venezky, & Chapman, 1969; Ehri, 1991, 1997; Moats, 1995; Treiman, 1993, 1998, 2006; Venezky, 1976, 2000). For instance, hard *c* as in *cat* is mastered earlier than soft *c* as in *city*, and hard *g* as in *girl* is learned before soft *g* as in *gem*. A list of words designed to test the decoding skill should, therefore, contain words that assess a wide range of GPC rules utilized by children as they grow older. Based on this observation, Shearer and Homer (1994) suggest that a child's stage of spelling development could be judged by examining spelling errors. A child could be in the phonemic, letter–name spelling, early phonetic, phonetic, and correct spelling stage. Of course, the misspellings by children usually can be in more than one stage.

A word of caution here. Even though early researchers in spelling such as the University of Virginia group (Bissex, 1980; Henderson & Beers, 1980; Morris, Nelson, & Perney, 1986; Read, 1971, 1986) proposed that spelling development progresses in predictable stages, more recent research studies (Cassar, Treiman, Moats, Pollo, & Kessler, 2005; Ehri, 1998, 2000) have pointed out that perhaps spelling development could be viewed as a "continual amalgamation of phonological, morphological, and orthographic knowledge" (Moats, 1995, p. 14), rather than as distinct stages. Of course, these development processes were based on English-speaking monolingual children and may not be true for speakers of other languages. For instance, Carbonell de Grompone, Tuana, Peidra de Moratoria, Lluch de Pintos, and Corbo de Mandracho (1980) observed three phases of spelling development among native speakers of Spanish beginning with the simple one-to-one correspondence between phonemes and graphemes followed by "rule-governed" phonemes, where the graphemes vary based on the context, and finally phonemes that have more than one representation. There are fewer exceptions in Spanish because Spanish orthography is more transparent than English orthography. Caravolas (2006) reviewed studies of beginning spelling in four languages: Czech, French, German, and English. French and English are considered as having deeper orthographies compared to Czech and German. It was found that speakers of English developed spelling at a slower rate than speakers of transparent languages such as Czech and German. This phenomenon was true for both basic and advanced spelling and was largely explained in terms of orthographic depth. Rolla San Francisco, Mo, Carlo, August, and Snow (2006) and Sun-Alperin and Wang (2007) found that Spanish speakers substitute the Spanish vowel sound while spelling English vowels. (In English one vowel letter has more than one sound, while in Spanish one vowel letter has one vowel sound.)

Furthermore, qualitative analyses of spelling errors could also be helpful in designing corrective instruction. A detailed phonological analysis of spelling errors such as substitution of consonant phonemes, omission of consonants in blends, omission of unaccented vowels (schwa), or syllable omission can be useful in identifying the source of spelling (and decoding) errors of the child whose attention could be drawn to those errors (Joshi, 2003).

In summary, spelling, as a recall task, is a more rigorous test of decoding skill than nonword reading. The validity of spelling tests could be improved by administering only those words the child could read aloud correctly and by using qualitative or quasi-qualitative analyses of spelling errors. The outcome of a qualitative analysis of spelling errors can also be successfully utilized in remedial spelling instruction.

Again, as mentioned under phonological awareness, decoding, and word recognition, a child's home language will have an influence on English spelling, so that factor must be taken into consideration. Because *st, sm*, or *sn* blends do not appear at the beginning of the words in Spanish, it is not uncommon for Spanish-speaking children to add an *e* at the beginning of words in *snake* and *smile* and spell them as *esnake* and *esmile* or reduce the blends thus spelling *stars* as *tars* (Goldstein, 2001). In one of our studies (Joshi, Hoien, Feng, Chengappa, & Boulware-Gooden, 2006), it was observed that when children from India and Norway were not sure of the correct spelling, they would attempt to spell the word and were successful in producing a few of the phonetic equivalents, whereas Chinese children tended to skip the word entirely or their misspellings were off the target word when they were uncertain about the word. For example, for the word *world,* Norwegian children wrote *word, world, vold,* and *vorld;* Indian children wrote *word, volte, wold,* and *owed;* but the Chinese children wrote *work, worker, wall,* and *what,* all of which are real words. This could be because the phonological nature of the Norwegian and Kannada orthography might have facilitated the production of an approximation to the target word while Children exposed to Chinese orthography may view the word as a whole unit; hence when Chinese children did not know the correct spelling of the target word, they wrote another real word.

COGNITIVE DOMAIN, COMPONENT 2: COMPREHENSION

Comprehension is a generic term that includes both reading and listening comprehension.

Listening Comprehension

A number of studies have shown that, except for modality differences, reading comprehension and listening comprehension are mediated by the same cognitive processes. As noted earlier, the correlation between reading and listening comprehension is impressive. Savage (2001) found the correlation coefficient between listening and reading comprehension to be 0.81. Listening comprehension, therefore, can be used to assess comprehension without being confounded by decoding skill. This finding seems to be true for second-language learning as well. Proficiency in listening comprehension in the second language is a significant predictor of second-language reading comprehension as well (Reese, Garnier, Gallimore, & Goldenberg, 2000; Royer & Carlo, 1991). Proctor, August, Carlo, and Snow (2005) directly tested the cognitive component of the component model with ELLs by administering various measures of decoding, listening comprehension, and reading comprehension to 132 Spanish–English bilinguals in grade 4. Even though there was significant relationship among the three variables, vocabulary knowledge and listening comprehension were most predictive of reading comprehension, which led the authors to conclude that "positive changes in vocabulary knowledge had direct effects on reading comprehension but also on listening comprehension, through which reading comprehension was further affected" (p. 253). The discrepancy between reading comprehension and listening comprehension can tell us whether decoding or comprehension per se is the source of the reading problem.

Listening comprehension can be assessed by more than one test and, consequently, results can vary somewhat depending on the test used (Joshi, Williams, & Wood, 1998). One test that has both listening and reading comprehension subtests is the Woodcock Language Proficiency Battery. Both comprehension subtests were normed on the same population and use the same cloze format. This makes reading and listening comprehension comparable. The Diagnostic Achievement Battery (Newcomer, 1999) and the Wechsler Individual Achievement Test–III (WIAT-III; The Psychological Corporation, 2009) also have subtests of listening comprehension and measures of academic language proficiency.

Reading Comprehension

A common misconception is that all standardized tests of reading comprehension are alike. This is not true, because tests differ in the strategy they use for assessing comprehension. For example, the Stanford Diagnostic Reading Test (Karlsen & Gardner, 1995) and the Gates–MacGinitie Reading Tests (MacGinitie, MacGinitie, Maria, & Dreyer, 2000) require children to read passages and answer questions that are in multiple-choice formats. Under such a format, the ability not only to comprehend but also to remember the passage read plays a role in performance. Memory ability, therefore, can become a confounding factor.

Another strategy used for assessing reading comprehension is the cloze procedure, where the reader is required to furnish words that are systematically deleted from sentences. The assumption is that the reader cannot supply the correct word unless he or she understands the meaning of the sentence. Tests that follow this format do not usually impose time restrictions. A weakness of this form of assessment is that it is somewhat removed from the reading of a paragraph or a story. Thus scores obtained using sentences in cloze format may not be ecologically valid measures of comprehension. The Woodcock Reading Mastery Test—Revised (Woodcock, 1998), the Woodcock Language Proficiency Battery—Revised (Woodcock, 1994), and the Woodcock Diagnostic Battery (Woodcock, 1997) have subtests that assess reading comprehension by relying on the cloze format.

The Peabody Individual Achievement Test—Revised (Markwardt, 1998) follows a different technique to assess reading comprehension. In this test, the individual reads a sentence and chooses one picture from among four that fits the sentence. Even though this form of testing reduces memory load, correct understanding of the pictures requires a good deal of reasoning ability. This is particularly true at higher grades.

Many of these tests take 45 minutes or more to complete and are meant to be given in a single session. Blanchard, Di Cerbo, Oliver, and Albers (2001) found that when the test was split into halves and administered in two separate sessions, the reading comprehension scores improved, particularly for students with poor reading skills.

Because comprehension is the ultimate goal of reading, various aspects related to comprehension, such as syntactical complexity and cultural factors, should be considered while assessing comprehension.

Vocabulary

Even though in the component model "vocabulary" is not accorded the status of a separate component, vocabulary knowledge is a prerequisite of overall comprehension skill. Developing a larger vocabulary is often a critical factor in improving reading comprehension (Anderson & Freebody,

1981; Anderson & Nagy, 1992; Davis, 1944; Joshi, 2005; Snow, Burns, & Griffin, 1998). Nevertheless, vocabulary knowledge is a prerequisite of comprehension skill. Good decoding skills are required for comprehending written material; however, once decoding skills are mastered, comprehending written material depends on how well the meaning of the words (semantic relationships) are understood.

The coefficients of correlation between vocabulary and reading comprehension range from 0.66 to 0.75 (Just & Carpenter, 1987). A meta-analysis of vocabulary studies by Stahl and Fairbanks (1986) suggested that vocabulary knowledge very likely played a causal role in comprehension. Not surprisingly, the reading vocabulary of children with specific reading disability tended to be lower than that of their normally achieving peers. In order to obtain a true estimate of the students' vocabulary knowledge, it is desirable to administer tests of both reading and listening vocabulary. The Woodcock Language Proficiency Battery—Revised (WLPB-R; Woodcock, 1994) has subtests of both listening and reading vocabularies. Many of these tests are also available as Spanish version. For instance, the Batería III Woodcock–Muñoz (Woodcock et al., 2006) is a comprehensive set of tests that assesses both cognitive abilities and achievement levels of Spanish-speaking individuals between the ages of 2 years and 90+ years. Tejas Lee is the Spanish version of the Texas Primary Reading Inventory. The Center for Applied Linguistics has developed a website called Development of Literacy in Spanish Speakers (DeLSS) (www.cal.org/delss/products/delss-tests.html) that provides information for the different types of reading tests available for Spanish speakers. The Peabody Picture Vocabulary Test–IV (PPVT-IV; Dunn & Dunn; 2007) and the Spanish version of the same (Test de Vocabulario en Imágenes Peabody [TVIP-H]; Dunn, Padilla, Lugo, & Dunn, 1986) are used by researchers to measure vocabulary knowledge. It should be noted, however, that because these instruments are in multiple-choice formats, they assess recall of familiar items and may not accurately measure the depth of one's vocabulary knowledge.

August and Shanahan (2006) warn that tests normed on monolingual English-speaking children may not be suitable for ELLs. Quinn (2001) administered two tests that measured comprehension of grammar that were standardized on native English speakers to ELLs. The results showed that there were no clear developmental patterns for ELLs, which has led Quinn to conclude that the language development, both comprehension and production, of ELLs is significantly different from native speakers of English. In addition, a distinction must be made between conversational English and academic English (Collier & Thomas, 1989; Cummins, 1984, 1991). Academic English is the language used in textbooks, and decisions about assessment and placement should be based on students' competence in academic English. Several studies have shown that a mismatch between English spoken at home and academic English can adversely affect reading achievement

(Charity, Scarborough, & Griffin, 2004; Horton-Ikard, & Ellis Weismer, 2007). More important, when students were taught to use academic English in their conversation, reading scores and overall academic achievement improved (Charity et al., 2004; Craig & Washington, 2004)

Strengths and Weaknesses of Frequently Used Tests

It was noted earlier that tests of listening comprehension and reading comprehension play a key role in identifying the weak component of reading. For this reason, standardized batteries, which test both reading comprehension and listening comprehension, have an advantage. Two examples of such tests are the Woodcock Language Proficiency Battery (Woodcock, 1994) and the Wechsler Individual Achievement Test–III (WIAT-III; The Psychological Corporation, 2009). In addition, the WIAT-III is linked to the Wechsler Intelligence Scale for Children–IV (WISC-IV, The Psychological Corporation, 2003), which makes a comparison of achievement and IQ scores possible.

Measures of Decoding and Spelling

Precautions to be exercised when evaluating tests of decoding and spelling were noted earlier in this chapter. That is, tests of decoding should take into consideration the time it takes for the student to read the nonwords. In addition, nonwords used as test items for decoding should not have many similar-sounding or rhyming cohorts.

Measures of Reading Comprehension

Tests of reading comprehension use different strategies to assess comprehension. Each strategy has its own advantages and disadvantages. Tests that utilize the cloze strategy reduce the memory load of the reader, but tests in the Woodcock series are not timed and, therefore, do not assess speed of comprehension. Being limited to one or two sentences, such tests also are also not designed well to assess inferential comprehension and, therefore, are somewhat removed from true reading.

Tests such as the Stanford Diagnostic Reading Test–IV (SDRT-IV; Karlsen & Gardner, 1995) and the Gates–MacGinitie Reading Tests–IV (MacGinitie et al., 2000), use paragraphs of varying lengths followed by multiple-choice test questions. Performance on these type of tests depends not only on the comprehension ability of the reader but also the memory power of the reader. These tests can be administered to groups of children and, therefore, save much time and expense. A major weakness of tests in multiple-choice formats is that they allow for guessing, which can misrepresent the true ability of the reader. For instance, under ordinary circumstances, if there are four choices for every question, the chance of guessing the correct answer is 25%. The chances of successful guessing increase when the questions are independent of the passage to be read and answered ("passage independent"). These so-called passage-independent questions can be answered correctly from past experience and prior knowledge even without reading the passage. For example, the probabilities of correctly answering the question "What did Jack do at McDonald's?" are high without even reading a passage about "Our Visit to McDonald's." In contrast, a passage-dependent question such as "How many people went to McDonald's with Jack?" cannot be correctly guessed without reading and comprehending the passage. The problem of passage-independent comprehension was studied as early as 1964 by Preston; however, the topic has not been studied on a consistent basis (e.g., Hanna & Oaster, 1978; Katz, Lautenschlager, Blackburn, & Harris, 1990; Kennan & Betjemann, 2006). Nevertheless, it has been recognized as a confounding factor that should be considered when selecting tests.

Another strategy for testing reading comprehension is adopted by the Peabody Individual Achievement Test—Revised (PIAT-R; Markwardt, 1998). Although this format may benefit individuals who may not be able to respond orally but can point to the pictures that correspond to the sentence, the reading comprehension subtest involves a great deal of reasoning. At higher levels, some of the test items are very similar to items seen in tests of intelligence. Moreover, the picture format cannot be used to assess comprehension of central ideas and themes contained in connected prose. More information about the different types of tests such as achievement tests, diagnostic tests, informal measures, curriculum-based measures, and portfolios can be found in Aaron, Joshi, and Quotrochi (2008).

We have outlined various instruments that could be used to identify reading problems in ELLs based on the component model, which has empirical support and is pragmatic (Aaron, Joshi, Boulware-Gooden, et al., 2008; Aaron, Joshi, & Quotrochi, 2008; Adlof et al., 2006; Barth, Catts, & Anthony, 2009). We have also provided some pitfalls to avoid while assessing the reading skills of ELLs. Below, we outline some research evidence about the reading disability in the second language to answer the question of whether it is a cognitive problem or a reading problem. That is, if a student has a reading disability in the first language, would s/he also have reading problem in the second language?

Reading Disability in the Second Language

Regarding reading disability in the second language, there are two views. One is the script-dependent hypothesis, according to which the patterns of reading disability may depend on the orthographic complexity of the language (Gholamain & Geva, 1999). The other view is the central deficit hypothesis, which is an upshot of Cummins's (1981) interdependence hypothesis. According to this hypothesis, underlying cognitive factors such as verbal knowledge and phonological skills are important in reading, and thus when children have reading difficulties in one language, they will also exhibit reading difficulties in the other language because the two languages are interdependent.

There is support for both of the hypotheses in the literature. While reviewing the literature on reading disabilities in bilinguals, it was observed that in almost all of the studies bilinguals had reading problems in both of their languages (see Joshi, Prakash, & Surendranath, 2010; Obler, 1984). Based on the limited evidence available on bilingual dyslexia in 1984, Obler suspected that "if a child is dyslexic in learning to read one language, then he or she is as a rule dyslexic in learning to read the next" (p. 493). Klein and Doctor (2003) studied three cases of biscriptal dyslexics of English and Afrikaans, a shallow orthography, and found that there were problems with phonological processing in both languages. Their findings led them to the conclusion that bilinguals do not develop special mechanisms for processing print that are different from those employed by monolingual readers and spellers. These findings would support the central deficit hypothesis. However, Wydell and Butterworth (1999) studied a developmental bilingual dyslexic who was dyslexic only in English but not in Japanese, even though he had studied Japanese as a second language later. This would support the script-dependent hypothesis.

Perhaps the severity of the reading problem may depend on the orthographic distance between the two languages; that is, when the two languages are similar, such as Italian and Spanish, then a child with a reading problem in one language may have a reading problem in the other language as well. On the other hand, if the child is bilingual in two dissimilar languages, such as Spanish and Chinese, there may not be transfer of the reading problem from one language to the other.

SUMMARY

We have outlined the assessment procedures for ELLs based on the component model, which is based on psychological and linguistic facts related to reading and can be used by classroom teachers, speech–language pathologists, and school psychologists. According to this model, acquisition of reading skills depends on components from three domains: the cognitive domain, the psychological domain, and the ecological domain. In this chapter we have focused on the cognitive domain, which consists of two components: word recognition and comprehension. We have also outlined the various tests that could be used for assessing the components that belong to the cognitive domain and described some of the precautions that need to be taken in interpreting test scores. Information obtained through these tests should guide the teacher and the speech–language pathologist toward appropriate remedial instruction.

Lesaux and Geva (2006) reviewed studies that compared word-level skills that included word reading and spelling as well as text-level skills of monolinguals and ELLs and concluded that the performance of these two groups on word reading, phonological awareness, and spelling was very similar. For instance, ELLs who had word reading difficulties or spelling difficulties performed poorly on phonological awareness tasks, and their performance was similar to monolinguals who had reading or spelling difficulties (Chiappe & Siegel, 1999; Chiappe et al., 2002; Everatt, Smythe, Adams, & Ocampo, 2000; Wade-Woolley & Siegel, 1997). This trend was also found among monolingual Dutch and Dutch second-language learners (Verhoeven, 2000).

Even though Geva (2000) did not outline a theoretical model, she did recommend that two assessments be required for assessing the reading performance of ELLs: (1) the assessment of phonological processing and rapid basic reading skills, and (2) measuring the gap between reading and listening comprehension. A small gap between reading and listening comprehension, with reading comprehension being slightly lower, may be normal. A large gap indicates that while the student is able to understand vocabulary and ideas, s/he is having trouble making sense of words and ideas in print, which may be due to decoding deficits. As Lesaux and Geva (2006) expressed, "given the overrepresentation of language-minority students among struggling readers, it is important to find mechanisms for early identification of those likely to struggle, so as to provide prevention services before they fall behind" (p. 54). We hope that this chapter has provided an outline to identify the reading problems of ELLs in a systematic way.

NOTE

1. Detailed description of the component model is discussed in Aaron and Joshi (1992); Aaron, Joshi, Boulware-Gooden, and Bentum (2008); and Aaron, Joshi, and Quotrochi (2008).

REFERENCES

Aaron, P. G., & Joshi, R. M. (1992). *Reading problems: Consultation and remediation*. New York: Guilford Press.

Aaron, P. G., & Joshi, R. M., Ayotollah, M., Ellsberry, A., Henderson, J., & Lindsey, K. (1999). Decoding and sight-word reading: Are they two independent components of word recognition skill? *Reading and Writing: An Interdisciplinary Journal, 14,* 89–127.

Aaron, P. G., Joshi, R. M., Boulware-Gooden, R., & Bentum, K. (2008). Diagnosis and zAn Alternative to the Discrepancy Model of Learning Disabilities, *Journal of Learning Disabilities, 41,* 67–84.

Aaron, P. G., Joshi, R. M., & Quotrochi, D. (2008). *the professional reading teacher.* Baltimore: Brookes.

Adams, M. (1990). *Beginning to read: Thinking and learning about print.* Cambridge, MA: MIT Press.

Adlof, S. M., Catts, H. W., & Little, T. D. (2006). Should the simple view of reading include a fluency component? *Reading and Writing: An Interdisciplinary Journal, 19,* 933–958.

Alliance for Excellence in Education. (2003). Adolescent literacy. Retrieved October 31, 2005, from *www.all4ed.org/adolescent_literacy.*

Anderson, R. C., & Freebody, P. (1981). Vocabulary knowledge. In J. Guthrie (Ed.), *Comprehension and teaching: Research reviews* (pp. 77–117). Newark, DE: International Reading Association.

Anderson, R. C., & Nagy, W. (1992). The vocabulary conundrum. *American Educator, 16*(4), 14–18, 44–47.

August, D., Kenyon, D., Malabonga, V., Caglarcan, S., Louguit, M., Francis, D., et al. (2001). *Test of Phonological Processing in Spanish (TOPPS).* Washington, DC: Center for Applied Linguistics.

August, D., & Shanahan, T. (2006). *Developing literacy in second-language learners.* Mahwah, NJ: Erlbaum.

Ball, E., & Blachman, B. (1991). Does phoneme awareness training in kindergarten make a difference in early word recognition and developmental spelling? *Reading Research Quarterly, 26,* 49–66.

Barth, A. E., Catts, H. W., & Anthony, J. L. (2009). The component skills underlying reading fluency in adolescent readers: A latent variable analysis, *Reading and Writing, 22,* 567–590.

Berninger, V. W., Abbottt, R. D., Abbott, S. P., Graham, S., & Richards, T. (2002). Writing and reading: Connections between language by hand and language by eye. *Journal of Learning Disabilities, 35,* 39–56.

Berninger, V. W., Dunn, A., Lin, A. S., & Shimada, S. (2004). School evolution: Scientist practitioner educators creating optimal learning environments for all students. *Journal of Learning Disabilities, 37,* 500–508.

Bissex, G. (1980). *Gnys at wrk: A child learns to write and read.* Cambridge, MA: Harvard University Press.

Blachman, B. A., Tangel, D. M., Ball, E. W., Black, R., & McGraw, C. K. (1999). Developing phonological awareness and word recognition skills: A two-year intervention with low-income, inner-city children. *Reading and Writing: An Interdisciplinary Journal, 11,* 239–273.

Blanchard, J. S., Di Cerbo, K. E., Oliver, J., & Albers, C. A. (2001, July). *Can divided time administration raise test scores?: The relation between attention and standardized reading comprehension tests.* Paper presented at the annual meeting of the Society for the Scientific Studies of Reading, Boulder, CO.

Bowers P., & Wolf, M. (1993). Theoretical links among naming speed, precise timing mechanisms, and orthographic skill in dyslexia. *Reading and writing: An Interdisciplinary Journal, 5,* 60–85.

Bradley, L., & Bryant, P. E. (1985). *Rhyme and reason in reading and spelling.* Ann Arbor: University of Michigan Press.

Calfee, R. C., Venezky, R. L., & Chapman, R. S. (1969). *Pronunciation of synthetic words with predictable and nonpredictable letter–sound correspondence* (Technical Report No. 111). Madison: Research and Development Center, University of Wisconsin.

Caravolas, M. (2006). Learning to spell different languages: How orthographic variables might affect early literacy. In R. M. Joshi & P. G. Aaron (Eds.), *Handbook of orthography and literacy* (pp. 497–511). Mahwah, NJ: Erlbaum.

Caravolas, M., Hulme, C., & Snowling, M. J. (2001). The foundations of spelling ability: Evidence from a 3-year longitudinal study. *Journal of Memory and Language, 45,* 751–774.

Carbonell de Grompone, M. A., Tuana, E. J., Peidra de Moratoria, M., Lluch de Pintos, E., & Corbo de Mandracho, H. (1980). Evolucion de la ortografia segun la classificacion estructural de los errors ortograficos [Spelling development according to the structural classification of spelling errors]. *Lectura y Vida, 1*(4), 11–17.

Carver, R. P., & Clark, S. W. (1998). Investigating reading disabilities using the Rauding diagnostic system. *Journal of Learning Disabilities, 31,* 453–471.

Cassar, M., Treiman, R., Moats, L. C., Pollo, T. C., & Kessler, B. (2005). How do the spellings of children with dyslexia compare with those of nondyslexic children? *Reading and Writing: An Interdisciplinary Journal, 18,* 27–49.

Castles, A., & Coltheart, M. (2004). Is there a causal link from phonological awareness to success in learning to read? *Cognition, 91,* 77–111.

Catts, H. W., & Kamhi, A. G. (2005). Causes of reading disabilities. In H. W. Catts & A. G. Kamhi (Eds.), *Language and reading disabilities* (pp. 94–126). Boston: Allyn & Bacon.

Catts, H. W., & Kamhi, A. G. (2006). (Eds.). *The connections between language and reading disabilities.* Mahwah, NJ: Erlbaum.

Chiappe P., & Siegel, L. S. (1999). Phonological awareness and reading acquisition in English- and Punjabi-speaking Canadian children. *Journal of Educational Psychology, 91,* 20–28.

Chiappe, P., Siegel, L. S., & Gottardo, A. (2002). Linguistic diversity and the development of reading skills: A longitudinal study. *Scientific Studies of Reading, 6,* 369–400.

Cho, J. R., & McBride-Chang, C. (2005). Correlates of Korean Hangul acquisition among kindergartners and second graders. *Scientific Studies of Reading, 9,* 3–16.

Cisero, C. A., & Royer, J. M. (1995). The development and cross-language transfer of phonological awareness. *Contemporary Educational Psychology, 20,* 275–303.

Collier, V. P., & Thomas, W. P. (1989). How quickly can immigrants become proficient in school English? *Journal of Educational Issues of Language Minority Students, 5,* 26–38.

Compton, D., & Carlisle, J. (1994). Speed of word recognition as a distinguishing characteristic of reading disabilities. *Educational Psychology Review, 6,* 115–140.

Cossu, G., Gugliotta, M., & Marshall, J. C. (1995). Acquisition of reading and written spelling in a transparent orthography: Two non parallel processes? *Reading and Writing: An Interdisciplinary Journal, 7,* 9–22.

Charity, A. H., Scarborough, H. S., & Griffin, D. (2004). Familiarity with "school English" in African-American children and its relationship to early reading achievement. *Child Development, 75,* 1340–1356.

Craig, H. K., & Washington, J. A., (2004). Grade-related changes in the production of African American English. *Journal of Speech, Language, and Hearing Research, 47,* 450–463.

Cummins, J. (1981). The role of primary language development in promoting educational success for language minority students. In California State Department of Education (Ed.), *Schooling and language minority students: A theoretical framework.* Los Angeles, CA: National Dissemination and Assessment Center.

Cummins, J. (1984). Bilingualism and special education: Issues in assessment and pedagogy. San Diego, CA: College Hill Press.

Cummins, J. (1991). Interdependence of first- and second-language proficiency in bilingual children. In E. Bialystok (Ed.), *Language processing in bilingual children* (pp. 70–89). Cambridge, UK: Cambridge University Press.

Cunningham, A. C., & Stanovich, K. E. (1990). Assessing print exposure and orthographic processing in children: A quick measure of reading experience. *Journal of Educational Psychology, 88,* 733–740.

Davis, F. B. (1944). Fundamental factors of comprehension in reading. *Psychometrika, 9,* 185–197.

DeFries, J., Fulker, D., & LaBuda, C. (1987). Evidence for a genetic etiology in reading disability in twins. *Nature, 329,* 537–539.

de Jong, P. F., & Van der Leij, A. (2002). Effects of phonological abilities and linguistic comprehension on the development of reading. *Scientific Studies of Reading, 6,* 51–77.

de Jong, P. F., & Van der Leij, A. (2003). Developmental changes in the manifestation of a phonological deficit in dyslexic children learning to read a regular orthography. *Journal of Educational Psychology, 95,* 22–40.

Denckla, M. B., & Rudel, R. G. (1976). Rapid automatized naming (RAN): Dyslexia differentiated from other learning disabilities. *Neuropsychologia, 14,* 471–479.

Dudley-Marling, C. (2004). *A classroom teacher's guide to struggling readers.* Portsmouth, NH: Heinemann.

Dunn, L. M., & Dunn, L. M. (2007). *Peabody Picture Vocabulary Test–IV.* San Antonio, TX: Psychological Corporation.

Dunn, L. M., Padilla, E. R., Lugo, E. E., & Dunn, L. M. (1986). *Test de Vocabulario en Imágenes Peabody.* Circle Pines, MN: American Guidance Service.

Durgunoğlu, A. Y., Nagy, W. E., & Hancin-Bhatt, B. J. (1993). Cross-language transfer of phonological awareness. *Journal of Educational Psychology, 85,* 453–465.

Ehri, L. C. (1991). Development of the ability to read words. In R. Barr, M. L.

Kamil, P. Mosenthal, & P. D. Pearson (Eds.), *Handbook of reading research* (Vol. 2, pp. 383–417). New York: Longman.

Ehri, L. C. (1997). Learning to read and learning to spell are one and the same, almost. In C. A. Perfetti, L. Reiben, & M. Fayol (Eds.), *Learning to spell: Research, theory, and practice across languages* (pp. 237–269). Mahwah, NJ: Erlbaum.

Ehri, L. C. (1998). Grapheme–phoneme knowledge is essential for learning to read words in English. In J. L. Metsala & L. C. Ehri (Eds.), *Word recognition in beginning literacy* (pp. 3–40). Mahwah, NJ: Erlbaum.

Ehri, L. C. (2000). Learning to read and learning to spell: Two sides of a coin. *Topics in Language Disorders, 20*(3), 19–49.

Everatt, J., Smythe, I., Adams, E., & Ocampo, D. (2000). Dyslexia screening measures and bilingualism. *Dyslexia, 6,* 42–56.

Ferroli, L. J., & Krajenta, M. (1989). Validating a Spanish developmental spelling test. *National Association for Bilingual Education Journal, 14,* 41–61.

Fitzgerald, J., & Shanahan, T. (2000). Reading and writing relations and their development. *Educational Psychologist, 35,* 39–50.

Frith, U., & Snowling, M. (1983). Reading for meaning and reading for sound in autistic and dyslexic children. *British Journal of Developmental Psychology, 1,* 320–342.

Frost, R., Katz, L., & Bentin, S. (1987). Strategies for visual word recognition and orthographic depth: A multilingual comparison. *Journal of Experimental Psychology: Human Perception and Performance, 13,* 104–115.

Geva, E. (2000). Issues in the assessment of reading disabilities in L2 children—Beliefs and research evidence. *Dyslexia, 6,* 13–28.

Gholamain, M., & Geva, E. (1999). Orthographic and cognitive factors in the concurrent development of basic reading skills in English and Persian. *Language Learning, 49*(2), 183–217.

Goldstein, B. (2001). Transcription of Spanish and Spanish-influenced English. *Communication Disorders Quarterly, 23*(1), 54–60.

Gough, P. B., & Tunmer, W. (1986). Decoding, reading, and reading disability. *Remedial and Special Education, 7,* 6–10.

Hanna, G. S., & Oaster, T. R. (1978). Toward a unified theory of context dependence. *Reading Research Quarterly, 14,* 226–243.

Hannon, B., & Daneman, M. (2001). A new tool for measuring and understanding individual differences in reading comprehension. *Journal of Educational Psychology, 93,* 103–128.

Hearing on Measuring Success. (2001). *Using assessments and accountability to raise student achievement.* Retrieved November 23, 2006, from *edworkforce. house.gov/hearings/107th/edr/account3801/lyon.htm.*

Henderson, E. H., & Beers, J. W. (Eds.). (1980). *Developmental and cognitive aspects of learning to spell: A reflection of word knowledge.* Newark, DE: International Reading Association.

Holm, A., & Dodd, B. (1996). The effect of first written language on the acquisition of English literacy. *Cognition, 59,* 119–147.

Hoover, W., & Gough, P. (1990). The simple view of reading. *Reading & Writing: An Interdisciplinary Journal, 2,* 127–160.

Horton-Ikard, R., & Ellis Weismer, S. (2007). A preliminary examination of vocabu-lary and word learning in African American toddlers from middle- and low-socioeconomic status homes. *American Journal of Speech–Language Pathol-ogy, 16*, 381–392.

Hulme, C., Snowling, M. J., Caravolas, M., & Carroll, J. (2005). Phonological skills are (probably) one cause of success in learning to read: A comment of Castles and Coltheart. *Scientific Studies of Reading, 9*, 351–365.

Joshi, R. M. (2003). Misconceptions about the assessment and diagnosis of reading disability. *Reading Psychology, 24*, 247–266.

Joshi, R. M. (2005). Vocabulary: A critical component of comprehension. *Reading and Writing Quarterly, 21*, 209–219.

Joshi, R. M., & Aaron, P. G. (1991). Developmental reading and spelling disabilities: Are these dissociable? In R. M. Joshi (Ed.), *Written language disorders* (pp. 1–24), Boston: Kluwer Academic Publishers.

Joshi, R. M., & Aaron, P. G. (2000). The component model of reading: Simple view of reading made a little more complex. *Reading Psychology, 21*, 85–97.

Joshi, R. M., & Aaron, P. G. (2002). Naming speed and word familiarity as confounding factors in decoding. *Journal of Research in Reading, 25*, 160–171.

Joshi, R. M., & Aaron, P. G. (Eds.). (2006). *Handbook of orthography and literacy.* Mahwah, NJ: Erlbaum.

Joshi, R. M., & Aaron, P. G. (2007, July). *Can componential model be applied to Spanish orthography?* Paper presented at the annual meeting of the Society for the Scientific Studies of Reading, Prague, Czech Republic.

Joshi, R. M., Hoien, T., Feng, X., Chengappa, R., & Boulware-Gooden, R. (2006). *Learning to spell by ear and by eye: A cross-linguistic comparison.* In R. M Joshi & P. G. Aaron (Eds.), *Handbook of orthography and literacy* (pp. 569–577). Mahwah, NJ: Erlbaum.

Joshi, R. M., Padakannaya, P., & Nishanimath, S. (2010). Dyslexia and hyperlexia in bilinguals. *Dyslexia, 16*, 99–118.

Joshi, R. M., Williams, K., & Wood, J. (1998). Predicting reading comprehension from listening comprehension: Is this the answer to the IQ debate? In C. Hulme & R. M. Joshi (Eds.), *Reading and spelling: Development and disorders* (pp. 319–327). Mahwah, NJ: Erlbaum.

Juel, C. (1994). *Learning to read and write in one elementary school.* New York: Springer-Verlag.

Just, M. A., & Carpenter, P. A. (1987). *The psychology of reading and language comprehension.* Boston: Allyn & Bacon.

Karlsen, B., & Gardner, E. F. (1995). *Stanford Diagnostic Reading Test–IV.* San Antonio, TX: Harcourt Brace.

Katz, S., Lutenschlager, G., Blackurn, A., & Harris, F. H. (1990). Answering read-ing comprehension items without passages on the SAT. *Psychological Science, 1*, 122–127.

Kennan, J. M., & Betjemann, R. S. (2006). Comprehending the Gray Oral Reading Test without reading it: Why comprehension tests should not include passage-independent items. *Scientific Studies of Reading, 10*, 363–379.

Klein, D., & Doctor, E. A. L. (2003). Patterns of developmental dyslexia in bilinguals. In N. Goulandris (Ed.), *Dyslexia in different languages* (pp. 112–136). London: Whurr.

Leach, J. S., Scarborough, H., & Rescorla, L. (2003). Late-emerging reading disabilities. *Journal of Educational Psychology 95*, 211–224.

Lesaux, N., & Geva, E. (2006). Synthesis: Development of literacy in language-minority students. In D. August, T. Shanahan (Eds.), *Developing literacy in second-language learners* (pp. 53–74). Mahwah, NJ: Erlbaum.

Levy, B. A., & Carr, T. H. (1990). Component process analysis: Conclusions and challenges. In T. H. Carr & B. A. Levy (Eds.), *Reading and its development: Component skills analysis* (pp. 423–438). New York: Academic Press.

Leybaert, J., & Content, A. (1995). Reading and spelling acquisition in two different teaching methods: A test of the independence hypothesis. *Reading and Writing: An Interdisciplinary Journal, 7*, 65–88.

Limbos, M. M., & Geva, E. (2001). Accuracy of teacher assessments of second-language students at risk for reading disability. *Journal of Learning Disabilities, 34*, 136–151.

Lundberg, I., Frost, J., & Petersen, P. (1988). Effects of an extensive program for stimulating phonological awareness in preschool children. *Reading Research Quarterly, 23*, 263–284.

MacGinitie, W. H., MacGinitie, R. K., Maria, K., & Dreyer, L. G. (2000). *Gates–MacGinitie Reading Tests–IV*. Chicago: Riverside.

Markwardt, F. C. (1998). *The Peabody Individual Achievement Test—Revised*. Circle Pines, MN: American Guidance Services.

Marshall, J. C., & Newcombe, F. (1973). Patterns of paralexia. *Journal of Psycholinguistic Research, 2*, 179–199.

McBride-Chang, C., & Kail, R. V. (2002). Cross-cultural similarities in the predictors of reading acquisition. *Child Development, 73*, 1392–1407.

Moats, L. C. (1995). *Spelling, development, disabilities, and instruction*. Baltimore: York Press.

Morris, D., Nelson, L. J., & Perney, J. (1986). Exploring the concept of "spelling instructional level" through the analysis of error-types. *Elementary School Journal, 87*, 181–200.

Muter, V. (1998). Phonological awareness: Its nature and its influence over early literacy development. In C. Hulme & R. M. Joshi (Eds.), *Reading and spelling: Development and disorders* (pp. 343–367). Mahwah, NJ: Erlbaum.

National Assessment of Educational Progress. (2007). *The nation's report card*. Retrieved October 31, 2005, from *www.nces.ed.gov*.

National Center for Education Statistics. (2004). *Condition of education*. Washington, DC: U.S. Department of Education, Office of Educational Research and Reform.

National Reading Panel. (2000). *Report of the National Reading Panel: Teaching children to read: An evidence-based assessment of the scientific research literature on reading and its implications for reading instruction. Reports of the subgroups*. Rockville, MD: National Institute of Child Health and Human Development Clearinghouse.

Newcomer, P. (1999). *Diagnostic Achievement Battery–3*. Austin, TX: PRO-ED.

Oakhill, J. V., Cain, K., & Bryant, P. E. (2003). The dissociation of word reading and text comprehension: Evidence from component skills. *Language and Cognitive Processes, 18*, 443–468.

Obler, L. (1984). Dyslexia in bilinguals. In R. N. Malatesha & H. A Whitaker (Eds.), *Dyslexia: A global issue* (pp. 477–496). The Hague: Martinus Nijhoff.

Olson, R. K. (2006). Genetic and environmental influences on the development of reading and related cognitive skills. In R. M. Joshi & P. G. Aaron (Eds.), *Handbook of orthography and literacy* (pp. 693–707). Mahwah, NJ: Erlbaum.

Palmer, J., McCleod, C., Hunt, E., & Davidson, J. (1985). Information processing correlates of reading. *Journal of Memory and Language, 24*, 59–88.

Perfetti, C. A. (1988). Verbal efficiency theory in reading ability. In M. Daneman, G. E. MacKinnnon, & T. G. Waller (Eds.), *Reading research: Advances in theory and practice* (pp. 109–143). New York: Academic Press.

Pinheiro, Â. M. V. (1995). Reading and spelling development in Brazilian Portuguese. *Reading and Writing: An Interdisciplinary Journal, 7*, 111–138.

Pressley, M. (2000). What should comprehension instruction be the instruction of? In M. L. Kamil, P. B. Mosenthal, D. Pearson, & R. Barr (Eds), *Handbook of reading research* (Vol. 3, pp. 545–561). Mahwah, NJ: Erlbaum.

Preston, R. C. (1964). Ability of students to identify correct responses before reading. *Journal of Educational Research, 58*, 181–183.

Proctor, C. P., August, D., Carlo, M., & Snow, C. (2005). Native Spanish-speaking children reading in English: Toward a model of comprehension. *Journal of Educational Psychology, 97*, 246–256.

The Psychological Corporation. (2009). *Wechsler Individual Achievement Test–III.* San Antonio, TX: Author.

The Psychological Corporation. (2003). *Wechsler Intelligence Scale for Children–IV.* San Antonio, TX: Author.

Quinn, C. (2001). The developmental acquisition of English grammar as an additional language. *International Journal of Language and Communication Disorders, 36*(Suppl.), 309–314.

Quiroga, T., Lemos-Britton, Z., Mostafapour, E., Abbott, R. D., & Berninger, V. W. (2002). *Journal of School Psychology, 40*, 85–111.

Rand Reading Study Group (2002). *Reading for understanding: Toward an R&D program in reading comprehension* (C. Snow, Ed.). Santa Monica, CA: RAND.

Read, C. (1971). Preschool children's knowledge of English phonology. *Harvard Educational Review, 41*, 1–34.

Read, C. (1986). *Children's creative spelling.* London: Routledge/Kegan Paul.

Reese, L., Garnier, H., Gallimore, R., & Goldenberg, C. (2000). Longitudinal analysis of the antecedents of emergent Spanish literacy and middle school English reading achievement of Spanish-speaking students. *American Educational Research Journal, 37*(3), 633–642.

Rolla San Francisco, A., Mo, E., Carlo, M., August, D., & Snow, C. (2006). The influences of language of literacy instruction and vocabulary on the spelling of Spanish–English bilinguals, *Reading and Writing 19*, 627–642.

Royer, J. M., & Carlo, M. S. (1991). Transfer of comprehensions skills from native to second language. *Journal of Reading, 34*(6), 450–455.

Savage, R. S. (2001). The "simple view of reading": Some evidence and possible implications. *Educational Psychology in Practice, 17,* 17–33.

Sebastian-Gallés, N., & Vacchiano, A. P. (1995). The development of analogical reading in Spanish. *Reading and Writing: An Interdisciplinary Journal, 7,* 23–38.

Shankweiler, D., Crain, S., Katz, L., Fowler, A. E., Liberman, A., Brady, S., et al. (1995). Cognitive profiles of reading-disabled children: Comparison of language skills in phonology, morphology, and syntax. *Psychological Science, 6,* 149–156.

Shearer, A. P., & Homer, S. P. (1994). *Linking reading assessment to instruction.* New York: St. Martin's Press.

Snow, C., Burns, M., & Griffin, P. (Eds.). (1998). *Preventing reading difficulties in young children.* Washington, DC: National Academy Press.

So, D., & Siegel, L. S. (1997). Learning to read Chinese: Semantic, syntactic, phonological, and working memory skills in normally achieving and poor Chinese readers. *Reading and Writing: An Interdisciplinary Journal, 9,* 1–21.

Spache, G. (1940). A critical analysis of various methods of classifying spelling errors: I. *Journal of Educational Psychology, 31,* 111–134.

Stahl, S., & Fairbanks, M. (1986). The effects of vocabulary instruction: A model based meta-analysis. *Review of Educational Research, 56,* 72–110.

Stahl, S., & Murray, B. (1994). Defining phonological awareness and its relationship to early reading. *Journal of Educational Psychology, 86,* 221–234.

Stage, S. A., & Wagner, R. K. (1992). Development of young children's phonological and orthographic knowledge as revealed by spellings. *Developmental Psychology, 28,* 287–296.

Sun-Alperin, M. K., & Wang, M. (2007). Spanish-speaking children's spelling errors with English vowel sounds that are represented by different graphemes in English and Spanish words. *Contemporary Educational Psychology, 33,* 932–948.

Tangel, D. M., & Blachman, B. A. (1995). Effect of phoneme awareness instruction on kindergarten children's invented spelling. *Journal of Reading Behavior, 24,* 133–161.

Torgesen, J. K., & Bryant, B. R. (1995). *Test of Phonological Awareness.* Austin, TX: PRO-ED.

Torgesen, J. K., Wagner, R. K., & Rashotte, C. A. (1999). *Test of Word Reading Efficiency.* Austin, TX: PRO-ED.

Treiman, R., (1993). *Beginning to spell.* New York: Cambridge University Press.

Treiman, R., (2006). Knowledge about letters as a foundation for reading and spelling. In R. M. Joshi & P. G. Aaron (Eds.), *Handbook of orthography and literacy* (pp. 581–599). Mahwah, NJ: Erlbaum.

U.S. Department of Education. (2003, February 3). *FY 2004 budget summary.* Retrieved October 23, 2006, from *www.ed.gov/about/overview/budget/budget04/summary/edlite-section.html.*

U.S. Department of Education. (2007). *State education indicators with a focus on Title 1 2002–2003.* Retrieved May 4, 2010, from *www.ccsso.org/content/pdfs/SEI_02-03.pdf.*

Vellutino, F., Scanlon, D. M., Sipay, E. R., Small, S. G., Pratt, A., et al. (1996).

Cognitive profiles of difficult-to-remediate and readily remediated poor readers: Early intervention as a vehicle for distinguishing between cognitive and experienced deficits as basic causes of specific reading disability. *Journal of Educational Psychology, 88,* 601–638.

Venezky, R. (1976). *Theoretical and experimental base for teaching reading.* The Hague: Mouton.

Venezky, R. (2000). *The American way of spelling.* New York: Guilford Press.

Verhoeven, L. T. (2000). Components in early second-language reading and spelling. *Scientific Studies of Reading, 4,* 313–330.

Wade-Woolley, L., & Siegel, L. S. (1997). The spelling performance of ESL and naïve speakers of English as a function of reading skill. *Reading and Writing: An Interdisciplinary Journal, 9,* 387–406.

Wagner, R. K., Torgesen, J. K., & Rashotte, C. A. (1999). *Comprehensive Test of Phonological Proficiency.* Austin, TX: PRO-ED.

Wang, M., & Geva, E. (2003). Spelling acquisition of novel English phonemes in Chinese children. *Reading and Writing: An Interdisciplinary Journal, 16,* 325–348.

Waters, G., Bruck, M., & Seidenberg, M. (1985). Do children use similar processes to read and spell words? *Journal of Experimental Child Psychology, 39,* 511–530.

Wolf, M., & Bowers, P. (1999). The double-deficit hypothesis for the developmental dyslexias. *Journal of Educational Psychology, 91,* 415–438.

Woodcock, R. W. (1989). *Woodcock–Johnson Psychoeducational Battery.* Austin, TX: DLM.

Woodcock, R. W. (1994). *Woodcock Language Proficiency Battery—Revised.* Chicago: Riverside.

Woodcock, R. W. (1997). *Woodcock Diagnostic Battery—Revised.* Chicago: Riverside.

Woodcock, R. W. (1998). *Woodcock Reading Mastery Tests—Revised.* Circle Pines, MN: American Guidance Service.

Woodcock, R. W., McGrew, K. S., & Mather, N. (2001). *Woodcock–Johnson Tests of Achievement.* Rolling Meadows, IL: Riverside.

Woodcock, R. W., Muñoz-Sandoval, A. F., McGrew, K. S., & Mather, N. (2006). *Batería III Woodcock–Muñoz.* Chicago: Riverside.

Wydell, T. N., & Butterworth, B. L. (1999). A case study of an English–Japanese bilingual with monolingual dyslexia. *Cognition, 19,* 491–514.

Ziegler, J. C., & Goswami, U. (2005). Reading acquisition, developmental dyslexia, and skilled reading across languages: A psycholinguistic grain size theory. *Psychological Bulletin, 31,* 3–29.

PART V

∎   ∎   ∎

Conclusion

CHAPTER 13

■ ■ ■

The Policy Context of Research on Basic Processes in Bilingual Children in the United States

KENJI HAKUTA

In this chapter, I have been asked to comment on the practical and policy implications of the work presented in this book. To address the task, I am going to take several steps back and look at the broad sweep of research on bilingualism and its relationship to educational policy and practice. The questions addressed by the chapters are classic problems: What is the nature of language transfer? What are the effects of different orthographic systems? What is the nature of language shift? Are there possible detrimental or beneficial effects of bilingualism? What is the relationship between first language (L1) and second language (L2)? How do we best assess bilingual students, given that most assessments are developed for monolingual populations? Several chapters identify ways in which basic reading processes are similar among children learning to read in their first and second language (e.g., Manis & Lindsey, Chapter 11; Geva & LaFrance, Chapter 10). This is very important because it suggests that, at least for some aspects of literacy instruction, similar approaches and strategies are appropriate for both English-speaking and English-learning students. But there are some differences as well. Much smaller vocabularies and less-developed receptive and expressive skills can not only interfere with the acquisition of literacy skills but also obscure the presence of other fundamental difficulties children might have, such as poor phonological skills and rapid naming ability, both of which have more pronounced impact on the development of early reading abilities. We also learn that the relationship between L1 and L2 reading can vary depending on whether one or both are alphabetic (vs. logographic) scripts (e.g., Cheung, McBride-Chang, Tong, Chapter 7; Leong, Chapter 8). Students literate in logographic scripts use different kinds of strategies and demonstrate different types of errors, or interference, associated with their L1 than do students whose L1 is alphabetic. Although this sort of "contrastive analysis" (Gass & Selinker, 2003) fell out of favor some years ago, it might be poised for a comeback.

These are all welcome developments in a field that sorely needs serious long-term work to advance our understanding and devise effective programs and interventions for students who far too often are largely struggling in school. Presumably the insights from this research will inform policy and practice and lead to improvements in student outcomes. But in order to appreciate more fully how findings such as those reported between the covers of this book fit into, I will paint my understanding of the big picture.

My views are based on 35 years of having been involved in some way with research on bilingualism and its practical and policy implications, starting with a paper I published in 1974 on a case study of a Japanese girl learning English (Hakuta, 1974). In that paper, I observed patterns of English that were neither fully productive in the grammatical sense nor fully imitated, something that I termed *prefabricated patterns*. I have been amused by seeing fragments of that concept reappear in current pedagogy as sentence frames in explicit direct instruction of English language development. I was also reminded of this finding as I read in several chapters that learning to read in L2 is in many ways like learning to read in L1, but not entirely; the patterns learned in your L1 can help provide a foundation so that you are not learning everything for the first time, but there is plenty to learn that is particular to the L2. In any case, shortly after this work, I got involved in a study of bilingualism and cognitive development, and then my work shifted more and more into the area of bilingual education, language maintenance and shift, and into the areas of practice and policy. At the same time, I had the opportunity to get directly involved in federal education policy, including the reauthorization of the Bilingual Education Act as well as federal education research funding through the U.S. Department of Education. These experiences all form the basis from which I provide this account.

PART C COORDINATING COMMITTEE

During the 1970s and into the 1980s, spanning the creation of the U.S. Department of Education by President Jimmy Carter in 1979, there was a

committee of bureaucrats representing three offices of the federal government: the Office of Bilingual Education and Minority Languages Affairs
(OBEMLA), the Office of Planning, Budget, and Evaluation (OPBE), and
the National Institute of Education (NIE). OBEMLA was an office created
under the Bilingual Education Act, enacted as Title VII of the Elementary
and Secondary Education Act (ESEA), and its principal functions were to
run grants programs to local and state education agencies to develop and
support teacher professional development and bilingual education programs for limited English-proficient students. There was a section in Title
VII, Part C, which provided modest funding for research to accompany the
programs. To enable coordination with the office charged with program
evaluation (OPBE) and with basic research (NIE), a coordinating committee
of representatives of these offices was formed to help distribute the funds
(see Kaestle, 1991, 1993).

I was fortunate enough to receive funding in the late 1970s and
early 1980s during the basic research phase of my career to look at second-language acquisition and the cognitive effects of bilingualism. These
were all funded and administered by NIE, but the funds came from Part
C. As a relatively junior person in the field at the time, simply trying to
build my research portfolio, I was scarcely aware of the sources of these
funds—just happy to have external funding. I remember attending some
Part C conferences in which I met other researchers who were feeding
from the same trough. Many of us had backgrounds in the traditional
disciplines of psychology, sociology, anthropology, and applied linguistics. But there were others who were working in the area of educational
program evaluation asking questions about the efficacy of different kinds
of programs.

As I have documented elsewhere (Moran & Hakuta, 1995), funding
priorities in Part C shifted just as I was getting used to the idea of funding for my own basic research, overtaken by the agenda of OPBE that
was responding to political forces. Basic questions, such as the nature of
second-language acquisition and the role of the native language, the consequences of bilingualism on cognitive flexibility, the nature of biliteracy,
or the cultural influences of language and literacy practices in immigrant
communities—questions that had been at the core of the NIE agenda—
were phased out of the funding portfolio. These questions were replaced
by whether there was evaluation research evidence to support bilingual
education programs.

What swirled behind this shift were complex winds of policy debates
around the nature of Title VII, the Bilingual Education Act. In its original formulation, and appropriate to the "bilingual" label of the act,
the purpose was to encourage programs through grants to teach limited English-proficient students through the native language, and either
maintain bilingualism (a lofty and controversial goal, given the history of

immigrant languages in the nation) or transition into English-only within a few years through transitional bilingual programs. While the rhetoric was on maintenance, the reality was transitional for the most part (see Hakuta, 1986).

The law during that period also allowed programs that did not use the native language (i.e., were English only), known as Special Alternative Instructional Programs (SAIPs), but funding for SAIPs was capped at 8% of total appropriated funds. Bilingual education was the default, SAIPs were allowed but capped, and Congress was already suspicious about whether bilingual approaches were better than English-only approaches. A study by AIR (Danoff, Coles, McLaughlin, & Reynolds, 1977), commissioned by Congress and released in 1977, compared English achievements of students in bilingual and ESL programs and found few differences between them. The study contained many design flaws (e.g., some subjects who were in ESL programs had been previously in bilingual programs), but it did point to the intense interest in the question: Does bilingual education work, and should policy favor it?

The knowledge base at that time was severely limited. There had been documentation of the first bilingual programs for Cuban refugees in Dade County in the 1960s (Mackey & Beebe, 1977). This study demonstrated feasibility and success, but these programs were mostly for the first wave of refugees—the Cuban elites with a firm determination to return eventually after the fall of the Castro regime. There were the Canadian experiences in French immersion whose goal was to attain bilingualism, but through exclusive instruction in French provided to middle-class Anglophones (Lambert & Tucker, 1972)—this would be parallel to immersing middle-class native English speakers in Spanish-only programs, where risk to the native language is low and bilingualism is additive (Lambert, 1975). The French immersion programs were developed with the accompaniment of considerable research armamentarium, much to the credit of psychologists at McGill University led by the late Wally Lambert (we miss you, Wally), who seized the opportunity to amass an impressive research line of evaluation and basic research on the development of children in these programs. With a significant information vacuum, a rapidly emerging need where the growth in the bilingual student population was already predicted by demographers, and a fabulous model of research established by the McGill researchers, the early 1980s was a time when educational knowledge for U.S. English learners could have flourished.

The Part C researchers during this time, including myself, Lily Wong Fillmore, Henry Trueba, Rudy Troike, Muriel Saville-Troike, and Guadalupe Valdés, were funded by the NIE. At the same time, William Tikunoff and colleagues were conducting case study work on characteristics of effective schools. The NIE agenda was decidedly liberal in orientation and very broad in its conception of bilingual students and their needs.

On the federal policy front, though, there was agitation about bilingual programs. The Carter administration tolerated and occasionally promoted the programs, even going so far as to propose bilingual education as the preferred if not required program under the Lau Remedies in 1980 (although this was also considered an election year ploy for Latino votes, since the administration did not act on this until the election year; see Crawford, 1999). Conservative irritation over bilingual education and questioning of its effectiveness hit stride with the election of Ronald Reagan, which immediately withdrew the proposed Lau Remedies. Alan Ginsburg, who headed OPBE at the time, was quick to respond to political shifts, and his staff members soon produced a review of studies addressing this problem (published eventually as Baker & de Kanter, 1983, but circulated in mimeo form for several years). The methodology was poor and unscientific, but the study did its job, raising questions about the efficacy of bilingual over English-only programs and therefore throwing into doubt existing policy. This led to Education Secretary William Bennett declaring a war on the 8% cap on SAIPs, claiming: "After 17 years of federal involvement, and after $1.7 billion in federal funding, we have no evidence that the children whom we sought to help—that the children who deserve our help—have benefited" (reported in Hertling & Hooper, 1995).

This policy environment, in which proponents for bilingual education became pitted against advocates for English-only programs, created the shift in priority for how Part C funds were used. This coincided with the demise of NIE, an independent research organization modeled after the National Institutes of Health (NIH) and its transformation into the Office of Educational Research and Improvement (OERI). Horse-race studies evaluating the relative efficacy of the program types became the emphasis, at the expense of fundamental research on bilingualism. In this environment, even the Canadian research was interpreted to fit the political question, because if French immersion was possible without any use of the native language, why would English immersion not be as well for U. S. language minorities? The real answer, of course, is that the sociolinguistic circumstances are completely different—in Canada, the dominant group is being immersed in the language of the minority group without any threat of loss of the native language, whereas in the United States the minority group is being immersed in the language of the dominant culture with the assumption that the native language will be extinguished. Sociolinguists are particularly sensitive to these differences, but of course, social sciences are not thought of as real scientists, especially if their theories are inconsistent with the political paradigm.

Part C funds were used for two ambitious large-scale studies. One was a nationally representative, descriptive study of program variations and outcomes, with longitudinal data collection (Development Associates, 1986).

The hope was to apply the cutting-edge causal analytic tool of the time (LISREL, a structural modeling technique developed to make causal inference from complex data). The other was a systematic comparison of early-exit, late-exit, and structured English immersion programs using a quasi-experimental design (Ramirez, Yuen, Ramey, & Pasta, 1991a; Ramirez, Pasta, Yuen, Billings, & Ramey, 1991b). These research studies absorbed almost all of the federal dollars available through Part C, with the goal of definitively answering the question of the moment. They did not, and were heavily critiqued and generally deemed as failures by a committee of the National Academy of Sciences (Meyer & Fienberg, 1992).

By the time Title VII was reauthorized in 1988, in the aftermath of the Bennett attacks and the failure of the evaluation studies, the cap on SAIPs was increased to 25%. More important, faith in the horse-race studies comparing program types was eroded, as it became increasingly evident that what really mattered was the variation within the program types, not the program types themselves. There was, once again, an important niche created for basic research.

During this period, I had the opportunity to receive spontaneous and unintended postdoctoral training on the policy process, thanks to high visibility given to my study that looked at the relationship of bilingualism with cognitive flexibility (Hakuta & Diaz, 1985). I was reporting on the work establishing correlations as well as some longitudinal analyses on how degree of bilingualism was positively related to some cognitive measures at the American Psychological Association convention in 1985. At a press conference after the paper, I was asked what I thought about bilingual education programs and whether they were effective. I said that I did not know that much about bilingual education programs (this part was never reported) but that I thought bilingualism was good, that the research suggested that bilingualism could be a positive boost for children, and that programs should promote bilingualism. The latter part was reported in the *New York Times*, which then merited me a call from the Reagan administration as well as the democratically controlled Congress asking me to clarify or expand on my remarks. The Reagan administration was especially interested, I later found out, because William Bennett was about to launch his attack on bilingual education programs, and I kind of got in the way. And Congress was interested because I was supposed to help boost bilingual education.

I was invited to a hearing in Congress with all kinds of hoopla that amused me, although I was a bit intimidated about the position in which I had found myself—the short movie, *Bambi Meets Godzilla*, which was popular in the Orson Welles Cinema in Cambridge when I was a student, kept flashing through my mind (this can be readily seen on YouTube by searching for the title, e.g., *www.youtube.com/watch?v=tAVYYe87b9w*— warning, it is a short film). I went there armed with a set of bullets, trying to help the committee appreciate the differences between evaluation and basic research, what we know or think we know from basic research, and I reproduce these points in Table 13.1. What's amusing looking at this list now is how little the broad set of questions and points have changed, and that the main changes are in the certainties and complexities entailed. The lessons of Part C remain the tensions between wanting to know whether certain policies work, and fundamental questions about how things work and why they work. These should not really be choices made, though in a

TABLE 13.1. Research Conclusions about Bilingualism and Bilingual Education (Circa 1985)

- Double standards exist about bilingualism: good for some children, but not for others; expectations about speed of second language learning are different too.
- Evaluation of bilingual education programs is very political; often, it is not clear what is being compared with what—apples with oranges. We have to be very careful about interpreting program evaluations.
- Instead of looking only at evaluation research, we should be looking at what basic research has to say about bilingualism in children.
- Bilingualism is a good thing for children of all backgrounds—when bilingual children are compared with monolingual children on different kinds of skills, bilingual children are superior.
- To be "proficient, to be fluent, to know" a language means many different things: you can have good conversational skills, but that is different from being able to use it in other settings, such as in school.
- Bilingual children are often informally evaluated in their conversational skills, but not in how they can use English in school.
- The two languages of the bilingual child are interdependent—they do not compete for limited space and resources.
- The stronger the native language of the children, the more efficiently they will learn English.
- Knowledge and skills learned in one language transfer to the other language—they do not have to be relearned.
- It is a myth that children are like linguistic sponges; they may take anywhere from 2 to 7 years, especially to master the academic uses of English.
- It is a myth that the younger children are, the faster they learn a second language.
- Bilingual program evaluations, although problematic, suggest that (1) bilingual programs are more effective than alternative programs, and (2) good bilingual classrooms have the same features as any good monolingual classroom.
- When we talk about bilingual education, we are entrapped by myths and labels; we should try not to get worked up about the labels of programs, because the issue becomes primarily political; we know from basic research that a good education in two languages is achievable, that it can have many benefits, and all we need to do is to build the commitment to establish programs that *get* us out of the imprisoning mentality that the two languages have to be in competition.

Note. Reported in Hakuta (1991).

zero-sum budget situation, that is how they play out. We need both kinds of knowledge—in the language of clinical drug trials, we need to know not just whether a drug works, but also why it works.

STANDARDS-BASED REFORM

Enter standards-based reform, circa 1990 (Smith & O'Day, 1991). This movement, based on the theory that education standards setting would help align the system (teachers, curriculum, testing, and resources) in a consistent and hopefully positive direction, caught the attention of governors, Congress, and the incoming Clinton administration. The standards-based approach became incorporated into the reauthorization of the Elementary and Secondary Education Act as the Improving America's Schools Act (IASA) of 1994. Along with its companion legislation, Goals 2000, the IASA required states to develop standards and accountability systems. The legislation had a systemic focus in which all students, including limited English-proficient students, are included. This had the effect, potentially, of moving the policy focus for bilingual children away from the language of instruction to effectiveness of the system, whatever the approach.

The standards-based approach was also more consistent with civil rights law, especially with how the Office for Civil Rights had come to interpret important court cases, including Lau v. Nichols (1974) and Castañeda v. Pickard (1981). This approach basically said that an appropriate program for limited English-proficient students was one that met three standards: (1) the program is based on sound educational theory; (2) the program is implemented with adequate resources; and (3) the program is evaluated after a period of time, and modifications are made to the implementation or theory if the desired outcome is not achieved. It was agnostic as to the approach—as long as it was thoughtful, well implemented, and adequately evaluated.

The standards-based approach also resulted in an increased attention to the inclusion of limited English-proficient students in the accountability system. The law "requires States to assess LEP students, to the extent practicable, in the language and form most likely to yield valid results," putting pressure on questions such as the appropriate language of testing, and representational questions such as how knowledge is learned, stored, and expressed vis-à-vis language.

Importantly, the standards-based approach, originally intended for the canonical content areas (English language arts, math, sciences, history, and social studies as the core), expanded to English as a second language. Teachers of English to Speakers of other languages (TESOL) developed standards in the early 1990s. Some states, such as California, followed with the development of state standards in English language development. Enough state activity around English language standards had taken place by the time IASA came up for reauthorization such that the next iteration, No Child Left Behind (NCLB) in 2001, included a requirement that all states develop English language proficiency standards, and tests aligned to these standards to be used for accountability purposes for limited English-proficient students. These policy issues have surfaced a number of critical questions that can look to basic research. How well do these standards address the fundamental nature of language proficiency? How adequately do they incorporate different components and aspects of language? How is language variation addressed? What are the expectations about language transfer? What expectations are realistic about how long it takes children to develop different aspects of language proficiency? Should the expectations vary based on the linguistic and social backgrounds of the students? How do we look at the relationship between aspects of English language proficiency development and reading/literacy expectations for all students?

The standards-based movement moved the efficacy questions away from the horse-race question of bilingual versus English-only questions, at least at the federal level. That said, the language of instruction issue continues to smolder, and it has popped to the surface at the state level in ballot initiatives in California in 1997 (Proposition 227), Arizona in 2000 (Proposition 203), Massachusetts in 2002 (Question 2), Colorado in 2003 (Proposition 31), and Oregon in 2008 (Measure 58). It is clearly a well-defined and easy political opportunity that is difficult to resist. When questions are defined in this simple way, it is difficult for research of any kind—basic, applied, evaluation—to hold any sway as it is overwhelmed by the cauldron of symbolic politics.

SCIENTIFICALLY BASED RESEARCH IN EDUCATION

Some of the strongest language criticizing the nature of education research comes from Reid Lyon (1999), who used it to shake more positivism into education research—and, some would say, to advance his own goals of championing his agency's program in reading research. Lyon testified to Congress in 1999 in his capacity as Chief of the Child Development and Behavior Branch of the National Institute of Child Health and Human Development. It's a doozie (pardon the technical language), so worth quoting at length:

> It must be concluded that too little education research conducted over the past century has been based on scientific principles that have proven successful in expanding our knowledge in other arenas critical to child health and development. Indeed, much of the educational research conducted over the past 20 years has been predicated on the notion that scientific

findings are relative—in the eyes of the beholder—and that science is not
the process of discovering the ultimate truth of nature, but rather a social
construction that changes over time. These types of anti-scientific ideolo-
gies and philosophical positions have been expressed within a culture of
postmodern thinking where a major premise is that there is no genuine
scientific method, but rather a sense that anything and everything goes.
This is unfortunate.

He added:

Educational research is at a crossroads. The educational academic community can choose to be part of the modern scientific community or it
can isolate itself and its methods from mainstream scientific thought and
progress. The scientific method has been adapted to study and understand
the most complex of physical, biological, social, and behavioral systems
and interactions. Surely, the teaching and learning process deserves no
less. In order to develop the most effective instructional approaches and
interventions, we must clearly define what works, the conditions under
which it works, and what may not be helpful. This requires a thoughtful
integration of experimental, quasi-experimental and qualitative/descrip-
tive methodologies. Education research can be strengthened by beginning
to define an exact set of conditions—variables that can be quantified and
manipulated—and determine what happens in the presence and absence
of these conditions. These observations, no doubt, must be enriched with
qualitative insights that add ecological context to the quantitative scaffold. Education research must be open to taking the next step of formu-
lating specific hypotheses that can be tested and *confirmed* or *refuted*.
By careful experimentation, we now understand and can treat complex
conditions that reflect a confluence of biology and environment. If educational research is to participate in and contribute to the scientific community and the lives of our children, leaders within the academic educational
establishment must be willing to show the next generation of educational
researchers the way. I am confident it can be done, and hopeful that it will
occur in the near future.

This caricature of educational research came as a bit of a surprise to
those of us who thought we were operating within the scientific paradigm—
as surely the authors of the chapters in this volume would assume, as well.
Sure, we have colleagues who are postmodern and layer interpretation upon
interpretation and frame it all within a social constructivist paradigm, and
we may engage with them in interpreting educational research, but the basis
of our work is squarely scientific.

My direct engagement with these issues came while I served as chair
of the policy board for OERI, formally named the National Education
Research Policy and Priorities Board (NERPPB, 2000) during the Clinton

administration, as policy debates began emerging around the reauthorization of OERI. Comments such as those of Reid Lyon were common, and echoed in forums such as the Brookings Institution (1999) that served as a lovefest for randomized field trials in education. It marked a new tone for educational research in Washington. There were even more extreme versions of this equating of science with randomized experiment, where one Congressional staffer drafted legislative language mandating random assignment, minimum sample sizes, and power analysis. At one moment of exasperation, I remember remarking, "They might as well mandate that the hypotheses be random as well!"

After hearings and deliberations, especially with the influence of balance from Donald Stokes's book *Pasteur's Quadrant,* in which he argued that the traditional continuum between basic and applied research is less useful than thinking of educational research as "use-inspired" basic research (Stokes, 1997), the NERPPB (2000) was able to separate science from method:

> The power of science comes from a combination of strong theory and data that bear on the theory. This implies endorsement of explicit ideas and agreed-upon methods for exploring and testing these ideas based on observation that has internal and external consistency. Experiments, as a classification of research, should not be scattershot or universal. Rather, they should be justified by a cumulative record of rigorous naturalistic observation and piloting. This requires knowledge of context in addition to adherence to scientific canons. While experiments in education may not be used as frequently as they should as a preferred means for investigation—for a variety of reasons, perhaps, but availability of funds is surely one such reason—"science" should not be equated with "experiments."

The NERPPB also commissioned a study by the National Academy of Sciences, asking to look at this question from the perspective of the "hard" sciences. This report was eventually published in 2002 as *Scientific Research in Education* (Shavelson & Towne, 2002), and independently supported the views expressed by the board.

This setting of a "gold standard" for evidence played out particularly strongly in the area of reading research, such as in the work of the National Reading Panel (2000), but worked its way to second-language learners through the National Literacy Panel, chaired by Diane August and Timothy Shanahan (August & Shanahan, 2006). One would appropriately describe research in this area as being very much the mix of the scientific portfolio, including some randomized trial experiments and quasi-experiments, as well as highly theoretically oriented work within the Pasteur's quadrant that contains the problems of bilingualism.

As a final and somewhat ironic footnote, as Claude Goldenberg (2008) so eloquently and directly notes in his summary paper of some of the leading syntheses of the scientific literature on programs for English learners, the strongest evidence lies in the area of language of instruction. His most important finding is as follows: "Teaching students to read in their first language promotes higher levels of reading achievement *in English.*" In spite of the call for scientific basis for education research, when the evidence that best meets these criteria are inconsistent with political beliefs about the appropriateness of bilingual instruction, then politics still trumps the research. Thus the peer-reviewed "practice guides" published by the U.S. Department of Education entirely skipped the bilingual issue. Interestingly, some of the researchers engaged in this issue are honest about wanting to avoid the political nature of bilingual education, but as Claude Goldenberg pointedly asked in a public forum with some of these researchers: "How could you drop it off the radar screen?" (reported in Zehr, 2006).

This indeed does seem to be the main lesson that we have learned about the value of a strong base in both the basic kinds of research on bilingualism contained in this book, and the evaluation research conducted. The field, although circling around a similar core set of questions, is doing so in a cumulative fashion and solidifying core knowledge about the nature, development, and measurement of bilingualism. It is indeed gratifying to see the sophistication of the work now being done analyzing relationships between L1 and L2, for example, Oller, Jarmulowicz, Pearson, and Cobo-Lewis's (Chapter 4) examination of the "language shift" and the consequences of the development of one language on the other; or Bialystok and Feng's (Chapter 5) complex portrait of interactions between bilingualism and skill acquisition in one or both languages. The motivational message should be this: Keep adding to the knowledge, but with a vigilant attitude to the policy context.

REFERENCES

August, D., & Shanahan, T. (Eds.). (2006). *Developing literacy in second-language learners.* Washington, DC: Center for Applied Lingusitics. Available at *www. cal.org/projects/archive/natlitpanel.html.*

Baker, K. A., & de Kanter, A. (1983). Federal policy and the effectiveness of bilingual education. In K. A. Baker & A. de Kanter (Eds.), *Bilingual education: A reappraisal of Federal policy* (pp. 33–86). Lexington, MA: Lexington Books.

Brookings Institution Forum. (1999, December 8). *Can we make education policy on the basis of evidence?: What constitutes high quality education research and how can it be incorporated into policymaking?* Washington, DC. Available at *www.stanford.edu/~hakuta/www/docs/brookings.html*

Crawford, J. (1999). *Bilingual education: History, politics, theory, and practice* (4th ed.). Los Angeles: Bilingual Education Services.

Danoff, M. N., Coles, G. J., McLaughlin, D. H., & Reynolds, D. J. (1977). *Evaluation of the impact of ESEA Title VII Spanish/English bilingual education program*. Palo Alto, CA: American Institutes for Research.

Development Associates. (1986). *Year 1 report of the longitudinal phase* (Technical report). Arlington, VA: Author.

Gass, S., & Selinker, L. (Eds.). (1992). *Language transfer in language learning*. Amsterdam: Benjamins.

Goldenberg, C. (2008). Teaching English language learners: What the research does—and does not—say. *American Educator* (Summer), 8–44.

Hakuta, K. (1974). Prefabricated patterns and the emergence of structure in second language acquisition. *Language Learning, 24,* 287–297.

Hakuta, K. (1986). *Mirror of language: The debate on bilingualism*. New York: Basic Books.

Hakuta, K. (1991). What bilingual education has taught the experimental psychologist: A capsule account in honor of Joshua A. Fishman. In O. García (Ed.), *Bilingual education: Focusschrift in honor of Joshua A. Fishman on the occasion of his 65th birthday* (pp. 203–212). Amsterdam: Benjamins.

Hakuta, K., & Diaz, R. (1985). The relationship between degree of bilingualism and cognitive ability: A critical discussion and some new longitudinal data. In K. E. Nelson (Ed.), *Children's language* (Vol. 5, pp. 319–344). Hillsdale, NJ: Erlbaum.

Hertling, J., & Hooper, S. (1995, October 9). District officials criticize Bennett's call for flexible bilingual-education policy. *Education Week*. Retrieved from *www.edweek.org/ew/articles/1985/10/09/06250005.h05.html*.

Kaestle, C. (1991). *Everybody's been to fourth grade: An oral history of federal research and development in education* (Report to the National Academy of Sciences, Committee on the Federal Role in Education Research). Madison: Wisconsin Center for Education Research.

Kaestle, C. (1993). The awful reputation of education research. *Educational Researcher, 22*(1), 23–31.

Lambert, W. E. (1975). Culture and language as factors in learning and education. In A. Wolfgang (Ed.), *Education of immigrant students* (pp. 55–83). Toronto: Ontario Institute for Studies in Education.

Lambert, W. E., & Tucker, G. R. (1972). *Bilingual education of children: The St. Lambert experiment*. Rowley, MA: Newbury House.

Lyon, G. R. (1999, October 26). *Education research: Is what we don't know hurting our children?* Statement to the Subcommittee on Basic Research of the House Science Committee, U.S. House of Representatives.

Mackey, W., & Beebe, V. N. (1977). *Bilingual schools for a bicultural community: Miami's adaptation to the Cuban refugees*. Rowley, MA: Newbury House.

Meyer, M., & Fienberg, S. (Eds.). (1992). *Assessing evaluation studies: The case of bilingual education strategies*. Washington, DC: National Academy Press.

Moran, C., & Hakuta, K. (1995). Bilingual education: Broadening research perspectives. In J. Banks (Ed.), *Handbook of multicultural education* (pp. 445–462). New York: MacMillan.

National Education Research Policy and Priorities Board. (2000). *Investing in research: A second policy statement with further recommendations for research in education by the National Educational Research Policy and Priorities Board.* Washington, DC: U.S. Department of Education.

National Reading Panel. (2000). See *www.nationalreadingpanel.org.*

Ramirez, D. J., Pasta, D. J., Yuen, S. D., Billings, D. K., & Ramey, D. R. (1991). *Final report: Longitudinal study of structured-English immersion strategy, early-exit, and late-exit transicional bilingual education programs for language-minority children: Vol. I* (Technical report). San Mateo, CA: Aguirre International.

Ramirez, D. J., Yuen, S. D., Ramey, D. R., & Pasta, D. J. (1991). *Final report: Longitudinal study of structured-English immersion strategy, early-exit, and late-exit transicional bilingual education programs for language-minority children: Vol. II* (Technical report). San Mateo, CA: Aguirre International.

Shavelson, R., & Towne, L. (2002). *Scientific research in education.* Washington, DC: National Academy Press.

Smith, M. S., & O'Day, J. (1991). Systemic school reform. In S. H. Fuhrman, & B. Malen (Eds.), *The politics of curriculum and testing (Politics of Education Association Yearbook, 1990)* (pp. 233–267). London: Taylor & Francis.

Stokes, D. (1997). *Pasteur's quadrant: Basic science and technological innovation.* Washington, DC: Brookings Institution.

Zehr, M. (2006, November 3). Guides avoid bilingual vs. English-only issue. *Education Week.* Retrieved from *www.edweek.org/ew/articles/2006/11/08/11ell.h26. html.*

Index

Page numbers followed by an *f*, *n*, or *t* indicate figures, notes, or tables.